CAMBRIDGE

Altered States

The Globalization of Accountability

Is globalization good for democracy? Or has it made our governing institutions less accountable to citizens? Located at the intersection of international relations and comparative politics, this book explores the effects of globalization on national governance. Under what circumstances do the transnational forces that embody globalization encourage or discourage political accountability? Among the transnational forces discussed in the book are the International Monetary Fund, the World Bank, multinational corporations, the United Nations, private military contractors, peacekeepers, the European Court of Human Rights, and several transnational social movements. Using in-depth case studies of situations in which these transnational institutions interact with national governments and citizens, Valerie Sperling traces the impact of economic, political, military, judicial, and civic globalization on state accountability and investigates the degree to which transnational institutions are themselves responsible to the people whose lives they alter.

Valerie Sperling is Associate Professor of Government and International Relations at Clark University. She is the author of *Organizing Women in Contemporary Russia: Engendering Transition* (Cambridge University Press, 1999) and the editor of *Building the Russian State* (2000). Her research on the Russian women's movement, as well as on militarism and patriotism in Russia, has been published in *Nations & Nationalism, Women & Politics, Signs: Journal of Women in Culture and Society,* and numerous edited volumes.

Altered States

The Globalization of Accountability

VALERIE SPERLING
Clark University

CAMBRIDGE
UNIVERSITY PRESS

CAMBRIDGE UNIVERSITY PRESS
Cambridge, New York, Melbourne, Madrid, Cape Town, Singapore, São Paulo, Delhi

Cambridge University Press
32 Avenue of the Americas, New York, NY 10013–2473, USA

www.cambridge.org
Information on this title: www.cambridge.org/9780521541817

First published 2009

Printed in the United States of America

A catalog record for this publication is available from the British Library.

Library of Congress Cataloging in Publication data
Sperling, Valerie.
    Altered states : the globalization of accountability / Valerie Sperling.
        p.   cm.
    Includes bibliographical references and index.
    ISBN 978-0-521-83400-1 (hardback) – ISBN 978-0-521-54181-7 (pbk.)
        1. Globalization – Economic aspects.   2. World politics.   3. Democracy.
    4. Civil society.   I. Title.
    JZ1318.S667 2009
    303.48′2–dc22   2008041980

ISBN 978-0-521-83400-1 hardback
ISBN 978-0-521-54181-7 paperback

Contents

Acknowledgments

Trying to make a useful contribution to a veritable ocean of literature on globalization seemed at times like the height of academic folly. When a friend on a Fulbright fellowship to the Russian city of Volgograd learned by email that I was writing a book on globalization, she replied with oddly threatening encouragement: "Go to it! As long as you promise it's the one book I can read in order to get a grasp of the issues!" I made no such promise. In fact, as my research led me in one direction after another, I began to think of the topic as something resembling an outsize amoeba. I would poke the project in one area and it would bulge out in another, demanding attention. Rather than getting a firm grasp of the innumerable aspects of the topic of globalization and accountability, readers of this book will, I hope, be led to pursue further many of the fluid and challenging issues raised herein.

I am grateful to the many people who helped *me* get a grasp of those issues. They include: Brad Adams, Anton Burkov, Eva Busza, Jeff Checkel, Matt Evangelista, Steve Fish, Eric Gordy, Evan Gottesman, Henry Hale, Steve Hanson, Pauline Jones Luong, Pam Jordan, Diederik Lohman, Sarah Martin, Susan McLucas, Sarah Mendelson, Joel Ostrow, Margo Picken, Paul Posner, Jim Richter, Kathleen Schneider, Martina Vandenberg, Celeste Wallander, and Kristen Williams. I owe much to the book's two anonymous reviewers for their careful reading of my text, their insightful comments, and their uncanny ability to distill (and then tell me) what I was *really* arguing. I am fortunate to have worked with Lew Bateman, my editor at Cambridge University Press; his interest in my initial book proposal and ongoing support of the project helped me pursue it to completion. I also thank my parents, and my good friends and colleagues in the Government Department (and elsewhere) at Clark University for their encouragement of and interest in my work. A word of appreciation must also go to copy editor Andrew Saff, who (among other things) sent a virtual shoebox filled with commas back to the bank on my behalf.

The book has benefited from several sources of institutional sustenance. Funding from Tom Hillery (through Clark University) paid for research assistance for the project. A course release granted by Clark's administration enabled me to finish the manuscript sooner rather than even later. A grant from the Francis A. Harrington Public Affairs Fund at Clark University paid for the book's index. The Davis Center for Russian and Eurasian Studies at Harvard University welcomed me with a faculty associateship over the duration of my research on the project.

My caring and talented partner Sam Diener gave me the extraordinary gifts of his patience and insight, read every bit of the manuscript with loving attention, brought much fitting information my way, and continues to encourage me to think about questions of justice and accountability every day. I'm beyond grateful for that and more. Last, I thank Sasha Diener Sperling, who provided frequent and welcome breaks from my writing process by climbing into my lap and demanding to see photographs of garbage trucks and penguins on the computer. Later, he graduated to requesting videos of fire engines, cooking, and manufacturing processes (jelly beans, graham crackers, and pasta in particular). Soon enough, Sasha will be surfing the web, making connections with children in other countries – probably founding a cross-border society for the appreciation of throwing fastballs indoors. The world – whether poorly or accountably governed – will one day be run by his generation. I hope they create a more favorable global balance between impunity and accountability than the one described in the pages that follow.

Transnational Institutions and Accountability

In an early scene of the 1987 film *Roxanne*, Steve Martin places some coins into a newspaper box on the street, pulls out a paper, glances at the front page, and shrieks in horror. He digs furiously in his pocket, presses more change into the slot, opens the box, and hurriedly shoves the offending newspaper back inside. My desire to write this book was driven by similar sentiments.

A glance at the "international" section of any major daily newspaper tends to reveal stories of war-related losses, devastating poverty, corrupt and abusive government, and social injustice in myriad forms. Dictators throw dissidents into prison cells and torture them. Men with guns rape and murder civilian women in Iraq, Somalia, Liberia, Bosnia, and too many other states. Women with rusted razors scrape off little girls' genitals. Frustrated jihadists fly airplanes into buildings. And every day, approximately 4,900 more children under age five perish from disease borne by the lack of clean water and sanitation.[1]

I found the news rather depressing. The committers of violence, the enforcers of injustice, and the promoters of poverty were often anonymous and frequently got off the hook. Sometimes they were locals, citizens of the states in which they committed their human rights violations; often, they represented the state itself. Other times, the problem seemed to originate beyond a state's borders, traceable to a transnational agency, an amorphous global ideology, an absence of empathy.

The persistence of such stories, combined with seemingly casual indifference on the part of the economically and politically powerful,

---

[1] United Nations Development Program, *Beyond Scarcity: Power, Poverty, and the Global Water Crisis* (New York: Palgrave Macmillan, 2006), p. 42.

eventually generated a largely unprintable research question in my mind. In its cleaned-up form, it reads something like, "What is *wrong* with the world?" This may be (as I have explained to my seminar students) a lousy research question, but it was a good starting point. Why were people suffering unnecessarily? Specifically, what could the parents of a young man "disappeared" by paramilitary forces in Chechnya do when Russia's law enforcement system refused to pursue the case? To whom might a refugee, raped by a peacekeeper in exchange for food, report the abuse? What options would be open to a pregnant woman denied employment in one of Mexico's foreign-owned textile assembly plants? What recourse would a Bangladeshi prostitute have when the international organization supporting the health clinic she uses suddenly withdraws its funds? More generally, how might the powerful be held accountable?

Imagine a worldwide ledger, a balance sheet, weighing the relative proportions of accountability and impunity. Clearly, much of the impunity we observe is firmly rooted in domestic politics, generated by governments that, in many countries, treat parts of the populace with benign neglect – or worse, with outright cruelty. But the contemporary world also boasts a great deal of transnational activity. The International Monetary Fund (IMF), transnational corporations, the United Nations, private military companies, the European Court of Human Rights (ECHR), transnational social movements, and many other border-crossing institutions exert enormous influence on states and citizens around the globe. What impact might these transnational forces – economic, political, military, judicial, and civic – have in the impunity-accountability equation?

A variety of transnational forces are engaged in promoting state accountability, broadly construed. Some transnational institutions, such as the World Bank, are explicitly trying to fight corruption. Others, such as the European Court of Human Rights, and a number of transnational social movements, aim to promote human rights and push governments to abide by the rule of law. The United Nations seeks, in some cases, to jump-start democratization in deeply troubled states, making governments accountable to citizens through elections. Private military companies (PMCs) claim to foster military security as a precondition for democratization. Some transnational forces, such as multinational corporations, do not profess to increase states' accountability to citizens and can even present barriers to it.

The question motivating this book is what roles transnational, as opposed to domestic, forces play in affecting the balance between accountability and impunity worldwide.[2] Within this inquiry, I address not only accountability relations between governments and populations but also those between transnational forces and the people whose lives they affect. With illustrative analyses of a wide range of transnational forces, I illuminate the complicated and sometimes unexpected creation and unraveling of accountability relationships. This book looks at five kinds of transnational forces (economic, political, military, judicial, and civic) and asks under what conditions they encourage or discourage a particular aspect of liberal state-building and democracy – namely, accountability – in a variety of countries, as well as whether they practice accountability in their own activities.

In the chapters that follow, I argue that economic, political, military, judicial, and civic forms of transnational action (or "globalization") are unquestionably altering accountability relationships – within states, between states and transnational institutions, and between those institutions and the people they affect. As their reach expands, transnational forces have gained influence in policy areas formerly reserved for domestic institutions and actors. International financial institutions such as the IMF and the World Bank exercise growing power over economic policy in borrower countries. The United Nations (UN) and other international political institutions lead democratization campaigns in postconflict states. Private (and typically transnational) military contractors widen the scope of their activities into realms previously covered by national military forces. Transnational judicial institutions such as the ECHR have become available even to citizens of nondemocratic states. Civic activism, too, has been transformed; transnational social movements mobilize to affect national governments and transnational institutions alike.

The involvement of transnational forces in these areas may be detrimental to democratic accountability, as well as providing opportunities to reinforce it. On the whole, however, the impact of these varied types of globalization on accountability provides considerable cause for concern. *In many cases, the effect of transnational involvement on accountability is negative, and in others, where a net positive impact is in evidence, the effectiveness of transnational institutions and actors in provoking or bolstering*

[2] Following Thomas Olesen, I prefer "transnational" to "global" as a way to describe the border-crossing entities discussed here. Referring to social movements, Olesen writes that *transnational* "refers to interactions…across borders" and *global* "implies something evenly distributed on a global scale." See Thomas Olesen, "The Uses and Misuses of Globalization in the Study of Social Movements," *Social Movement Studies*, Vol. 4, No. 1 (May 2005), p. 59.

governmental accountability is fundamentally limited. The constituents of
national governments and transnational institutions alike often find themselves metaphorically knocking on the doors of empty or invisible offices,
unable to render their governing institutions – whether domestic or transnational – accountable to the people their decisions most affect.

Given the ongoing power of domestic governments, transnational action
may have only a marginal impact on the accountability-impunity ledger. In
people's lives, however, that impact can be significant. To the Chechen parents of sons abducted and killed by Russian military forces, it makes a difference when Russia's government is pushed to atone for its unaccountable
behavior by paying out thousands of euros in fines levied by the European
Court of Human Rights. When the efforts of foreign mercenaries helped
bring Sierra Leone's civil war to a temporary halt, it made a difference to the
villagers who had been terrorized by machete-wielding rebels. The largely
peaceful transition to (initially) pluralist elections in Cambodia, organized
by the United Nations, constituted a welcome change from the bloodthirsty
dictatorship and foreign occupation that preceded the UN's intervention.
Transnational union organizing to save workers' jobs can make the difference between a continued income and impoverishment. These forms of
transnational action have a direct impact on individuals' lives. But one of
the most important ways in which transnational forces influence people's
lives is *indirect* – namely, by encouraging or discouraging governments that
interact with transnational forces to rule in a more accountable fashion.

What makes a state move toward more accountable government? The
answer lies in a combination of agency (rulers' choices), domestic pressures,
and influences from the transnational environment. Although such processes
are hard to disentangle, it is primarily some combination of individual conscience or calculation and domestic pressure that leads rulers to embrace a
more accountable style of governance.[3] But what role might transnational
factors play in that process?[4] Even if their actions are not determinative,

[3] In accounting for democratization, Charles Tilly argues for the primacy of "contentious
politics" – the "collective making of claims among constituted political actors," over
leaders' "democratic intentions." Charles Tilly, *Contention and Democracy in Europe,
1650–2000* (New York: Cambridge University Press, 2004), pp. 9, 15. State leaders may
opt to increase officially and institutionally the accountability of their governments for
many reasons. For a summary of these, see Andreas Schedler, "Restraining the State: Conflicts and Agents of Accountability," in Andreas Schedler, Larry Diamond, and Mark F.
Plattner, eds., *The Self-Restraining State: Power and Accountability in New Democracies*
(Boulder: Lynne Rienner, 1999), pp. 333–50.
[4] Recent scholarship emphasizes the relevance of transnational forces in domestic democratization processes. See Jon C. Pevehouse, *Democracy from Above: Regional Organizations*

in what ways do transnational forces promote or hinder accountability in democratic and not-so-democratic states? Transnational forces may not be decisive in struggles against nondemocratic government, but neither are they insignificant. They deserve consideration when we study the conditions under which movement toward accountability takes place.

A more familiar way to conceptualize the impact of transnational forces on accountability is in terms of "globalization." As a concept, globalization is typically disaggregated into three (interrelated) categories: economic, cultural, and political. The first two refer to the technologically facilitated, cross-border spread of goods and money, on the one hand, and ideas and identities, on the other, and are the subjects of a vast literature.[5] Although globalization is often discussed as if it were limited to economics and culture, this book adopts the perspective that globalization is multidimensional, cutting across the many realms of human interaction, including political life.[6]

Globalization's political aspect has received less attention than its economic and cultural counterparts, but it is no less important. As a transborder or "supraterritorial" phenomenon,[7] globalization has had dramatic effects on national politics. In the past few decades, the conventional areas of concern for national government – politics, economics, civic organizing, military activity, and judicial decision making – have all become "supraterritorial," or, put differently, have undergone "deterritorialization."[8] This is the essence of globalization's political aspect: the impact of transnational forces on national-level political processes and decision making. The transnational forces under discussion in this book – including the United Nations,

---

and Democratization (Cambridge, UK: Cambridge University Press, 2005); Hans Peter Schmitz, "Domestic and Transnational Perspectives on Democratization," *International Studies Review* 6 (2004), pp. 403–26; Tilly, *Contention and Democracy*, p. 237.

[5] Some scholars denote the diversity of global processes as a plural: globalizations. See John A. Guidry, Michael D. Kennedy, and Mayer N. Zald, eds., *Globalizations and Social Movements: Culture, Power, and the Transnational Public Sphere* (Ann Arbor: University of Michigan Press, 2000). On economic globalization and popular resistance to it, see Michael Hardt and Antonio Negri, *Empire* (Cambridge, MA: Harvard University Press, 2000); James H. Mittelman, *The Globalization Syndrome: Transformation and Resistance* (Princeton: Princeton University Press, 2000); Joseph E. Stiglitz, *Globalization and Its Discontents* (New York: W.W. Norton, 2002). For a history and analysis of globalization in multiple areas (economics, the environment, military action, culture, politics, and migration), especially as advanced capitalist states and societies are affected, see David Held, Anthony McGrew, David Goldblatt, and Jonathan Perraton, *Global Transformations: Politics, Economics and Culture* (Stanford: Stanford University Press, 1999).

[6] Held et al., *Global Transformations*, p. 12.

[7] Jan Aart Scholte, *Globalization: A Critical Introduction* (New York: Palgrave, 2000), p. 3.

[8] Ibid., p. 16.

the IMF and the World Bank, multinational corporations, private military companies, the European Court of Human Rights, and transborder civic groups – all fall under the rubric of supraterritorial organizations.[9]

In addition to their economic and cultural effects, the impact of such organizations has been profoundly political. Although in the chapters that follow I address transnational forces in the areas of economics and culture as well as those with a more explicitly political profile, I do so with an eye toward investigating their influence on accountability. Within this book, then, my main interest is in globalization as an expressly political phenomenon, encompassing a broad array of transnational forces and institutions that create opportunities for and obstacles to accountable governance, both within states and within the transnational entities themselves.

ALTERED STATES

Perhaps most affected by globalization in the last twenty-five years is the notion of state accountability. Hence the book's title, *Altered States*. Some transnational forces, such as private military companies, privatize state functions, taking them out of the public sphere and making it harder to maintain an accountability relationship between the public and those exercising military power on behalf of the government. Others, like transnational courts and international financial institutions (such as the IMF and the World Bank), render decision making transnational instead of leaving it within the purview of a state's own citizens, leading to a situation that one could label "accountability once removed." State leaders – depending on the relative power of their state in the global system – have in some cases become more responsive to multinational corporations or other transnational entities than to their putative domestic constituents. Popular awareness of accountability has also grown in the last several decades as communications technology blossomed. Not long ago, if some gross injustice impinged upon the lives of people living hundreds or thousands of miles distant, chances were that knowledge of those events would creep

---

[9] Ibid., p. 53. Although Scholte does not include PMCs in his analysis, they may fairly be considered as a subset of multinational corporations (MNCs), although they raise different accountability issues. Scholte also categorizes regional organizations like the ECHR as supraterritorial; the ECHR promotes "global" (supraterritorial) norms on human rights, reinforcing its transborder nature. See ibid., p. 147. Although the UN could be regarded as an intergovernmental, rather than transnational, organization, Bruce Cronin persuasively argues that it is both. See Bruce Cronin, "The Two Faces of the United Nations: The Tension Between Intergovernmentalism and Transnationalism," *Global Governance*, 8 (2002), pp. 53–71.

only slowly – if at all – beyond the zone of oppression into the consciousness of the wider world. But states no longer have private lives. When governments commit acts of violence against individuals or groups, it quickly becomes public knowledge. Transnational institutions also step in to try and put a stop to abuses of various kinds and, like states, are themselves targeted when their actions appear to violate people's rights.

Altered states, then, refers to two separate but linked processes. First, in our ever more transnationally governed world, the relationship of states to accountability has changed. Not only are national governments supposed to be accountable to their populations, but they are increasingly also subject to accountability claims by transnational social movements, where noncitizens act (ostensibly) on behalf of, or in coalition with, the affected population. States are also expected to demonstrate their responsiveness to transnational governance institutions, to exhibit accountability "upward." Governments are under increasing pressure to respond to transnational economic institutions in particular, altering economic policies in the direction of greater trade openness, for instance. Member states are also accountable to regional judicial institutions such as the European Court of Human Rights and are expected to change their policies and laws in accordance with international instruments of human rights law. Second, the world's population – or growing segments of it – is living in an "altered state" of consciousness facilitated by the rapid development of communications technology. Connected by the Internet and by satellite technology that enables video of a massacre to be uploaded instantly from a witness's cell phone to the eyes of the world, people live in a relatively novel state of awareness about the actions of governments and transnational institutions and are more able to make a collective response to injustices far from home.[10] The altered state of the world's citizens, along with the norms that globalization spreads regarding human rights and social justice, generates resistance to unaccountable behavior by transnational institutions and states alike.

GLOBALIZATION AND ACCOUNTABILITY

Whereas economic, political, and military interconnectedness have a long history, one of the novelties of present-day globalization is that it is taking place in a world that embraces at least a rhetorical commitment to democracy at the state level. The tenets of democracy, however,

---

[10] Such use of technology is addressed in Brian Martin, *Justice Ignited: The Dynamics of Backfire* (Lanham, MD: Rowman & Littlefield, 2006).

are "only rarely extended to cover aspects of multilateral regulation and global governance."[11] As one group of globalization scholars writes, "It is readily understood that the quality of democracy depends on rendering political decision-making accountable to citizens in a delimited political community."[12] The boundaries of that political community may change once decision making transcends the state level (as occurs when regional and transnational institutions exercise power within states), raising questions about how and whether to hold transnational institutions accountable to the people whose lives they affect.[13]

Defining Accountability

Accountability is a central aspect of political democracy.[14] Philippe Schmitter and Terry Lynn Karl define "modern political democracy" as "a system of governance in which rulers are held accountable for their actions in the public realm by citizens, acting indirectly through the competition and cooperation of their representatives."[15] In consolidated, functioning democratic states, a series of accountability relationships restrains government behavior. But how, precisely, does accountability work to preserve democracy? At base, an accountability relationship is a power relationship.[16] As it is traditionally understood, accountability in a democratic context has two aspects. First, public officials are obliged to provide information about their actions, and to explain and justify publicly the decisions on which their actions are based. This is known as "answerability." The second component of accountability is "enforcement," where "powerholders who have violated their public duties" are subject to sanctions such as impeachment or elections ending their term in office.[17]

---

[11] Held et al., p. 431.

[12] Ibid., p. 446.

[13] Ibid., pp. 446–7.

[14] Anne-Marie Goetz and Rob Jenkins, *Reinventing Accountability: Making Democracy Work for Human Development* (New York: Palgrave Macmillan, 2005), p. 11, ft. 7, citing Robert S. Barker, "Government Accountability and Its Limits," *Issues of Democracy*, Vol. 5, No. 2 (2000); Susan Rose-Ackerman, *From Elections to Democracy: Building Accountable Government in Hungary and Poland* (New York: Cambridge University Press, 2005), p. 1.

[15] Philippe Schmitter and Terry Lynn Karl, "What Democracy Is…and Is Not," *Journal of Democracy*, Vol. 2, No. 3 (Summer 1991), p. 76.

[16] A clear and thorough explication of accountability is provided in Goetz and Jenkins, pp. 8–14.

[17] Andreas Schedler, "Conceptualizing Accountability," in Schedler, Diamond, and Plattner, eds., p. 14.

More precisely, democracy involves "vertical" and "horizontal" forms of accountability. Vertical accountability refers to the process wherein the voting public is informed by its government leaders about decisions, and decides whether those leaders' justification of their actions is sufficient to warrant their continued presence in office or not.[18] For a vertical accountability system to work, the active participation of civil society is required. This should ensure adequate pressure on rulers to engage in the information and justification processes, and motivate voters to act according to their preferences, given the rulers' actions.[19]

Vertical accountability, then, relies on certain conditions, such as the widespread right to free speech and assembly as well as freedom of information. It also requires that the basic electoral elements of democracy be in place, such as the right to vote, run for office, and join political parties and other political groups (not controlled by the state) whose right to exist is generally protected by law. Robert Dahl's criteria for a modern political democracy – what he calls "polyarchy" – constitutes a set of prerequisites for vertical accountability, and provides a more concrete understanding of democracy as a form of rule where political rights (participation in elections) are made real by the guarantee of civil liberties (freedoms of speech, publication, and association).[20] Among states there is, of course, a range of compliance with Dahl's criteria. "Democratic" states, as I use the term in this book, are those that abide by Dahl's conditions. By contrast, states that hold regular elections but do not guarantee civil liberties enable unaccountable government in the guise of democratic rule.[21] Likewise, as used in this book, an "accountable" government is understood to be a

---

[18] Larry Diamond and Leonardo Morlino, "The Quality of Democracy: An Overview," *Journal of Democracy*, Vol. 15, No. 4 (October 2004), p. 25.

[19] Ibid., p. 25. Loss of office is not the only sign that accountability is functioning; those who keep the public informed are less likely to suffer legitimacy problems and suffer electoral sanctions. See Philippe Schmitter, "The Ambiguous Virtues of Accountability," *Journal of Democracy*, Vol. 15, No. 4 (October 2004), p. 49.

[20] I draw here on M. Steven Fish's discussion of democracy as a concept. M. Steven Fish, *Democracy Derailed in Russia* (New York: Cambridge University Press, 2005), p. 16. For a pithy summary and analysis of "democracy" as it has been used by political scientists, see ibid., pp. 15–20. For the six criteria by which "polyarchy" can be identified, see Robert A. Dahl, *Dilemmas of Pluralist Democracy* (New Haven: Yale University Press, 1982), p. 11, as cited in Fish.

[21] My endorsement of "democracy" as a desirable position toward which states are sometimes pushed by both domestic and transnational pressures should not be interpreted as a particular fondness for liberal democracy (as opposed to another political system that might rely less heavily on economic influence or involve more direct popular decision making). Still less should it be seen as suggestive of a belief that the West, or the United States in particular, has achieved an ideal state of "democracy" in its political system.

democratic government, but may exhibit limitations in its accountability to
a variety of groups even though their political rights and civil liberties are
not circumscribed by law.

The instruments of vertical accountability, such as citizen organizing,
media pressure, and elections, are insufficient as constraints on rulers'
abuse of power.[22] Mechanisms of "horizontal accountability" – whereby
government institutions check each other's power – also play a critical
role in democratic governance. These include electoral commissions and
human rights commissions, as well as the historical division of power
between judiciaries, legislatures, and executives.[23] Neither vertical nor
horizontal accountability, however, constitutes a strong means of control
over politicians. Term limits on elected officials undermine the use of vertical accountability's enforcement mechanism; politicians in their last term
in office can no longer be subjected to electoral sanction.[24] Some forms
of horizontal accountability are similarly weak. Executives asked by legislators to justify their decisions may resist divulging the evidentiary basis
for their decisions or may simply lie. The power of a free press in such
an instance, should, in time, help to reestablish the horizontal accountability relationship. Motivated and informed by media reports of executive wrongdoing, citizens can pressure the legislature to hold the executive
branch accountable. Vertical and horizontal accountability mechanisms
are thus interdependent.[25]

Accountability is often discussed in terms of "principals" and "agents,"
where the latter act on behalf of the former. In the context of democratic
government, the "agents" are elected officials, such as a president or legislator, and the "principals" are voters. Technically, it is only when both the
principals and the agents acknowledge their relationship that accountability can be said to exist. The advent of transnational governance institutions

---

[22] Larry Diamond, Marc F. Plattner, and Andreas Schedler, "Introduction," in Schedler,
Diamond, and Plattner, eds., p. 3. The term "horizontal accountability" originates with
Guillermo O'Donnell. See Guillermo O'Donnell, "Horizontal Accountability in New
Democracies," in Schedler, Diamond, and Plattner, eds., pp. 29–51.

[23] Ibid.

[24] James D. Fearon, "Electoral Accountability and the Control of Politicians: Selecting Good
Types Versus Sanctioning Poor Performance," in Adam Przeworski, Susan C. Stokes, and
Bernard Manin, eds., *Democracy, Accountability, and Representation* (Cambridge, UK:
Cambridge University Press, 1999), p. 82. Term limits may provide other benefits, such as
preventing individuals' accumulation of undue political power.

[25] Although it does not consider accountability in a transnational context, Przeworski,
Stokes, and Manin, eds., *Democracy, Accountability, and Representation,* provides a
variety of thoughtful treatments of the complex relationship between accountability and
democracy.

and their growing reach, however, has provoked significant debate over accountability relationships. Should transnational institutions such as the International Monetary Fund be accountable to those who are affected by their policies or only to the finance ministers of the Fund's member states? Institutionalized accountability relationships, such as those between the IMF's management (the "agents") and the member states' finance ministers (the "principals"), can be distinguished from a type of relationship increasingly common in world politics, where groups or individuals believe an agent *should* be accountable to them, but the agent disagrees. In such cases, an accountability relationship has not been institutionalized between the agent and the "would-be principals" or "accountability-seekers."[26]

Robert Keohane's distinction between "internal" and "external" accountability captures this tension.[27] Unlike the "internal" institutionalized form of accountability that arises between principals and the agents to whom they delegate power, an "external" accountability relationship may arise when "a person or community is substantially affected by the actions of an individual or organization."[28] External accountability, then, is motivated by "impact" rather than by the explicit delegation of authority from one person or group of people ("principals") to an agent.[29] Along these lines, the editors of a study analyzing attempts to hold the World Bank accountable to local communities define accountability nonspecifically as "the process of holding actors responsible for actions," reflecting the ambiguity in contemporary understandings of accountability relationships.[30]

Also increasingly open for discussion is the range of actions and outcomes for which "powerholders" may legitimately be held accountable. In particular, accountability mechanisms are no longer "expected [only] to satisfy concerns with outcomes, but also to examine outcomes of a particular kind – those that improve social justice and the realization of rights. This means, among other things, holding state and non-state actors

---

[26] Goetz and Jenkins, p. 10; Robert O. Keohane, "Global Governance and Democratic Accountability," in David Held and Mathias Koenig-Archibugi, eds., *Taming Globalization: Frontiers of Governance* (Oxford: Polity Press/Blackwell, 2003), p. 140.

[27] Keohane, p. 141.

[28] Mathias Koenig-Archibugi, "Transnational Corporations and Public Accountability," *Government and Opposition*, Vol. 39, No. 2 (April 2004), p. 236, citing David Held, *Democracy and the Global Order* (Cambridge, UK: Polity Press, 1995).

[29] Keohane, p. 141.

[30] Jonathan A. Fox and L. David Brown, "Introduction," in Jonathan A. Fox and L. David Brown, eds., *The Struggle for Accountability: The World Bank, NGOs, and Grassroots Movements* (Cambridge, MA: MIT Press, 1998), p. 12.

accountable for whether they contributed to improving poor people's levels of human development."[31] States and transnational institutions are subject to what Anne-Marie Goetz and Rob Jenkins call a "new accountability agenda," where pressure has mounted for an "expansion" of accountability along multidimensional lines, with the goal of increasing justice, particularly for the world's poor.[32] The World Social Forums, large activist gatherings that began in Porto Alegre, Brazil, in 2001 and occurred yearly thereafter, as well as spinning off regional, national, and local Social Forums, embody the notion that transnational corporations, financial institutions, and national governments alike should be held accountable for the effects of global capitalism on the poor. Using the slogan "Another World Is Possible," the Social Forums embrace the idea that global "solidarity" can change transnational institutions, such that the latter will operate on a democratic, accountable basis and will promote human rights, social justice, egalitarianism, and popular sovereignty.[33] Increasingly, material well-being and human rights are seen as conditions that accountability mechanisms are supposed to protect.

Deterritorialization, Privatization, and Accountability

As the power of transnational institutions expands, accountability has become globalized – or "deterritorialized" – in three fundamental ways. First, some *transnational institutions now attempt to hold states accountable*; states are not just hypothetically accountable to their own citizens, but are also hypothetically held accountable (and, often, are responsive) to transnational economic, political, judicial, and civic forces. This "upward accountability" implies that a transnational force can require "answerability" from a national government, and can also impose sanctions in the event that the government does not justify its actions to the liking of the transnational institution. States are upwardly accountable in this way to transnational financial institutions that extend loans (such as the IMF and the World Bank) and to regional judicial bodies such as the European Court of Human Rights, although those institutions' powers of enforcement are limited. Second, *transnational forces can promote governmental*

---

[31] Goetz and Jenkins, p. 146.

[32] Ibid., pp. 3–4.

[33] The World Social Forum Charter of Principles can be found at http://www.forumsocialmundial.org.br/main.php?id_menu=4&cd_language=2. On the first World Social Forum, see William F. Fisher and Thomas Ponniah, eds., *Another World Is Possible: Popular Alternatives to Globalization at the World Social Forum* (London: Zed, 2003).

accountability to citizens in particular countries. Transnational pressure for governmental accountability can come from above and from below. Promoting accountability from above suggests a "supraterritorial" source of pressure for accountability, such as from a transnational court like the ECHR or an international financial institution that links its loans to anti-corruption programs. Transnational forces may also promote accountable behavior in states from below. This occurs when grassroots activists in a given country organize social movements with support from transnational allies, pressuring the government to alter its behavior. Transnational forces aiming to increase state accountability – particularly, the observance of human rights – often work in tandem, from above and below simultaneously. Human rights organizations in Russia, operating on foreign grants, for instance, bring cases of their government's human rights violations to the ECHR. Finally, *transnational institutions themselves are increasingly viewed as legitimate targets of accountability* by the populations they affect, whether these institutions wield military power (such as United Nations peacekeepers and private military companies), economic power (such as the IMF, World Bank, and multinational corporations), or civic power (such as transnational social movements and nongovernmental organizations).

Deterritorialization has clearly altered accountability relationships, provoking a surge of academic literature about the "democratic deficit" engendered by transnational institutions and their growing power. Scholars concerned about the democratic deficit point to two fundamental problems with transnational institutions (such as the IMF and the World Bank) that play significant roles in national politics: "democracy at the national level has become increasingly meaningless as real decisions are made at a higher level, and these higher-level institutions are largely exempt from democratic oversight or accountability."[34] The "subsidiarity principle" of democratic theory similarly dictates that "governing power [be] located at the closest possible point to the citizen," which is not the case when transnational institutions (particularly bureaucracies) make decisions.[35]

---

[34] Marc Lynch, "Globalization and International Democracy" (a review essay), *International Studies Review*, Vol. 2, No. 3 (Fall 2000), p. 96. Ian Shapiro and Casiano Hacker-Cordón, eds., *Democracy's Edges* (Cambridge, UK: Cambridge University Press, 1999), also contains several chapters analyzing international institutions and the democratic deficit.

[35] Scholte, *Globalization: A Critical Introduction*, p. 33. Also see David Held, "Democratic Accountability and Political Effectiveness from a Cosmopolitan Perspective," *Government and Opposition*, Vol. 30, No. 2 (April 2004), pp. 369–74.

Among other critics concerned about popular disenfranchisement, Robert Dahl argues that international organizations (IOs) lack the mechanisms for accountability and transparency that could make them democratic, and that in such large institutions, so distanced from the main body of the populations they affect, accountability and control over decision making are necessarily lacking.[36] By contrast, Andrew Moravcsik contends that it is unfair to hold international institutions to a democratic ideal; rather, we should compare them with democracy as it is practiced, complete with its flaws (such as the delegation of decision making rather than direct participation) in the "existing advanced democracies."[37] Moravcsik dismisses concerns about the democratic deficit in the European Union, arguing that the institution is no less democratic (on several measures) than the world's contemporary advanced democracies.[38] He restricts his argument about international organizations' "democratic legitimacy" to the European Union, however, expressing skepticism about its application to other IOs, particularly those where the nation-states involved are not sufficiently "influential, democratic and technically competent," as is often the case, given the paucity of democratic regimes.[39]

Like Moravcsik, Goetz and Jenkins are careful not to fault globalization for accountability deficits. In their view, democratic deficits largely reflect "flaws" in democratic processes at the national level, which antedate the intensification of globalization. Specifically, accountability mechanisms, even in democratic systems, are structurally biased against marginalized groups, particularly the poor.[40] These biases are manifested in numerous ways. For instance, state officials regularly close their eyes to violations of policies intended to protect the poor (such as workplace safety standards).[41] The search for fair treatment, particularly for the marginalized, is also significantly retarded by oppression outside of the state's official institutions; racism, sexism, and other forms of discrimination provide the background against which official institutions maintain their own discriminatory behavior.[42] Globalization, then, is not the sole force driving the absence

---

[36] Robert Dahl, "Can International Organizations Be Democratic? A Skeptic's View," in Shapiro and Hacker-Cordon (eds.), *Democracy's Edges,* pp. 19–36.
[37] Andrew Moravcsik, "Is There a 'Democratic Deficit' in World Politics? A Framework for Analysis," *Government and Opposition,* Vol. 39, No. 2 (April 2004), p. 337.
[38] Ibid., p. 349.
[39] Ibid., p. 363.
[40] Goetz and Jenkins, p. 6.
[41] Ibid., pp. 36, 45–76.
[42] Goetz and Jenkins note this "spillover" effect (p. 14) and discuss it with respect to gender on pp. 158–79.

of accountability. Rather, the globalization of ideas has helped spread the twin notions of accountability and democracy, inspiring greater numbers of people to demand accountability from their flawed institutions – both domestic and transnational.[43]

Globalization entails changes in accountability relationships due not only to deterritorialization but also to privatization. Legal theorist Alfred Aman sees the increasing pressure on states to privatize their public sector responsibilities as one of the main components of globalization, and as a significant sponsor of the "democracy deficit."[44] When democratic states transfer (or "outsource") formerly public functions and services to the private sector, citizens largely relinquish their powers of oversight. Moving public services into the realm of the market decreases citizens' opportunity to hold their government accountable for decisions and for the outcomes of public policies now implemented by private entities.[45] Markets, moreover, "simply do not offer the transparency and accountability necessary for a vibrant democratic society."[46] If the private providers of formerly public services (such as prisons run by the private sector, or welfare eligibility administration run by private corporations) made available sufficient "information on which their policies are based and according to which those policies might be assessed," it would enable them to undergo proper citizen scrutiny, but private corporations are not required to do so.[47] Aman's remedy for this accountability gap – in the United States, at least – is to expand the Administrative Procedures Act (APA) "to include private actors carrying out public responsibilities" and to make the Freedom of Information Act applicable "at least to those private entities engaged in providing services previously provided by government."[48] In nondemocratic states, however, this would not be a tenable solution.

Privatization is, in a way, a form of deterritorialization, in that it moves decision making into a private realm, inaccessible to citizens (much as decisions at the IMF lie beyond the control of citizens in borrower countries). As state services are privatized and as state control over economic choices is increasingly ceded to multinational corporations and international financial institutions, the "shrinking state" may decline as a "target for popular

---

[43] Ibid., p. 6.
[44] Alfred Aman, *The Democracy Deficit: Taming Globalization Through Law Reform* (New York: New York University Press, 2004), p. 90.
[45] Ibid., pp. 6–7.
[46] Ibid., p. 12.
[47] Ibid., p. 13, p. 139.
[48] Ibid., p. 141, p. 150.

discontent," leaving no accessible institutions to which to protest.[49] State accountability to a population can then slowly evaporate.

Both deterritorialization and privatization have ramifications for state sovereignty as well as for democracy. The modern state is commonly understood as governing a territory, deriving the rules under which life in that territory proceeds, and enjoying "supreme authority" there vis-à-vis other states in the international system.[50] Although the "modern polity was built on the idea of the modern state and a system of state-based accountability," this notion has become outdated in the era of global institutions and their growing jurisdiction.[51] State sovereignty, though legally intact, has correspondingly also declined in practice; "states do not retain sole command of what transpires within their own territorial boundaries."[52]

Sovereignty, however, varies with state power. Less powerful states retain control over fewer areas of policy and to a lesser extent than more powerful states.[53] Robert Keohane and Joseph Nye thus advise caution when theorizing about the effects of globalization on states and governance; these effects "vary with the size, power, and domestic political culture of the states involved."[54] These variations are particularly obvious in states' interactions with economic forms of globalization. Whereas higher levels of economic development provide a relative "degree of insulation" from economic shocks and challenges to state sovereignty, more "vulnerable" states may find that their economic policy options are constrained, with some choices (such as "expansionary macroeconomic policies") taken off the table altogether.[55] States also retain varying levels of control over

---

[49] T. David Mason, *Caught in the Crossfire: Revolutions, Repression, and the Rational Peasant* (Lanham, MD: Rowman & Littlefield, 2004), p. 268, citing Richard Snyder, "The End of Revolution?" *Review of Politics* 61 (Winter 1999), pp. 5–28, at p. 13.

[50] See Valerie Sperling, "Introduction," in Valerie Sperling, ed., *Building the Russian State* (Boulder: Westview Press, 2000), pp. 1–23, at pp. 2–7; Andrew Vincent, *Theories of the State* (Oxford: Basil Blackwell, 1987), p. 20.

[51] Held, pp. 364, 367.

[52] Ibid., p. 367. States as such rarely have complete autonomy; state institutions confront other claimants contending for power within the territory, limiting state autonomy. See Joel Migdal, "Strong States, Weak States: Power and Accommodation," in Myron Weiner and Samuel P. Huntington, eds., *Understanding Political Development* (Boston: Little, Brown, 1987).

[53] Some states, such as Myanmar and North Korea, retain relatively more control due to their isolation from the world system.

[54] Robert O. Keohane and Joseph S. Nye, Jr., "Introduction," in Joseph S. Nye and John D. Donahue, eds., *Governance in a Globalizing World* (Washington: Brookings Institution Press, 2000), p. 17.

[55] The inflation associated with expansionary policies invokes punishments from global financial markets in the form of high interest rates. See Held et al., pp. 18, 440; Vicky

economic decision making in the face of transnational capital flows.[56] Regional judicial bodies and cross-border civic associations may also erode states' sovereignty by compelling governments to act in particular ways, whether it be altering laws that violate human rights or disposing of nuclear waste more safely.[57] In short, the current proliferation and range of transnational forces can impinge upon state sovereignty in ways that circumscribe democratic politics. But in nondemocracies, the transnational forces that reduce state sovereignty offer citizens new mechanisms and approaches by which to attempt to hold the domestic and transnational institutions that govern them accountable.

Synopsis of the Study

This book investigates the impact of globalization on political accountability in the contemporary world. More concretely, under what conditions do an array of transnational forces – economic, political, military, judicial, and civic – encourage or discourage the deepening of an accountability relationship between state rulers and citizens? And given that transnational forces are playing ever more "state-like" roles in the world (whether by replacing state functions – as private military companies may do – or by formulating national economic policy, as the IMF does), I also ask to what degree they, too, act in more or less accountable ways.

To explore these issues, I draw on a wide range of cases – specific instances in which states and citizens interact with the transnational forces under discussion. My analysis of these cases reveals the range of internal and external accountability exhibited by transnational forces, and also concretely illustrates those forces' impact (whether positive or negative) on the political accountability of national governments to citizens. Each chapter focuses on one type of globalization, and the book on the whole brings in cases from the diverse political terrain of states in Europe, Asia, Africa, and the Americas. The chapters are enriched by data from my interviews with activists, researchers, and lawyers involved in the pursuit of human rights and democratic accountability in Russia, Bosnia, Cambodia, and West Africa.

Randall and Robin Theobald, *Political Change and Underdevelopment: A Critical Introduction to Third World Politics*, 2nd edition (London: Macmillan, 1998), p. 255.

[56] Mittelman, *The Globalization Syndrome*, p. 225.

[57] Sperling, "Introduction," p. 3. For able summaries of the "hyperglobalist" and "skeptical" perspectives on the novelty of economic globalization and the power of states, see Held et al., pp. 2–28; Scholte, *Globalization: A Critical Introduction*, pp. 13–40.

The chapters that follow thus trace the impact of transnational economic, political, military, judicial, and civic institutions on state accountability, as well as exploring the political accountability of the institutions themselves. Some parts of the project allow for an explicitly comparative framework. In Chapter 2, for instance, which explores the effects of economic globalization, I draw on several quantitative studies to shed light on the relationship between economic liberalization and democratic accountability more broadly. The chapter then considers the extent to which a series of transnational economic institutions (the IMF, the World Bank, the World Trade Organization [WTO], multinational corporations, and the North American Free Trade Agreement [NAFTA]) are accountable, and to whom, and under what conditions they help to foster state accountability to citizens.

The impact of other transnational forces on accountability does not lend itself to statistically rigorous comparative methodologies. When exploring cases of domestic politics explicitly taken over by transnational forces, for instance, there is an extremely small universe from which to choose.[58] Only Bosnia, Cambodia, and East Timor have experienced this profound level of transnational political intervention. Of these, the Cambodian and Bosnian cases have had the longest period of time to "ripen," making them the more sensible targets of inquiry.[59] Chapter 3, on the forces of political globalization, therefore investigates two major cases in which the organization of domestic politics became the province of transnational actors: the United Nations–run elections in Cambodia in 1993 and their aftermath, and the transnationally led process set up to facilitate democratization in Bosnia following the 1995 Dayton Accords. I consider the transnational impact on democratic accountability in each case.

Transnational military forces (in the form of private military companies and UN peacekeepers), by contrast, operate in many states. Chapter 4, on military globalization, explores the interactions between political accountability and the use of PMCs in Sierra Leone's civil war and in Iraq under U.S. occupation, and considers the ramifications of licensing U.S.-based PMCs to work for foreign governments such as Croatia and Equatorial Guinea. I examine the effects of PMCs on accountability in these particular cases to show that the use of privatized and transnational

---

[58] I am explicitly not considering *inter*national instances of politics run from outside, such as postwar foreign occupation, only transnational cases.

[59] Conflict between factions of the army and national police in East Timor erupted in 2006, and the general consensus was that the presence of the UN Transitional Administration in East Timor from 1999 to 2002 had not been sufficient. See Jane Perlez, "A Nation-Building Project Comes Apart in East Timor," *New York Times*, July 14, 2006, p. A4.

military force affects the prospects for democracy in the developing states where PMCs operate, as well as the quality of democracy in the developed states where they are based. The chapter then explores several cases of peacekeeping (in Bosnia, Cambodia, and Liberia) through the lens of accountability to women, highlighting the difficulty of holding peacekeepers accountable for their violations of women's human rights.

Chapter 5, on the globalization of judicial institutions, examines the European Court of Human Rights' effect on accountability within Russia's political and judicial systems. Aside from United Nations conventions (which have little enforcement power), there are few transnational judicial institutions that can call states to task, so my selection of the European Court of Human Rights and its impact on Russia is necessarily illustrative rather than representative.

Chapter 6 covers the globalization of civic organizing, investigating cases where transnational social movements have pressured national governments and multilateral institutions to enforce human rights norms and increase their political accountability. The chapter begins with examples from China, Mexico, Argentina, Kenya, and Nigeria illustrating the advantages and disadvantages of organizing transnationally to demand humane treatment and democratic accountability from national governments. The success of a small transnational alliance currently fighting female genital mutilation in Mali then demonstrates the importance of internal accountability within transnational advocacy coalitions, an issue further highlighted by four transnational campaigns targeting World Bank projects (where the campaigns exhibited varying levels of accountability to their ostensible constituents). The chapter also takes up the related problems of donor dependency and accountability faced by transnational service–providing NGOs operating in developing countries.

The concluding chapter, "Altered States and Altered Citizens," addresses this study's implications for our understanding of accountability amid growing transnational political and economic interconnection, and imagines the further development of a nascent global conscience as a way to tip the scales away from impunity and toward greater political accountability in both national and transnational governance.

2

For Richer, for Poorer

Economic Globalization

The most visible manifestation of economic globalization is the flow of manufactured goods across national borders. Shoes conceived of at Nike's headquarters in Oregon are produced in far-flung factories in China, Vietnam, Indonesia, and Thailand, to avoid high labor costs in the United States, and then sold to consumers the world over who possess sufficient disposable income to afford sneakers priced at up to $300 a pair. Even services have become globalized, and for similar reasons. Dial a toll-free number in the United States to purchase airline tickets and you may find yourself talking with an airline reservations agent located in India. And, to avoid U.S. regulations, phone sex calls by U.S. residents are routed through poor countries like Guyana, a practice that generates up to 40 percent of Guyana's gross domestic product (GDP).[1]

Our global economy is not a new phenomenon. Trade between countries and between continents is a centuries-old process that grew considerably during the latter half of the nineteenth century.[2] Yet the intensity of that exchange has grown in the past several decades at quite high speed. Today's global market bears little resemblance to the world's economic system in the mid-twentieth century, at which point it was "an aggregation of reasonably distinct domestic economies."[3] For the most part, at that time, manufacturing took place in the industrialized countries (the "First

[1] Gary Schanman, "Technologically Transmitted Smut: On the Cutting Edge of Technology, 'Cyber-sex' Is Big Business," *Monroe Street Journal*, February 10, 1997, accessed November 15, 2007, at http://www.umich.edu/~msjrnl/backmsj/021097/tech.html.
[2] See Eric Hobsbawm, *The Age of Capital 1848–1875* (London: Weidenfeld & Nicholson, 2000).
[3] Gary Gereffi, "The Elusive Last Lap in the Quest for Developed-Country Status," in James Mittelman, ed., *Globalization: Critical Reflections* (Boulder: Lynne Rienner, 1997), p. 53.

World") – the United States, Europe, and Japan – where manufactured goods were sold as well as being widely exported abroad. The "less-developed" or "Third World" states, for their part, exported raw materials (such as minerals, metals, oil, coffee, and other agricultural products) to the industrialized states, in the economic pattern typical of colonialism.[4]

Over the past half-century, these processes of production and trade underwent significant change. Manufacturing became a transnational process, with companies headquartered in the First World frequently operating or subcontracting to factories in the developing states. The shift toward global manufacturing, in addition to appealing to large companies' profit margins, was welcomed in part as an opportunity to solve the economic problems that plagued many developing states. Under the "export-led industrialization" model that took off in the 1980s, developing states would attempt to find their "comparative advantage," producing some product for the world market and earning foreign exchange through these exports. The "invisible hand" of the market imagined by eighteenth-century economist Adam Smith, now grew to encompass an ever larger and denser economic network – what most people imagine when they hear the term "globalization."

The economic theory accompanying this transnational trend over the past few decades has been termed "neoliberalism," to capture both its basis in liberal thought – particularly the inviolability and centrality of private property – and the novel global context in which it operates.[5] Among the precepts of economic neoliberalism – also sometimes labeled "market reforms," "economic liberalism," or "the Washington Consensus" – are the following.[6] First, market forces are assumed to be more efficient and

[4] Ibid., p. 53.
[5] "Neoliberal" – in the economic sense – has acquired a perjorative connotation; few scholars characterize themselves as proponents of neoliberal economics despite the term's widespread usage. See Taylor C. Boas and Jordan Gans-Morse, "Neoliberalism: From New Liberal Philosophy to Anti-Liberal Slogan," *Studies in Comparative International Development*, Vol. 44, No. 2 (forthcoming, Summer 2009). Note that I am not using "neoliberalism" as it is used in international relations theory, where it refers to "neoliberal institutionalism," a school of thought that examines the role that multilateral institutions (such as the IMF and the World Trade Organization [WTO]) can play in helping states cooperate with each other. See Robert O. Keohane and Joseph S. Nye, *Power and Interdependence: World Politics in Transition* (Boston: Little, Brown, 1977).
[6] John Williamson, who originated the phrase "Washington Consensus," distinguishes it from neoliberalism, which he paints as a more radical "ideological agenda" supposedly being foisted on countries around the globe (cited in Boas and Gans-Morse). The Washington Consensus denotes the substantial agreement among Washington, D.C.-based economic institutions (such as the IMF, World Bank, and several U.S. government agencies) on the policy instruments favored in addressing indebted countries' economic

more effective than governments at solving economic problems. Governments are therefore enjoined to encourage private enterprise and trade and to avoid regulation beyond the point of maximizing market efficiency (this often entails some degree of deregulation). Markets are deemed superior in transnational economic relations as well; free trade (involving the elimination of most state subsidies, price controls, wage floors, and restrictions on imported goods) is therefore preferred to protectionism (where domestic producers are somewhat shielded from outside competition). Second, states running large deficits are advised to adopt fiscal austerity and reduce their public spending. Similarly favored is the expansion of the private sector into areas previously controlled by the state. State-owned enterprises (such as factories, hospitals, and utility companies) are sold to the private sector with the aim of reducing the waste and corruption often associated with state bureaucracies.[7]

Since 1990, neoliberal economics has become embodied in a set of policies widely imposed by governments and international financial institutions (IFIs). As developing countries, mired in debt, pursued export-led industrialization, many sought loans from IFIs such as the International Monetary Fund (IMF) and the World Bank, which now made their loans conditional on governments' compliance with neoliberal policies, as specified in the Structural Adjustment Programs (SAPs) that accompanied the loans. Simultaneously, hoping to keep the prices of their exports competitive and to attract foreign companies, many governments sought to keep wages low, preserving their comparative advantage in labor costs.

The pressures of the global market, in concert with free trade policy, have affected not only states' economies but their politics as well. This chapter explores several aspects of economic globalization, focusing on its ramifications for political accountability. To whom are the transnational institutions most commonly viewed as the sponsors and promoters of economic "openness" – such as the IMF, the World Bank, multinational corporations, and multilateral trade agreements – accountable? What accountability mechanisms do they feature? And under what conditions do these varied institutions foster or impair states' accountability to their citizens?

In this chapter, I begin by reviewing arguments about the general relationships among neoliberalism, economic development, and democratization.

problems. See John Williamson, "What Washington Means by Policy Reform," in John Williamson, ed., *Latin American Adjustment: How Much Has Happened?* (Washington: Institute for International Economics, 1990), accessed June 11, 2008, at http://www.iie.com/publications/papers/paper.cfm?researchid=486.

[7] See ibid.

I then explore the accountability of the IMF and the World Bank as institutions, as well as their negative and positive effects on state accountability. Similar issues are then more briefly discussed regarding the World Trade Organization (WTO), multinational corporations (MNCs), and the North American Free Trade Agreement (NAFTA). Finally, I consider various transborder responses to economic globalization, aimed at securing accountability for the citizens of an increasingly borderless world economy. On the whole, the transnational economic forces evaluated in this chapter do little to deepen and much to undermine the accountability relationship between national governments and their citizens and exhibit only meager mechanisms of accountability to the people whose economic – and even political – lives they increasingly govern.

GLOBAL NEOLIBERALISM, GROWTH, AND INEQUALITY

From the mid-1970s on, the world's countries' economic openness expanded, picking up speed over time.[8] Despite initial enthusiasm about the potential for free market reforms to remedy the economic woes of the developing world (based, in large part, on impressive growth rates in South Korea, Singapore, Taiwan, and China), economic openness and economic growth proved to have a complex relationship.

The connection between growth in GDP and economic openness remains disputed. A 2005 United Nations Development Program (UNDP) report, for example, found that a central component of neoliberalism – namely, import liberalization (cutting tariffs) – was not correlated with growth in GDP.[9] Indeed, the East Asian states that had made such progress in economic growth and poverty reduction had done so while avoiding import liberalization. Instead, they used protectionism. Trade liberalization was implemented for exports (the increase in which is good for economic growth) but only slowly when it came to "removing impediments to imports." Financial and capital markets were liberalized only gradually, and governments took seriously the need to keep inequality limited and

---

[8] Roland Paris, *At War's End: Building Peace After Civil Conflict* (New York: Cambridge University Press, 2004), p. 21, citing Jim Gwartney and Robert Lawson, with Dexter Samida, *Economic Freedom of the World: 2000 Annual Report* (Vancouver: Fraser Institute, 2000), Exhibit 3, accessed November 27, 2007, at http://oldfraser.lexi.net/publications/books/econ_free_2000/.

[9] United Nations Development Program (UNDP), *Human Development Report 2005: International Cooperation at a Crossroads: Aid, Trade and Security in an Unequal World* (2005), p. 119, accessed November 27, 2007, at http://hdr.undp.org/en/reports/global/hdr2005/.

promote education, in order to advance "social cohesion" and a "climate favorable to investment and growth." In short, the East Asian states' governments played an active role, rather than getting out of the way of the market.[10] China and several of the other developing economies most successful in the globalization era had expanded their exports, but maintained protection of their industries until new jobs in export sectors were created. Lowering barriers to imports without creating jobs to make up for those inevitably lost when imports drive local businesses in some sectors to bankruptcy would only reduce economic growth. Only after the economy grew under protected conditions did the Chinese government begin "dismantling its trade barriers, twenty years after its march to the market began, a period in which it grew extremely rapidly."[11]

Likewise disputed was a 2002 study by the World Bank, which claimed that individual countries' level of economic integration ("globalization") was positively correlated with those countries' economic growth, as well as with declining poverty and inequality.[12] Analyzing developing countries according to the change in their ratio of trade to GDP between 1977 and 1997, the study categorized its subjects as "globalizing or more globalized" states and "less globalized countries or weak globalizers," where the "globalizing countries [were] found to have had faster economic growth, no increase in inequality, and faster reduction of poverty than the weak globalizers."[13] Former World Bank economist Robert Wade critiqued the Bank's use of *change* in the ratio of trade to GDP as the indicator for globalization, arguing that instead the appropriate variable should be the *level* of a state's integration. The Bank's method places China and India in the "globalizers" category, skewing the results, because both China and India increased their trade-to-GDP ratio *not* by using "liberal trade and investment policies," but by applying protectionism. Similarly, the Bank's study placed poor countries ("dependent on a few natural resource commodity exports") with high – but not *increasing* – ratios of trade to GDP in the weak or nonglobalizing category, which hides the fact that for many countries, high levels of integration into the global economy do not correlate with economic growth.[14] The World Bank study itself included a

---

[10] Joseph Stiglitz, *Globalization and Its Discontents* (New York: W. W. Norton), p. 92.
[11] Ibid., p. 60.
[12] Robert Hunter Wade, "The Disturbing Rise in Poverty and Inequality: Is It All a 'Big Lie'?" in David Held and Mathias Koenig-Archibugi, eds., *Taming Globalization: Frontiers of Governance* (Oxford: Polity Press/Blackwell, 2003), p. 30.
[13] Ibid., p. 30.
[14] Ibid., p. 31.

disclaimer undermining its conclusion about the benefits of trade openness: "We label the top third 'more globalized' [that is, bigger increase in trade/ GDP] without in any sense implying that they adopted pro-trade policies. The rise in trade may have been due to other policies or even to pure chance."[15] Recommending trade liberalization to developing countries as a prescription for growth thus rests on a shaky foundation.

The relationship between income inequality and economic globalization is also contested.[16] Still, significant evidence points to growing income inequality in recent decades, both within and among countries around the world. By 1989, the gap in income and wealth between the richest 10 percent of the world's people and the poorest 10 percent had grown to ten times its size in 1980.[17] Using several methodologies, Wade convincingly illuminates a trend toward increasing inequality between 1980 and 2001. Using purchasing power parity (PPP) figures, Wade puts forth three claims. First, if one looks at the polarization of incomes across the globe (comparing the richest and poorest deciles of the world's population to the median), it is clear that polarization of income has "increased unambiguously" over that time period. More of the world's inhabitants are "living at the ends of the world income distribution; and a rising share of the world's income is going to those at the top." Second, weighting countries equally (e.g., Belgium counts the same as India), "inequality between countries' average PPP-adjusted income has also *increased* since at least 1980," as has the dispersion of per capita GDP. Finally, although weighting countries by population seems to show that inequality is "*constant* or *falling* since around 1980," Wade notes that this result is a statistical artifact based on the inclusion of "fast average growth in China and India. If they are excluded, even this measure of inequality shows inequality widening since 1980."[18]

The data on inequality within countries over time are less ambiguous. Between 1985 and 2005, indicators measuring domestic income inequality showed a distinct increase. According to the Human Development Report in 2005, "Of the 73 countries for which data are available, 53 (with more than 80% of the world's population) have seen inequality rise, while only 9

---

[15] Cited in ibid., p. 32.
[16] For a brief summary of various positions on this question see Valentine M. Moghadam, *Globalizing Women: Transnational Feminist Networks* (Baltimore: Johns Hopkins University Press, 2005), pp. 24–5.
[17] Stephen Gill, "Globalization, Democratization, and the Politics of Indifference," in Mittelman, ed., *Globalization: Critical Reflections*, p. 215.
[18] Wade, pp. 26–8.

(with 4% of the population) have seen it narrow. This holds true in both high- and low-growth situations (such as China in the first case and Bolivia in the second) and across all regions."[19] A growing income gap is evident even within the wealthiest countries. In the United States, for example, income inequality has been on the rise in tandem with the ascent of neoliberalism. Between 1970 and 1998, the top (richest) .01 percent of taxpayers went from holding .7 percent of total income (earning 70 times as much as the average income in the United States) to receiving over 3 percent of total income, earning 300 times as much as average families. "That meant the 13,000 richest families in America had almost as much income as the 20 million poorest households."[20]

Trying to pin down the relationship between economic liberalization and inequality, poverty, or growth in any given country over time (and hence in all countries over time) is a vexing exercise. Sound scholarly studies on this issue have reached opposite conclusions. For instance, M. Steven Fish's analysis of the relationship between liberal economic policies and social welfare in twenty postcommunist countries between 1990 and 2001 found a positive relationship between economic liberalization and improvements in social welfare.[21] By contrast, M. Rodwan Abouharb and David Cingranelli conducted another long-term, quantitative study of the same question in 131 developing countries (1981–2003) that revealed a negative relationship over time between social welfare and the implementation of market reforms via structural adjustment programs.[22] One obstacle to clarity on these matters is that convenient time series data on economic liberalization in particular is absent. One indicator, the Economic Freedom Index (EFI), which scores countries on their relative economic liberalism versus statist control of the economy (measuring protectionism, government spending and economic intervention, monetary policy, and so forth) would be useful in this regard, but its data begin only

---

[19] UNDP, *Human Development Report 2005*, p. 55.
[20] Paul Krugman, "For Richer: How the Permissive Capitalism of the Boom Destroyed American Equality," *New York Times Magazine*, October 20, 2002.
[21] M. Steven Fish, *Democracy Derailed in Russia* (Cambridge, UK: Cambridge University Press), pp. 152–5. Fish used the Cumulative Economic Liberalization Index (developed for the postcommunist region) to measure economic liberalization and the Human Development Index (HDI) to measure social welfare.
[22] M. Rodwan Abouharb and David Cingranelli, *Human Rights and Structural Adjustment* (Cambridge, UK: Cambridge University Press, 2007), pp. 142–9. The study's authors used the Physical Quality of Life Index (PQLI), which partially overlaps with HDI, as the measure of change in social well-being.

in 1995.[23] Because there is, as Fish put it, a "paucity of data on economic liberalization over the 1990s that cover the whole world," as well as for the two preceding decades, it remains for further research to uncover the precise relationship between economic liberalization and inequality over time.[24] Such research would show whether movement from less economic liberalism to more in any given country was accompanied by declining inequality or not, in the general context of a world economy increasingly focused on liberalization.

NEOLIBERALISM AND DEMOCRATIZATION: PEANUT BUTTER AND JELLY, OR OIL AND WATER?

The interactions between poverty, inequality, growth and the rise of liberal economics globally are not straightforward. Less consideration has been given to the relationship between economic liberalization and democratization, and those studies that do treat the relationship are decidedly ambivalent about the direction of the causal arrows.

One careful crossnational empirical study of this question reveals a positive relationship between openness in the polity and in the economy from 1995 to 2005. Using the World Bank's Voice and Accountability index to measure political freedom and the Economic Freedom Index to measure economic openness, Fish found that "economic freedom is a good predictor of political openness" irrespective of a country's level of development.[25] Whether this connection is a matter of correlation or causation (or which way the causal arrow might run between economic liberalism and political openness) is unclear.[26]

---

[23] For an explanation of the EFI, see Fish, p. 135.

[24] Ibid., p. 152.

[25] Ibid., pp. 135–47. For a summary of the components of the Voice and Accountability measure, and of alternative methods of scoring countries on political openness and democracy, see ibid., pp. 21–3.

[26] Ibid., p. 150. In one study of economic liberalization and democratization confined to postcommunist countries, economic liberalization is shown to have a long-term positive impact on democratization, but no short-term impact. See M. Steven Fish and Omar Choudhry, "Democratization and Economic Liberalization in the Postcommunist World," *Comparative Political Studies*, Vol. 40 (2007), pp. 254–82. Another study, looking only at democracies, finds that the more integrated a country is into the global economy (measured by trade openness and capital flows), the less "retrospective accountability" there is for incumbents on economic issues (that is, in the face of poor economic performance, voters punish incumbents less in open economies than they do in relatively more closed ones, possibly because politicians are able to blame globalization and economic openness for

Even if economic liberalization is positively correlated with democratization, the increased income inequality that has accompanied the rise of free market reforms may well amount to an unequal distribution of political accountability among the citizenry of individual countries. The rise of inequality, in combination with the contraction in government spending on public services (such as education) and social welfare "has meant that the very social and material basis for greater political equality – central to the very idea of democracy – has been undermined in many countries."[27] Under a system of liberal democracy, one's opportunity to influence policy is to some degree limited in proportion to the amount of property and other social and economic resources in one's possession.[28] Accountability is not equally distributed in the political-economic marketplace. Those in the bottom tier of income and wealth often find their political choices restricted.

In a wide-ranging study on accountability, Anne-Marie Goetz and Rob Jenkins argue that even nominally democratic political structures do not reliably tend to address the needs of the poor.[29] A 2002 UNDP study echoed this finding, drawing on the fact that per capita income (PCI) in more than sixty states was lower in 2002 than it had been in 1990. In the words of the UNDP director, Mark Malloch Brown, "Democracy doesn't seem to be responding to the real agenda of the world's poor." The report noted the relative power of corporations in democratic elections; 80 percent of the funding for India's major political parties stemmed from large corporate donors in 1996, for example.[30] For this reason, the World Bank's Voice and Accountability index may be a poor measure of political accountability, as it seeks to measure "the extent to which citizens of a country are able to participate in the selection of governments," without taking into consideration the fact that "voice," in the form of voting, lobbying political parties, participating in "community forums," and so on, does not necessarily provoke accountability, at least for the poor.[31]

---

their state's economic troubles). See Timothy Hellwig and David Samuels, "Voting in Open Economies: The Electoral Consequences of Globalization," *Comparative Political Studies* Vol. 40 (2007), pp. 283–306.

[27] Gill, p. 214.

[28] Ibid., p. 215.

[29] Anne-Marie Goetz and Rob Jenkins, *Reinventing Accountability: Making Democracy Work for Human Development* (New York: Palgrave Macmillan, 2005).

[30] Barbara Crossette, "U.N. Report Says New Democracies Falter," *New York Times*, July 24, 2002, p. A8.

[31] Goetz and Jenkins, p. 28; World Bank, "Questions and Answers: Government Indicators," accessed November 27, 2007, at http://info.worldbank.org/governance/kkz2005/q&a.htm#2.

The political power that corporations wield is only one point at which political accountability and economic forces intersect. Even in democracies, political elites' accountability to the population may be limited by transnational forces, constraining elite choices over economic and social policy. But democratic governance (in its ideal form) requires that "the main conditions affecting the social life of the members of the political community need to be under their collective control" – including the conditions affecting their economic lives.[32] As economic globalization has spread – and with it, the potential for capital flight and decreased investment – domestic economic policies are no longer adopted without an eye toward international markets.[33] The range of viable economic policy options for states has decreased; citizens' meaningful choices over their economic lives are thus limited.

As areas formerly governed by country-level decisions move into the sphere of issues governed in part by transnational institutions (from trade policy to money supply to the level of state expenditure allowed under structural adjustment programs), citizens may be frustrated by the circumscribed terrain of national politics and policy making. Some of the most controlling "global governance" institutions are the IFIs. SAPs with which states are obligated to comply as a condition for loans require governments to restrict their spending and shrink their economic role. Although the economic policy prescriptions of the Washington Consensus – christened by economist John Williamson and embodied in SAPs – embraced investment in primary education and basic health care,[34] governments often choose to pursue SAP-mandated budget targets by cutting state funding for social services across the board. This leads to higher costs for education, health care, housing, utilities, and basic commodities, especially to poorer citizens, as well as to layoffs and wage cuts for public employees.[35] Many such policy changes occur after little or no popular debate, and sometimes amidst the repression of protests against them. Under such conditions, state accountability to the population suffers. In exploring the issue of comparative citizen trust in democratic government, Pippa Norris suggests that the "increasing globalization of governance, and the weakening independence

---

[32] Mathias Koenig-Archibugi, "Introduction: Globalization and the Challenge to Governance," in Held and Koenig-Archibugi, eds., *Taming Globalization*, p. 3.

[33] Ibid., p. 4.

[34] Williamson, "What Washington Means by Policy Reform."

[35] Abouharb and Cingranelli, *Human Rights and Structural Adjustment*, pp. 138–42; International Monetary Fund (IMF), "Structural Conditionality in Fund-Supported Programs," February 16, 2001, accessed June 11, 2008, at http://www.imf.org/external/np/pdr/cond/2001/eng/struct/cond.pdf.

of the nation-state, may also reduce the ability of citizens to use party choice in national elections as a mechanism to determine public policy," thereby depressing citizens' sense that their governments are able to live up to their vision of representative democracy.[36]

Not only may the party spectrum be limited by the available policy options, restricted by economic competition among states for foreign investment and so on, but even candidates who oppose economic liberalization while on the campaign trail may become neoliberals once in office. Carlos Menem, running for the presidency of Argentina in 1989, had decided "to pursue austerity and large scale privatizations" far in advance of the election, but hid this intention from the voting public in order to retain the support of significant voter blocks, such as unions and state employees. Similarly, Alberto Fujimori, victorious in Peru's 1990 presidential elections, had campaigned against tight fiscal policy and in favor of "continued state intervention in the economy," but reversed himself once in office, implementing an austerity program almost immediately.[37] Such "switches" are not uncommon:

In twelve of the forty-four presidential election campaigns that took place in Latin America between 1982 and 1995, the winning candidate pronounced himself in favor of some combination of job creation, growth, higher real wages, industrial policy, a gradualist approach to inflation stabilization, and limited repayment of the foreign debt, only to impose austerity and a withdrawal of the state from the economy immediately upon coming to office.[38]

In other Latin American cases where presidential candidates did endorse "pro-market policies," they did so primarily when "no credible opponent could pronounce welfare beliefs and hence threaten their election," as in the Chilean case in 1989. There, Patricio Aylwin, a candidate of the coalition that displaced the dictatorial Augusto Pinochet regime (which had implemented neoliberal policies) endorsed the neoliberal model despite voters' displeasure, secure in the knowledge that the right-wing Pinochet "could not credibly shift to a welfare position."[39]

Even without direct pressure from IFIs, some developing countries successful in the liberalizing global economy have exhibited an uneasy

---

[36] Pippa Norris, ed., *Critical Citizens: Global Support for Democratic Government* (Oxford, UK: Oxford University Press, 1999), p. 23.
[37] Susan C. Stokes, "What Do Policy Switches Tell Us About Democracy?" in Adam Przeworski, Susan C. Stokes, and Bernard Manin, eds., *Democracy, Accountability, and Representation* (New York: Cambridge University Press, 1999), p. 99.
[38] Ibid., pp. 99–100.
[39] Ibid., pp. 106–8.

relationship to democracy. Markets, on their own, do not necessarily promote democratization or accountability.[40] Although, as Thomas Friedman asserts, "[G]lobal markets today are demanding, in return for their investments, the rule of law, transparency, predictability, cooperation and pluralism in financial affairs," markets do not insist on pluralism in *political* affairs.[41] In fact, some of the developing countries most successful at competing in the global market over the past few decades, demonstrating high growth rates, have been dictatorships.[42] Taiwan and South Korea, for example, maintained authoritarian rule until 1987, and the governments of Malaysia and China continue to repress political opposition, keeping labor unions tightly controlled.

Economic liberalization is not inconsistent with democratization, however. In countries where state ownership of the economy is extensive, corruption may be high, and economic power may reside in few hands. Under those circumstances, privatization of the economy could distribute not only economic but political power. But, although privatization of assets may be important as a means of spreading power beyond the pockets of state leaders, economic liberalism can also decrease workers' rights and their power to organize as citizens, making privatization an economic process that benefits some more than others when it comes to the distribution of political power and accountability.

The economic liberalization that swept Latin America, starting with the consolidation of neoliberal reforms in Chile in the 1980s, highlights this process.[43] There, free market reforms promoted growth, but also had the effect of lowering wages for workers and considerably reducing the power of trade unions, with important political ramifications up to the present

---

[40] Nor are markets themselves accountable institutions. Benjamin Barber, commenting on the dangers of "market fundamentalism," notes that the ideology of beneficent privatization "tricks people into believing...that buying power is the same as voting power. But consumers are not citizens, and markets cannot exercise democratic sovereignty.... Democracy is more than consumer polling. It demands the consideration not only of what individuals want (private choosing) but also of what society needs (public choosing)." See Benjamin R. Barber, "A Failure of Democracy, Not Capitalism," *New York Times*, July 29, 2002, p. A23.

[41] Cited in James Mittelman, *The Globalization Syndrome: Transformation and Resistance* (Princeton: Princeton University Press), p. 247.

[42] Bernard Cassen, "To Save Society," in Frank J. Lechner and John Boli, eds., *The Globalization Reader* (Malden, MA: Blackwell, 2000), p. 15.

[43] Market reforms were initiated in Chile after 1973, when the socialist government of Salvador Allende was overthrown and replaced by a military dictatorship under General Augusto Pinochet. Neoliberal policies began to dominate economic and social policy in the early 1980s. See Paul Posner, "Development and Collective Action in Chile's Neoliberal Democracy," *Political Power and Social Theory*, Vol. 18 (2007), pp. 85–129.

day. The pro-market reforms implemented by Latin America's military regimes were kept essentially intact by the postauthoritarian governments. These policies privileged the business elite at the expense of labor, eviscerating worker rights. Political scientist Paul Posner posits that the staying power of antidemocratic elements in Latin American politics ("the persistent lack of accountability of civilian and military leaders") stems in part from neoliberal economic policies, which, in turn, have a demobilizing effect on collective action.[44]

When it comes to persistent poverty and income inequality, both of which exist in Chile, grassroots action and public protest are among the best means of keeping or making state leaders accountable, particularly for populations too poor to influence policy makers in other ways. Yet, under neoliberal policies and the concomitant privatization of many public goods, the "range of issues and public policy options around which social and political actors can mobilize" is greatly reduced.[45] Governmental accountability to citizens is rendered toothless if little is left in the realm of debate. Privatization thus threatens accountability as formerly "common goods" exit the public sphere and become commodities. Moreover, neoliberal reforms have also disabled the supply side of left-leaning collective action by producing "a decline in the formal sector of the economy, a weakening of organized labor, and an expansion of the informal sector," which itself is fragmented and notoriously difficult to organize.[46] The outcome, in the Chilean case, is that in an effort to sustain Chile's international competitiveness, governments from Pinochet through the democratically elected administrations that followed have adopted neoliberal reforms that "have imposed substantial constraints on the development options open to the public" and diminished the political voice of the working class.[47]

Others claim that the judicious application of markets and privatization can support development and economic growth. Nobel Prize–winning economist Amartya Sen, for instance, puts faith in market capitalism as a contributor to both economic growth and to freedom – "the freedom of exchange and transaction."[48] But as an important corollary, Sen

[44] Ibid., p. 1.
[45] Paul Posner, *State, Market and Democracy in Chile: The Constraint of Popular Participation* (New York: Palgrave Macmillan, 2008).
[46] Ibid.
[47] Paul Posner, "Development and Collective Action in Chile's Neoliberal Democracy," conference paper presented at "Democracy in Latin America Thirty Years After Chile's 9/11," State University of New York (SUNY)–Albany, October 10–12, 2003, p. 18.
[48] Amartya Sen, *Development as Freedom* (New York: Anchor, 1999), p. 6.

acknowledges the inadequacy of markets as a means of providing for "public goods" such as health care, education, and security, and points to the danger of applying fiscal conservatism to the provision of such public goods.[49] Markets are simply not accountable to the population on the matter of labor and social rights. Political freedom, therefore, is crucial to the formation of policy that meets popular needs: "Governmental response to the acute suffering of people often depends on the pressure that is put on the government, and this is where the exercise of political rights (voting, criticizing, protesting and so on) can make a real difference."[50] Governmental accountability to the population is critical to development success. Sen's discussion of famine as a phenomenon alien to democratic regimes is a compelling illustration of this point. Dictators are unaffected by famine, but rulers in a democracy will be subject to criticism by the press and by popular disapproval at the voting booth. This leads democrats to forestall famine by providing emergency employment to people at risk of famine, so that they can purchase food and avoid its movement to wealthier areas, as the market would otherwise demand.[51] Markets, in short, ignore popular suffering. Economic liberalization, then, is compatible with democracy and accountability only to the extent that it does not function to excise from the public sphere the voices of significant groups of people.

Many states, of course, permit only the narrowest range of political participation, independent of the economic policies they adopt. The U.S.-based think tank, Freedom House, in its 2006 evaluation of the world's political systems, identified 123 "electoral democracies" (meeting the bare minimum standards of procedural democracy) among the world's 193 countries, whereas only 90 states received the rank of "free" (denoting a more thorough combination of political rights and civil liberties than "electoral democracy" alone). In that year, 58 countries were deemed "partly free," and 45 were "not free," implying some form of dictatorial rule. That "freedom" is in the minority among the world's governments is nothing new. The number of states categorized as "free" reached its apparent zenith in 1998 and, almost a decade later, remained at a plateau described by Freedom House's executive director, Jennifer Windsor, as a period of "freedom stagnation."[52] Why should this be the case?

[49] Ibid., pp. 128, 145.
[50] Ibid., p. 151.
[51] Ibid., pp. 160–88.
[52] Freedom House, "Freedom in the World, 2007," accessed June 28, 2007, at http://www.freedomhouse.org/template.cfm?page=363&year=2007.

A variety of domestic plagues, ranging from governmental corruption and civil war to abject poverty and inequality, are more than sufficient to keep democratization and accountable government at bay. The direction of the causal arrows, though, remains something of a puzzle. Do states disintegrate into ethnic conflict because democracy is absent, or does ethnic conflict make democratic governance impossible? Does poverty cause dictatorship, or is it the other way around?[53] Is corruption a cause or consequence of inequality?

Certainly the lion's share of the obstacles to governmental accountability lies at the domestic level, often with a state's leadership. Political scientist Stephen Hanson argues that without an ideology inspiring state officials to prioritize the state's interests over their own interests, corrupt practices will continue. Belief in the virtues of "belonging to Europe," for example, was instrumental in promoting accountable behavior among officials in some Eastern European countries after the fall of communist dictatorship in 1989, thereby fostering democratic consolidation.[54] Absent the belief in an ideology that convinces state officials to behave in accountable ways or to support the development of accountable institutions, such institutions are unlikely to be built or to be long-lasting.[55]

Poverty, inequality, corruption, the violent repression of political protest – all these may be symptoms of unaccountable government. The accepted practices of national sovereignty typically render such problems domestic – to be solved at the state level. But state policy and governance do not take place in isolation. The vast majority of states are tied into the global economy, affected to differing degrees by the institutional carriers of economic liberalization – international financial institutions such as the IMF and the World Bank, multinational corporations (MNCs), and transnational trade agreements. To the extent that these transnational economic institutions promote or detract from accountability to the people affected by them (whether directly or indirectly, by way of their effects on state accountability), they deserve our attention here.

---

[53] Statistical analyses of the relationship between political liberties and economic growth generate mixed results, suggesting no reliable relationship between them. See Sen, p. 328, ft. 4.

[54] Stephen E. Hanson, "Defining Democratic Consolidation," in Richard D. Anderson, Jr., M. Steven Fish, Stephen E. Hanson, and Philip G. Roeder, *Postcommunism and the Theory of Democracy* (Princeton: Princeton University Press, 2001), pp. 141–8.

[55] Ibid., p. 142, citing Arthur Stinchcombe, "On the Virtues of the Old Institutionalism," *Annual Review of Sociology*, Vol. 23 (1997), pp. 1–19.

INSTITUTIONS OF ECONOMIC GLOBALIZATION:
THE IMF AND THE WORLD BANK

Founded as World War II drew to a close, the IMF and the World Bank (sometimes called the "Bretton Woods" institutions, after the United Nations conference in Bretton Woods, New Hampshire, at which they were established) constituted an institutional attempt to create a transnational economic atmosphere conducive to growth. The World Bank's initial mandate was to provide reconstruction loans to Japan and the European states devastated by World War II, whereas the IMF was initially conceived as an organization supporting international trade (by regularizing the system of payments between countries engaging in trade) and also as a source of loans to remedy balance-of-payments problems in the advanced industrial countries. In the 1960s, the IMF's client base shifted, as many recently decolonized countries sought loans. Many of these newly independent states lacked the economic institutions more commonly found in the industrialized world, and were floundering in long-term economic straits.[56] Under these new lending circumstances, the IMF began to impose ever-larger numbers of conditions on its loans, "to compel governments to adopt the desired economic policies."[57] The conditions started to include various means to "increase export productivity," such as "improving infrastructure, diversifying exports, liberalizing trade, eliminating price controls, enforcing wage restraint, and changing tax policy and government expenditure patterns."[58] Traditionally, these policy areas had been addressed by states rather than by transnational lenders.

Distinct from each other at first, the lending profiles of the IMF and the World Bank converged over time. Until the 1980s, the World Bank lent funds to states for large-scale development projects, whereas the IMF restricted itself to short-term lending to solve balance-of-payments difficulties. Loans from the latter organization came along with financial austerity conditions, whereas World Bank funds largely carried no such constraints. This line between IMF and World Bank lending deteriorated in the 1980s, as IMF loans became more long term and World Bank loans acquired conditionalities similar to those placed on borrowers from the IMF. Both institutions had become lenders mandating structural adjustment programs

---

[56] Michael Barnett and Martha Finnemore, *Rules for the World: International Organizations in Global Politics* (Ithaca: Cornell University Press, 2004), p. 59.
[57] Ibid., pp. 56–7.
[58] Ibid., p. 59.

in the developing countries that borrowed from them, and are two of the world's major institutional promoters of economic liberalization.[59]

The origins of structural adjustment programs lie largely in the oil crisis of 1973. As oil prices rose, profits flowed from the oil-exporting countries to Western banks, which sought to lend the money out and benefit from interest on their loans. Many such loans were made to the governments of developing countries, enabling them to pay for the increasingly expensive oil, and also to buy Western goods, fund large development projects, increase military spending, and, in some cases, pocket the funds themselves. Encouraged by Western governments and the IMF, "[u]naccountable military dictators were supported by loans from equally unaccountable bankers."[60] Interest rates rose at the end of the 1970s, as did oil prices, and the loan recipients were unable to pay off their debts, as prices for their raw material and agricultural exports declined. The IMF and the World Bank loaned money to these states, imposing structural adjustment programs designed to push states to increase exports, cut state spending, and pay back their debts using their export earnings – in short, to liberalize their economic policies.[61]

What effects have IMF and World Bank structural adjustment programs had on economic growth and inequality? Michel Camdessus, a former managing director of the IMF, and his successor, Horst Kohler, claim that IMF loans and the conditions attached to them are designed at least in part to promote economic growth in borrower countries.[62] Yet former World Bank economist William Easterly, analyzing IMF and World Bank adjustment loans from 1980 to 1998, found "no direct effect of structural adjustment on growth," and that the amount of change in poverty rates given a certain amount of growth is lower when a country is operating under structural adjustment loans than when it is not.[63] Looking at the effects of IMF agreements alone on growth, political scientist James Vreeland revealed a consistent picture. After controlling for selection bias from relevant variables (such as economic conditions, because countries

[59] Paris, p. 21. For a coherent explanation and critique of IMF conditionality policies, see Stiglitz, *Globalization and Its Discontents*.

[60] Jean Somers, "Debt: The New Colonialism," in Bill Bigelow and Bob Peterson, *Rethinking Globalization: Teaching for Justice in an Unjust World* (Milwaukee: Rethinking Schools Press, 2002), p. 79.

[61] Ibid., pp. 78–81.

[62] James Vreeland, *The IMF and Economic Development* (New York: Cambridge University Press, 2003), p. 2.

[63] William Easterly, "IMF and World Bank Structural Adjustment Programs and Poverty," World Bank, 2001.

with low growth might be the ones applying for IMF loans in the first place), Vreeland found that IMF programs "have a negative effect on economic growth" across time.[64] Specifically, "on average, economic growth is roughly 1.5 percent slower when countries are under an IMF program than otherwise."[65]

IMF programs not only have a negative impact on economic growth, but they also increase income inequality. Although growth declines overall, "those at the upper end of the income distribution" may gain financially "because of distributional shifts" away from economically disadvantaged groups like labor and the poor.[66] Put differently, working-class incomes tend to decline under IMF agreements. International creditors evaluate low wages for workers as "a good sign, indicating a willingness or commitment to repay debt." One 1990 study showed that "wage repression in a given country is positively associated with loans to that country."[67]

Why might IMF loans and the conditions associated with them decrease economic growth and exacerbate the gap between rich and poor in a given country? According to Vreeland, growth declines due to cuts in public investment, increased interest rates (leading to bankruptcy among local businesses), and capital flight:

There is no reason to assume that upward shifts in income distribution should result in *domestic* investment. Increased income of the owners of capital may simply result in savings abroad. If this is the case then the distributional consequences of IMF programs may exacerbate this pattern.[68]

[64] Vreeland, p. 8.
[65] Kendall W. Stiles, "The IMF and Economic Development: Book Review," *Perspectives on Politics*, Vol. 2, No. 3 (September 2004), p. 644.
[66] Vreeland, pp. 134, 151. See also Gopal Garuda, "The Distributional Effects of IMF Programs: A Cross-Country Analysis," *World Development*, 28 (2000), pp. 1031–51; Manuel Pastor, Jr., "The Effects of IMF Programs in the Third World: Debate and Evidence from Latin America," *World Development* 15 (1987), pp. 365–91; idem, *The International Monetary Fund and Latin America: Economic Stabilization and Class Conflict* (Boulder: Westview Press, 1987).
[67] Vreeland, p. 157, citing Gary A. Dymski and Manuel Pastor, Jr., "Bank Lending, Misleading Signals, and the Latin American Debt Crisis," *International Trade Journal* 6 (1990), pp. 151–92.
[68] Vreeland, p. 155, italics in the original. Trade liberalization hypothetically improves growth by opening up the country to imports that would then push inefficient local industry to close down and be replaced by more productive industry. But, as Stiglitz explains, this does not occur in the absence of capital and sufficient entrepreneurship, and capital is unavailable because IMF conditions require high interest rates – "sometimes exceeding 20 percent, sometimes exceeding 50 percent, sometimes even exceeding 100 percent." New jobs thus fail to materialize, replacing low productivity jobs with no jobs at all. See Stiglitz, *Globalization and Its Discontents*, p. 59.

Reasons for rising income inequality include the unemployment and lower wages that tend to occur under SAPs, as well as the increased costs of imported goods (because devaluation of the local currency makes imports more expensive). Cutbacks in state subsidies along with increased taxes (to raise state revenue) also increase the income gap, in part because the effort to raise taxes often focuses on sales tax and value-added tax, the rates of which are the same for every consumer but the burden of which therefore "fall more heavily" on the poor.[69]

Awareness of such issues may have provoked changes in IMF and World Bank loan agreements. The 1990s brought the advent of IMF and World Bank restructuring programs featuring "social safety nets" to offset the programs' adverse effects on the poor. And in 1999, the IMF renamed its Enhanced Structural Adjustment Facility; it is now the Poverty Reduction and Growth Facility, reflecting at least a rhetorical commitment to poverty reduction.[70]

In their literature, the IMF and the World Bank put forth an explicit commitment to reducing poverty and promoting economic growth in the developing world.[71] The World Bank in particular also expresses concern about corruption and other markers of unaccountable government in its borrower states. But both organizations are frequently criticized for their own lack of accountability. To whom and through what mechanisms are these powerful institutions accountable? And in what ways do the IMF and the World Bank promote or detract from states' accountability to their citizens?

Accountability and the IMF

Whereas democratic theory has extensively addressed the question of legitimacy and what constitutes it within a nation-state, scholars "have far fewer notions about how or why global governance and rule by

[69] Paris, pp. 166–7, citing Manuel Pastor, Jr., and Michael Conroy, "Distributional Implications for Macroeconomic Policy: Theory and Applications to El Salvador," in James K. Boyce, ed., *Economic Policy for Building Peace* (Boulder: Lynne Rienner, 1996), p. 159. In contrast to Vreeland's broader data, one study examining SAPs in Latin America found a weak association between structural adjustment and growth, as well as a somewhat positive impact of structural adjustment on poverty and inequality reduction. Brian F. Crisp, Michael J. Kelly, "The Socioeconomic Impacts of Structural Adjustment," *International Studies Quarterly*, 43 (1999), pp. 533–52.
[70] Jan Aart Scholte, *Globalization: A Critical Introduction* (New York: Palgrave), pp. 141, 215.
[71] International Monetary Fund, "What Is the IMF?" accessed September 30, 2006 at http://www.imf.org/external/pubs/ft/exrp/what.htm#do.

international organizations might be legitimate."[72] Debate has therefore arisen regarding the legitimacy and accountability of transnational organizations, from the European Union to the IFIs, over their putative "democratic deficit."

What is the evidence for a "democratic deficit" with respect to the IMF? One set of arguments focuses on the IMF's role as a promoter of economic liberalization. In this view, international institutions that promote neoliberal policies are undemocratic to the degree that they undermine state responsiveness to the population, especially in the area of welfare provision.[73] Rising inequality, from this perspective, would be addressed by governments if they were not restrained by IMF conditionalities and the free trade policies that the IMF supports.

A second argument pointing to a democratic deficit at the IMF turns on the organization's internal accountability. To whom, precisely, is the IMF accountable in its policy decisions and their effects? Internally, the IMF is accountable to its Board of Governors, typically the ministers of finance or central bank governors of the 185 countries that constitute the IMF's membership. These "governors," appointed by the member states, are presumably accountable to their own governments. The governors, however, attend only yearly meetings, which do not conduct "real managerial or policy business."[74] At the daily level, the IMF is run by a twenty-four–member executive board composed of representatives (the "executive directors") of various member states, plus the managing director (chair of the executive board). The United States, the United Kingdom, Japan, Germany, France, Russia, China, and Saudi Arabia all have their own executive directors; other states form groups and share an executive director.[75] The executive board meets three times a week in Washington, D.C., and approves all the IMF's actions and reports. It is the executive directors "who formally make the decisions regarding the disposition of funds and other key matters of policy."[76]

---

[72] Barnett and Finnemore, p. 166.

[73] For a critical summary of the "social democratic" critique of international organizations, see Andrew Moravcsik, "Is There a 'Democratic Deficit' in World Politics? A Framework for Analysis," *Government and Opposition*, Vol. 39, No. 2 (April 2004), p. 357.

[74] Barnett and Finnemore, p. 48.

[75] Ibid., p. 48. For a list of the executive directors and their alternates, see http://www.imf.org/external/np/sec/memdir/eds.htm.

[76] See Joseph S. Nye, Jr., et al., *The "Democracy Deficit" in the Global Economy: Enhancing the Legitimacy and Accountability of Global Institutions* (A Report to the Trilateral Commission) (Washington, Paris, Tokyo: Trilateral Commission, 2003), p. 15.

In decision making, states' votes are weighted according to their "quota subscriptions" – the sum of money that each country pays to the IMF upon joining the organization. These "quotas" are calculated in accordance with the size of each state's economy; quotas for states with larger economies far outweigh those of developing countries.[77] Because each state's percentage of votes is tied to economic indicators, IMF votes "reflect not just the preferences of states but the preferences of the Fund's richest and most powerful members."[78] According to the Articles of Agreement (section 5), decisions are typically made by majority vote.[79] In accordance with the distribution of voting power on the IMF's executive board, the United States holds just under 17 percent of the votes. Japan, Germany, France, and the UK, which wield the next largest number of votes, together control nearly 22 percent. By contrast, developing countries are underrepresented in decision making at the IMF; as of July 2008, forty-four African states shared just two seats on the executive board and wielded a combined total of 4.4 percent of the total votes.[80] The distribution of decision-making power among member states is important because of the powerful role that the IMF plays in international finance. Based on "objective" indicators, the IMF categorizes countries' economies in normative ways, and those determinations "can affect the ability of a state to get external financing at reasonable rates, to get access to IMF funds, or to escape the IMF's conditionality demands."[81]

[77] For information on how quotas are determined and the formula by which they are converted into voting power, see International Monetary Fund, "IMF Quotas: A Factsheet," October 2007, accessed November 27, 2007, at http://www.imf.org/external/np/exr/facts/quotas.htm.

[78] Barnett and Finnemore, p. 49. The IMF is self-financing: its administrative costs are covered by interest on its loans and by investing the funds that member states contribute upon joining the organization. See ibid., pp. 49, 186, ft. 9. On the IMF's financing, see International Monetary Fund, "Financing the Fund's Operations," April 11, 2001, accessed November 27, 2007, at http://www.imf.org/external/np/tre/ffo/2001/fin.htm. A table showing each IMF member country's quota and votes held (as a percentage of the total) can be found at International Monetary Fund, "IMF Members' Quotas and Voting Power, and IMF Board of Governors," November 2007, accessed November 27, 2007, at http://www.imf.org/external/np/sec/memdir/members.htm.

[79] Barnett and Finnemore, p. 49. Although its decision-making process is generally referred to as "voting," the executive board "rarely votes on most matters. Instead, the managing director simply concludes the discussions with a statement about 'the sense of the meeting,' which constitutes the board's decision." See ibid., p. 185, ft. 5. The managing director holds only a tiebreaker vote. See IMF, "Articles of Agreement of the International Monetary Fund," Article XII, accessed July 29, 2008, at http://www.imf.org/external/pubs/ft/aa/aa12.htm#5.

[80] International Monetary Fund, "IMF Executive Directors and Voting Power," accessed July 31, 2008, at http://www.imf.org/external/np/sec/memdir/eds.htm.

[81] Barnett and Finnemore, p. 32.

These categorizations are crucial to the developing countries seeking loans on international markets.

Based on the preceding, the IMF appears to be internally accountable to the member states that fund it.[82] Despite a voting process that lends some states more power than others, membership in the IMF is voluntary, superficially suggesting intact lines of accountability between the organization and its member states, mediated through their finance ministers.[83] But are IFIs (such as the IMF) tools of the national governments that participate in them, or are they proxies for the government of a global polity?[84] If they are merely tools of their member states, then they present no accountability problem, because the IFIs in that case are analogous to national-level regulatory agencies to which decision-making power is delegated. In short, if national governments delegate authority to IFIs, then the IFIs are accountable to those governments (the "shareholders").[85] In this view, IMF "interventions" in the developing world, such as membership in the IMF itself, are voluntary, occurring at the behest of states seeking IMF assistance. Agreement by a national government to adopt any loan conditionalities thus suffices as evidence of IMF accountability to its member states, and demands for greater IMF accountability are misplaced.[86]

But if the IMF and other international financial institutions are in fact institutions of global governance, creating government policies and circumscribing policy choices in exchange for financing (as a national legislature might do in an appropriations bill), then they may fairly be regarded as insufficiently accountable to the "stakeholders" – those affected by the policies that they promote.[87] From this perspective, there are many obstacles to the IMF's external accountability as an institution. First, whereas there are few links in the chain of accountability between decision makers at the IMF and those in the finance ministries of member states, there are many more (or none) between those decision makers and the people affected by their decisions. Vreeland suggests that the accountability chains between

---

[82] In Keohane's terms, the IMF is subject to internal accountability because its member states control it by means of "authorization" and "support." See Robert O. Keohane, "Global Governance and Democratic Accountability," in Held and Koenig–Archibugi, eds., *Taming Globalization*, pp. 144–5.

[83] "Voluntary" participation in the IMF is rather constrained, because most developing countries cannot get by without IMF assistance. See Barnett and Finnemore, p. 167.

[84] Miles Kahler, "Defining Accountability Up: The Global Economic Multilaterals," *Government and Opposition*, Vol. 39, No. 2 (April 2004), p. 136.

[85] Ibid., p. 136.

[86] Ibid., p. 138.

[87] Ibid., p. 136.

domestic constituents and IMF staff creating conditions for loans are extremely complex and therefore weak: "Taken in sum, it might be a miracle if there is any accountability at all."[88] In democratic polities adopting IMF conditions, the accountability chain may be tortuous (from IMF staff, to the executive board, to the Board of Governors, to the government of the member state that appointed [or elected] its governor to the IMF, to the voter who can oppose that government in the next election). But in nondemocratic states under adjustment programs, the accountability chain between the IMF and the citizenry is broken, because the citizens of such states neither voted for nor may vote against the leaders who made those particular financial agreements with the IMF under a free and fair electoral system.[89]

Regardless of the type of government under which they live, the people most likely to experience the results of IMF policies are in effect excluded from the locus of decision making. Accountability to them – even indirect accountability – is largely absent: "many people are stakeholders in global political problems that affect them, but remain excluded from the political institutions and strategies needed to address these problems."[90] Even in democratic, representative states, IFIs such as the IMF are not legitimated by national governments in their entirety, but in reality, only by "parts of" those governments. Under the "club model of international organization," the IMF is a "club" of finance ministers (just as the WTO is a "club" of trade ministers), leaving out other parts of the governments that participate in IMF and WTO agreements (such as the sectors of the state responsible for environmental or labor standards).[91]

The limited range of people involved in IMF decision making (compared to the organization's reach) strikes former World Bank chief economist Joseph Stiglitz as fundamentally unfair. Because taxpayers in borrower countries pay back the loans received from the IMF (the default rate is extremely low), it has, in effect, imposed "taxation without representation."[92] This constitutes a situation of political unaccountability:

[The] mind-set of an institution is inevitably linked to whom it is *directly* accountable.... The IMF's actions affect the lives and livelihoods of billions throughout

---

[88] Vreeland, pp. 157–8.
[89] Authoritarian government cannot, of course, be blamed on the IMF, and, as will be discussed in this chapter, IFIs' accountability mechanisms can serve as an important way for citizens to affect indirectly the actions of their nondemocratic governments.
[90] David Held, "Democratic Accountability and Political Effectiveness from a Cosmopolitan Perspective," *Government and Opposition*, Vol. 30, No. 2 (April 2004), p. 370.
[91] Nye et al., p. 4.
[92] Stiglitz, *Globalization and Its Discontents*, pp. 20, 62.

the developing world; yet they have little say in its actions. The workers who are thrown out of jobs as a result of the IMF programs have no seat at the table; while the bankers, who insist on getting repaid, are well represented through the finance ministers and central bank governors. The consequences for policy have been predictable: bailout packages which pay more attention to getting creditors repaid than to maintaining the economy at full employment.[93]

Another obstacle to the IMF's external accountability is its lack of institutional transparency. Without sufficient information, accountability cannot be enforced. The IMF is subject neither to direct accountability by citizens nor to the equivalent of a transnational Freedom of Information Act that would make more citizens aware of the details of the agreements that their governments sign as well as the positions taken at the IMF by the representatives of their governments.[94] Legislators, too, are often out of the loop when it comes to IMF decision making. Despite the fact that in 2000, the U.S. Congress passed legislation requiring the U.S. executive director at the IMF to vote against proposals to include "user fees" for elementary school students in loan agreements, the U.S. executive director "ignored the law" and voted in favor of imposing such fees. Had the information not been leaked, the closed nature of IMF deliberations and votes would have "made it difficult for Congress – or anyone else – to see what was going on."[95] As a public institution, the IMF should be subject to public accountability and transparency, rather than shielded by secrecy.[96] Other scholars agree that national legislatures and parliaments need better information about the IFIs and their activities and that greater transparency would facilitate the process of keeping the public and their representatives well informed.[97]

The IMF's lack of transparency also enables unaccountable behavior by member states' governments, in that member governments often disavow responsibility for decisions made at the IMF. Based on his own experience at the IMF, one participant in a 2001 Trilateral Commission meeting about

[93] Ibid., p. 225.
[94] Joseph Stiglitz, "Globalization and Development," in Held and Koenig-Archibugi, eds., *Taming Globalization*, p. 63.
[95] Stiglitz, *Globalization and Its Discontents*, pp. 51–2; see also Celia W. Dugger, "In Africa, Free Schools Feed a Different Hunger," *New York Times*, October 24, 2004, accessed July 31, 2008, at http://www.nytimes.com/2004/10/24/international/africa/24africa.html? pagewanted=1&_r=1&sq=user%20fees%20october%202000%20congress&st=cse& oref=slogin&scp=2.
[96] Stiglitz, *Globalization and Its Discontents*, p. 52.
[97] See Nye et al., pp. 5–6.

IFI accountability bemoaned the tendency of governments to be two-faced on matters of IMF policy:

Let me say that it is an infuriating dereliction of duty to have a government sit in the board of the IMF, push in one direction, and six weeks later criticize the institution for going in the direction which they pushed....I think it is a major cause of the [IMF's] perceived lack of accountability that governments simply will not stand up and defend the things they do in private.[98]

In the words of international relations scholar Joseph Nye, "The democratic deficit really does start at home."[99]

Although such arguments may make it appear that the IMF is, in fact, accountable to member governments – who only pretend to be powerless – in a study of transnational bureaucracies, including the IMF, Michael Barnett and Martha Finnemore argue that IFI accountability to states is largely illusory. Such organizations tend, over time, to become autonomous from the states that created them, resulting in unintended side effects and undesired consequences. Transnational bureaucracies are fully accountable neither to their member states nor to local populations. Barnett and Finnemore debunk the idea that international organizations (IOs) are merely the reflection of states' desires. Instead, as bureaucracies, they not only "develop their own ideas and pursue their own agendas," but even carry out counterproductive policies in contradiction to their own missions.[100]

Using the IMF for illustration, Barnett and Finnemore show how transnational bureaucracies expand their roles within states without a concomitant increase in accountability to the citizens of those states. In trying to determine why its past remedies for fixing balance-of-payments problems in the advanced industrial countries failed to work in the developing world, the IMF ended up expanding its mandate to interfere more and more in domestic economies, establishing conditionalities and technical assistance programs that contributed to vast structural changes in the economies of its client states.[101] Although conditionalities imposed on deficit states (states with international balance-of-payments problems) were not foreseen in the IMF's original Articles of Agreement, the conditions placed on IMF loans expanded over time as deficits proved intractable. "In the 1970s the number of performance criteria in IMF stabilization programs averaged six. In the 1980s it averaged ten. By 1999

[98] Ibid., p. 15.
[99] Ibid., p. 18.
[100] Barnett and Finnemore, p. 2.
[101] Ibid., p. 13.

there were an average of twenty-five performance criteria attached to IMF stabilization programs required of borrowers for use of IMF resources."[102] These included specific "fiscal and monetary conditions...containing not just targets but both ceilings and floors," as well as policies such as wage restraint and the removal of state subsidies.[103] Despite these encroachments on domestic economies, decreased balance of payments deficits were still elusive in many cases. The IMF turned to another set of factors at that point, aimed at improving the capacity, transparency, and general "good governance" of loan recipients.[104] Given its initially narrow mandate, the IMF's level of accountability to states likely seemed sufficient for the tasks first delegated to it. As its purview expanded, the IMF's increasing intervention into national economies turned the IMF into a domestic political player, warranting more accountability to the affected populations.

The absence of such accountability in the face of growing popular education about structural adjustment programs exposes the legitimacy failures of the IMF and other IFIs. Recognizing these legitimacy gaps has led international organizations to try to increase the participation of borrower governments in the development of their policies (to promote policy "ownership"). Also, to enhance the informational side of accountability, the IMF has begun to provide a great deal of information on its website, including the text of loan agreements. Its internal discussions, however, remain largely inaccessible to the public.[105]

In an attempt to redress the perceived accountability gap further, in 2001 the IMF created an Independent Evaluation Office (IEO).[106] The IEO revisits and evaluates particular IMF programs and policies, "selecting operations for review based on suggestions from stakeholders inside and outside the IMF."[107] The IEO reports do not sugar-coat their negative findings. A report on the success of the IMF's exchange rate policy advice from 1999 to 2005, for instance, found that the IMF "was simply not as effective as it needed to be in both its analysis and its advice, and

---

[102] Ibid., pp. 56–9.
[103] Ibid., pp. 60–1.
[104] Ibid., pp. 61–2.
[105] Ibid., p. 170.
[106] With reference to institutions of global governance, Keohane asks, "Which entities should be held accountable, to whom, in what ways?" And what should be done in the event of "'accountability gaps' – situations in which actual practice differs greatly from a desirable state of affairs?" See Keohane, "Global Governance and Democratic Accountability," p. 132.
[107] See International Monetary Fund, "What Is the IMF?"

in its dialogue with member countries," and also noted the accountability problems that can arise when country officials insist on the confidentiality of their discussions with IMF staff, such that the information cannot be shared with the IMF's executive board. On this issue, the report concluded, "Simply pretending that no issue exists is not a responsible response."[108] In 2005, the IEO undertook an evaluation of the effectiveness of structural conditionality in IMF programs, reflecting awareness of the extensive criticism that its policies have received since the early 1990s, when structural conditionality expanded, leading to increased intervention in national politics.[109] The founding of the IEO bespeaks a certain consciousness on the part of IMF management about the importance of monitoring the effects of IMF interventions and of involving outside "stakeholders" in the process and may improve the internal and external accountability of the institution overall.

At base, international institutions are only as publicly accountable as their member states allow them to be. In that sense, as Jessica Einhorn notes, the "democratic deficit stems most acutely from the unrepresentative nature of some member governments of these organizations, and from the imperfect democracy in every country."[110] However, to the extent that they lack accountability to the people they affect, transnational economic institutions such as the IMF contribute to the democratic deficit. Some IFIs have attempted to shrink their accountability gaps by setting up internal and external accountability mechanisms and by releasing information about their activities to the public. By using undemocratic processes, transnational economic institutions can reinforce member states' lack of accountability to their citizens. But IFIs also have the power to challenge the accountability gaps that governments perpetuate at home. The next section examines the ways in which the IMF both supports and detracts from states' accountability to their citizens.

State Accountability and the IMF

One way in which the IMF can detract from governmental accountability is by privileging the executive branch, enabling the latter to push

---

[108] Independent Evaluation Office (IEO), "IMF Exchange Rate Policy Advice 1999–2005," May 17, 2007, pp. 2, 9.

[109] Independent Evaluation Office, "Evaluation of Structural Conditionality in IMF-Supported Programs," May 17, 2005, p. 2, accessed November 27, 2007, at http://www.ieo-imf.org/eval/ongoing/051805.pdf.

[110] Jessica Einhorn, in Nye et al., p. 28.

through unpopular policies enshrined in IMF agreements, and sidelining the legislature in the process. As Vreeland established, IMF adjustment programs often depress economic growth. Why might governments sign on to such agreements? Some states do so out of economic difficulty such as debt, deficits, lack of investment, and the fact that "they are desperate for foreign reserves and are forced to accept IMF conditions in exchange."[111] But there is also a political reason: The executive branch may bring in the IMF as a means of pushing through economic policies that would not be supported at home. In short, "they may want conditions to be imposed."[112] Based on statistics, including the finding that countries seek IMF programs irrespective of their level of foreign reserves, Vreeland argues: "The imposition of conditions may not be a stick but a carrot, attracting unpopular governments seeking to impose economic policy changes. The IMF may tend to be an ally for right wing governments."[113]

An IMF agreement is signed by a representative of a country's executive branch, the finance minister. The IMF concludes its agreements "with this branch of government alone, even if the approval of other parties, such as a legislature, are [sic] required for the policy changes laid out in the agreement."[114] An accountability problem therefore arises. If the executive branch favors market reforms (a desire that may be shared in the short term by a narrow group of wealthy supporters in the export sector) but the majority of the population – in a democratic setting – does not, the legislative branch may be unwilling to engage in economic reforms. However, once the executive branch agrees to IMF conditions, the legislature must pass laws to make the policy changes; otherwise, the IMF will fail to make the loan, which in turn, sends a negative message to other creditors as well as to investors from abroad.[115] The legislature in that case can be said to behave as if it were accountable to the executive branch – or, indirectly, to the IMF – rather than to its domestic constituents. Given that governments often spend years at a time under IMF loans and conditions, this is not a trivial accountability gap. Between 1971 and 1990, the average period spent under consecutive agreements was 5.3 years, with many states under agreements for longer periods.[116]

---

[111] Vreeland, pp. 126, 153.
[112] Ibid., p. 16.
[113] Ibid., p. 103.
[114] Ibid., p. 12.
[115] Ibid., p. 14.
[116] Ibid., p. 18.

IFIs such as the IMF thus behave as "enablers" to state leaders seeking to short-circuit their accountability to groups such as labor that may be powerful within the legislative branch. An IMF agreement (and the financial ramifications of a legislative refusal to implement it) allows the executive to abdicate responsibility for unpopular economic policies. In this way, governments can use IFIs "to skew policy outcomes away from those that are likely in the national political arena."[117]

Although this may disenfranchise parts of the population, it enhances the power of executives, who generally seek to avoid domestic opposition.[118] It is for this reason – to avoid accountability to their domestic audience – that governments resist reform of the IMF's policy of safeguarding the confidentiality of negotiations and decision making. Despite reforms such as the creation of the IEO, "information that might embarrass a government at the hands of its domestic opponents has remained carefully guarded at the IMF."[119] By abjuring transparency in its decision-making process, the IMF enables state executives to evade accountability to their populations.

In states featuring a modicum of vertical accountability, voters can eventually remove the executive who agreed to IMF conditions (whether they did so under duress or as an end-run around likely domestic opposition). But IMF agreements can extend beyond the term of the executive branch that initiated it. Because such agreements can provoke significant changes in economic policy, including reductions in social welfare spending (in order to meet hard targets in deficit reduction), the accountability picture becomes more complicated when agreements extend over time to political administrations that have not yet been elected. Political control over the Brazilian economy, for example, was at stake when in 2002 the existing government signed a loan agreement for $30 billion in the face of elections planned for several months later. The agreement stipulated that $24 billion of the loan would be disbursed in 2003, after the elections, only under the condition that the new – as yet unelected – government would achieve "certain budgetary targets" or face a cutoff of much-needed funds. This fact effectively compelled both of the left-leaning opposition candidates in Brazil's election to "reluctantly [endorse] the loan deal" despite popular dissatisfaction with eight years of neoliberal policies. The economic adviser to the Workers' Party candidate who eventually won

---

[117] Kahler, pp. 141–2.
[118] Ibid., p. 141.
[119] Ibid., pp. 143–4, 156.

office, Luiz Inacio da Silva (known as Lula), commented that the IMF agreement would restrict a future Worker's Party government like "a plaster cast" and prevent its candidate from fulfilling campaign promises about social welfare spending.[120] When an election cannot significantly affect a government's budgetary choices due to external restraints, accountability is in question.

The governments of developing countries often sign IMF agreements in the absence of other options. The prime minister of post-independence Jamaica, Michael Manley, initially scorned the IMF, stating: "the Jamaican government will not accept anybody, anywhere in the world telling us what to do in our own country. Above all, we're not for sale." Manley had been elected in 1976 on an anti-IMF platform, but in 1977, lacking other options, he reluctantly signed Jamaica's first loan agreement with the IMF.[121]

Governments adopting IMF programs because they need the loan may discover that they are under significant pressure to restrict debate over the program's conditions. In late 1997, in the throes of the East Asian currency crisis, South Korean state officials were "scared to disagree openly [with the policies being imposed on Korea by the IMF]." Not only might they risk losing the IMF loan, but public hesitation on Korea's part could provide fuel for the IMF to "discourage investments from private market funds" in the Korean economy. The executive branch's approval of a loan agreement is not evidence of democratic consent, because the latter implies informed public debate. By contrast, Stiglitz contends, "In dictating the terms of the agreements, the IMF effectively stifles any discussions within a client government – let alone more broadly within the country – about alternative economic policies," thereby obstructing governmental accountability.[122]

Any narrowing of public debate over policy options under conditionality is particularly problematic for state accountability because IMF loan agreements may require legislation on economic issues of considerable importance to the public. Some agreements even specify the laws that a state's legislature "would have to pass to meet IMF requirements or 'targets' – and by when."[123] In Haiti, for example, where the IMF sought to

[120] Larry Rohter, "Brazilians Find Political Cost for Help from I.M.F.," *New York Times*, August 11, 2002, p. 3.
[121] See Stephanie Black, "About the Film," 2001, accessed November 27, 2007, at http://www.lifeanddebt.org/about.html.
[122] Stiglitz, *Globalization and Its Discontents*, pp. 42–3.
[123] Ibid., pp. 43–4.

increase Haitian exports, one of the IMF's loan conditions was to maintain Haitian wages at poverty level: "In 1991 and 1994, the IMF conditioned loan assistance on wage restraint. Then, in 1996, the IMF gave the Haitian government technical assistance to revise its labor code. Haitian labor law had required an increase in the minimum wage if inflation were to exceed 10 percent. The IMF had that law changed, even as inflation hit 30 percent."[124] Direct pressure from the IMF to cap or decrease the wages of low-income workers is not uncommon.[125]

In effect, because poor and indebted states are so dependent on loans, such policy changes render the government more accountable to transnational economic institutions than to domestic constituents.[126] This "donor-driven" accountability gap is widespread in the developing world. In Mozambique, for instance, in the early 1990s, a majority of gross national product (GNP) consisted of development aid, coming in exchange for political and economic reforms. Arrangements made with the IMF and the World Bank for structural adjustment mandated cuts in "human resource development" in order to free up funds that could go toward paying some fraction of Mozambique's $5.8 billion debt, representing 443.6 percent of GNP in 1995.[127] James Mittelman explains:

An ever-tightening web of conditionality constricts Mozambique's economic and political options. This vulnerability severely limits the state's ability to formulate policies appropriate to national needs. (Hence, when IMF and World Bank officials came to Maputo and told Mozambicans to tighten their belts, local authorities were incredulous. Knowing full well that many of their compatriots are so threadbare that they must substitute potato sacks for clothing, the government's negotiating team matter-of-factly responded that the people do not have belts to tighten.)[128]

---

[124] Global Exchange, "How the International Monetary Fund and the World Bank Undermine Democracy and Erode Human Rights: Five Case Studies," September 2001, accessed March 1, 2006, at http://www.globalexchange.org/campaigns/wbimf/imfwbReport2001.html.

[125] Paul W. Drake, "Introduction: The Political Economy of Foreign Advisers and Lenders in Latin America," in Paul W. Drake, ed., *Money Doctors, Foreign Debts, and Economic Reforms in Latin America from the 1890s to the Present* (Wilmington: Scholarly Resources, 1994), pp. xi–xxxiii.

[126] Goetz and Jenkins, p. 10.

[127] Mittelman, *The Globalization Syndrome*, pp. 98–9, 101.

[128] Ibid., p. 99. The power of IFIs may be exaggerated when it comes to economic policy and the conditionalities attached to loans. Although conditionality can be construed as detracting from a borrower country's sovereignty, low compliance rates suggest that in some cases the IFIs are "purchasing" policy reform – rather than rewarding it with aid – and are not getting much for their money. Governments frequently reverse the "good" policies that they promise to the lenders, aware that they can "resell" them to the IFIs later on. See Paul Collier, "Learning from Failure: The International Financial

Mozambique's state officials chose to adopt austerity measures without popular debate:

> We explain the [adjustment] measures after they have been taken. You must understand that given their nature, these matters cannot be announced before taking effect since the people would act in such a way to cancel their effect. We explain frankly to the people why the measures have been taken and they understand that additional sacrifices are necessary and that we are rehabilitating our economy in a time of war.[129]

Mittelman contrasts this externally driven "post facto" approach to popular participation with the early postcolonial period when the same political party (FRELIMO) had used "extensive grassroots participation in decisionmaking." In short, the extensive involvement of transnational financial institutions had spurred decay in government's political accountability.[130] The state had relinquished control to outside forces at the expense of popular participation.

Referring to the African context, but arguably applicable elsewhere, Peter Wilkin contends that the "imposition...and acceptance" of liberalization, privatization, and deregulatory policies "diminishes the democratic character of national, regional, and international political institutions by placing key decisions over policymaking in the hands of ever further removed officials and institutions."[131] As IFIs pressure indebted states to repay their loans, the role of these states shifts. In addition to restricting wages, IFI-mandated policies often lead to reduced spending on public goods, resulting in the degeneration of public education and health care, sometimes referred to as "social rights."[132] Governmental accountability entails a responsibility to maintain the public goods that are part and parcel of the state's *raison d'etre*. But state accountability for the provision of such goods "becomes problematic when the hands of the state are

---

Institutions as Agencies of Restraint in Africa" in Andreas Schedler, Larry Diamond, and Marc F. Plattner, eds., *The Self- Restraining State: Power and Accountability in New Democracies* (Boulder: Lynn Rienner), pp. 313–30.

[129] Cited in Mittelman, *The Globalization Syndrome*, pp. 101–2.

[130] Ibid., p. 102.

[131] Peter Wilkin, "Human Security and Class in a Global Economy," in Caroline Thomas and Peter Wilkin, eds., *Globalization, Human Security and the African Experience* (Boulder: Lynne Rienner, 1999), p. 39.

[132] See Radhika Balakrishnan, "Why MES with Human Rights? Integrating Macroeconomic Strategies with Human Rights" (Marymount Manhattan College, 2005), p. 19; J. Ann Tickner, "Feminist Perspectives on Security in a Global Economy," in Thomas and Wilkin, eds., *Globalization, Human Security and the African Experience*, p. 45.

tied by fiscal and monetary policies imposed by international financial institutions."[133]

It is the least powerful sectors of the population who rely on such goods most heavily, but have little influence over the structural adjustment programs that result in limiting them. For example, although the IMF has ceased to promote user fees for elementary school students, many impoverished countries operating under structural adjustment programs reduce their budgets for social services and continue to charge user fees for secondary schooling.[134] The impact on marginalized groups is predictable. In Uganda, the school fee is roughly $30 per month, but poverty keeps such fees out of reach for many girls. Some choose instead to sell their bodies to older men who pay their school fees, but risk gaining their education at the price of sexual exploitation and, often, HIV infection.[135] IFI policies can also have a hand in famine. A famine raging in Niger in 2005 was made worse by the imposition of increased taxes on food, imposed by the government under pressure from a structural adjustment program created by the IMF and the European Union (EU).[136] In addition to the provision of education and health care, food security constitutes a fundamental way in which governments should be accountable to the population.

Vreeland suggests that if the IMF is "truly interested in poverty reduction and growth, then safeguarding the incomes of labor and the poor can become a condition of IMF programs like any other condition." Rather than reducing state spending, IFIs could prioritize human security. Explains Vreeland, "In the past, the IMF has shied away from issues of distribution, arguing that the Fund should stay out of domestic politics. Yet, the moment the IMF demands that budget deficits be cut and interest rates raised, the Fund has entered into domestic politics."[137] Often, this entrance spurs a decline in state accountability to marginalized groups, cutting back on the social rights that could help reduce poverty in the longer term. States are notoriously unaccountable to their least powerful citizens,[138] and IFIs

---

[133] Balakrishnan, p. 17.

[134] "Cry for Action: Shameful Neglect and the Search for Hope in AIDS-Ravaged Africa: An Interview with Stephen Lewis," *Multinational Monitor*, Vol. 28, No. 2 (March–April 2007), accessed July 31, 2008, at http://www.multinationalmonitor.org/mm2007/032007/interview-lewis.html.

[135] Marc Lacey, "For Ugandan Girls, Delaying Sex Has Economic Cost," *New York Times*, August 18, 2003, p. A4.

[136] Andrew Riedl, "Stop Famine in Niger," Peacework (August 2005), p. 11.

[137] Vreeland, p. 165. "Distribution," here, signifies the redistribution of wealth to the poor.

[138] Goetz and Jenkins, *Reinventing Accountability*.

frequently legitimate and encourage that lack of accountability through their policies.

What about instances where IMF actions have had a positive effect on governmental accountability? On occasion, IMF practices have led to more accountable government, if inadvertently. Structural adjustment programs accompanying loans from IFIs in the late 1980s, for instance, helped provoke the collapse of many authoritarian neopatrimonial regimes across sub-Saharan Africa. Rulers saw their budgets shrink, leaving fewer resources with which to support patronage networks. "With few sources of control apart from material inducement or coercion, many governments were vulnerable to opposition challenges from disaffected elites and popular groups," creating an opportunity to introduce more accountable government.[139] But such external effects could not determine the paths that each state took after the initial collapse of its patronage regime. The strict budget and other IFI requirements may have contributed to the collapse of neopatrimonial governments, but the form of the regimes that took their places ranged from nascent democracies (Benin) to collapsed states (Liberia), depending on the relationship among domestic political forces (opposition and incumbents) in each case.[140]

At other times, the IMF and other IFIs have made an overt effort to increase governmental accountability to citizens and, at the same time, to improve the institutions' external accountability. Such efforts are most effective and significant in the context of authoritarian regimes little inclined to incorporate public opinion in their policy making. One such joint initiative by the IMF and the World Bank involves the Heavily Indebted Poor Countries program, intended to remove debt burdens from the poorest IMF loan recipient states. The receipt of debt relief is conditional on a government's preparation of a Poverty Reduction Strategy Paper (PRSP), a document describing "that country's strategy for reducing poverty and how the money it's going to get as a result of debt reduction will be used." The improvement in accountability stemming from the use of PRSPs hypothetically arises because the IMF and the World Bank mandate that the PRSP be a collaborative effort between a state's government and its citizens' groups.[141]

---

[139] Peter M. Lewis, "Economic Reform and the Discourse of Democracy in Africa: Resolving the Contradictions," in Crawford Young and Mark Beissinger, eds., *Beyond State Crisis? Postcolonial Africa and Post-Soviet Eurasia in Comparative Perspective* (Washington: Woodrow Wilson Center Press, 2002), p. 297.

[140] Ibid., p. 298.

[141] Nye et al., p. 63.

The PRSP process, initiated in 1999, aimed to engage citizens' groups in strategizing about national development and to better guarantee that governments would direct the "savings" garnered from debt reduction toward the public good (such as education and health care). But as an accountability mechanism, the PRSP is weak. The IMF and the World Bank retain the final say over a PRSP's approval, and nongovernmental participation often has been impaired by a lack of access to the relevant documents and data. PRSPs have not altered the fundamentally closed process by which loans are negotiated: "Citizens groups which are involved in so-called 'participatory' processes joke that they are learning a new conjugation of the verb 'to participate' – namely, 'I participate, you participate, he/she participates, we participate, you participate and *they* decide.'"[142] To the extent that the PRSP initiative enables civil society groups and legislatures to gain a voice in designing IMF agreements, the accountability of the IFIs and the state's government will increase.

Accountability and the World Bank

Compared to the IMF, the World Bank has been more responsive to demands for accountability, particularly external accountability.[143] Internally, the accountability structure of the World Bank is organized much like that of the IMF and is subject to many of the same critiques. As at the IMF, the World Bank's member states wield voting power in proportion to their financial contributions to the Bank, in a "one-dollar, one vote" system.[144] Member states are represented at the Bank by a "governor" (typically, a finance minister), although the governors meet only once a year and have little influence over concrete decisions. The Bank's member states are represented continually by "executive directors" (sometimes shared among a group of states), who make decisions about concrete loans.[145] But even the

---

[142] Nancy C. Alexander, "Paying for Education: How the World Bank and the International Monetary Fund Influence Education in Developing Countries," *Peabody Journal of Education*, Vol. 76, Nos. 3–4 (2001), p. 329. On PRSPs and accountability, also see Goetz and Jenkins, pp. 184–5.

[143] Jonathan A. Fox and L. David Brown, "Introduction," in Jonathan A. Fox and L. David Brown, eds., *The Struggle for Accountability: The World Bank, NGOs, and Grassroots Movements*, p. 35, ft. 5.

[144] Jonathan A. Fox, "Introduction: Framing the Inspection Panel," in Dana Clark, Jonathan A. Fox, and Kay Treakle, eds., *Demanding Accountability: Civil Society Claims and the World Bank Inspection Panel* (Lanham, MD: Rowman & Littlefield, 2003), p. xiv.

[145] David A. Wirth, "Partnership Advocacy in World Bank Environmental Reform," in Fox and Brown, eds., *The Struggle for Accountability*, p. 55.

most powerful of the member states do not completely control the World Bank; its managers appear to have more direct control and authority than the executive board.[146] States joining the World Bank must first be members of the IMF, but beyond that, the World Bank is an equal opportunity lender; its mandate requires that it distribute loans without taking the politics of recipient governments into account.[147] Democratic and authoritarian regimes alike may turn to the World Bank for assistance.

The World Bank made loans worth $23 billion in 2006 alone, and thus deserves scrutiny from an accountability standpoint. However, those affected by the projects financed, as well as the donor countries' taxpayers, have enjoyed little access to information about World Bank projects. Even the executive directors, who have the power to approve World Bank loans, are frequently "denied access to critical information" about projects.[148] As at the IMF, the confidentiality of agreements between the Bank and the borrower country is the reason most typically provided when the Bank refuses to reveal information publicly.[149]

In 1993, the World Bank altered its information policy in response to demands for greater access to project information. Before that time, the Bank had been notorious for withholding nearly all the data about its projects:

[T]he Bank consistently restricted almost every type of document regarding Bank projects, policy-based lending, economic programs, as well as much environmental and social information.... Attempts to gain access to information – by the public and particularly by people directly affected by Bank projects and programs – were consistently met with refusals and red tape.[150]

The 1993 policy produced a new type of document, the Project Information Document (PID), "written specifically for public consumption" in the early stages of project development. Although these proved disappointingly vague at first, neglecting even to state the location of the proposed project or to provide a contact person, within a few years of the new policy's implementation, the quality and detail of PIDs improved.[151] Like the IMF, the Bank now publishes a multitude of project documents on its website (www.worldbank.org).

---

[146] Fox and Brown, "Introduction," p. 13.
[147] Nye et al., p. 34.
[148] Lori Udall, "The World Bank and Public Accountability: Has Anything Changed?" in Fox and Brown, eds., *The Struggle for Accountability*, pp. 391–2.
[149] Wirth, "Partnership Advocacy," p. 74, ft. 7.
[150] Udall, p. 404.
[151] Ibid., p. 406.

Although its reputation is as a development bank financing large infra-structure projects (such as dams) and providing technical assistance in developing countries, the World Bank, like the IMF, has also embraced structural adjustment policies in its loans, with the same set of ramifications for the accountability of the states adopting them. From 1980 to 2001, the World Bank was signatory to 442 structural adjustment agreements, compared to 414 by the IMF.[152] The ramifications for the accountability of the governments that adopt World Bank structural adjustment agreements are the same as those previously elaborated with respect to governments adopting IMF loan conditionalities.

The World Bank's portfolio extends beyond the economic macrostability around which IMF programs center. Since 1990, raising living standards, reducing poverty, and promoting environmentally sustainable development have taken center stage in the World Bank's promotional literature, in part as a reaction to popular protests against the negative effects of World Bank–financed projects. By the mid-1990s, lending for human resource development averaged about 15 percent of the Bank's operations, up from only 5 percent in the 1980s.[153]

The World Bank's internal accountability can be measured not only by the institution's responsibility to its member states but also by the degree to which World Bank policies are consistent with its own "social and environmental reform goals."[154] Specifically, Bank guidelines established in the early 1990s under pressure from transnational activists call explicitly for Bank-financed projects to abide by a set of operational policies on the rights of indigenous people, to mitigate the effects of involuntary resettlement, to protect the environment, and to attend to "the social costs of macro-economic structural adjustment."[155] Bank projects conform to those policies in differing degrees.

Although structural adjustment programs implemented under the tutelage of the IMF and the World Bank have been widely criticized as detracting from accountability, because – among other things – they are generally agreed upon without much public discussion, multilateral financial institutions can

[152] M. Rodwan Abouharb and David L. Cingranelli, "The Human Rights Effects of World Bank Structural Adjustment, 1981–2000," *International Studies Quarterly*, 50 (2006), p. 236.

[153] Jonathan A. Fox and L. David Brown, "Assessing the Impact of NGO Advocacy Campaigns on World Bank Projects and Policies," in Fox and Brown, eds., *The Struggle for Accountability*, p. 493.

[154] Fox and Brown, "Introduction," p. 13.

[155] Ibid., p. 8.

also play a role in trying to enforce a borrower state's accountability to its population. In 1993, under pressure from transnational activists, the World Bank established an Inspection Panel to which citizens in borrower countries can complain if they have been (or fear that they will be) adversely affected by a World Bank–funded project that did not comply with the Bank's operational policies and procedures, such as on indigenous rights or environmental protection.[156] Claims brought to the Inspection Panel have in several cases stopped the World Bank from endorsing, legitimating, and funding projects that would have enabled national governments to run roughshod over the rights of some segment of their populations. Establishing this external accountability mechanism has helped the World Bank abide by its own policies and has (on occasion) made borrower governments more accountable to their citizens. The following sections explore the World Bank's external accountability as an institution and the ways in which the Bank has detracted from and enhanced governmental accountability.

The Inspection Panel

One feature of the World Bank that distinguishes it from the IMF (in terms of its external accountability mechanisms) is the Inspection Panel. The Inspection Panel was established as a result of intense opposition to a World Bank–financed project – the Sardar Sadovar dam on the Narmada River – in the early 1990s. The multimillion dollar project, funded in part by the Bank, was disrupted by mass protests in India over the inadequate resettlement of people displaced by the dam, as well as by transnational protests urging the Bank to reevaluate the project and cease its funding. In 1992, an independent evaluation of the project at the Bank's behest (the Morse Commission report) brought to light the various ways in which the Bank's own policies had been violated in the project. Transnational advocacy groups used the Narmada fiasco and subsequent report as a means to extract concessions from the World Bank, including the eventual creation of the Inspection Panel and the consistent release of additional information about Bank projects.[157]

The Inspection Panel set "an important precedent in international law by making an international financial institution directly accountable

---

[156] Ibid., p. 4.
[157] Ibid., p. 8. For a comprehensive history of the pressures leading to the formation of the Inspection Panel and the continuing contestation over its operation, see Dana Clark, "Understanding the World Bank Inspection Panel," in Clark, Fox, and Treakle, eds., *Demanding Accountability*, pp. 1–24.

to citizens for the first time."[158] In brief, claims must stem from at least two people who purport to be (or expect to be) harmed materially by a World Bank–financed project as a result of the violation of Bank policies and procedures. Claimants must first address Bank officials, and may only turn to the Inspection Panel if the Bank's initial response is unsatisfactory. Claims may be made only up to the point where a loan is 95 percent disbursed, creating the equivalent of a statute of limitations. Decisions about whether claims were worthy of investigation initially lay with the World Bank's executive board, but this was later changed (as a result of divisive conflicts among the executive directors over particular cases); the Inspection Panel now decides whether claims should be investigated and recommends inspections of eligible claims to the board, which generally approves the investigation.[159] The Bank has endeavored to make the claims process transparent and publishes annual reports (available on the Web) detailing requests for inspection and the process and outcomes of Inspection Panel investigations.

The power of the Inspection Panel, however, is quite limited. First of all, investigations on-site are at the discretion of the borrower government – clearly an obstacle to the potential investigative power of the Inspection Panel.[160] Second, because loans are, in essence, partnerships between the Bank and borrower governments, when violations of Bank policies are uncovered, borrowers and Bank staff alike can claim that the other bears responsibility.[161] Similarly, even after an investigation, the Inspection Panel has no power to monitor the implementation of whatever remedial action the executive board might approve; grotesque violations could be found, but the Inspection Panel lacks a means by which to ensure that the Bank would address them.[162] Nor can the Inspection Panel stop a project; all it can provide is a public assessment about the Bank's violations of its policies. In several cases, failure to resolve the claimant's problems has led to claims being resubmitted to the Inspection Panel.[163]

Between its inception in 1994 and July 2007, forty-six requests for inspection were submitted to the Inspection Panel. Claims are most commonly based on alleged violations of the environmental assessment, project

---

[158] Udall, p. 414.
[159] Clark, "Understanding the World Bank Inspection Panel," pp. 16–17.
[160] Ibid., p. 10.
[161] Fox, "Introduction," p. xiv.
[162] Clark, "Understanding the World Bank Inspection Panel," pp. 16–17.
[163] Kay Treakle, Jonathan A. Fox, and Dana Clark, "Lessons Learned," in Clark, Fox, and Treakle, eds., *Demanding Accountability*, p. 266.

supervision, involuntary resettlement, indigenous peoples, and information disclosure policies.[164] But although it constitutes a mechanism to broadcast the lack of accountability to groups potentially marginalized by their own governments – and by transnational financial institutions more broadly – the Inspection Panel does not resolve the disproportion in the power of affected citizens versus that of the Bank's management. Claimants may not "appeal either the panel recommendation or the board's decision about how to respond to their claim," nor are claimants consulted about remedial measures adopted by the Bank.[165]

Despite these flaws, the Inspection Panel should make the World Bank more accountable to the public by allowing citizens adversely affected by its projects to file complaints and receive a hearing.[166] A review of several cases – the Arun III dam project, the China Western Poverty Reduction Project, and Argentina's Garden program – serves to illustrate the strengths and weaknesses of the Inspection Panel as an external accountability mechanism.

The World Bank's approval process for the Bank-funded Arun III dam project in Nepal was the first to undergo scrutiny by the Inspection Panel. As the project evolved, the Bank consistently withheld documents on "finances, alternatives [to the dam], or cost-benefit analysis," making outside analysis of the project nearly impossible.[167] In Nepal, nongovernmental organizations (NGOs) had wanted to ensure that the project would be subjected to public discussion before it was approved, because it was projected to cost $1 billion and would likely have a detrimental impact on spending in other areas. By withholding information from the public until after Nepal's parliamentary elections in November 1994, "the Bank was, in effect, obstructing the democratic processes of public participation, debate, and consultation inside Nepal."[168] Finally, a Nepali NGO, the Arun Concerned Group, brought its case to the newly created Inspection Panel.[169] The Arun Concerned Group filed its complaint in October 1994, alleging that the World Bank was "violating its own policies and procedures on environmental impact assessment, resettlement, indigenous peoples, energy, economic evaluation of projects, and information."[170]

---

[164] Ibid., p. 251.
[165] Ibid., p. 267.
[166] Ibid., p. 247.
[167] Udall, p. 409.
[168] Ibid., p. 410.
[169] Ibid., p. 414.
[170] Ibid., p. 416.

The claim was accepted for investigation and resulted in the World Bank, under its new president, James Wolfensohn, withdrawing its support for the project.[171]

Wolfensohn's decision provoked considerable resistance and denial from Bank management, and during the ensuing period of almost five years, the executive board consistently refused to authorize the Inspection Panel to conduct another full investigation, often as a result of obstruction by executive directors from borrower countries.[172] Finally, after some particularly egregious instances of conflict-ridden board meetings over proposed Inspection Panel investigations, the executive board decided that the Inspection Panel was not functioning as the "fig leaf" that several directors had clearly hoped it would (e.g., as a means of deflecting environmentalist and other civic criticism of Bank loans) and ordered a review of the Inspection Panel process in 1998–1999.[173] The outcome was mixed as far as improving the Bank's external accountability. The review recommended that the Bank's executive board no longer decide whether or not an investigation take place, leaving that instead to the Inspection Panel. The board did not obstruct subsequent recommendations by the Inspection Panel to investigate.[174] But the Inspection Panel lost ground on the "harm standard," such that claimants would now have to argue persuasively that their position was (or would be) worse under the project than if the project had not been implemented at all.[175]

The first claim submitted under the Inspection Panel's new rules (after the 1998–1999 reevaluation) was the China Western Poverty Reduction project, a thinly disguised attempt by the Chinese leadership to gain World Bank funding for the government's ongoing policy of resettling Chinese settlers on land inhabited by Tibetans. The executive board abided by the new understanding and authorized an investigation by the Inspection Panel, resulting ultimately in the World Bank's refusal to make the

---

[171] Ibid., p. 421. The Inspection Panel claim and the protests that spurred it were not the sole factor in discouraging Wolfensohn's support of the project; "[it] was especially vulnerable because it was to be funded by the Bank's concessional, low-interest aid window, the International Development Association (IDA), whose budget was under sharp attack in the [then-]Republican-controlled U.S. Congress." See Fox and Brown, "Assessing the Impact of NGO Advocacy Campaigns on World Bank Projects and Policies," p. 489.

[172] Clark, "Understanding the World Bank Inspection Panel," pp. 12–13.

[173] Richard E. Bissell, "The Arun III Hydroelectric Project, Nepal," in Clark, Fox, and Treakle, eds., *Demanding Accountability*, p. 40.

[174] Clark, "Understanding the World Bank Inspection Panel," pp. 17–18.

[175] Ibid., pp. 16–17.

loan in question.[176] However, by initially supporting and defending the project – a Chinese government resettlement policy seeking to move fifty-eight thousand people onto Tibetan land, "displacing at least four thousand local people, including Mongol and Tibetan nomadic peoples" – the Bank's project staff created a situation where the Bank appeared to provide "an international seal of approval of China's population transfer program as a legitimate form of development."[177] Had it gone through, the Bank's loan would have not only violated Bank policies but also endorsed the Chinese occupation of Tibet. Moreover, it would have facilitated the authoritarian behavior of China's government, which actively repressed the Tibetan population and permitted no free speech on the matter.

The Inspection Panel's analysis of the case revealed that China's request had been classified as a Category "B" loan, although loans supporting involuntary resettlement and other issues raised by the China project were generally classified as Category "A," requiring a full Environmental Assessment as well as a plan to mitigate the negative effects of the project on the population. The Bank staff had not filed an Indigenous Peoples' Development Plan, nor had they consulted the local Mongol and Tibetan minorities, despite a World Bank policy that mandated including "the informed participation of the indigenous people themselves" when staff created a plan for protecting indigenous interests.[178] Nor did the Bank provide sufficient public information about the project, in large part because Bank staff had "simply failed to require the Chinese government to prepare the detailed project documents required by [Bank] policies."[179] The Panel's investigation revealed that China was consistently held to a lower standard of accountability and that the sketchy quality of the Bank staff's plan for the China/Tibet project was, according to the Bank's management, "very much in line with Bank practice in applying social and environmental policies to projects in China *in the context of its political and social systems.*"[180]

In short, the China Western Poverty Reduction investigation showed that the Bank not only loaned to authoritarian regimes (as per its "apolitical" mandate) but was willing to lower its policy standards for those regimes. Such practices actively privileged governmental authoritarianism over

---

[176] Ibid., pp. 17–18.
[177] Dana Clark and Kay Treakle, "The China Western Poverty Reduction Project," in Clark, Fox, and Treakle, eds., *Demanding Accountability*, pp. 212, 214.
[178] Ibid., p. 218.
[179] Ibid., p. 220.
[180] Cited in ibid., p. 229. Italics in the original.

accountability as well as diminishing the external accountability of the Bank toward the population its project would have affected. The Inspection Panel investigation thus interrupted a long-standing Bank habit of legitimating the practices of China's repressive government. The subsequent decision by the executive board to steer clear of the project promoted the Bank's external accountability.

A rather different issue was raised by an Inspection Panel claim regarding a structural adjustment program in Argentina in July 1999. Until this claim was filed, the adverse affects of structural adjustment loans on populations seemed to be something for which international financial institutions could not be held accountable. Yet such loans make up over one-third of the World Bank's lending and facilitate a number of policies that, at least in the short term, can adversely affect the material well-being of the country's poor in the name of making the overall economy more competitive.[181]

In the mid-1990s, in recognition of these problems and reflecting its ostensible interest in poverty reduction, the Bank began more regularly to include "social conditionality clauses in structural adjustment loan agreements," the purpose of which was to preserve funding for programs that met the needs of the poorest population groups.[182] According to the World Bank's operational directive on poverty reduction at that time, "Bank-supported adjustment programs…include measures to protect the most vulnerable from declines in consumption and social services – with particular attention paid to food and nutritional security – in the context of an agreed public expenditure program."[183]

In 1998, Argentina was the recipient of such a loan, including a social conditionality clause that set aside $680 million in the state's budget for support of various programs for the poor, including a seed-distribution and community garden program. When the budget for this program was cut by about two-thirds in 1999, a handful of the garden program's beneficiaries, collaborating with a local human rights group, filed a claim with the Inspection Panel on the basis of the Bank's failure to comply with its own policies on "poverty reduction, project supervision, and public access

---

[181] Victor Abramovich, "Social Protection Conditionality in World Bank Structural Adjustment Loans: The Case of Argentina's Garden Program (Pro-Huerta)," in Clark, Fox, and Treakle, eds., *Demanding Accountability*, p. 191.

[182] Ibid., p. 191. The Bank's structural adjustment programs now often include clauses protecting spending on social programs for the poor, but these "conditions are often discretionary." See Alexander, "Paying for Education," p. 290.

[183] Cited in Abramovich, pp. 201–2.

to information."[184] The group included in its claim a request for the Panel to recommend that further distribution of the loan money to Argentina be halted until the situation could be investigated.

Before the Inspection Panel could investigate the claim, the Argentine government allotted further funds to the garden program, resolving the material problem, at least temporarily. The Panel reviewed the claim regardless, and found the claimants eligible to bring to the Inspection Panel a claim related to a structural adjustment loan. This finding set an important precedent.[185] Apparently, the Bank would now have to take public responsibility for the adverse effects of structural adjustment loans if the harm arose as a result of noncompliance with a social conditionality clause.

Although the fact that the claim was deemed eligible appears to represent an improvement in external accountability, the Inspection Panel did not question structural adjustment programs and their effects on governmental accountability more broadly.[186] The Inspection Panel ultimately recommended against inspection, given that the very threat of a suspension of the loan was enough to motivate the Argentine government to shift money into the endangered program, thereby eliminating the problem.[187] Yet, in accepting the eligibility of the garden program's complaint, the Inspection Panel "legitimated the claims" of people affected by structural adjustment programs, allowing citizens potentially to "hold the bank accountable both to its poverty alleviation mandate and to the negative consequences of its macroeconomic development model."[188]

Even claims rejected by the Inspection Panel have had a positive impact on establishing accountability relationships between lending institutions and affected communities. A 1995 claim objecting to the violation of World Bank policies toward indigenous people (in this case, the Pehuenche of Chile, whose land was encroached upon by a dam project on the Biobio River) was rejected by the Inspection Panel because the loan was made by one of the World Bank Group's private lending agencies, the International Finance Corporation (IFC), which – unlike the World Bank Group's two main lending arms, the International Bank for Reconstruction and Development (IBRD) and the International Development

---

[184] Ibid., p. 192.
[185] Ibid., p. 193.
[186] Ibid., pp. 207–8.
[187] Ibid., pp. 203–4.
[188] Fox and Treakle, p. 283.

Association (IDA) – was not covered by the Inspection Panel's mandate.[189] The Bank's president then authorized a review of the project's environmental and social impact in order to determine whether Bank policies had been violated. When the report was released, even its redacted form was a scathing "indictment of IFC's handling of the [dam] projects" financed by IFC loans.[190] Largely as a result of this case, the IFC began to take seriously the need to apply social and environmental standards to its loans and established a unit for that purpose. However, the IFC continues to balk at making information and loan agreements accessible to the public, citing "business confidentiality."[191]

The filing of the Chilean Inspection Panel claim was also successful in provoking the World Bank Group to establish an external accountability procedure for its private-sector lending agencies – the IFC and the Multilateral Investment Guarantee Agency (MIGA) – creating the Compliance Advisor and Ombudsman (CAO) office in 2000. The CAO reports to the World Bank's president, and is thus autonomous of IFC officials. As the institution of the CAO is relatively new, its effectiveness is still unclear, but its recalcitrance in making information public limits its utility as an accountability mechanism.[192] Although the private-sector branches of the World Bank Group are less externally accountable than its IBRD and IDA, the founding of the Inspection Panel helped to spread the concept of accountability to affected populations.

---

[189] The International Bank for Reconstruction and Development (IBRD) lends to "middle income and creditworthy poor countries" at low rates, and the International Development Association (IDA) provides long-term low- or no-interest credits and grants to poor countries (www.worldbank.org). Such loans frequently go toward the repayment of old loans, such as from the IMF. The World Bank Group also includes the International Finance Corporation (IFC), which extends loans at market rates and promotes privatization (including the privatization of public services), "encourag[ing] holders of local and foreign capital to invest in the private sector in underdeveloped countries." See Jacques B. Gélinas, "The Pillars of the System," in Robin Broad, ed., *Global Backlash: Citizen Initiatives for a Just World Economy* (Lanham, MD: Rowman & Littlefield, 2002), p. 108; David Tannenbaum, "Obsessed: The Latest Chapter in the World Bank's Privatization Plans," *Multinational Monitor*, Vol. 23, No. 9 (September 2002), accessed November 27, 2007, at http://multinationalmonitor.org/mm2002/02september/sept02corp1.html. Finally, the Multilateral Investment Guarantee Agency (MIGA) encourages foreign direct investment, offering "private investors technical assistance and insurance against losses incurred because of non-commercial risks." See Gélinas, p. 108.

[190] David Hunter, Cristian Opaso, and Marcos Orellana, "The Biobio's Legacy: Institutional Reforms and Unfulfilled Promises at the International Finance Corporation," in Clark, Fox, and Treakle, eds., *Demanding Accountability*, p. 129.

[191] Ibid., p. 135.

[192] Ibid., p. 135.

In another move accentuating external accountability, the IFC in 2006 adopted a new set of standards regulating loans, such that all companies borrowing from the IFC will have to observe the "core labor standards" (CLS) defined by the International Labor Organization (ILO). These standards "prohibit the use of forced labour, child labour and discriminatory practices, and require recognition of freedom of association and the right to collective bargaining."[193] If implemented, observed, and enforced, these standards would represent a significant effort by a transnational lending institution to improve corporate accountability to workers – something states have been reluctant to do. A cautionary tale, however, is provided by the experience of Haitian workers fired from a factory for attempting to form a union, despite the fact that a CLS condition was included (as part of an IFC pilot project) in the loan received by the clothing manufacturer operating the factory. The company ultimately recognized the union and brought the workers back onto the payroll, but only after pressure from the union. This experience suggests that unless the IFC takes the CLS requirement seriously, its inclusion in loan agreements may have little effect without substantial organizing efforts by workers.[194]

Even if indirectly, the Inspection Panel claim process provoked new accountability mechanisms at the IFC and MIGA. The establishment of the Inspection Panel also led the Inter-American Development Bank (IDB) and the Asian Development Bank (ADB) to establish inspection mechanisms (although not standing ones) in 1994 and 1995, but their inspections are board-authorized, as they were in the Inspection Panel's early years. The European Bank for Reconstruction and Development (EBRD) and the Japan Bank for International Cooperation are also developing accountability mechanisms in light of the pressure generated by civil society and the standing example of the Inspection Panel.[195]

The Inspection Panel itself has become a more independent instrument for fomenting World Bank accountability over time. The process, however, has been contentious, and setbacks in the Inspection Panel's power have occurred in some areas while its autonomy has in other ways increased.

---

[193] ICFTU Online, "Action by World Bank's IFC on Workers' Rights a Major Step Forward," February 22, 2006, accessed February 26, 2006, at http://www.icftu.org/displaydocument.asp?Index=991223448&Language=EN.

[194] Ibid. Other branches of the World Bank have not introduced such standards for their public infrastructure loans (loans to governments), despite evidence in a 2004 report from Indonesia that "child labour, discrimination against women workers, and denial of freedom of association" were occurring in Bank-financed projects. See ICFTU Online.

[195] Treakle, Fox, and Clark, p. 274.

Moreover, the impact of cases taken up by the Inspection Panel has varied considerably. A few claims led the Bank to withdraw its support for projects that it had previously endorsed. A handful of claimants were satisfied by the outcome of their claims, whereas others were physically beaten by representatives of their home governments as a result of filing a claim.[196] Such responses could have a chilling effect on citizens' willingness to bring issues to the Inspection Panel's attention.

On occasion, Bank management actively attempted to "subvert the panel findings and avoid accountability."[197] One such case involved a complaint about the Bank's funding of the Yacyretá hydroelectric power project, a vast construction project along a river between Argentina and Paraguay. In 1996, people from communities affected by the filling of the reservoir registered a claim with the Inspection Panel, contending that the Bank had failed to observe its policies on resettlement of affected communities and mitigation of negative environmental effects, among other things. An investigation by the Panel confirmed multiple policy violations. But in March 1998, Bank management intentionally distorted the Panel's findings, publishing a letter in a Paraguayan newspaper, stating, "The Bank is satisfied with the conclusions of the [Inspection Panel's] report, which confirm that the Bank policies on resettlement, the environment, community participation and all other areas were fully met and implemented in the Yacyretá case," when, in fact, the opposite was true.[198]

One important result of the Inspection Panel's tenure has been to increase the Bank's external accountability: "...[W]hen panel reports publicly verify claims of grassroots critics, they create a new crosscutting accountability relationship, constituting a form of 'answerability' of the bank to directly affected communities."[199] The Panel may also help to improve governmental "answerability" to citizens. Because the Inspection Panel process requires that claims be filed by people directly affected (rather than by environmental or human rights groups outside the country), borrower governments are less able to deny the problems raised or to claim that the complaints are the work of outsiders.[200] The Inspection Panel thus adds to the potential for both the Bank's and the borrower governments'

---

[196] Fox, "Introduction," p. xix.
[197] Treakle, Fox, and Clark, p. 254.
[198] Cited in World Bank, *Accountability at the World Bank: The Inspection Panel, 10 Years On* (Washington: World Bank, 2003), p. 67.
[199] Jonathan A. Fox and Kay Treakle, "Concluding Propositions," in Clark, Fox, and Treakle, eds., *Demanding Accountability*, p. 280.
[200] Ibid., p. 280.

accountability, because it provides an arena in which local communities are given a voice.

In a 2007 case of such local protest, the Ugandan National Association of Professional Environmentalists (NAPE) brought a complaint to the Inspection Panel concerning the Uganda Private Power Generation (Bujagali) Project, a hydroelectric dam being built on the Nile near Bujagali Falls, in Uganda. In August 2008, the Panel released its report on the Bujagali project, finding violations of several Bank policies.[201] In its response to the Inspection Panel report, the Bank's executive board acknowledged that, among other things, the project had not complied with Bank policies on resettlement and had not properly compensated the 2,500 families adversely affected by the project for their material losses. After discussions with the Inspection Panel and Bank management, the board reported that the Bank managers on the project would take several additional actions in light of the Panel's report, including carrying out an "enhanced socio-economic study to support and fully achieve livelihood restoration."[202] Staff at International Rivers, a California-based environmental NGO, however, expressed surprise at the relatively weak response by the board to the Panel's report, and were skeptical that significant changes would be made to the project.[203] Local voices raised against Bank projects, even when amplified by the Inspection Panel, may not be loud enough to echo persuasively in the Bank's inner sanctum.

Within the IBRD and IDA, staff acknowledge that internal compliance with the Bank's environmental and social policies was taken more seriously after the establishment of the Inspection Panel and the potential threat of repercussions for staff who failed to incorporate those policies into project plans as required. In October 2001, the Bank introduced Integrated Safeguards Data Sheets (ISDS), designed to be filled out by Bank staff working on project planning, as a means to force "staff to go on record regarding which, if any, safeguard policies are acknowledged to apply to a specific project under consideration."[204] However, the Bank "still lacks a track record of sanctioning individual staff members for violations of

---

[201] Inspection Panel, "Inspection Panel Investigation Report: Uganda – Private Power Generation (Bujagali) Project," August 29, 2008, accessed December 15, 2008, at http://internationalrivers.org/en/node/3568.

[202] World Bank, "News Release: World Bank Board Discusses Investigation by the Independent Inspection Panel of Power Project in Uganda," December 12, 2008, accessed December 15, 2008, at http://siteresources.worldbank.org/EXTINSPECTIONPANEL/Resources/Bujagali_Press_Release_Final_121208_Clean.pdf.

[203] In addition to compensation issues, other concerns about the project include its escalating (and potentially unaffordable) cost to the Ugandan government. Phone interview with Lori Pottinger, staffperson at International Rivers, December 15, 2008.

[204] Treakle, Fox, and Clark, pp. 269–70.

its social and environmental policies," and insufficient data exists to be able to judge whether compliance has increased since these institutional changes were implemented.[205]

One significant flaw in the Inspection Panel's accountability process is that the safeguard policies themselves are the subject of dispute. When diluted, they weaken the Inspection Panel's ability to hold the Bank's management accountable for harm incurred on the ground. Soon after establishing the Inspection Panel,

the bank embarked on a process to convert its hundreds of pages of bank policies and Operational Directives into a standardized format consisting of three related documents: the Operational Policy (OP) and Bank Practice (BP) documents, which outline mandatory requirements for staff, and the Good Practice (GP) document, which is considered to be merely "guidance" for staff and not actionable through the panel process.

Designed to make staff compliance with policy more feasible and more likely, the changes may have had a more sinister motivation. As "the senior bank manager initially responsible for the process divulged in an internal memo in 1996, 'Our experiences with the Inspection Panel are teaching us that we have to be increasingly careful in setting policy that we are able to implement in practice.'" Through the conversion process, "management's tendency has been to weaken the mandatory language or move important provisions into the Good Practice section of the policy to avoid being accountable to tough standards."[206] Whereas the "mandatory" category incorporates the Bank's environmental assessment and resettlement policies, for example, other standards with a direct relationship to external accountability – such as incorporating "informed participation by poor people" – fall under the "good practices" rubric.[207] Because the Inspection Panel is charged with holding the Bank to its own standards, when those standards are diluted or made less stringent, this reduces the accountability of the Bank to local communities. The Panel will have "far fewer standards to hold the Bank to, and ultimately, the scope of the Inspection Panel's mandate will be greatly narrowed."[208] Institutional mechanisms of accountability, therefore, are only as good as their mandates and the policies and rules that underlie them. Similarly worrisome is the Bank's plan

---

[205] Fox and Treakle, p. 282.
[206] Treakle, Fox, and Clark, p. 272.
[207] Jonathan Fox, "Advocacy Research and the World Bank: Propositions for Discussion," *Development in Practice*, Vol. 12, No. 4 (November 2003), p. 523.
[208] Udall, p. 426.

to "avoid accountability by shifting more responsibility for policy compliance to the borrower," as discussed in a 2002 World Bank strategy paper. Yet governments are notoriously unable and unwilling to implement safeguard measures on their own without pressure from the Bank (and from civil society – which is often subject to repression under the authoritarian regimes receiving World Bank loans).[209]

State Accountability and the World Bank

Through accountability mechanisms such as the Inspection Panel, citizens can attract more attention and even defend their human rights to a greater extent than they could within the confines of the national political arena. For the inhabitants of nondemocratic states or the disenfranchised citizens of semidemocratic states, transnational institutions such as the World Bank can provide a means of promoting state accountability to citizens. Despite lofty rhetoric along these lines, the World Bank's effects on fostering political accountability have been mixed. This section examines the impact of World Bank programs on governmental corruption, the effectiveness of the Bank's "safeguard policies" (intended to protect the environment and living standards of people in project-affected communities), the results of Bank-sponsored SAPs on the state's protection of labor rights and human rights, and the Bank's (indirect) role in strengthening civil society against unaccountable states.

World Bank Loans and State Corruption
In the 1990s, the blossoming of technologies enabled the movement of "information and monies instantaneously and discreetly around the planet," facilitating "corruption without frontiers," and making the pursuit of accountability more difficult.[210] Within the World Bank, proposals were made to address corruption in borrower countries, but "[r]epresentatives felt that to tackle corruption would clearly interfere with the Bank charter's requirement to abstain from political considerations in lending decisions, and was therefore not an option." Over time, under Wolfensohn's leadership, the World Bank did adopt an anticorruption agenda, bringing in Transparency International as a consultant to develop an anticorruption

[209] Treakle, Fox, and Clark, p. 273.
[210] Fredrik Galtung, "Transparency International's Network to Curb Global Corruption," in Gerald E. Caiden, O. P. Dwivedi, and Joseph Jabbra, eds., *Where Corruption Lives* (Bloomfield: Kumarian Press, 2001), p. 193.

strategy for the Bank and dedicating funding to build accountable political institutions in borrower states.[211]

According to former World Bank president Paul Wolfowitz, the Bank first recognized corruption's corrosive effect on development in 1996.[212] A decade later, the World Bank's efforts to address corruption as a central obstacle to poverty reduction had become increasingly public. On a trip to Indonesia in April 2006, Wolfowitz, then president of the World Bank, expounded upon the Bank's interest in promoting development by quashing corruption and improving governance. "Good governance," explained Wolfowitz,

is essentially the combination of transparent and accountable institutions, strong skills and competence, and a fundamental willingness to do the right thing. Those are the things that enable a government to deliver services to its people efficiently. An independent judiciary, a free press, and a vibrant civil society are important components of good governance. They balance the power of governments, and they hold them accountable for delivering better services, creating jobs, and improving living standards. Some countries can achieve growth for many years without all of those factors. Indeed, Indonesia's history in the 1970s and 1980s is an illustration of that. But the devastating economic crisis that followed here shows how fragile growth can be when institutions that keep governments accountable, transparent, and responsible, are systematically weakened.[213]

Wolfowitz made clear his intention to bring fighting corruption to the fore within World Bank programs and operations. After his appointment to the Bank's presidency in 2005, Wolfowitz oversaw the cancellation and suspension of multiple loans to countries in response to instances of corruption in the way that the loans were used. Wolfowitz's anticorruption rhetoric was accompanied by the development of "anti-corruption teams" to conduct direct observation of Bank-funded projects in the developing world, the expansion of the World Bank's institutional integrity department, and plans to increase loans designed to build or reform domestic courts. Such concrete signs of World Bank attention to corruption suggest

[211] Celia W. Dugger, "World Bank Chief Outlines a War on Fraud," *New York Times*, April 12, 2006, p. A7; Galtung, pp. 195–6.
[212] Paul Wolfowitz, "Good Governance and Development: A Time for Action," Jakarta, Indonesia, April 11, 2006, accessed July 5, 2006, at http://web.worldbank.org/WBSITE/ EXTERNAL/NEWS/0,,contentMDK:20883752~pagePK:34370~piPK:42770~theSitePK: 4607,00.html. The Bank had, in fact, begun to link its loans to a "good governance" requirement in borrower states as early as 1990, stressing the importance of the rule of law and citizen participation in policy making. See Paris, p. 30, citing World Bank, *Advancing Social Development: A World Bank Contribution to the Social Summit* (Washington, DC: World Bank, 1995).
[213] Wolfowitz, "Good Governance and Development."

that the institution could play a useful role in building domestic political accountability.[214] Bank programs fighting corruption and promoting good governance in borrower states increased considerably under Wolfowitz's leadership. In 2005, only about 5 percent of new projects featured an accountability or anticorruption plank, up from less than one-half of 1 percent (.4 percent) a decade earlier. By fiscal year 2006, nearly half of the Bank's "new lending operations included support for strengthening governance, amounting to...19.2 percent of the Bank's new lending for the year."[215]

Yet loans are not necessarily made conditional on states' anticorruption and "good governance" measures. As evidenced by a document leaked from the Bank's vice president's office, the Bank had not as of mid-2006 determined how to resolve the conflict between "raising the bar" on anticorruption in borrower states, on the one hand, and tying the lending process to standards that would make loan procedures "too slow or bureaucratic," if not leading governments to shun the Bank as a source of funds altogether, on the other. Evidently aware of the Bank's "reputational risks" on the corruption issue, the document questioned whether governance and anticorruption should "become more central for decisions on aid volumes...across countries" and asked whether anticorruption efforts within World Bank financed projects "should...be more systematic."[216]

The cost of corruption in World Bank lending alone is enormous. A U.S. Senate Committee study found in 2004 that the Bank had "lost about 100 billion dollars slated for development in the world's poorest nations to corruption since 1946 – nearly 20 percent of its total lending portfolio."[217] Indeed, a study examining bilateral and multilateral aid programs between 1975 and 1995, as well as debt relief programs, uncovered no evidence that such aid "goes disproportionally to less corrupt governments."[218] Holding

---

[214] The World Bank is pouring money into rule of law and governance programs, but these are focused on courts that handle business relationships and property rights in particular, suggesting the Bank's support for a narrowly construed accountability. Anne-Marie Goetz, "Gender and Accountability," Lecture at Fletcher School, Tufts University, April 10, 2006.

[215] Wolfowitz, "Good Governance and Development."

[216] Emad Mekay, "World Bank Weighs Risks of Anti-Graft Drive," Inter Press Service News Agency, June 2, 2006, accessed July 5, 2006, at http://www.ipsnews.net/news.asp?idnews=33476.

[217] Ibid. For links to the World Bank's anticorruption and good governance activities and data, see World Bank, "Governance and Anti-Corruption," accessed December 4, 2008, at http://www.worldbank.org/wbi/governance/.

[218] Alberto Alesina and Beatrice Weder, "Do Corrupt Governments Receive Less Foreign Aid?" *American Economic Review*, Vol. 92, No. 4 (September 2002), p. 1126. "Aid" includes loans and below-market rate "grants," as well as debt forgiveness.

other variables constant, the study's authors found that states receive multilateral foreign aid irrespective of their level of corruption, and that the receipt of increased foreign aid probably increases corruption as well (because the pot of resources potentially to be appropriated increases). Multilateral lending agencies have exhibited consistent support for corrupt governments.[219]

Although the World Bank and IMF have tried for well over a decade to promote good governance, World Bank loans continue to flow to governments grossly implicated in corruption scandals.[220] In Kenya, for instance, the World Bank announced a new $145 million loan to the government in January 2006, $25 million of which was designated for anticorruption work, just as protestors in Kenya were calling the government to account for its failure to address corruption.[221]

Among the Bank's stated methods of "minimizing the risk of corruption in World Bank funded projects" is the practice of devolving control over projects to local communities. In an April 2006 speech in Indonesia, Wolfowitz cited examples:

During this short visit, I have seen tsunami survivors in Aceh managing their own reconstruction projects, I have seen widows using microfinance to improve their families' lives, and I have talked to local villagers in Sulawesi who have been deciding which development projects to pursue. In all of these projects, the communities determine where the investments are made. They control the funds and monitor the results of the projects. The result has been more value for each rupiah spent, and demonstrable reductions in the levels of corruption.[222]

Bringing into the planning stage the communities that are the intended beneficiaries has likely helped to improve the outcomes of World Bank

---

[219] Ibid., p. 1135. Although corruption may not affect the distribution of aid, it does affect negatively the distribution of foreign direct investment. See Mohsin Habib and Leon Zurawicki, "Corruption and Foreign Direct Investment," in Transparency International, *Global Corruption Report 2004* (London: Pluto Press, 2004), pp. 313–15. Because FDI is correlated with improved collective labor rights (see Layna Mosely and Saika Uno, "Racing to the Bottom or Climbing to the Top? Economic Globalization and Collective Labor Rights," *Comparative Political Studies*, Vol. 40 (2007), pp. 923–48), World Bank efforts to combat corruption could have multiple positive impacts.

[220] Hans Peter Schmitz, "Domestic and Transnational Perspectives on Democratization," *International Studies Review*, Vol. 6 (2004), p. 415.

[221] Dugger, "World Bank Chief Outlines a War on Fraud." Anticorruption protests continued in 2007, when the Kenyan parliament attempted to strip Kenya's anticorruption agency of its authority to investigate major instances of corruption before 2003. See Adam Mynott, "Politics Sinks Kenya's War on Graft," BBC News, September 14, 2007, accessed October 10, 2007, at http://news.bbc.co.uk/2/hi/africa/6993826.stm.

[222] Wolfowitz, "Good Governance and Development."

projects. As of the mid-1990s, a third of Bank-sponsored project outcomes "fail[ed] to create any enduring benefits."[223] To the extent that it promotes local decision making, the World Bank may foster accountability as well as poverty reduction.

State Violation of the World Bank's "Safeguard" Policies

Particularly in the context of nondemocratic government, grassroots input into policy programs can promote accountability. The World Bank's guidelines (reformed in the 1990s) on mitigating any negative environmental, social, and economic impact of their projects set a certain standard for governmental accountability to local populations. The Bank's conditions include participation and consultation on projects by people likely to be affected. Yet, the World Bank's "capacity to force compliance with its famous loan conditionalities is actually quite uneven."[224] Moreover, "[b]ecause the bargaining processes between national governments and the Bank are not public, it is difficult to ascertain in any given case whether Bank officials actually try to use their political capital in an effort to prevent or mitigate social and environmental damage," even when they are aware of the likelihood of such damage in advance. But in nondemocracies, where citizens cannot hold their governments accountable for observing the World Bank's conditions, Bank pressure on a state's government may constitute the best hope for compliance.[225] When the Bank fails to conduct assessments properly before making a loan, or does not withhold loan disbursements when safeguard policies are ignored, the Bank legitimates unaccountable behavior on the part of the borrower state.

The Bank's reformed "safeguard policies" were designed to press borrower governments "to become responsive to social and environmental concerns" by using World Bank leverage over loan disbursement to encourage compliance.[226] Borrower governments, however, resist social and environmental conditionalities, seeing them as violations of national sovereignty – a convenient excuse for perpetuating unaccountable government.[227]

---

[223] Richard W. Stevenson, "A Chief Banker for Nations at the Bottom of the Heap," *New York Times*, September 14, 1997, Section 3, p. 1.

[224] Fox and Brown, "Introduction," p. 14.

[225] Ibid., p. 15.

[226] Ibid., p. 7.

[227] See Deborah Moore and Leonard Sklar, "Reforming the World Bank's Lending for Water," in Fox and Brown, eds., *The Struggle for Accountability*, p. 366.

Historically, the World Bank's enforcement of its safeguard policies has been less than rigorous. The Bank's resettlement policy, for instance, which "encourages project managers to minimize involuntary resettlement in the first place, and then details how to 'rehabilitate' those who are resettled in order to leave them at least as well off as they were before relocation," was initiated in 1980, but was implemented only sporadically.[228] Notable improvements in resettlement planning were visible only after 1992, in the wake of extensive local and transnational protest over the dramatic failure of a resettlement policy in India where the Bank-financed Narmada River dam project was under way.[229] Bank projects were supposed to include resettlement plans before approval, but "only 50 percent of 1986–1991 projects had such plans."[230] By 1994, 100 percent of projects featured resettlement plans. However, because over 85 percent of Bank loans did not include funds to cover the cost of resettlement or rehabilitation, the Bank's commitment to its own policy appeared weak to borrower governments (which often then failed to comply with the policy).[231] The World Bank's own assessment of resettlement outcomes in its projects found that the Bank was woefully inadequate in enforcing its own policies on resettlement – that accountability, or "compliance with official reform commitments," was lacking.[232] By not sufficiently stressing the importance of borrower governments abiding by the Bank's resettlement policies (and by approving loans that did not include plans to abide by those policies), the Bank facilitated and legitimated borrower governments' absence of accountability to their populations.

Compliance with indigenous and environmental safeguard policies has been similarly irregular. The World Bank's policy on indigenous peoples, initiated in 1982 and strengthened in 1991, imposed certain protective conditions on development projects on indigenous territory. The 1991 policy, Operational Directive on Indigenous Peoples, "mandates not only protecting indigenous peoples from the harmful effects of projects, but also providing them with the opportunity to participate in the development process,

---

[228] Jonathan A. Fox, "When Does Reform Policy Influence Practice? Lessons from the Bank-wide Resettlement Review," in Fox and Brown, eds., *The Struggle for Accountability*, p. 304.

[229] Fox, "When Does Reform Policy Influence Practice?" pp. 305, 308. See also William F. Fisher, ed., *Toward Sustainable Development?: Struggling over India's Narmada River* (Armonk, NY: M. E. Sharpe, 1995).

[230] Fox, "When Does Reform Policy Influence Practice?" p. 318.

[231] Ibid., p. 318.

[232] Ibid., p. 303.

which would involve a recognition of their own distinctive needs."[233] In effect, making local participation in decision making mandatory increases state accountability to the population because it implies information sharing and participation, both components of accountable government. However, states often ignore the conditions specified in the loan agreements, and the Bank does not force the issue, thereby failing to meet its own standards and holding neither itself nor the borrower government accountable.

The Bank's record on holding borrowers accountable for compliance with environmental conditionalities is also inconsistent. A World Bank review in 1995 showed that "progress was made in mitigation of direct impacts," but that the "'weakest aspects of EA [environmental impact assessment] work continue to be public consultation and analysis of alternatives'" along with a weak record on supervision, "which suggests that the Bank has limited information about the degree to which mitigation plans are actually implemented." The Bank's review of its EA policy "downplays the systematic lack of implementation of recommended measures by borrowing governments."[234] By not making conditionality "real" (by withholding loan disbursements in the face of noncompliance), the Bank in effect fails to use its power to press governments to behave accountably (to observe the conditions to which they agreed).

Insufficiently rigorous environmental impact assessments sometimes lie at the root of this problem. The analysts who conduct environmental impact assessments are selected by the Bank official whose job it is to "[get] the project designed and approved." Analysts can be hired from outside the Bank as well, so it is not in the interest of an in-house evaluator to be "too socially and environmentally rigorous" because they may find themselves unpopular with project managers.[235] The Bank's own lack of compliance with its rules facilitates unaccountable action on the part of borrower governments.

The World Bank does use its leverage to enforce a certain degree of compliance with social conditionalities. In 1999, the Bank extended a large loan to Chad's government for its share in an oil pipeline being built by a consortium of transnational corporations led by Exxon Mobil. World Bank financing was contingent upon the Chadian government's setting aside 80 percent of its pipeline profits for development and poverty reduction

[233] Andrew Gray, "Development Policy, Development Protest: The World Bank, Indigenous Peoples, and NGOs," in Fox and Brown, eds., *The Struggle for Accountability*, p. 287.
[234] Fox and Brown, "Assessing the Impact of NGO Advocacy Campaigns on World Bank Projects and Policies," pp. 526–7.
[235] Ibid., p. 529.

and 10 percent for the benefit of "future generations." But in early 2006, Chad's parliament "seriously weakened" the law setting aside the lion's share of oil revenue for development, provoking the World Bank to suspend loan disbursements.[236] In May 2005, the "independent accountability board" set up by the World Bank, designated to carry out oversight on oil revenue spending, "laid out a damning catalog of malfeasance and bungling," and documented extensive corruption.[237] Although the Bank was willing to hear Chad's explanation for wanting to alter the law to free up more funds for expenditures outside of their designation, the Chadian government officials refused to justify their decision, and the loans were withdrawn.

In July 2006, the World Bank reached a negotiated agreement with Chad, reducing the amount of oil revenues to be set aside for poverty reduction to 70 percent, allowing the state to increase its expenditures on "security" and to eliminate altogether the previously agreed-upon fund for "future generations." It is likely that the initial funding for the pipeline should not have gone through, given the fact that Chad is, according to Transparency International, tied with Bangladesh for the dubious honor of being the most corrupt government in the world.[238] Private financing alone, however, would not have mandated the set-aside of funds or the oversight committee to monitor the government's compliance, making the World Bank's involvement potentially useful in the service of promoting the Chadian government's accountability to its impoverished population.

Willingness to use its leverage on behalf of local citizens is often the result of activist pressure on the World Bank. Loan disbursements to the Brazilian government were held up in 1985 when the government faced protests from poor rural Brazilians displaced by the World Bank–financed Itaparica dam project. These protests had gained the attention and support of transnational organizations, including Oxfam and the U.S.-based Environmental Defense Fund, which pressured the Bank to use its leverage. As a result of this pressure, the Bank "made approval of the second and third tranches of its $500 million national electric power sector loan conditional on improved resettlement terms for those affected by the dam."[239]

---

[236] Lydia Polgreen and Celia W. Dugger, "Chad's Oil Riches, Meant for Poor, Are Diverted," *New York Times*, February 18, 2006, pp. A1, A6.

[237] Ibid. See also Goetz and Jenkins, pp. 144–6.

[238] Lydia Polgreen, "World Bank Reaches Pact with Chad over Use of Oil Profits," *New York Times*, July 15, 2006, p. A5.

[239] Fox and Brown, "Assessing the Impact of NGO Advocacy Campaigns on World Bank Projects and Policies," p. 512.

World Bank Programs and the Deterioration of Labor Rights and Human Rights

Even when it attempts to hold governments in compliance with Bank safeguard policies, ill effects on state accountability and human rights protection may still occur as a result of World Bank programs. Trade openness – often endorsed by structural adjustment programs – is negatively correlated with labor rights such as collective bargaining.[240] World Bank programs that intend to raise the level of a state's exports frequently aim to increase labor market flexibility – "code" for lower wages and decreased job protection.[241] Bank-supported "labor law reform programs...[may] require governments to decentralize their collective bargaining systems so that workers are only able to bargain at the enterprise level rather than at the company or industry level," as occurred in the adjustment program in Argentina, eviscerating workers' power of collective bargaining.[242]

Human rights, specifically the right to physical integrity, are also undermined by World Bank (and IMF) structural adjustment programs. A study examining the effects of World Bank structural adjustment agreements (SAAs) from 1981 to 2000 found that "receiving and implementing a SAA from the World Bank had the net effect of worsening government respect for all types of physical integrity rights." The study's authors found that in the year that an SAA is negotiated with the World Bank, a state's observance of physical integrity rights improves, but then deteriorates in the years during which the implementation of the agreement occurs.[243] This cumulative negative effect of SAAs suggests that the Bank could (and should) make ongoing government respect for physical integrity rights a condition of loan receipt[244] and thereby support governmental accountability and rule of law.

Strengthening Civil Society

The impact of transnational pressure from multilateral financial institutions such as the World Bank is necessarily limited; grassroots mobilization – in

---

[240] Mosely and Uno, "Racing to the Bottom or Climbing to the Top?"

[241] Stiglitz, *Globalization and Its Discontents*, p. 84.

[242] AFL-CIO et al., "Responsible Reform of the World Bank," April 2002, p. 13, accessed July 17, 2007, at http://www.bicusa.org/bicusa/issues/Responsible_Reform_of_the%20_World_Bank.pdf. One large-scale study found that the longer a state's exposure to structural adjustment was, the less it protected worker rights. Abouharb and Cingranelli, *Human Rights and Structural Adjustment*, p. 200.

[243] Physical integrity rights entail "citizens' rights to freedom from torture, political imprisonment, extra-judicial killing, and disappearances." Abouharb and Cingranelli, "The Human Rights Effects of World Bank Structural Adjustment," pp. 233–5, 256.

[244] Ibid., p. 256.

states reliant on their populations as a source of labor and taxes – has a more direct effect on movement toward accountable government. But World Bank pressure can play an auxiliary or catalytic role in promoting state accountability to the population, acting directly on the government or as a spur for the development and strengthening of local civic organizations.

The Bank's Inspection Panel has played a role in the latter regard. In addition to being an external accountability mechanism for the World Bank, the Inspection Panel has helped indirectly to hold national governments accountable to local communities. In one example, the process and aftermath of submitting a claim to the Inspection Panel "galvanized local citizens [adversely affected by the Yacyretá hydroelectric dam project] to press for greater political space in Paraguay to assert their rights."[245] After Panel representatives visited the site in 1997, talking with displaced persons who had not been compensated in accordance with the Bank's resettlement policy, the agency in charge of building and managing the dam stopped intimidating and refusing compensation to local people affected by the dam, and began to meet with community leaders.[246] An activist involved in filing the Inspection Panel claim found that the Panel's existence presented citizens with a legitimate means of challenging powerful institutions both abroad and at home. The presence of the Inspection Panel was not determinative, however. Although the Inspection Panel report validated the citizens' complaints, civic groups were unsuccessful in pressuring their government (along with the development banks) to create an "independent monitoring mechanism to assess the impacts of the dam...[and that would] incorporate their full participation in the design and implementation of solutions."[247] Citizen empowerment is critical if governments are to be held accountable to citizens; to the extent that local voices are amplified by Bank involvement, the potential for political accountability to citizens increases.

The Inspection Panel claim process can help promote the development of domestic accountability, irrespective of a claim's outcome. Filing a claim can "empower a local organization" and motivate the formation of civic coalitions that, through the claim process, gain experience in policy advocacy, preparing them for future engagement with the state and multilateral

---

[245] Kay Treakle and Elias Diaz Peña, "Accountability at the World Bank: What Does It Take? Lessons from the Yacyretá Hydroelectric Project, Argentina/Paraguay," in Clark, Fox, and Treakle, eds., *Demanding Accountability*, p. 69.
[246] Ibid., p. 77.
[247] Ibid., p. 87.

development banks alike.[248] In Brazil, for example, groups active in filing a 1995 claim with the Inspection Panel (regarding the Rondonia Natural Resources Management Project) helped to found the Brazilian Network on Multilateral Financial Institutions (Rede Brasil) in 1995. Rede Brasil then took part in filing an Inspection Panel claim in 1997 regarding the government's failure to compensate villagers for their losses due to flooding in the Itaparica dam resettlement project.[249] Such domestic mobilization is critical: "The panel – or any external reform conditionalities – cannot take the place of national political processes for social monitoring of bank projects."[250] In short, domestic civic mobilization at home is central to compelling governments to act accountably.[251]

A Word on the WTO

A third global governance institution of central importance in the economic realm is the WTO. Activists drew public attention to the WTO in 1999 when more than fifty thousand protesters mobilized in Seattle to disrupt the WTO's third Ministerial Conference. Critical of the WTO's decision-making processes and of its reluctance to incorporate environmental and labor standards into trade agreements, the protests highlighted the lack of accountability in transnational economic institutions.[252]

The WTO shares several of the accountability deficits exhibited by the IMF and the World Bank. All three organizations are "intrusive" in the domestic policy arena; where the IMF and World Bank impose

---

[248] Aurelio Vianna, Jr., "The Inspection Panel Claims in Brazil," in Clark, Fox, and Treakle, eds., *Demanding Accountability*, p. 147.

[249] Ibid., p. 153. For elaboration on these examples, also see Maria Guadalupe Moog Rodrigues, "The Planafloro Inspection Panel Claim: Opportunities and Challenges for Civil Society in Rondonia, Brazil," in Clark, Fox, and Treakle, eds., *Demanding Accountability*, pp. 45–68.

[250] Vianna, p. 163.

[251] Participation in filing an Inspection Panel claim is no guarantee of civic groups' positive reception by the state. Indian citizens lodged a complaint with the Inspection Panel in 1997 about the adverse environmental impact and resettlement/rehabilitation failures of a coal-development project in Singrauli, India, where villagers who refused resettlement were met with violent opposition and harassment. After the claim was filed, the World Bank loan recipient – India's National Thermal Power Corporation (NTPC) – retaliated by raising the level of violence: "people were beaten and physically restrained while their homes were bulldozed in the presence of and at the behest of NTPC." Dana Clark, "Singrauli: An Unfulfilled Struggle for Justice," in Clark, Fox, and Treakle, eds., *Demanding Accountability*, p. 176.

[252] Jim Lobe, "Unions Assail WTO for Ignoring Worker Rights," *OneWorld.net*, 2003, accessed June 12, 2008, at http://www.commondreams.org/headlines03/0908-02.htm.

"conditionalities," the WTO requires compliance with open trade policies. The European Community, for instance, was not allowed to put up an import barrier against U.S. beef fed with growth hormones, despite concerns about the health risks to consumers.[253] Similarly, for several years, the United States attempted to protect the profits of U.S.-based pharmaceutical companies by using WTO agreements on intellectual property to discourage the sale of generic HIV drugs from countries such as India to developing states racked by HIV/AIDS epidemics.[254]

Like the IMF and World Bank, the WTO is internally accountable to its member states, but the chain of accountability relationships between the trade ministers who comprise its highest decision-making body and the communities affected by WTO decisions is convoluted at best. Trade negotiations at the WTO are handled by representatives of member states (unlike the decision-making processes at the IMF and World Bank, where there is significant staff input), and although this shortens the accountability chain, it does not make it direct by any means (because, even in democratic member states of the WTO, voters neither select nor exercise powers of recall over their state's delegation). Decision-making processes at all three institutions are still relatively closed-door affairs, characterized by informality rather than by a transparent, accessible, participatory process.[255]

Even in the face of a restrictive decision-making process, transparency and well-institutionalized forms of monitoring can provide some measure of accountability for transnational economic organizations.[256] Under pressure from NGOs, the WTO (like the IMF and World Bank)

[253] Michael Mason, "The World Trade Regime and Non-Governmental Organisations: Addressing Transnational Environmental Concerns" (London: LSE Research Online, 2003), p. 22, accessed June 11, 2008, at http://eprints.lse.ac.uk/571/1/RPESA-no84(2003).pdf; Ngaire Woods and Amrita Narlikar, "Governance and the Limits of Accountability: The WTO, the IMF, and the World Bank," *International Social Science Journal*, Vol. 53, No. 170 (2001), pp. 569–83, at p. 569.

[254] Ian F. Fergusson, "The WTO, Intellectual Property Rights, and the Access to Medicines Controversy," Congressional Research Service, November 5, 2007, accessed June 12, 2008, at http://italy.usembassy.gov/pdf/other/RL33750.pdf; see also John S. James, "WTO Accepts Rules Limiting Medicine Exports to Poor Countries," *AIDS Treatment News*, September 12, 2003, accessed June 12, 2008, at http://www.thebody.com/content/art31751.html. As a prerequisite to India's accession to the WTO, the Indian parliament passed legislation delaying the production of new generic drugs for export. See John Lancaster, "In Bow to WTO, India Targets Drug Copying," *Washington Post*, March 24, 2005, p. E6, accessed June 12, 2008, at http://www.washingtonpost.com/wp-dyn/articles/A61757-2005Mar23.html.

[255] Woods and Narlikar, pp. 572–3.

[256] Ibid., pp. 574–9.

has made public increasing amounts of previously classified information, "de-restricting" more documents and doing so more quickly than in the past, although member states balk at this greater insistence on transparency. The aftermath of the Seattle protests also brought increased opportunities for interaction and consultation between NGOs and the WTO on various issues, including environmental standards, and increasing numbers of NGOs have been accredited to attend WTO ministerial conferences over time.[257] Such contact points between NGOs and the WTO, however, are fewer and less institutionalized than those between NGOs and the IMF or World Bank. The WTO also lags behind the IMF and World Bank in terms of having mechanisms for evaluating and monitoring its effects (such as the IMF's Independent Evaluation Office or the Bank's Inspection Panel).[258] On balance, the WTO falls short of the already low external accountability standard exhibited by the IFIs.[259]

MULTINATIONAL CORPORATIONS

In addition to international financial institutions, multinational corporations (MNCs) constitute a cornerstone of economic globalization. MNCs – sometimes called TNCs, or transnational corporations – dominate the world economy, producing and marketing their goods and services across national borders. As of 2002, there were roughly 64,000 MNCs located around the world, with 840,000 subsidiaries operating outside of their parent corporation's home state.[260] The economic scale of many of these corporations is immense. In 1998, the "hundred largest MNCs control[led] about 20 per cent of global foreign assets...and account[ed] for almost 30 per cent of the total world sales of all MNCs."[261]

---

[257] Mason, "The World Trade Regime and Non-Governmental Organisations," p. 12.

[258] Woods and Narlikar, p. 578.

[259] From a different perspective, the WTO and its dispute settlement/enforcement process acts as an accountability mechanism within the system of international trade and is hence a valuable addition to the institutions of global governance, offsetting to some degree the previous "unilateralism" of U.S. power in world trade. See Keith Griffin, "Economic Globalization and Institutions of Global Governance," *Development and Change*, Vol. 34, No. 5 (2003), pp. 789–808, at p. 797.

[260] United Nations Conference on Trade and Development (UNCTAD), "World Investment Report 2002: TNCs and Export Competitiveness," Geneva, United Nations, 2002, as cited in Mathias Koenig-Archibugi, "Transnational Corporations and Public Accountability," *Government and Opposition*, Vol. 39, No. 2 (April 2004), p. 234.

[261] David Held et al., *Global Transformations: Politics, Economics and Culture* (Stanford: Stanford University Press, 1999), p. 236.

At the upper end of the scale, MNCs wield more financial clout than some countries. Fifty-one of the world's one hundred largest economies in 1998 were corporations, and only forty-nine were states.[262] Spanning the economic gamut from the extraction of oil and other natural resources to manufacturing and services, MNCs affect the world's population not only as consumers and laborers, but also as citizens of the states where MNCs operate. This section asks whether MNCs are – or should be – accountable (and to whom) and in what ways they have used their economic power to affect states' accountability to citizens.

The Accountability of MNCs

Multinational corporations are privately owned entities, not public institutions. Thus, although there is a theoretically direct accountability relationship between corporations' leaders and their shareholders, it is "less obvious why corporations should be accountable to the general public, since no delegation of authority seems to occur between them." Yet the fact that each corporation is granted a charter by the state and that its owners' liability is therefore limited would seem to justify a certain measure of corporate accountability to the public. Moreover, a relationship of accountability may be said to exist not only where authority is delegated but also where "a person or community is substantially affected by the actions of an individual or organization," a situation that applies to the actions of MNCs worldwide.[263]

As the role of MNCs in the world's economy has grown, so have calls for corporate accountability. The growing power of MNCs in the public sphere – in the decision-making calculus of governments – "has subjected firms to a demand that they be treated as holders of the public trust, and therefore a growing insistence that they answer to ordinary people, not just state institutions, for their actions, and perhaps suffer direct sanctions

---

[262] Amnesty International USA, "AI on Human Rights and Labor Rights," in Frank J. Lechner and John Boli, eds., *The Globalization Reader* (Malden: Blackwell, 2000), p. 187. This statistic relies on the comparison of corporate sales to country GDP. Using the "value added" of corporations instead of sales generates a different result: In 2000, thirty-seven of the top one hundred economies were corporations. However, this methodology still shows that a group of large corporations are significantly "bigger" economically than many countries. Walmart, the largest corporation on the list (in terms of "value added"), weighs in at $67.7 billion, well larger than many states' economies. See P. De Grauwe and F. Camerman, "How Big Are the Big Multinational Companies?" *Tijdschrift voor Economie en Management*, Vol. XLVII, No. 3 (2002), pp. 311–26.

[263] Koenig-Archibugi, "Transnational Corporations and Public Accountability," p. 236.

as well."[264] Powerful corporations "such as Enron or Microsoft may be of such economic significance that they operate, in a sense, like governing bodies and have a correspondingly greater obligation to the public for transparency and accountability relative to smaller business entities."[265] As states increasingly turn the provision of social services over to private corporations – often to MNCs – the ramifications of private investment choices on public life merit an inquiry into the external accountability relationship between MNCs and citizens.

The trend toward privatization of state-run water systems, for instance, has led to increased (and often unaffordable) price raises, where the profits go not to the state but to foreign multinationals, who, after completing the project, cannot be held accountable for failures the same way that a government potentially could be. In the suburbs of Buenos Aires, after control of the water supply was privatized, the MNC in charge of making water available and then managing the system failed to install sufficient sewers, leading to flooding. Regulatory agencies were not put into place when control was turned over to the private water company. "In the early phase, a regulatory agency was not in place," said Abel Fatala, the engineer in charge of public services in the municipal government of Buenos Aires. "When it did start up, it was made in the image of the water company. The concrete result was that there was no control at all."[266] Pressure on states to put citizen interests over corporate ones occasionally results in a victory for civic protest. Such a case arose in 1999 in Cochabamba, Bolivia, when the Bolivian government privatized the city's water system to a consortium owned in part by the U.S.-based Bechtel Corporation. The population protested vehemently against the ensuing and dramatic increase in water prices, holding mass demonstrations that led the Bolivian government to break its contract with the consortium.[267]

Blaming multinational corporations and other transnational actors for development failures and poverty (in its many forms), however, particularly when the corporation in question has not done anything illegal, can let the state off the hook. Assuming that states are powerless vis-à-vis

---

[264] Goetz and Jenkins, p. 11.
[265] Alfred Aman, *The Democracy Deficit: Taming Globalization Through Law Reform* (New York: New York University Press, 2004), pp. 179–80.
[266] Quoted in John Tagliabue, "As Multinationals Run the Taps, Anger Rises over Water for Profit," *New York Times*, August, 26, 2002, p. 1.
[267] Bechtel took the Bolivian government to court at the World Bank, but dropped the claim in early 2006 under heavy pressure from transnational activists. See Jim Shultz, "Bechtel vs. Bolivia: The People Win!" *Peacework* (February 2006), accessed July 18, 2007, at http://www.peaceworkmagazine.org/pwork/0602/060208.htm.

corporations "[reduces] pressure on states, individually and collectively, to regulate in ways that promote human development."[268] Although MNCs may encourage unaccountable regimes to continue their practices, they can also have a positive impact on political accountability.

The Impact of MNCs on State Accountability

The growth and global spread of MNCs' operation in the past fifty years have contributed to an increasing "accountability gap" between corporations and the citizens affected by their activities, whether they are workers, consumers, or local people living in proximity to corporate activity. Although a state should be able to represent its citizens' interests against those of a corporation violating labor rights or environmental regulations, "[g]lobalization means that it is more difficult for national governments to hold corporations accountable than in the past."[269] Corporate mobility and the growing trend among developing countries' governments to engage in "deregulatory competition" (e.g., lowering or exempting taxes on corporations; ignoring or decimating environmental standards) have even "turn[ed] the accountability relationship upside down by making governments accountable to [MNCs], or at least by increasing the bargaining power of [MNCs] vis-à-vis the governments."[270] As governments, especially in the developing world, compete for foreign capital investment and its attendant potential for technology transfer and employment opportunities, the deregulatory race "impairs the accountability relationship between governments and TNCs," because the incentive is for governments to limit their "demands on the agent and to abstain from punishment for fear that the agent will move to the jurisdiction of another principal." This kind of competition affects developing countries more than others. Although states belonging to the Organization for Economic Cooperation and Development (OECD) "are able to resist the downward pressure of competitive regulation," resistance is weaker outside of the advanced industrialized world.[271]

Typically, corporations can be held accountable to the public "through state institutions – legislatures, bureaucracies and courts." In weak states, or in states where MNCs collude with authoritarian rulers (the former

[268] Goetz and Jenkins, p. 144.
[269] Robert Keohane, as cited in Koenig-Archibugi, "Transnational Corporations and Public Accountability," p. 235.
[270] Ibid., p. 242.
[271] Ibid., pp. 242–3.

support the latter's monopoly on power, for instance), that accountability relationship does not hold. Even under less conspiratorial circumstances, governments may feel pressured to meet corporate demands rather than imposing regulations that a transnational corporation finds distasteful. In short, if a government is weak relative to a corporation, it may not play its proper role in holding the latter accountable or may find itself behaving as if it were accountable to the MNC operating on its territory rather than to the constituents who elected it.[272] The state's accountability failure is particularly clear in the area of labor rights.

MNCs and Labor Rights

The degree to which states – particularly states with relatively weak economies – can bargain with corporations for the protection of their citizens' labor rights may be limited. One effect of inter-state competition for corporate investment is the expansion of the private sphere at the expense of the public sphere. As the public sphere shrinks, so may the area of state accountability. Often, looking at issues through a "gender-sensitive lens" will highlight the broader picture.[273] Using women's employment as a lens on workplace rights and state accountability illustrates how mobile the dividing line is between the public and private spheres. In particular, MNCs' preference for "flexible" labor has resulted in the expansion of the informal sector of the economy, where MNCs function under fewer regulatory standards and hire workers without the contracts and benefits that would be available to them in the formal sector. As of 2005, only one-third of Mexico's economically active population worked in the formal economy: "This means the majority of workers have no legal recourse to guarantee their rights in the workplace."[274] Workplace rights guaranteed by the state in the formal sector of the economy go unobserved in the informal sector. As the state bows to pressure from transnational corporations (and lending institutions), as the informal economy grows, the state shrinks the public space in which rights are guaranteed, effectively turning the informal economy into a private space where women – who are the majority of informal-sector workers – can be exploited with near impunity.

---

[272] Ibid., pp. 237–9.

[273] V. Spike Peterson and Anne Sisson Runyan, *Global Gender Issues*, 2nd edition (Boulder: Westview Press, 1999), p. 1; also see Cynthia Enloe, *The Curious Feminist: Searching for Women in a New Age of Empire* (Berkeley: University of California Press, 2004).

[274] Linda S. Stevenson, "Gender Equality and Globalization: Cooperation and Conflict," unpublished paper, presented at Women's Caucus for Political Science APSA Pre-Conference, Washington, D.C., 2005, p. 10.

One such "privatized" space is the export processing zone (EPZ), where local workers are hired by MNCs to produce manufactured goods for export. Although men dominate the industrial labor market worldwide, EPZs – particularly those that focus on textiles, clothes, and electronic components – boast a dramatically feminized workforce.[275] The predominance of developing country exports produced by women led one economist to pronounce the Third World industrialization process "as much *female* led as *export* led."[276] The female-dominated EPZs of the Philippines, for instance, where 85 to 90 percent of employees are women, offer wages lower than those in other industrial sectors. Forty percent of the women working in EPZs are paid salaries below the legal minimum wage, compared to 17 percent of men. One factory manager in a Philippine EPZ justified the recruitment of women for such low-wage jobs, explaining: "[they] endure poverty well."[277]

Labor standards, and the right to organize and bargain collectively to improve them, are typically limited in EPZs and "free trade zones." In Jamaica, for instance, the government agreed to bar unionization from its free trade zones. Women who attempted to organize collectively to better their wages and working conditions were fired.[278] Similarly, when the Malaysian government was seeking to attract foreign investment in the 1980s, electronics industry unions were repressed under pressure from U.S. business executives.[279] Within China's Special Economic Zones and Mexico's *maquiladoras* (assembly plants) as well, workers' rights are routinely violated and unions suppressed or banned.[280] The repression of unions reinforces MNCs' ability to hire workers at low wages, whether inside or outside of EPZs. In China, for instance, 3 million women "working for wages as low as 12 cents an hour make 80 percent of the sporting goods and toys sold in the United States each year."[281]

Although some transnational corporations engaged in extractive industries such as mining are limited in their mobility, those in manufacturing have more bargaining power over the benefits that they receive from

---

[275] Mittelman, *The Globalization Syndrome*, p. 86.
[276] Susan Joekes, cited in Moghadam, *Globalizing Women*, p. 53.
[277] Mittelman, *The Globalization Syndrome*, p. 86.
[278] Black, "About the Film."
[279] William Greider, "Wawasan 2020," in Lechner and Boli, eds., *The Globalization Reader*, pp. 148–54, at p. 152.
[280] Robert J. S. Ross, "The 'Race to the Bottom' in Imported Clothes," *Dollars and Sense* (January/February 2002), pp. 46–7.
[281] Tom Hayden and Charles Kernaghan, "Pennies an Hour, and No Way Up," *New York Times*, July 6, 2002, p. A27.

host countries, such as tax breaks or wage ceilings. In the context of a "borderless world," MNCs "play national governments against each other in order to get the best financial deals. Wages and environmental regulations are undermined as firms threaten to leave in search of cheaper labor and lower restrictions."[282] Empirical evidence lends credence to the race-to-the-bottom hypothesis. One study of the clothing industry found that export production has shifted toward states offering lower wages. Between 1998 and 2001, the share of clothing imported by the United States from low-wage countries – including Bangladesh, Burma, Guatemala, Indonesia, Nicaragua, and Peru – increased, while imports from higher-wage countries such as Canada and Israel fell.[283] The average wage in the textile industry across the thirty-four countries from which the United States imports 94 percent of its clothing fell by about 6 percent (with the 2001 average hourly wage for apparel producers across the countries studied landing between $1.76 and $1.63).[284]

The presence of MNCs, however, can also have a countervailing, positive impact on labor rights. A recent study examining the effects of economic globalization on labor rights in ninety developing countries between 1986 and 2002 found that foreign direct investment (FDI) has a "positive and significant" relationship with workers' enjoyment of the right to organize unions, engage in collective bargaining, and strike.[285] MNCs headquartered in the "first world" and operating subsidiary enterprises in developing states may bring along "best practices for workers' rights," or lead governments to observe the rule of law more generally (perhaps to make the legal environment more secure for corporate property and dispute resolution).[286] Not all MNC involvement is beneficial to the protection of labor rights, however. In sectors where MNCs' primary interest is in keeping labor costs low (such as in the textile industry, which operates largely through subcontracting, not through FDI), the effects on labor rights are negative, as is generally the case whenever MNC subcontracting to locally owned enterprises prevails over FDI. The effects of MNCs on encouraging the debilitation of labor rights is mixed, and most likely varies by industry, as well as by the proportion of FDI to local subcontracting. Where MNCs require a skilled labor force or are engaged in capital intensive industry, they are less

---

[282] Tickner, p. 45.
[283] Ross, "The 'Race to the Bottom' in Imported Clothes," pp. 46–7.
[284] Robert J.S. Ross, "The Declining Average Wage in Imported Clothes," *Dollars and Sense* (July 2002), p. 6.
[285] Mosely and Uno, p. 923.
[286] Ibid., p. 925.

liable to press governments for lower wages or to move elsewhere in search of cheaper labor; in labor-intensive industries such as textiles, countries may well compete to provide a low-waged and deregulated atmosphere, to the detriment of labor rights.[287]

MNCs and Authoritarian Government

Although FDI seems to favor democratic governments over dictatorships, cases of "collusion" between MNCs and dictators persist, particularly when corporations are engaged in extractive industry in the developing world.[288] Such companies can help keep authoritarian rulers in power by "[providing] the government with resources – royalties and tax revenues – that are vital for maintaining the political status quo."[289]

Multinational oil companies have been among the worst offenders in this regard. The history of oil company symbiosis with authoritarian rule in oil-rich Nigeria included ongoing environmental destruction and human rights violations against indigenous people inhabiting the Niger Delta in the 1990s.[290] In 1998, for instance, the Chevron oil company brought the Nigerian military in to counter unarmed demonstrators in Ilajeland in the Niger Delta, killing two protestors and injuring roughly thirty others. In 1999, the Nigerian military used a Chevron-owned helicopter and boats to attack Niger Delta villages.[291]

One reason for the Nigerian government's violent treatment of the Niger Delta population has been the state's ongoing reliance on oil exports for over 95 percent of its foreign exchange earnings: "This fact has rendered much of the country's population superfluous to the regime's pursuit of patronage resources, except insofar as individuals or groups contest the

---

[287] Ibid., pp. 927, 941. "Cheap labor" is a misnomer; low-waged workers are labor "*made cheap*" by structural circumstances as well as conscious choices by manufacturers and governments. See Cynthia Enloe, *Globalization and Militarism* (Lanham, MD: Rowman & Littlefield, 2007), p. 20.

[288] Nathan Jensen, 'Democratic Governance and Multinational Corporations; Political Regimes and Inflows of Foreign Direct Investment," *International Organization*, Vol. 57, No. 3 (2003), pp. 587–616, cited in Koenig-Archibugi, "Transnational Corporations and Public Accountability," p. 240.

[289] Keonig-Archibugi, "Transnational Corporations and Public Accountability," p. 240.

[290] Cyril I. Obi, "Global, State, and Local Intersections: Power, Authority, and Conflict in the Niger Delta Oil Communities," in Thomas Callaghy, Ronald Kassimir, and Robert Latham, eds., *Intervention and Transnationalism in Africa* (Cambridge, UK: Cambridge University Press, 2001), pp. 173–93.

[291] Amy Goodman (with David Goodman), *The Exception to the Rulers: Exposing Oily Politicians, War Profiteers, and the Media That Love Them* (New York: Hyperion, 2004), chapter 3.

regime's control over oil."[292] Accountability to the population under such conditions would only threaten the government's monopolization of power and resources – used to retain the support of local "strongmen" for the Nigerian government.[293]

Transnational corporations – even oil companies – can also undermine unaccountable governments. Although state corruption may be mutually beneficial to rulers and corporate executives in the short term, some companies have supported "good governance" reforms intended to reduce corruption and bribery and hence to reduce the costs of business. In 2001, British Petroleum (BP), an oil company operating in Angola, decided to make public its tax payments to the Angolan government, "so that Angolans could demand answers from their government about where this money went." The infuriated Angolan government threatened to call an end to BP's contracts.[294] In this case, a corporation voluntarily lifted the lid on proprietary information, enabling local citizens to at least try to hold their government accountable for its expenditures.

NAFTA AND STATE/CORPORATE ACCOUNTABILITY

Multilateral trade agreements such as the North American Free Trade Agreement (NAFTA) are another vector transmitting neoliberalism and facilitating one of its central components, free trade. NAFTA has been widely criticized on the left as a vehicle for increasing corporate profit while spurring a race to the bottom in wages and undermining labor rights and environmental standards. NAFTA, however, was implemented along with an accountability mechanism – the North American Agreement on Labor Cooperation (NAALC). Although the NAALC has created a public forum in which to raise accountability issues, it has presented few opportunities to hold states and corporations accountable for their treatment of labor.

NAFTA's accountability mechanism, commonly referred to as the "labor 'side agreement,'" mandated the formation of a National Administrative Office (NAO) in the labor departments of each of the three countries party

---

[292] William Reno, "Mafiya Troubles, Warlord Crises," in Young and Beissinger, eds., *Beyond State Crisis?*, pp. 116–17. In the first quarter of 2006, only about 2 percent of Nigeria's foreign exchange earnings came from non-oil exports. See Central Bank of Nigeria, *Economic Report for the First Quarter of 2006*, pp. 17–18, accessed November 21, 2007, at http://www.cenbank.org/out/publications/reports/rd/2006/mrp-03–06.pdf.

[293] Reno, "Mafiya Troubles, Warlord Crises," p. 117.

[294] Goetz and Jenkins, p. 119.

to NAFTA. The NAOs were designed as repositories for complaints about violations of labor and environmental standards by transnational companies operating within the NAFTA states and were entrusted to address such complaints through inter-state labor department collaboration, presumably coordinated through the NAO.[295] In their first few years, the NAOs either dismissed or resolved any complaints of violations that they received through "high-level consultations between labor ministers." Then, in 1997, a Human Rights Watch (HRW) report on gender discrimination in the U.S.-owned *maquiladoras* on the Mexican–U.S. border led to the engagement of the U.S. NAO, which convened a committee to investigate the charges in July 1997. The HRW report alleged that the U.S. companies were violating the equal rights clauses of the Mexican Constitution, as well as Mexico's Federal Labor Law, by requiring pregnancy tests before hiring female workers (and then refusing to hire pregnant women), and by firing pregnant workers in order to avoid responsibility for the six-week paid maternity leave that the Mexican labor law required.[296]

The report by the U.S. NAO, released in January 1998, definitively acknowledged that the rights of pregnant women in the *maquiladoras* were being violated:

The review of Submission No. 9701 raises serious matters regarding the treatment of women workers who are pregnant in Mexico's *maquiladora* sector and the protection they are afforded by the Mexico authorities. Women are subjected to pregnancy screening and intrusive questioning. They are denied employment if they are pregnant. There are instances where they are dismissed from employment after becoming pregnant or are pressured into resigning for the same reason. The level of awareness amongst women of their rights is in question and they may lack confidence in the procedures and mechanisms by which those rights can be protected.[297]

Various Mexican government bodies disagreed about whether pregnancy screening was illegal, and Mexico's Federal District Human Rights Commission found evidence that even state agencies were using pre-employment pregnancy screening, in violation of the constitution.[298]

Although NAFTA had been designed to promote corporate interests, its "side agreement" created an institutional opportunity to highlight labor

---

[295] Linda S. Stevenson, "Confronting Gender Discrimination in the Mexican Workplace: Women and Labor Facing NAFTA with Transnational Contention," *Women and Politics*, Vol. 26, No. 1 (2004), p. 80.

[296] Ibid., pp. 80–1.

[297] Cited in ibid., p. 84.

[298] Ibid., p. 84.

rights, providing a potential forum in which to hold corporations account-able to local laws against discrimination. In this case, it also created an opportunity for Mexican citizens to hold their government accountable for implementing its own laws.[299] The pregnancy discrimination issue, how-ever, remained unresolved in the wake of the U.S. NAO report. Although the NAO provided an institutional space in which to investigate and pub-licize the violations, it had no enforcement power over the companies to impose a change in policy.

Meanwhile, as the NAO investigation was taking place, within the Mexican Congress a group of female legislators had created a Gender and Equity Commission with the intention of formulating policies that would address women's issues. In March 1998, the Commission sponsored a Women's Parliament where policy proposals were floated and discussed by politicians and women's civic groups alike, "including some on discrim-ination against pregnant women in the workplace." In August 1998, at a seminar organized by women's studies centers and NGOs to facilitate further discussion of policy proposals in advance of congressional debate on reforming Mexico's Federal Labor Law, a representative of the U.S. NAO "presented an in-depth analysis of the case of sex discrimination," which was followed by general agreement that "this would be a good time and issue on which to focus during the next legislative term." It is plausi-ble, then, that NAFTA, as a manifestation of the transnational neoliberal trade regime, had the unanticipated effect of helping to put discrimination against pregnant women on the Mexican congressional agenda.[300]

Further examples of transnational labor action involving the NAOs brought only mixed success at best against the companies in question. In 1994, for instance, the Postal, Telegraph and Telephone International Federation began a campaign against Sprint in response to the company's firing of Hispanic workers who sought to unionize at a factory in San Francisco.[301] Sprint closed the plant, prompting unions in Germany, France, and Nicaragua to pressure "their national telecom operators to force Sprint to adopt a code on labour standards as a condition for entering

[299] The use of the NAO to address gender discrimination was not an isolated case. A second instance where the U.S. and Canadian NAOs addressed the violation of Mexican work-ers' right to freedom of association and the right to choose a union is discussed in ibid., p. 82.

[300] Ibid., pp. 86–7. The labor law reforms discussion was ultimately tabled in the Congress due to interparty disagreements.

[301] Daphné Josselin, "Back to the Front Line? Trade Unions in a Global Age," in Daphné Josselin and William Wallace, eds., *Non-State Actors in World Politics* (Basingstoke: Palgrave, 2001), p. 178.

international alliances." Brazilian unions protested as well.[302] Utilizing NAFTA's accountability instrument, the NAALC, the Mexican Telephone Workers Union filed a case with the Mexican NAO regarding Sprint's violation of the San Francisco workers' right to organize. This resulted in ministerial consultations as well as a revealing report produced by the Secretariat of the Commission for Labor Cooperation (a body created by the NAALC). Titled "Plant Closings and Labor Rights," the report shed light on the widespread corporate tactic of plant closings (or threatened closings) in the face of union organizing campaigns.[303] NAFTA appeared to have opened up a new transnational space in which to curtail MNCs' violation of labor rights. But no further action was taken by the NAO against Sprint.

Success in the Sprint case proved ephemeral at the transnational and state levels alike. Amid the international solidarity organizing and the NAFTA consultations, the Communications Workers of America (CWA) filed a case against Sprint with the U.S. National Labor Relations Board (NRLB). Initially, in December 1996, the NRLB found that Sprint had "wrongfully closed its San Francisco subsidiary and ordered Sprint to reinstate the workers and to award them back pay." Sprint contested the ruling with an appeal in U.S. federal court. Less than a year later, in November 1997, the court reversed the NRLB's decision, "stating that there was overwhelming evidence that Sprint closed the plant because it was losing money, not because the company wanted to thwart the union organizing campaign."[304]

At best, the NAALC is a weak tool for rectifying violations of workers' rights. The agreement specifies eleven "labor principles" to which the signatory governments agreed, divided into three "tiers" of importance. The first tier includes "freedom of association and the right to organize[,]...the right to bargain collectively, and...the right to strike," but violations of these principles receive the "lowest level of treatment" – the side agreement stipulates only a "review" process for such violations, with "optional ministerial consultations." The suppression of unions, therefore, cannot be grounds for trade sanctions under the NAALC, and thus limits the agreement's utility as an accountability-promoting institution. The second tier of principles includes "prohibition of forced labor,

---

[302] Ibid., p. 186, ft. 17.
[303] Jacqueline McFadyen, "NAFTA Supplemental Agreements: Four Year Review," Working Paper 98–4, Institute for International Economics, accessed July 3, 2006, at http://www.iie.com/publications/wp/wp.cfm?ResearchID=145.
[304] Ibid.

nondiscrimination, equal pay for men and women, worker's compensation, [and] migrant labor protection," and merits both review and "evaluation." Only violations of three principles – child labor, minimum wage rights, and occupational health and safety – are entitled to "review, evaluation, and arbitration, with possible application of sanctions in cases of a 'persistent pattern of failure to effectively enforce' laws in those areas."[305]

The NAALC pertains only to individual countries enforcing their own laws on these issues. In a case where Mexican workers at a Sony factory registered a complaint about the obstacles that they faced (namely, being fired) when trying to form a union independent of the Mexican government, the "review" to which they were entitled resulted in the three labor ministers agreeing that the workers had a valid complaint. However, because the complaint was technically against the Mexican government's failure to enforce its own laws, Sony was not required to compensate the workers whose rights had been violated. The Mexican government's "punishment" was to hold public meetings and to "study...how to avoid this 'persistent' problem of nonenforcement." Although the NAALC agreement may be weak, one side-effect of the Sony case was that a Ford subsidiary in Mexico did not obstruct the formation of an independent union in the aftermath of the Sony case, seeking to avoid "the bad publicity that Sony received."[306]

While the availability of an NAO process may provide occasional opportunities to redress lapses in state and corporate accountability to workers, NAFTA itself has facilitated the suppression of union organizing in general. According to the 1996 study commissioned by the Secretariat of the Commission for Labor Cooperation, plant closing rates tripled as a response to unionization after NAFTA was initiated. Between 1993 and 1995, U.S. employers seeking to avoid unionization "threatened to close the plant in 50 percent of all union certification elections." This form of intimidation was effective; such employer threats were made "in 52 percent of all instances where the union withdrew from its organizing drive." Nor were the threats empty. In 15 percent of cases where the union won its certification election, within two years employers had closed all or part of the plant, a shutdown rate triple that found by studies of post-union-election shutdowns at the end of the 1980s, before NAFTA was implemented.[307]

---

[305] Lance Compa, "Another Look at NAFTA," in Broad, ed., *Global Backlash*, p. 136.
[306] See Broad, ed., *Global Backlash*, p. 122; Jerome I. Levinson, "NAFTA's Labor Agreement: Lessons," in Broad, ed., *Global Backlash*, pp. 142–9.
[307] The percentage of unionizing campaigns met by plant-closing threats was 62 percent in mobile industries such as manufacturing. Kate Bronfenbrenner, "We'll Close! Plant

NAO efforts alone are no match against governments and corporations, even when the NAO verifies that violations have occurred. The outcomes of NAO cases are "often ignored or deflected by home-country governments or firms."[308] The availability of the NAO process may even have had a demobilizing effect on labor rights activism, making successful challenges to violations less likely. In one illustrative case, the Coalition for Justice in the Maquiladoras (CJM), a group bringing together labor and human rights activists from Canada, the United States, and Mexico, spent ten years using a combination of local direct action (such as wildcat strikes) and pressure on corporations by means of phone and fax campaigns carried out by activists outside of Mexico. These tactics produced some improvements in conditions for Mexican workers in foreign-owned factories near the border. After the advent of NAFTA and the NAOs, however, "there was a decline in cross-border collaboration and in direct action," as cases were brought to national courts and the NAOs: "[A]s the locus of decision making moved upward, the principal actors – the workers at the point of production – were displaced by legal representatives and public officials with little knowledge of the issues and different concerns than those of the workers."[309]

Using transnational institutions as a means to resolve conflict in this case appears to have removed the conflict from the public realm of direct action. Collective action scholar Sidney Tarrow writes, "the decline of disruptive protest made it easier for decision makers to ignore workers' claims...[and] once direct action declined, institutional access alone was insufficient to advance their claims." Local pressure and mobilization (perhaps in combination with the use of transnational institutions like the NAOs) are thus shown to be important as a means of pressuring corporations and the state officials who collaborate with them in lowering labor standards.[310] For this reason, "sustainable change will only be achieved when national governments are continually pushed to live up to their claims and when the pressure 'from below' and 'from above' continues."[311]

Closings, Plant-Closing Threats, Union Organizing and NATFA, *Multinational Monitor*, Vol. 18, No. 3 (March 1997), accessed July 6, 2006, at http://multinationalmonitor.org/hyper/mm0397.04.html.

[308] Sidney Tarrow, *The New Transnational Activism* (New York: Cambridge University Press, 2005), p. 155.

[309] Ibid., p. 157, citing Heather Williams, "Of Labor Tragedy and Legal Farce: The Han Young Factory Struggle in Tijuana, Mexico," *Social Science History*, 27 (2003), pp. 525–50.

[310] Tarrow, pp. 157–8.

[311] Ibid., p. 159, citing Thomas Riise and Kathryn Sikkink, "The Socialization of International Human Rights Norms into Domestic Practices: Introduction," in Thomas Riise,

Harnessing free trade agreements in the service of state and corporate accountability to labor can succeed only when combined with grassroots activism – which has more direct effects on corporations than do mild reprimands by the NAOs. The involvement of grassroots activists is also more likely to guarantee that workers' concerns do not get lost in the process of taking a case into the legal (or quasi-legal) realm occupied by the NAOs.

RESISTANCE

Just as the formation of nation-states provided the space for national social movements to arise and contest existing power arrangements, the increasing concentration of transnational economic institutions – such as IFIs, trade agreements, and multinational corporations – has created a new set of opportunities and arenas for collective action.[312] And just as economic globalization is best seen not as a novel phenomenon but as a process of global economic integration taking place over centuries – albeit intensifying in the last quarter of the twentieth century – various resistance movements to "exploitative forms of global trade" developed well in advance of the 1970s. These include the transnational movement against the Atlantic slave trade and the human rights movement against the brutal colonization of the Belgian Congo from 1890 to 1910, among others.[313] Against this historical background, contemporary economic globalization has generated various forms of transborder resistance aimed at holding transnational economic institutions accountable to the people whose lives they most directly affect, whether they are working for MNCs or experiencing the effects of an IFI-sponsored adjustment program or development project. In this section, I examine several attempts to hold MNCs accountable to their workers (transnational social movements responding to IFI programs are addressed in Chapter 6).

As governments compete to create favorable environments for foreign business, it becomes more challenging to hold those governments accountable for how the MNCs on their territory treat labor. Groups concerned

Stephen C. Ropp, and Kathryn Sikkink, eds., *The Power of Human Rights: International Norms and Domestic Change* (Cambridge, UK: Cambridge University Press, 1999), p. 33.

[312] Tarrow, pp. 18–19.

[313] Zahara Heckscher, "Long Before Seattle: Historical Resistance to Economic Globalization," in Broad, ed., *Global Backlash*, pp. 86–91. On the movements regarding the Congo and the Atlantic slave trade, see Adam Hochschild, *King Leopold's Ghost* (Boston: Houghton Mifflin, 1998); idem, *Bury the Chains: Prophets and Rebels in the Fight to Free an Empire's Slaves* (Boston: Houghton Mifflin, 2005).

with workers' rights, like the U.S.-based Human Rights First (www. humanrightsfirst.org), argue that the relative decline of government power versus corporate power has created a new accountability problem:

> In the cold war...the main issue was how do you hold governments accountable when they violate laws and norms. Today the emerging issue is how do you hold private companies accountable for the treatment of their workers at a time when government control is ebbing all over the world, or governments themselves are going into business and can't be expected to play the watchdog or protection role?[314]

Often, such efforts fall to consumers.

Common forms of international consumer pressure on corporations include boycotts and "negative publicity" campaigns organized by non-governmental organizations. One relatively recent tactical development in the negative publicity field has been transnational organizing to pressure MNCs to observe a set of "minimum standards" – often called "corporate codes of conduct" – in the treatment of their workers. These range from banning child labor and maintaining health and safety conditions to allowing free speech and the formation of unions in their Third World factories. In short, by signing a corporate code of conduct, a company pledges to observe basic labor rights. The Fair Labor Association (FLA), a group of universities, NGOs, and MNCs organized in 1999 to monitor the behavior of U.S. clothing companies, is one such initiative. The FLA sets standards and then monitors factories operated by companies that agree to observe those standards, allowing brands that abide by the rules to sport an FLA label on the clothes they produce. This alerts consumers to the conditions under which the clothes were produced, enabling them to use their purchasing power to punish or praise companies as they see fit. The FLA also posts information about noncompliant companies on its website (http://www.fairlabor.org).

Founded in 1998, United Students against Sweatshops (USAS) similarly pressures MNCs to improve conditions for both workers and labor organizers in their factories. In 2003, a factory in the Dominican Republic producing baseball caps for universities and athletic companies was successfully pressured by students, as well as by Nike and Reebok, to allow the formation of a union after factory managers had fired unionizing employees. Wages were also raised by about 10 percent as a result of the organizing pressure to roughly $31 per week. Such victories are more than

[314] Cited in Thomas Friedman, "The New Human Rights," *New York Times*, July 30, 1999.

symbolic. The factory in question was the largest one located in a free trade zone across the states of Central America, Mexico, and the Caribbean.[315] This particular victory, however, was fleeting. In 2007, the BJ&B factory closed its doors; its owners had decided to shift production to Vietnam, where independent union organizing is outlawed.[316]

"Naming and shaming" methods, ranging from consumer boycotts to the negative publicity accompanying violation of a corporate code of conduct, are frequently used as a means to express transnational solidarity with workers laboring in unsafe conditions. The practice of naming and shaming multinational corporations and governments engaged in economic exploitation and corruption, respectively, "provides a sort of accountability," although it is more apt to change the behavior of an MNC than of a government.[317] After a large antisweatshop mobilization against the Nike Corporation and reports of unsafe factory conditions – not to mention poverty wages – in April 1998, Nike's CEO, Phil Knight, publicly declared that the company would change its contractor policies: "The Nike product has become synonymous with slave wages, forced overtime, and arbitrary abuse. I truly believe that the American consumer does not want to buy products made in abusive conditions." Although Knight promised that health and safety conditions would be improved, he made no mention of allowing unionization or raising wages to at least a subsistence level.[318]

Corporate codes of conduct and other name-and-shame methods constitute attempts to "establish mechanisms of accountability that would operate at the same global scale" as that of transnational corporations.[319] Corporate codes of conduct that rely on "co-regulation" (joint corporate and NGO participation) are increasingly viewed as "an effective way to

---

[315] David Gonzalez, "Latin Sweatshops Pressed by U.S. Campus Power," *New York Times*, April 4, 2003, p. A3; see http://www.studentsagainstsweatshops.org/ for recent campaigns. On codes of conduct, and on NGOs and student groups using transnational solidarity to improve working conditions and labor rights, see Robert J. S. Ross, *Slaves to Fashion* (Ann Arbor: University of Michigan Press, 2004).

[316] Clean Clothes Campaign, "Nike Supplier Closes Unionized Factory, Shifts Work to Vietnam," *Peacework* (October 2007), p. 17.

[317] Josselin, p. 185; Robert O. Keohane and Joseph S. Nye, "Introduction," in Joseph S. Nye and John D. Donahue, eds., *Governance in a Globalizing World*, p. 35. Also, on the failure of the "blame and shame" approach taken by transnational human rights groups to achieve either public awareness or state policy change when applied to the problem of sexual assault in Russia, see Janet Johnson, *The Global Campaign Against Gender Violence in the New Russia* (Bloomington: Indiana University Press, forthcoming).

[318] Arnie Alpert, "Bringing Globalization Home Is No Sweat," in John Feffer, ed., *Living in Hope: People Challenging Globalization* (London: Zed, 2002), pp. 50–1.

[319] Koenig-Archibugi, "Transnational Corporations and Public Accountability," p. 245.

address the accountability gap of [MNCs]." In the absence of governmental action to enforce (or create) standards of labor and environmental protection to which private corporations will be held, groups such as
the FLA and USAS attempt to fill the gap, operating as "accountability
entrepreneurs."[320]

Negative publicity, however, is an accountability mechanism of limited utility. Lacking a state's power and infrastructure, NGOs engaged
in corporate monitoring are necessarily in over their heads. The many
factories – and myriad "sweatshops" – in which manufacturing occurs
likely cannot be sufficiently monitored without a bureaucracy dedicated to
the task.[321] Corporations cannot be compelled to participate, and sanctions
for those that violate the standards typically do not extend beyond bad
publicity. Successful boycotts confront "serious collective action problems
when it comes to applying sanctions." Most importantly, while "[n]egative
publicity may work as an instrument of accountability,…it suffers from
the fact that the people who are able to punish companies (e.g. consumers
in rich countries) are frequently not the same people whose interests the
codes are supposed to protect (e.g. workers and communities in developing
countries)."[322] Transnational solidarity campaigns to improve labor rights,
in the form of consumer boycotts, for instance,

carry the risk that they might inadvertently weaken efforts to organize workers
to speak for themselves. The threat of consumer boycotts might get corporations'
attention, but they may also undermine worker organization in developing countries, especially if workers believe that a transnational boycott might threaten the
enterprise's survival – and thus their long-term job prospects.[323]

Relying on powerful consumers to defend labor is ultimately not as effective an accountability mechanism as "strengthening workers' capacity
to demand reasonable working conditions for themselves," making the
accountability relationship between labor and corporation more direct.[324]
Unions, in this view, are the best enforcers of labor standards. Writes
sociologist Robert J. S. Ross, "democratically organized workers are their
own best defenders."[325]

[320] Ibid., pp. 254–5.
[321] Ross, *Slaves to Fashion*, p. 319.
[322] Koenig-Archibugi, "Transnational Corporations and Public Accountability," pp. 256–257.
[323] Gay W. Seidman, "Deflated Citizenship: Labor Rights in a Global Era," in Alison Brysk
and Gershon Shafir, eds., *People out of Place: Globalization, Human Rights, and the
Citizenship Gap* (New York: Routledge, 2004), pp. 127–8.
[324] Ibid.
[325] Ross, *Slaves to Fashion*, p. 321.

Codes of conduct may provide some degree of corporate accountability to consumers, but only indirectly to laborers. When consumers lose interest and pressure declines, the accountability relationship dissolves. By contrast, transnational labor solidarity – in the form of transborder union activism – creates a more direct accountability relationship between MNCs and labor. Given their utility in extracting improvements in labor standards from corporations domestically, trade unions could well provide the best source of pressure on MNCs operating globally. Transnational labor organizations – both long-standing international unions and newer "transnational workers' networks" – have had mixed success promoting labor's interests to MNCs and states.[326]

Although transborder worker organizing has "remained fairly weak" despite a few stand-out cases of border-crossing labor solidarity, the enactment of NAFTA provoked U.S. unions "to reconsider international solidarity."[327] While cross-border labor organizing may seem counterintuitive (after all, if a plant in Indiana relocates to the Mexican border, one might expect the U.S. workers to resent rather than seek to cooperate with Mexican workers), U.S. labor unions began to engage in *maquiladora* solidarity actions in the late 1980s, before NAFTA, and have continued to do so.[328] As the secretary-treasurer of the United Electric, Radio and Machine Workers of America (UE), which entered an alliance with an independent Mexican union (the Authentic Labor Front, or FAT) organizing in *maquiladoras*, put it:

Workers in the United States and Canada share a common interest in ensuring that Mexico workers are successful in organizing democratic unions and improving wages and benefits....If they fail, we share a future of common misery. I prefer to think of a future where we sit together at the bargaining table with trade unionists from Mexico and Canada, and together take on transnational corporations such as General Electric and Honeywell.

In this spirit, one joint action taken by the UE, alongside the U.S.-based Teamsters union, with FAT support, was to file a complaint with the U.S. NAO about labor violations and firings (related to unionizing actions by workers) at GE and Honeywell *maquiladoras*.[329]

[326] Josselin, p. 170.
[327] Robin Alexander and Peter Gilmore, "The Emergence of Cross-Border Labor Solidarity," in Rachael Kamel and Anya Hoffman, eds., *The Maquiladora Reader: Cross-Border Organizing Since NAFTA* (Philadelphia: American Friends Service Committee, 1999), p. 73; Scholte, *Globalization: A Critical Introduction*, p. 173.
[328] Kamel and Hoffman, eds., *The Maquiladora Reader*, p. 66.
[329] Alexander and Gilmore, pp. 67–8.

The common goal of raising labor standards (to protect job loss in developed countries, as well as to improve living standards in less developed countries) has provoked organizing in support of unions at home and abroad. As one U.S. labor organizer noted:

We must insist that workers' rights to wages and benefits such as health, education, and environmental safety be protected everywhere. *As Americans and Mexicans alike, we are now less citizens of the nation in which we are born, and more citizens of the company for whom we work*. This makes us equal. We must insist that this equality be reflected in our paychecks, our work conditions, our living conditions, our environmental conditions – for which the common company is responsible. This should impact the security of our jobs here and in Mexico.[330]

Labor solidarity across state lines, where workers join forces within a given industry and/or act as citizens of specific corporations, constitutes a potential means to hold MNCs accountable.

Tracing the fortunes of union organizing attempts at a franchised Coca-Cola bottling plant in Guatemala reveals a representative case of international labor solidarity. From 1975 to 1980, a "union-busting" campaign (including the murder of three Coca-Cola union leaders) in Guatemala led to an international solidarity movement organized by the International Union of Food and Allied Workers' Associations (IUF), featuring work slowdowns and stoppages as well as boycotts of Coca-Cola products. In 1980, this movement resulted in a decision by the Atlanta-based headquarters of Coca-Cola to "finance the purchase of the franchise from its U.S. owners by a Mexico-based consortium, which then negotiated a contract with the...union."[331] The new owners proved to have a short-lived interest in the plant, shutting it down without notice in February 1984, "after having gradually moved production to non-union facilities."[332] In response, 460 union members occupied the plant, setting off a renewed international solidarity boycott organized by the IUF and also leading Coca-Cola workers in Scandinavian IUF-affiliated unions to

---

[330] Ibid., p. 69, emphasis added. Since more than a third of the world's largest economies are corporations, rather than states, the notion of corporate citizenship is far from ridiculous. See Amnesty International USA, "AI on Human Rights and Labor Rights," p. 187; De Grauwe and Camerman, "How Big Are the Big Multinational Companies?"

[331] Jonathan Fried, "In Guatemala, Things Go Worse with Coke," *Multinational Monitor*, Vol. 5, No. 4 (April 1984), accessed July 6, 2006, at http://multinationalmonitor.org/hyper/issues/1984/04/fried.html.

[332] Peace Brigades International, "Organizations in Guatemala," March 2000, accessed November 21, 2007, at http://web.archive.org/web/20060906163221/http://www.peacebrigades.org/guate.html.

threaten strikes.[333] A year later, Coca-Cola intervened again, to sell and reopen the plant, successfully resolving the union's quest.[334] Cross-border solidarity of this type could help factory workers contend with the gross power imbalance that pervades their relationship to MNCs, and to some small degree counterbalances their own governments' failures to enforce labor rights.

Transnational industrywide trade unions provide another means of countering the global influence of MNCs. In 1995, the leader of the International Confederation of Free Trade Unions (ICFTU), Bill Jordan, explained that in order to confront globally mobile MNCs, international minimum standards were necessary: "Just as a civilized society has laws, so a civilized economy should have minimum standards.... The world is now global in a way it's never been before, and to match that, you need a strong international trade union, perhaps for the first time in the history of the world."[335] One ongoing attempt to stop the deterioration of standards across a given industry was initiated by the International Transport Workers' Federation (ITF) in 1948 – the Flag of Convenience (FOC) campaign. "FOCs are ships that sail under the registries of countries like Liberia that turn a blind eye to the labor conditions of their seamen," creating ideal conditions for a race to the bottom. Yet the ITF's campaign interfered, establishing a minimum wage scale that is supposed to apply across the globe on FOC ships and employing ITF inspectors to investigate and pursue cases where such protections are violated.[336] Between 1996 and 2001, ITF inspectors were able to extract $163 million in wages due to seafarers on FOC ships.[337]

Whereas global-level action (such as to establish minimum wage and labor standards) may be desirable, and even achievable in the long term,

---

[333] Bob Stix, "Boycott Coke," *Multinational Monitor*, Vol. 5, No. 5 (May 1984), accessed July 6, 2006, at http://www.multinationalmonitor.org/hyper/issues/1984/05/newsroundup.html.

[334] Henry J. Frundt, "Guatemala in Search of Democracy," *Journal of Interamerican Studies and World Affairs*, Vol. 32, No. 3 (Autumn 1990), p. 34.

[335] Hugh Williamson, "Globalizing Trade Unions: An Interview with Bill Jordan," *Multinational Monitor*, Vol. 17, No. 6 (June 1995), accessed on February 26, 2006, at http://multinationalmonitor.org/hyper/issues/1995/06/mm0695_11.html.

[336] Tarrow, p. 46, citing Nathan Lillie, "A Global Union for Global Workers: The International Transport Workers' Federation and the Representation of Seafarers on Flag of Convenience Shipping," Ph.D. dissertation, Cornell University, New York State School of Industrial and Labor Relations, 2003.

[337] International Transport Workers' Federation, "What Do FOCs Mean to Seafarers?" accessed November 15, 2007, at http://www.itfglobal.org/flags-convenience/flags-convenien-184.cfm.

transnational activist organizing has not been able to replicate the speed, intensity, and power of global economic forces.[338] Transnational union organizing in particular faces serious obstacles. First, organizing a "global strike" across a given industry requires surmounting a serious collective action problem. Even if there were willingness across a worldwide industry to seek collective bargaining for better wages and conditions, in most cases there exists no "international framework for collective bargaining," which instead takes place on a state-by-state basis.[339] North–South competition between states constitutes another obstacle to cross-border union solidarity. States compete for the investment and jobs provided by MNCs, which appears to put national-level unions in competition with each other for work. Viewed from this competitive perspective, unions based in the developing and advanced industrial worlds have divergent priorities and interests. Northern unions (or northern-dominated international federations) demanding higher labor standards are perceived as "Westocentric," because developing countries could interpret the imposition of such standards as amounting to protectionism for Western countries.[340]

A different framing of the problem emphasizes international labor standards as a means to combat the devastating competition between poor countries.[341] Since the early 1990s and the advent of neoliberal strategies across much of the developing world, the level of inter-state competition, particularly between developing states, has driven compacts among states, business, and even labor, to maintain a workforce attractive to foreign investors: "...labor unions from Australia to Zambia have found themselves cooperating in 'social pacts,' accepting constant or even reduced wages and benefits in order to sustain investment."[342] Labor organizing at the transnational level seems a sensible response "if national states in developing countries are too weak and too dependent to enforce [labor] rights." National governments may still constitute labor's best hope for labor rights, given that the mechanisms for enforcing them are strongest at the state level (where those rights exist, having been won by national-level labor movements).[343] But transnational capital and its challenges to national political sovereignty increasingly render states – especially in the

---

[338] Mason, "The World Trade Regime and Non-Governmental Organisations," p. 272.
[339] Josselin, p. 175.
[340] Ibid., pp. 178–9.
[341] Ross, *Slaves to Fashion*, p. 332.
[342] Seidman, "Deflated Citizenship," p. 115.
[343] Ibid., pp. 121, 127.

developing world – less viable enforcers of private corporations' account-ability to labor.

CONCLUSION: SOVEREIGNTY AND CITIZENSHIP IN THE GLOBAL MARKET

Neoliberalism creates – or exacerbates – a variety of accountability gaps. Governments that accept loan conditions over widespread popular protest, or repress union organizing in order to appeal to foreign investors, become increasingly accountable to corporations and financial institutions, while their citizens find themselves one sizeable step removed from the places where major decisions affecting their lives are made. Labor, too, has become increasingly "borderless." The overall absence of means through which temporary migrant laborers – such as Pakistanis and Philippinos working in Saudi Arabia and the United Arab Emirates (UAE) – could hold either employers or state officials accountable for human rights violations constitutes another accountability gap, what Alison Brysk and Gershon Shafir call a "citizenship gap."[344] Similarly, the laboring "citizens of Coca-Cola" can point to no constitution to uphold their rights, and can take no action in a voting booth if and when their labor rights are violated by the corporation.

Developing states that compete with each other for investment, for jobs, for loans, and for debt relief experience some deterioration in their state sovereignty when important economic decisions are made at a significant remove from the national arena in which their citizens (may) have a politi-cal impact. There are few direct lines of accountability between citizens and corporations, citizens and multilateral development banks, citizens and IMF managers. Nor do states have many tools with which to discipline and mold the behavior of multinational corporations, because labor-intensive manufacturers are no longer reliant on a "home state" in order to profit.

Still, as sociologist Peter Evans argues, states are not only a constant feature of the global landscape, but are essential, even to multinational corporations.[345] Transnational corporations in the global economy largely

---

[344] Brysk and Shafir, eds., *People Out of Place*. In 1980, 90 percent of the UAE's total labor force was composed of temporary foreign workers. Mittelman, *The Globalization Syn-drome*, p. 67. As of the year 2000, the foreign population of Kuwait, Qatar, and the UAE exceeded the native population. Held et al., *Global Transformations*, p. 300.

[345] Peter Evans, "The Eclipse of the State? Reflections on Stateness in an Era of Globalization," *World Politics* (October 1997), pp. 74–87.

prefer countries with "high" measures of state capacity (that is, with strong public institutions). States that cannot "protect [transnational economic actors'] returns" through administrative competence are unlikely attractors of global capital.[346]

Neoliberal policies, however, may work at cross-purposes to the development or maintenance of high state capacity in the longer term. Following the model of fiscal austerity and free trade "constrains the ability of governments to protect ordinary citizens, especially those who bear the costs of shifts in the configuration of international production networks," as states cut spending on education and social welfare or throw their borders open to "goods and capital." In such countries, Evans writes, "The state is perceived, not as the ultimate representative of national interests, but instead as the instrument of dimly understood but somehow 'foreign' interests." When states cater to global capital (and to the international financial institutions that support it with structural adjustment programs), the decay in a state's perceived accountability and capacity goes hand in hand. Despite their need for stable, capable administration in the states where they invest, transnational corporations could, in their insistence on low levels of regulation, end up becoming

accomplice[s] in the destruction of the infrastructure of public institutions on which [their] profits depend. Up to a point, constricting the ability of states to intervene in global markets may produce increased profits. By the time state capacity is so reduced that the unpredictability of the business environment becomes intolerable, even to major actors who have wide latitude in choosing where to do business, reconstructing public authority could be a long and painful process, even an impossible one.[347]

The greater the extent to which decision-making power lies outside the national public sphere, the more difficult it may become for states to construct (or reconstruct) public accountability as well.

In this context, it is in the interests of the carriers of neoliberalism and the constituents of the world economy alike to harness the transnational instruments traditionally used to promote neoliberalism in the service of accountability. Accountability mechanisms such as those attached to the World Bank and NAFTA could be bolstered and then tied to structural

---

[346] Ibid., p. 78. For an alternate view, see William Reno, *Warlord Politics in African States* (Boulder: Lynne Rienner, 1998), pp. 217–28. Reno suggests that in some cases, nominal sovereignty is sufficient to enable the leaders of extremely weak states to make profitable deals with MNCs – particularly in natural resources – without even providing security (a service provided by the MNCs themselves).

[347] Evans, p. 73.

adjustment agreements and trade agreements. Such agreements could set minimum standards for the treatment of labor – especially as regards the freedom to organize – and incorporate robust means to enforce these standards.

At their best, accountability mechanisms such as the Inspection Panel and the NAOs are instruments of empathy with the potential to lead to recognition of the importance of citizen participation in political and economic decision making. If the problem is that citizens are increasingly falling into an accountability abyss lying between national governments and transnational economic institutions, then one solution is to enhance the accountability mechanisms at the transnational level. But the ruptured accountability relationship between transnational economic institutions and citizens affected by them is only one of the obstacles to governments' fulfillment of their accountability obligations to citizens. At its root is the absence of pluralist politics within the state itself. Where NGOs lack the financial and bureaucratic wherewithal to combat transnational capital, national governments may be the best hope for enforcing citizens' labor rights. But many citizens of many states are kept voiceless, whether by authoritarian rule or within "electoral democracies" that lack political pluralism, or by inter-state competition that silences (in effect) the working class and others marginalized from national politics. Until political pluralism takes root and is protected domestically, participants and observers in states taking part in the global economy enjoy a certain, albeit extremely limited, form of citizenship: as citizens of corporations and international financial institutions, which may – ironically – provide a means of limited political voice.

A number of transnational institutions address the lack of political pluralism within states, promoting "good governance" and democratization by various means. Large-scale transnational attempts to help political pluralism and accountability take root in two nondemocratic states constitute the subject of the next chapter.

3

Democracy from Abroad?

Political Globalization

An election is typically thought of as a national affair. Yet even elections and their organization are increasingly borderless phenomena. From providing election monitoring (which often complements, rather than supplants, indigenous monitoring organizations and civic groups), to conducting elections, and beyond, international organizations have stepped into ever more extensive roles in countries struggling to move from dictatorship toward democracy.

Bilateral (government-to-government) "political" aid played a backstage role during the Cold War, as the superpowers competed for the affections of Third World leaders and military basing rights. It was only in the post–Cold War era that the United Nations and other transnational political organizations such as the Organization for Security and Cooperation in Europe (OSCE) adopted an increasingly open policy of democracy promotion.[1] By 1990, the shift toward increased (and normatively accepted) transnational participation in elections was in evidence.[2] At that time, the UN began to experience an exponential increase in requests for election monitoring "from governments that felt compelled to prove their legitimacy by the new standards" – suggesting that the UN had come to be seen as a legitimator in the world of increasingly intrusive transnational institutions.[3] It is in this context

[1] Roland Paris, *At War's End: Building Peace After Civil Conflict* (New York: Cambridge University Press, 2004), p. 25.
[2] Robert Pastor, "The Third Dimension of Accountability: The International Community in National Elections," in Andreas Schedler, Larry Diamond, and Marc F. Plattner, eds., *The Self-Restraining State: Power and Accountability in New Democracies* (Boulder: Lynne Rienner, 1999), p. 125.
[3] Jessica T. Mathews, "Power Shift," *Foreign Affairs*, Vol. 76, No. 1 (January/February 1997), pp. 50–66.

that the role of supranational political institutions grew, making possible an unprecedented level of transnational political intervention in a handful of struggling states.

Two dramatic cases of such "political globalization" will be discussed here; the first took place in the early 1990s in Cambodia, and the second in Bosnia some years later, in the wake of Yugoslavia's collapse. In the first case, the United Nations Transitional Authority in Cambodia (UNTAC) was designated to rule Cambodia for several years, culminating in the UN-run 1993 elections. I consider the accountability benefits as well as the potential pitfalls of this process, which, paradoxically, left Cambodia's authoritarian leadership in place, legitimized by the imprimatur of the United Nations. In Bosnia, an even more extensive degree of transnational control over politics similarly brought a brutal civil war to an end. That intervention, however, led not only to a situation of "accountability once removed" but seemed to support a pattern of unaccountable politics, at least in the near term. These albeit extreme examples suggest that transnationally led efforts to move postconflict states toward democracy from the top down can lead instead to the victory of unaccountable regimes operating under an internationally conferred stamp of legitimacy. But even when transnational political institutions fail as the midwives of accountability in national politics, they can help to create a support structure for local democracy activists by reinforcing the ideas and practices of civil society. In examining each case, I begin with an outline of the relevant political history and then assess the transnational attempts to install accountable political systems in these troubled countries.

Cambodia's UN-assisted transition in the early 1990s provides a lens on this rare process. There, between 1991 and 1993, the United Nations undertook an enormous task, setting out to convert into a democracy the war-torn and brutalized country run by the dictatorial Cambodian People's Party (CPP). The UN applied $2.2 billion in the service of democratization – but it was not enough. In the end, the UN-organized election process had the unanticipated effect of helping to entrench an authoritarian regime in power.

CAMBODIA: 1953–1993

Cambodia's political history in the twenty-five years leading up to the UN's arrival in 1991 was distinguished by extraordinary violence and considerable international machination. Granted independence from France in 1953, Cambodia had by 1967 fallen into a civil war between the army of Cambodia's elected government, nominally headed by Prince Sihanouk, and the guerrilla forces of Cambodia's small communist movement, the Khmer Rouge.[4] The United States' engagement in neighboring Vietnam, and the Vietnamese communists' use of northeast Cambodian territory, led the United States in 1969 to initiate a "secret" bombing campaign in Cambodia and to invade the country in 1970, against the wishes of the prince.

Deposed in a U.S.-supported coup in 1970, a disgusted Sihanouk joined forces with his former enemies, the Khmer Rouge. By April 1975, the Khmer Rouge, with Sihanouk's backing, had defeated the puppet government of General Lon Nol, winning the civil war. Upon taking the capital, the Khmer Rouge ordered its inhabitants, between 2 and 3 million people – roughly half of Cambodia's population at the time – out of the city, sending them on a forced march into the countryside. From there, the Khmer Rouge embarked on a horrific killing spree. Over the course of their three-and-a-half-year rule, the Khmer Rouge presided over the killings and deaths of approximately 1.2 million people, from starvation, disease, forced ruralization, torture, and outright execution.[5]

The Khmer Rouge's reign of terror was brought to an end in late 1978 by invading forces from Vietnam, itself run by a less brutal but fully authoritarian communist dictatorship. Having partially routed the Khmer Rouge, the Vietnamese installed a closely controlled government – in essence, a military dictatorship – to run what would now be called the People's Republic of Kampuchea (PRK).[6] Most of the governmental officials in Cambodia's new government were former Khmer Rouge who had defected to the Vietnamese side either before or following the invasion.

---

[4] Elizabeth Becker, *When the War Was Over: Cambodia and the Khmer Rouge Revolution* (New York: PublicAffairs, 1998), pp. 102–4.

[5] The estimated death tolls for the brief period of Khmer Rouge rule fall between 1 and 3 million people, with a generally accepted estimate of 1.2 million dead. Of these, roughly one-third died from forced ruralization (meaning from disease, transit, and starvation through labor); about a third from executions; and the rest from deaths in prison after torture. Estimates of deaths within the population range between one in four and one in seven. One demographer estimates that as much as 26 percent of the population may have died during the Khmer Rouge regime: 34 percent of men died, and 16 percent of women died. Jean-Louis Margolin, "Cambodia: The Country of Disconcerting Crimes," in Stéphane Courtois et al., *The Black Book of Communism: Crimes, Terror, Repression* (Cambridge: Harvard University Press, 1999), p. 589.

[6] A superb analysis of party politics, economics, and social conditions under the Vietnamese-backed People's Republic of Kampuchea (1979–89) can be found in Evan Gottesman, *Cambodia After the Khmer Rouge: Inside the Politics of Nation Building* (New Haven: Yale University Press, 2002).

Hun Sen, who became Cambodia's prime minister in 1985, for instance, had defected to the Vietnamese in 1977.[7] The Vietnamese-backed government, though dictatorial, made for a considerable improvement in Cambodians' daily lives, and greatly reduced the death rate. By 1980, the new government had reestablished markets, schools, family farming, money, and Buddhism – all of which had been forbidden by the Khmer Rouge during their brief but ruinous political tenure.[8]

In the mid-1980s, the Soviet Union considerably reduced military and financial support for its communist ally, Vietnam, as part of Soviet leader Mikhail Gorbachev's commitment to defuse the Cold War and redirect funds to domestic needs.[9] The Vietnamese government, in turn, now lacking the resources to maintain their occupation of Cambodia, let it be known that they were willing to withdraw their troops and help contribute to a peace process. In 1989, the Vietnamese withdrew their army, leaving the party that they had backed for the past ten years in control of roughly 80 percent of the country, the rest of which was still contested or controlled by the Khmer Rouge.[10] Reflecting the change in its political alliances abroad, in 1989, Cambodia's National Assembly performed political surgery on the country's state symbols, excising the ideological content from the flag, the national anthem, and even the name of the state itself, which would no longer be the communist-inflected People's Republic of Kampuchea, but instead the straightforward title "preferred by Hun Sen" – the State of Cambodia (SOC).[11]

By 1990, after several years of peace conferencing between Cambodia's main political factions and various concerned states (including the five permanent member states on the UN security council), an agreement was reached that representatives of the factions would form a Supreme National Council – a transitional political body to run the country until

[7] Hun Sen joined the Khmer Rouge at the age of sixteen in 1970, as a courier. After the Khmer Rouge takeover, he served as a deputy regimental commander in the Eastern Zone of Cambodia before defecting to Vietnam. MacAlister Brown and Joseph J. Zasloff, *Cambodia Confounds the Peacemakers 1979–1998* (Ithaca: Cornell University Press, 1998), p. 29.

[8] On the ideology and practices of the Khmer Rouge, see Karl Jackson, ed., *Cambodia 1975–1978: Rendezvous with Death* (Princeton: Princeton University Press, 1989); Ben Kiernan, *The Pol Pot Regime: Race, Power, and Genocide in Cambodia under the Khmer Rouge, 1975–79* (New Haven: Yale University Press, 1996).

[9] In the mid-1980s, Soviet aid to Vietnam was running at a staggering cost of $2 billion per year. In exchange, the Soviets received military basing rights. Brown and Zasloff, p. 35.

[10] Henry Kamm, *Cambodia: Report from a Stricken Land* (New York: Arcade, 1998), p. 207.

[11] Gottesman, p. 303.

the UN could carry out a peace and reconciliation process on site. In 1991, Prince Sihanouk was named head of the Council, and in October 1991, the Paris Agreement was signed, establishing UNTAC. The "Agreement on a Comprehensive Political Settlement of the Cambodia Conflict" was designed to end the ongoing fighting with remnants of the Khmer Rouge, to reconcile Cambodia's various political factions, and, ultimately, to hold elections allowing Cambodia's long-oppressed people to choose a government.[12] UNTAC's thankless task was, in essence, to govern Cambodia while carrying out this reconciliation process and establishing a "neutral political environment" in which fair elections could be held.[13]

UNTAC

UNTAC represented the first time that the UN had taken the "authority to assume complete responsibility for the administration" of a state.[14] The mission was therefore scrutinized closely by scholars, policy makers, and participants alike. Despite (or perhaps because of) its thoroughgoing mandate, UNTAC failed to accomplish a number of its central tasks, aside from conducting the founding election itself. The May 1993 election was a success in that 90 percent of registered voters went to the polls, and, despite using widespread tactics of public intimidation, Hun Sen's Cambodian People's Party (CPP) lost out to the Royalist Party, FUNCINPEC (led by Prince Sihanouk's son, Prince Ranariddh), which won a plurality of the vote. Despite the encouraging tally of votes, however, both before and after the election, the State of Cambodia continued to be run by the CPP, and neither the Khmer Rouge nor Cambodia's other armed factions were disarmed. And rather than being transformed into an increasingly accountable government, in the ten years following UNTAC's efforts, Cambodia's political leadership became more authoritarian. In 2006, Hun Sen's CPP still monopolized control over a corrupt and repressive Cambodian state.

---

[12] The four factions that were party to the Paris Agreements in 1991 were FUNCINPEC (the National United Front for an Independent, Neutral, Peaceful and Cooperative Cambodia), founded in 1981 with Sihanouk as its head (Brown and Zasloff, p. 18); the KPNLF (Khmer People's National Liberation Front); the Khmer Rouge; and the State of Cambodia, controlled by Hun Sen.

[13] Kamm, p. 205.

[14] The UN had done so earlier in the Indonesian territory of West Papua. See Sue Downie, "The United Nations in East Timor: Comparisons with Cambodia," in Damien Kingsbury, ed., *Guns and Ballot Boxes: East Timor's Vote for Independence* (Victoria, Australia: Monash Asia Institute, 2000), p. 120.

Something in the UN-sponsored transition to democracy had evidently gone awry. But what?

UNTAC's mission of civilian administrative control gave it "an unprecedented degree of 'transitional authority' over Cambodia."[15] The mission covered everything from refugee repatriation to human rights defense and organizing the elections. This included developing the election laws and rules, and educating and informing the public about the Paris Agreements, the voting process, and the parties contesting the election. The election was to be held in a neutral political environment, to be attained through the twin Herculean tasks of controlling the administrative structures of the state and demobilizing and largely disarming Cambodia's military factions.[16] The not inconsiderable areas of civilian administration to be controlled by UNTAC were "defense, public security, finance, information, and foreign affairs."[17] Technically, UNTAC's mandate was to "control" rather than to "govern" Cambodia, although UNTAC's leader, Yasushi Akashi, a highly skilled Japanese diplomat, did have the power to remove from Cambodia's administration intractable local officials who "obstructed the peace process."[18]

From the start, UNTAC faced what were probably insurmountable obstacles to carrying out its assignment. The first obstacle was largely logistical. Akashi and the UN team's military commander, General John Sanderson of Australia, did not arrive in Cambodia until March 1992, and the requisite international staff, tasked with "controlling" or "supervising" the administrative bureaucracies of the country, did not arrive in Cambodia until October 1992 – a full year after the signing of the Paris Accords.[19] The delay in bringing UNTAC staff to Cambodia aggravated the already challenging task of "controlling" Cambodia's state administration, which was wholly dominated by Hun Sen's party, the CPP.[20] The delay also likely "permitted the party in power to grow in its conviction both that it not

---

[15] Michael W. Doyle, *UN Peacekeeping in Cambodia: UNTAC's Civil Mandate* (Boulder: Lynne Rienner, 1995), p. 13.

[16] Ibid., pp. 26, 29–30.

[17] Ibid., p. 35.

[18] Brown and Zasloff, p. 102; Doyle, p. 37. Akashi was apparently "loath to utilize" that power, and did not do so. See Paris, p. 196.

[19] Brown and Zasloff, p. 103; Kamm, p. 209. For a detailed history and evaluation of Cambodia's political history from UNTAC through the election of 1998, see Brown and Zasloff, *Cambodia Confounds the Peacemakers*.

[20] The party running Hun Sen's Cambodia, the Kampuchean People's Revolutionary Party was renamed the Cambodian People's Party (CPP) in October 1991, a few short weeks before the UN Advance Mission arrived in Cambodia. The name change occurred at a party congress at which the leadership also rhetorically endorsed noncommunist ideas

only could but should evade the scrutnizers." Even after UNTAC's staff had arrived, the small numbers of international staff were easy enough for CPP functionaries to evade – and overtly so, as in the case of a "reported *order* by the governor of Battambang province (a nephew of the chair of the CPP) that provincial officials *not* obey UNTAC directives."[21] Cambodia scholars MacAlister Brown and Joseph Zasloff write: "The word 'control' is really inappropriate. At best UNTAC achieved a degree of 'influence'" over Cambodia's administration.[22] The "centralized communist bureaucracy" run by the CPP was a key obstacle to UNTAC's ability to carry out its mission, because a preexisting set of state authorities was in place and proved unwilling to surrender control to UNTAC.[23] Moreover, regarding the elections, the Cambodian government monopolized the state-run media and showed no qualms about using government officials to campaign for the CPP, while restricting media access for opposition candidates in defiance of UNTAC's attempt to establish a politically neutral environment for the election campaign.[24]

UNTAC's inability to fulfill its mandate in the area of controlling Cambodia's administration was attributable in part to a failure of capacity. According to Boutros Boutros-Ghali, the UN secretary general at the time, the direct supervision mandate "turned out to be nearly impossible to achieve because of language problems, lack of enforcement measures and inadequate experience on the part of UNTAC personnel with the kind of bureaucratic structures and procedures employed by the SOC."[25] Indeed, the deputy director of UNTAC's Civil Administration component thought that the UN mandate to control and monitor such a vast swath of Cambodia's government "was totally unrealistic purely from the point of [view of] language skills alone."[26] Brown and Zasloff add that the failure to neutralize Cambodia's political environment, in part through supervision of the state's administration, stemmed from the negotiators' failure to "think through realistically" how hard it would be to wrest control from a regime unenthusiastic about releasing its hold on power.[27] In short, the

such as "a free market economy, separation of powers, 'liberal democracy,' human rights, and pluralism." Gottesman, p. 345.
[21] Brown and Zasloff, p. 103, emphasis in the original.
[22] Ibid., p. 107.
[23] Doyle, *UN Peacekeeping in Cambodia*, p. 40.
[24] Ibid., p. 56.
[25] Quoted in Downie, p. 123.
[26] Quoted in Brown and Zasloff, p. 108.
[27] Ibid., p. 273.

party controlling the state of Cambodia, the CPP, would not let go, and UNTAC was not in a position to take control by force.

The state's failure to cooperate in allowing UNTAC actual control over civilian administration was matched by the Khmer Rouge's refusal to cooperate in disarmament. In June 1992, the Khmer Rouge refused to demobilize their troops, and in January 1993, they declared their intention to boycott the elections.[28] As their excuse for not demobilizing, the Khmer Rouge argued that Vietnamese troops remained in Cambodia, despite all evidence and assurances to the contrary.[29]

The Khmer Rouge's noncompliance undermined the entire demobilization process set forth in the Paris Peace Accords:

The cantonment of the factional armies was to have been completed by the end of July [1992], but the three other Cambodian parties were reluctant to disarm their forces in the face of Khmer Rouge recalcitrance. As a result, by mid-November, only some 55,000 troops had reported to the cantonment site, most of whom appeared to be untrained teenagers with antiquated weapons, while superior forces and caches of weapons remained in the field.[30]

UNTAC tried several times to persuade the Khmer Rouge to abide by the Paris Agreement and demobilize their troops, but when it became clear that they would not cooperate, UNTAC "abandoned its demobilization effort and allowed the soldiers who had already been cantoned to return to their respective armies on 'agricultural leave.'"[31]

UNTAC's leadership elected not to use force to implement the demobilization mandate. In one symbolic episode where Khmer Rouge forces confronted Akashi and Sanderson, preventing UNTAC from entering a Khmer Rouge–controlled area near Pailin by lowering a mere bamboo pole to block their path, UNTAC's military forces could easily have decided the situation in their own favor. But in that event, UNTAC would not have been able to protect from Khmer Rouge reprisals "the thousands of civilians who were vital to the implementation of the UNTAC mandate."[32] Nor was there international support (from troop-supplying countries or from most of the countries involved in negotiating the Paris Agreements) for UNTAC to use force in support of its mandate.[33] The mandate was for

[28] Richard H. Solomon, *Exiting Indochina* (Washington: U.S. Institute of Peace Press, 2000), p. 91.
[29] Brown and Zasloff, p. 137.
[30] Paris, p. 84.
[31] Ibid., p. 84, citing Doyle, *UN Peacekeeping in Cambodia.*
[32] Doyle, *UN Peacekeeping in Cambodia*, p. 67.
[33] Brown and Zasloff, p. 138; Doyle, *UN Peacekeeping in Cambodia*, p. 68.

peacekeeping, not peace enforcement, according to General Sanderson, which meant that UNTAC's military force could be used exclusively for self-defense.[34] Demobilizing the Khmer Rouge by force was thus out of the question.

During UNTAC's mission, Cambodia's armed factions used their weapons not only against each other on the battlefield but also to disrupt the political process. The CPP carried out a number of violent attacks against supporters of Cambodia's other major parties – FUNCINPEC and the Buddhist Liberal Democratic Party (BLDP). In all, 159 "political opponents" were killed during the election campaign.[35] Minus its Vietnamese patron, Hun Sen's government participated in the UN process out of economic necessity, but kept up its practices of political repression:

[This] meant complying with the expectations of the international community, when necessary, and protecting power in undemocratic and frequently violent ways, when possible. In Phnom Penh, where the streets were soon filled with UNTAC soldiers and Western journalists, opposition politicians set up offices and campaigned more or less freely. In the provinces, away from foreign eyes...elements of the security apparatus terrorized citizens working with opposition parties.[36]

UNTAC was similarly unable to control the Khmer Rouge during the campaign. In the last month before the May 1993 elections, the Khmer Rouge killed several UNTAC members, used terror against the parties running for office, and "slaughtered many ethnic Vietnamese," provoking an exodus of ethnic Vietnamese from the country.[37] In short, UNTAC had failed to "bring peace" to Cambodia.[38]

Nearly all of the tasks for which UNTAC was responsible were ambitious at best. The civilian police (CIVPOL) deployed with UNTAC demonstrated a "complete lack of experience and training in international supervision (not to mention inability to speak Khmer)," making their task of training the local CPP-run police force "quixotic." Moreover, even when alleged lawbreakers or human rights violators were arrested by CIVPOL, there was no usable court system in which to prosecute them (the Cambodian courts hardly demonstrated the requisite political

[34] Brown and Zasloff, pp. 145–6.
[35] Becker, p. 513; Doyle, p. 47.
[36] Gottesman, p. 349.
[37] Yossi Shain and Lynn Berat, "The international interim government model revisited," in Yossi Shain and Juan Linz, *Between States: Interim Governments and Democratic Transitions* (New York, Cambridge: Cambridge University Press, 1995), p. 73.
[38] Grant Curtis, *Cambodia Reborn* (Washington: Brookings Institution Press, 1998), pp. 9–10, 150.

neutrality). This situation "produced a striking irony: UNTAC, sent to protect human rights and secure law and order, began holding prisoners in violation of habeas corpus."[39]

Nor was Cambodia's extreme poverty relieved by the huge influx of money accompanying the UNTAC mission. More than $2 billion was spent on UNTAC operations to settle the Cambodia conflict, much of which paid for the housing, transport, maintenance, and communications needs of the sixteen thousand soldiers and six thousand civilians who came to the country.[40] UNTAC's presence skewed the local economy considerably, introducing a situation of grossly disproportionate salaries and incomes between those associated with UNTAC and those who remained outside of it. The civilian police within UNTAC, for example, were paid a per diem of $130 – in addition to their salaries – which was the equivalent of the average Cambodian's yearly earnings.[41] This discrepancy provoked local inflation as well as jealousy (and new excuses for corruption) among Cambodian state officials.[42] Thousands of Cambodian civil servants and teachers left their jobs to work for UNTAC, resulting in significant gaps in service provision.[43]

By fall 1992, UNTAC despaired of achieving military demobilization and moved its military forces into the job of helping to implement the elections, which now became the focus of the mission. Given the failure to create political neutrality for the campaign environment, UNTAC's original goal of sponsoring a free and fair election was reduced to guaranteeing the elections' secret ballot system.[44]

The May 1993 elections, although not held under the ideal conditions envisioned by the Paris Agreements, still represented a remarkable event. The elections began on May 23, 1993, in a festive atmosphere, and lasted through May 28. The long-anticipated vote electing the Constituent Assembly (which was to pass a constitution and then be automatically

[39] Doyle, *UN Peacekeeping in Cambodia*, pp. 48–9.
[40] Kamm, p. 211.
[41] Sandra Whitworth, *Men, Militarism and UN Peacekeeping: A Gendered Analysis* (Boulder: Lynne Rienner, 2004), p. 62.
[42] Kamm, p. 213. It is likely that most of the peacekeepers in Cambodia did not receive their full per diem payment. On peacekeeping missions, funds are distributed to troop-contributing countries, the governments of which pass the money along to their troops as they see fit. Senior officers may also appropriate funds intended for troops. Brad Adams, Director of Human Rights Watch's Asia Division, and Chief of the Legal Assistance Unit of the UN High Commission for Human Rights (Cambodia) from May 1995–September 1998, phone interview by author, July 26, 2006.
[43] Curtis, p. 9.
[44] Doyle, *UN Peacekeeping in Cambodia*, pp. 54, 57.

converted into a parliament, the National Assembly) produced an outcome that Hun Sen's government had no doubt feared. FUNCINPEC, the party led by Prince Sihanouk's son, Prince Ranariddh, won 45 percent of the vote, thereby obtaining fifty-eight seats (48.3 percent of the assembly's seats), whereas Hun Sen's formerly monopolistic CPP won only 38 percent of the vote, and was awarded fifty-one seats (42.5 percent of the assembly's seats). Supporters of the BLDP pulled in 4 percent of the vote, attaining ten seats, or 8.3 percent of the seats in the assembly.[45] The rest of the vote was split among minor parties.

After the Vote

Accustomed to outright political domination, Hun Sen's party evinced considerable displeasure at the election results. The election was thus followed by objections from the CPP, citing fraud and demanding new elections in several provinces. A few days later, after discussions with Hun Sen, Prince Sihanouk "surprised UNTAC by announcing, on June 3, the formation of a new national government," with himself as prime minister and Ranariddh and Hun Sen as joint deputy prime ministers.[46] The CPP promptly dropped its objection to the election results, but FUNCINPEC and UNTAC did not accept the fait accompli, and Sihanouk reversed himself, publicly withdrawing his proposed new government.[47] On June 16, with Akashi's backing, Sihanouk then suggested a variant of his original proposal: He would become king of Cambodia in a constitutional monarchy, with Ranariddh and Hun Sen sharing the prime ministership as first and second "prime" ministers, respectively.[48] With this compromise achieved, Sihanouk was thereupon pronounced head of state by the Constituent Assembly, and an interim administration was formed with Prince Ranariddh and Hun Sen as co-chairs of the Council of Ministers.[49] When the constitution was adopted after several months of interim governance, Ranariddh and Hun Sen retained their slightly surreal titles of "premier premier ministre" and "deuxieme premier ministre," and their parties shared the ministerial portfolios, with a small number going to the BLDP.[50]

[45] Brown and Zasloff, p. 158.
[46] Ibid., p. 168; Kamm, pp. 223–4.
[47] Brown and Zasloff, p. 169.
[48] Becker, pp. 514–15.
[49] Brown and Zasloff, p. 174.
[50] Brown and Zasloff, p. 189; Kamm, p. 227. The ministerial portfolios were distributed as such: 45 percent to FUNCINPEC and the CPP alike, and 10 percent to the BLDP. Curtis, p. 12.

Dividing the ministries evenly between the two parties was not a just result, given that FUNCINPEC had won a plurality of the popular vote under an electoral system using proportional representation.[51] By all rights, Ranariddh should have been entitled to become prime minister and negotiate the formation of a cabinet dominated by his party, FUNCINPEC. The equal division of portfolios meant that, on the ground, the CPP retained nearly full control over the bureaucracy, police, army, and court system. "Thus, the popular mandate expressed in the election, with its remarkable 90 percent voter turnout, was not translated into political power," and a significant link in the chain of political accountability had been broken.[52]

On September 21, 1993, the Constitutional Assembly fulfilled its task of ratifying a new Cambodian constitution. A few days later, Prince Sihanouk was reinaugurated as king and named Prince Ranariddh and Hun Sen as dual prime ministers in a government that reflected the composition of the interim administration. On September 26, UNTAC's mission was over, and Yasushi Akashi took his leave of the newly appointed Cambodian leadership after an emotional speech at the airport.[53]

The political system that UNTAC left behind was soon paralyzed. The power-sharing agreement between the CPP and FUNCINPEC created dual patronage networks, now twice as big as the one managed by the CPP before the election. Cambodia still lacked a neutral civil service – a prerequisite for an accountable government. Moreover, the new FUNCINPEC officials discovered that the CPP civil servants staffing the ministries were reluctant to serve their new bosses, refusing to carry out policies as directed.[54] Rather than facilitating the sharing of power, the new system was proving that FUNCINPEC could take only as much power as the CPP was willing to relinquish.[55] One reason for the paralysis was that the transnational political planners had not thought through what would happen if there *was* no decisive electoral result; no one had planned on how to divide power, or on whether FUNCINPEC would be able to run the country if it won a majority.[56]

---

[51] In deliberating over the electoral rules for the Constituent Assembly, the Supreme National Council had settled on a proportional representation system, giving each party seats in the assembly in accordance with its share of the popular vote in each province. See Solomon, p. 77.

[52] Brown and Zasloff, p. 287.

[53] Ibid., p. 189.

[54] Curtis, pp. 24–5.

[55] Ibid., p. 21.

[56] Ibid., p. 15.

Cambodia's new legislature failed to counterbalance the power of the CPP-dominated executive branch. Despite the efforts expended on its election, the National Assembly met rarely and seemed powerless, initiating no legislation and voting unanimously ("just like under communism," according to one of its members).[57] Meanwhile, the parliamentarians voted themselves salaries of $650 per month "plus perks worth about another $1,000."[58] Against this background, the Khmer Rouge remained engaged in low-level warfare with the state of Cambodia, adding to popular insecurity. The Khmer Rouge also retained valuable timber and gem mining areas, thus diverting resources and income from the state.[59]

For all UNTAC's flaws, the election process – despite its outcome from the perspective of accountability – had preserved peace between Cambodia's two major parties. In that light, the decision to share the prime ministership after the elections between Ranariddh and Hun Sen "well reflected Cambodian realities" and was designed to purchase the CPP's support rather than destabilize the new government. It was also practical; approval of the constitution called for a two-thirds vote in the Assembly, which would have been unattainable without the coalition.[60]

Some Cambodian voters may have felt that the "way in which the CPP retained power despite losing the 1993 election undermined their faith in the democratic process."[61] But the UN's endorsement of the less-than-fair power-sharing agreement in the wake of the 1993 elections was only one of many impressions that Cambodians held about the UNTAC-sponsored elections. According to Evan Gottesman, the deputy director of the American Bar Association's Law and Democracy project in Cambodia in the mid-1990s:

After the UNTAC elections, Cambodians were very optimistic and very hopeful that things would be different. And notwithstanding the fact that the election results were not perfectly represented in the new government structure, there had been an election, there was a new constitution, the king was back, which meant a lot in terms of people feeling like there was a sort of return to pre-revolutionary Cambodia, and there were opposition parties who were in positions of at least nominal power. And there were NGOs, human rights organizations, journalists, and a lot of foreigners engaged in...a process that involved scrutiny and review of

---

[57] Ibid., p. 30.
[58] William Shawcross, *Cambodia's New Deal* (Washington: Carnegie Endowment For International Peace, 1994), p. 56.
[59] Curtis, p. 33.
[60] Doyle, *UN Peacekeeping in Cambodia*, p. 72, p. 98, ft. 133.
[61] Duncan McCargo, "Cambodia: Getting Away with Authoritarianism?" *Journal of Democracy*, Vol. 16, No. 4 (October 2005), p. 100, citing Caroline Hughes' interviews with Cambodian voters.

what was going on in Cambodia. The actual composition of the government, while certainly disappointing to some, was not the whole story.... There was no doubt some letdown from the expectation that there would be a real transition of power to the party that won the election, but not total despair by any means.[62]

That Cambodians would feel optimistic about the political future in 1993 is not surprising. For the duration of the election campaign, UNTAC had transformed the nature of political expression in Cambodia. Outside of the state-controlled media, UNTAC achieved an impressive degree of freedom of information, establishing Radio UNTAC (received across the state on 143,000 additional radios donated by private individuals in Japan) and thereby doing an end run around the state-and-CPP–dominated media and the political propaganda put forth by all four factions.[63] Radio UNTAC provided a means of distributing information to the population about the election from all of Cambodia's political parties, as well as being a source of independent news. UNTAC also presided over a relative explosion of print media in Cambodia in 1993: "The print media consisted of exactly one government controlled newspaper in 1991. In 1993 there were over 57 different newspapers, bulletins, and magazines produced by the political parties, indigenous human rights organizations, and independent publishers."[64] Several human rights groups also took advantage of the relatively more open atmosphere under UNTAC, establishing human rights monitoring and education programs. In December 1992, UNTAC showed its support for grassroots human rights organizing when its Human Rights Office held a "fair" to inform the public about Cambodian groups promoting human rights.[65] Among these were the Cambodian Human Rights and Development Association (ADHOC), founded in December 1991 by former political prisoners of Hun Sen's regime, and the Cambodian League for the Promotion and Defense of Human Rights (LICADHO), founded in 1992 by returning Cambodian émigrés, which undertook voter education campaigns in advance of the 1993 election.[66]

In addition to providing a temporarily protected space for civil society, UNTAC also succeeded in repatriating (in time for the 1993 elections) the

---

[62] Evan Gottesman, phone interview by author, July 3, 2006.

[63] Doyle, *UN Peacekeeping in Cambodia*, pp. 31, 55, 87.

[64] U.S. Department of State, "Cambodia Human Rights Practices, 1993," January 31, 1994, accessed July 20, 2006, at http://dosfan.lib.uic.edu/ERC/democracy/1993_hrp_report/93hrp_report&_eap/Cambodia.html.

[65] United Nations Transitional Authority in Cambodia (UNTAC), accessed November 21, 2007, at: http://www.un.org/av/photo/subjects/untac.htm.

[66] See http://www.licadho.org/aboutus.php and http://www.bigpond.com.kh/users/adhoc/about_adhoc/about_adhoc.htm, both accessed November 21, 2007.

roughly 350,000 refugees who had been effectively imprisoned in refugee camps in Thailand.[67] The repatriation process, however, was seen as insufficient, as people ran out of money and/or found that the land to which they sought to be repatriated was occupied by others – or by mines.[68]

Looking back at UNTAC's experience in Cambodia, Grant Curtis, a political scientist and senior program officer with UNTAC's Rehabilitation and Economic Affairs Component, concluded that setting the establishment of liberal democracy in Cambodia as UNTAC's goal had been unrealistic for many reasons, ranging from Cambodia's lack of experience with pluralistic politics to the social and economic devastation that pervaded the country. Instead, Curtis argued, UNTAC had done what was feasible. It had not established democracy, but rather had "launched a process of political change," creating new institutions in which democracy could then later potentially take root.[69]

CAMBODIAN POLITICS AFTER UNTAC

Curtis's hope would not be borne out in the decade following UNTAC's departure. Instead, democratic politics in Cambodia would take a sharp turn for the worse.

From Corruption to Coup

Following UNTAC's departure in September 1993, Cambodian politics quickly deteriorated into a struggle over the state's natural and other resources. The army, dominated by the CPP, but with the addition of new generals and high-ranking officers from FUNCINPEC, engaged in profitable deforestation, and state officials from both parties used their positions for self-enrichment.[70] Neither of the two "prime ministers" were, as Gottesman puts it, "eager to incorporate the principles of the new constitution into legislation," and thus anticorruption laws "were never sent to the legislature" and the courts "remained under the control of the executive branch."[71] Neither party's leadership was keen on political reform: "Pluralism in Cambodia did not evolve into a democratic exchange of ideas but into a tenuous compact among competing

[67] Becker, pp. 508–10.
[68] Whitworth, pp. 59, 61.
[69] Curtis, pp. 32, 154.
[70] Kamm, p. 234.
[71] Gottesman, p. 352.

patronage systems. Most FUNCINPEC officials were more concerned with satisfying their superiors than with changing the way the country was governed." The most visible exception, FUNCINPEC Finance Minister Sam Rainsy, who publicly objected to governmental corruption, was removed first from FUNCINPEC and then from his elected position in the legislature in 1995.[72]

The competition for resources soon became an overt armed struggle for power between Ranariddh and Hun Sen. In March 1996, frustrated by continued CPP control over the state bureaucracy, courts, police, and army, Ranariddh publicly demanded that the CPP share actual power with FUNCINPEC rather than continue the charade.[73] Speaking to a FUNCINPEC party conference in April, Ranariddh declared that he was "absolutely not happy" after two years in office as the nominal first prime minister, frankly stating: "Being first puppet prime minister, puppet vice-prime minister, puppet ministers, puppet governors and deputy governors and soon-to-be puppet chiefs of district... being a puppet is not so good."[74]

Meanwhile, Hun Sen and Ranariddh began building up independent military forces and recruiting Khmer Rouge leaders to their respective sides, hoping for military backup and electoral support in the national elections planned for May 1998.[75] The political contest soon turned violent. In March 1997, Sam Rainsy's newly formed Khmer Nation Party held a protest outside the National Assembly to demand that the courts become independent of the CPP. Grenades were thrown into the crowd of protestors, killing over a dozen people and wounding many others. The CPP was apparently responsible for the attack.[76]

By 1997, the dual prime ministers had split the armed forces among themselves, unit by unit, according to their political loyalties. They thus surrounded themselves with what amounted to two large private militias. Fighting began in June 1997, and in July the CPP-controlled armed forces seized FUNCINPEC headquarters, their military base, and Ranariddh's house, bringing a quick end to the shared prime ministership.[77] The CPP had regained full control of Cambodia as the result of a military

---

[72] Ibid., p. 353.
[73] Brown and Zasloff, p. 248.
[74] Quoted in Brown and Zasloff, p. 249.
[75] Ibid., p. 259.
[76] Kamm, p. 243; Sorpong Peou, *Intervention and Change in Cambodia: Towards Democracy?* (New York: St. Martin's Press, 2000), pp. 307–8.
[77] Kamm, p. 244.

coup. In the wake of the coup, several dozen high-ranking FUNCINPEC officials were executed, hundreds were arrested and tortured, and dozens fled abroad.[78]

The July 1997 coup provoked a reassessment of UNTAC's mission. UNTAC's laudable if "limited" success was now deemed "a failed rescue of a failed state."[79] Cambodia's fragile democracy had devolved into authoritarian rule – or worse. Brown and Zasloff write:

In light of the coup d'etat of Hun Sen in July 1997...the wisdom of creating two prime ministers to govern following the election but prior to the promulgation of the constitution is not self evident. The more usual parliamentary practice of naming a single prime minister from the party winning the most votes (FUNCINPEC) and inviting leaders from other parties garnering substantial votes (CPP, BLDP) to take cabinet posts in a coalition government might have reduced Hun Sen's tendency to think in July 1997 that he had a right to overthrow the "first" (but not superior) prime minister.[80]

UNTAC's military commander, General Sanderson, seemed to agree: Akashi's endorsement of the compromise, followed by UNTAC's rapid departure from Cambodia, had "set the course for the inevitable overthrow of the democratic process four years later."[81]

The 1998 Elections

Despite this turmoil, and under international pressure – Cambodia had lost considerable economic aid, as well as its UN seat in the wake of the coup – Hun Sen decided to abide by the constitution and hold elections to the National Assembly on schedule, in 1998.[82] Voting day (July 26) proved peaceful, with a high turnout of 93 percent.[83] Ranariddh and other opposition politicians were allowed to return safely to Cambodia before the elections, which were closely monitored by both foreign and domestic observers. Still, Kassie Neou, Cambodia's National Election Commission vice chair, reported that the CPP dominated the election commissions and apparatus at all levels and that Hun Sen's CPP-run government would not

[78] Ibid., p. 246; Peou, p. 305.
[79] Brown and Zasloff, p. 265.
[80] Ibid., p. 175. The dual prime ministership was incorporated in the constitution, intended to revert to a single prime ministership after the next scheduled elections in 1998. See ibid., p. 205.
[81] Quoted in Paris, p. 86.
[82] Brown and Zasloff, pp. 265, 301, 303.
[83] Ibid., p. 308.

relinquish control over the media.[84] As a result, the CPP monopolized the media coverage to the exclusion of all other parties, until the last month before the elections.[85] Nor was UNTAC radio there to provide a neutral informative voice; with access to TV time limited, the climate was therefore tougher for the opposition.[86]

Amid these obstacles, the two main opposition parties, FUNCINPEC and the Sam Rainsy Party (SRP), collectively defeated the CPP in the popular vote.[87] But due to a change in the formula used to translate votes into seats in the National Assembly, the opposition's advantage in the popular vote did not translate into a parliamentary majority. Although FUNCINPEC had won 31.7 percent of the votes, and the SRP had pulled in 14.3 percent of the votes, for a total of 46 percent compared to the CPP's 41 percent, the new formula, benefiting "the leading party," gave a total of fifty-eight seats to FUNCINPEC and the SRP combined, but sixty-four seats to the CPP, giving the latter a majority.[88] By contrast, if the National Election Commission had used the 1993 seat allocation formula, the CPP would have had fifty-nine seats, FUNCINPEC would have had forty-five seats, and the SRP would have had eighteen rather than fifteen seats, giving a majority of sixty-three seats to the opposition (see Table 1). The new rules reversed the outcome that might have been expected based on the popular vote.

TABLE 1. *Cambodian election results, 1998*

Party	Popular Vote	Number of Assembly Seats Won Using the 1993 Formula	Number of Assembly Seats Won Using the 1998 Formula
FUNCINPEC/ SRP combined	46% (32% and 14%, respectively)	63	58
CPP	41%	59	64

[84] Kassie Neou with Jeffrey C. Gallup, "Field Report: Conducting Cambodia's Elections," *Journal of Democracy*, Vol. 10, No. 2 (1999), p. 155.
[85] Ibid., p 158.
[86] Brown and Zasloff, p. 302.
[87] Sam Rainsy's Khmer Nation Party changed its name to the Sam Rainsy Party in advance of the 1998 elections in order to forestall further attempts by Hun Sen to divide and coopt the party's membership. Gottesman, phone interview, July 3, 2006.
[88] Brown and Zasloff, p. 312; Richard D. Fisher, Jr., "Don't Railroad Cambodia's Democrats," September 15, 1998, accessed November 21, 2007, at http://www.heritage.org/Research/AsiaandthePacific/BG1220.cfm.

The National Election Commission had announced to all the parties in May 1998, in advance of the election, that the seat formula would be changed. Although the "CPP could not have been certain that it would benefit from the change," it is certainly plausible that Hun Sen believed the CPP would win the election, given his party's control of the state and media, as well as the routing of the opposition during and after the July 1997 coup. His willingness to risk the election seems to suggest that he was confident of a win.[89]

Like its predecessor, the 1998 election was followed by political turbulence. Complaining of fraud, the opposition parties threatened to boycott the Assembly and organized peaceful demonstrations demanding that Hun Sen resign.[90] Bloodshed followed when "[a]fter a week of demonstrations and political uncertainty, the CPP trucked in iron-baton-wielding counterdemonstrators to disperse the protestors."[91] For four months, the CPP and the opposition failed to form a government or resolve the election disagreements.[92]

In November 1998, King Sihanouk brought Hun Sen and Ranariddh together and arranged another coalition government between the CPP and FUNCINPEC, led by Hun Sen as prime minister. This new coalition left out Rainsy's party, creating "an even more lopsided coalition" than that formed in 1993.[93] As part of the compromise, Ranariddh would become head of the National Assembly, and the CPP party leader (Chea Sim), who had held that post until then, became president of a new political body, the Senate, "created, it seems, mostly so that the CPP party secretary would have a prestigious position."[94]

Hun Sen had successfully split the opposition to his own advantage, and the process of jostling for power began anew. Having worked hard to hold a fair election under difficult circumstances, a dismayed Kassie Neou found that the process surrounding the formation of the coalition government after the 1998 elections "demonstrated all too clearly that much of Cambodia's leadership views elections not as the paramount political process through which people choose their leaders, but merely as one facet of a broader and relentless struggle for power."[95]

[89] Brown and Zasloff, pp. 303, 312.
[90] Neou, p. 161; Peou, p. 319.
[91] Gottesman, p. 355.
[92] Neou, p. 162.
[93] Gottesman, p. 355; Peou, p. 318.
[94] Gottesman, p. 355; Neou, p 162.
[95] Neou, p. 152.

The Politics of Pretense

Elections in Cambodia were fast becoming a veneer of accountability on an authoritarian regime. In 2002, the CPP won 98.6 percent of the vote in local elections, during which several opposition party members were killed.[96] The national parliamentary elections, held in July 2003, produced a less skewed vote than that in the local elections. The July vote showed increased support for the SRP, which won 22 percent of the popular vote, rivaling FUNCINPEC's 21 percent. With this combined 43 percent of the vote, the opposition won a total of 50 seats (of 123). The CPP, with 47 percent of the vote received 73 seats, again reflecting Cambodia's unusual votes-to-seats formula.[97]

As in 1998, Cambodians voting for the National Assembly found their efforts frustrated when, following the election, the three main parties failed to form a governing cabinet – this time, for eleven months. Initially, FUNCINPEC and the SRP joined forces in an "Alliance of Democrats," which offered to join the CPP in a "grand national-unity coalition government" on the condition that the CPP would remove Hun Sen and his close ally Sok An from the cabinet, but this demand went unmet. The stalemate was finally resolved when Hun Sen convinced Ranariddh of the merits of a two-party governing coalition in March 2004, leaving the SRP out of the picture; "Ranariddh did not bother to consult his party."[98] The new CPP-FUNCINPEC government was formed in July 2004. In exchange, FUNCINPEC officials were granted twice their previous number of senior government offices, suggesting that greed had outweighed principle for the semiroyalist party. Under the auspices of this new government, Sam Rainsy was stripped of his immunity by the National Assembly in February 2005 and fled Cambodia when faced with arrest, temporarily depriving Cambodia of its remaining opposition party.[99]

---

[96] Michael Massing, "In Failed States, Can Democracy Come Too Soon?" *New York Times*, February 23, 2003, p. A17; Seth Mydans, "Cambodian Leader Rules as If from the Throne," *New York Times*, March 19, 2002, p. A3.

[97] Central Intelligence Agency, *The World Factbook: Cambodia*, November 15, 2007, accessed November 21, 2007, at https://www.cia.gov/library/publications/the-world-factbook/geos/cb.html.

[98] McCargo, pp. 107–8.

[99] Ibid., pp. 108–9. Sam Rainsy was convicted in absentia of defamation. In December 2005, after retracting his allegations against Hun Sen, whom he had accused of being responsible for the 1997 grenade attack at a peaceful protest organized by the Khmer Nation Party, and against Ranariddh, whom he had accused of taking bribes in exchange for forming a coalition government with the CPP in 2004, he was pardoned and allowed to return to Cambodia, where he arrived in February 2006. See LICADHO (Cambodian League for the Promotion and Defense of Human Rights), *Threats to Human Rights*

The past decade of "electoral authoritarianism" under Hun Sen exhibits a pattern whereby elections in Cambodia have failed as a method of distributing political power in accordance with voters' expressed preferences. Instead, "Hun Sen [has] used the outward show of electioneering to legitimize the status quo, rather than let power change hands."[100] The CPP had technically lost the elections in 1993 to FUNCINPEC but was still equally (or more) empowered within the government formed afterward, thus setting the stage for the next two elections and their illegitimate aftermaths.[101]

Authoritarianism shows no sign of abating in Cambodia. According to local human rights groups, 2005 brought increased violations of human rights, suppression of free speech and association, and abuse of the legal process to facilitate such violations. Police broke up or prevented several dozen demonstrations, strikes, and public discussion forums, using force on multiple occasions. In a 2006 report, the Cambodian League for the Promotion and Defense of Human Rights (LICADHO) wrote:

In the face of such intimidation, human rights defenders fear violence and arrest when planning public events to promote human rights issues or when monitoring demonstrations held by others. By refusing permission for such events, on the spurious grounds that they pose a threat to national security and public order, the authorities seriously obstruct activities necessary for democracy and the defense of human rights.[102]

Human rights activists themselves are directly targeted by the Hun Sen regime; several activists, including Kem Sokha, the director of the Cambodian Center for Human Rights (CCHR), founded in 2002, were arrested at the end of December 2005 several weeks after a human rights rally "attended by thousands." Released on bail personally guaranteed by Hun Sen a few weeks later, the activists were told that the state would not act further on the case, but would allow the "statute of limitations" to

---

Defenders in Cambodia, 2005: Briefing Paper (June 2006), p. 5, accessed November 21, 2007, at http://www.licadho.org/reports/files/85HRDefenders2005.pdf; Sam Rainsy, "A Farcical Justice," December 22, 2005, accessed November 21, 2007, at http://www.samrainsyparty.org/national_assembly/2005/dec/051222_statement.htm.

[100] McCargo, pp. 98, 100.

[101] Cambodian politics continues to be pervaded by violence. Documentation of political murders (of people working for parties other than the CPP) between 1994 and 2005 can be found in a UN report: Cambodia Office of the High Commissioner of Human Rights (COHCHR), "Continuing Patterns of Impunity in Cambodia," October 2005, accessed July 27, 2006, at http://cambodia.ohchr.org/Documents/Reports/Thematic%20 reports%20by%20SRSG/English/242.pdf.

[102] LICADHO, *Threats to Human Rights Defenders in Cambodia, 2005*, p. 7.

expire after a three-year period. The activists could thus be rearrested if they behaved, in Hun Sen's words, "arrogantly." One human rights group summed it up: "The offer, seemingly, was freedom from imprisonment in return for three years' silence."[103] If political participation is a central component of accountability, the level of repression of free participation in Cambodia makes attainment of an accountable political relationship challenging indeed.

DEMOCRACY FROM ABROAD: ANALYZING ACCOUNTABILITY IN CAMBODIA

UNTAC cannot be blamed for Cambodia's disappointing and dictatorial political outcome. Dozens of states are beset by the political demons of "illiberalism" – many displaying the form, if not the content, of democracy – without having experienced a transnational intervention on the scale of UNTAC.[104] Certainly, Cambodia boasted an unusually intractable series of obstacles to democratization well before the arrival of UNTAC in 1992. These ranged from widespread poverty and illiteracy to the national trauma wrought by the Khmer Rouge and their decimation of the social, educational, and welfare infrastructure. Yet the severity of Cambodia's circumstances should not discourage an analysis of the ways in which UNTAC's practices and choices affected the conditions for improving political accountability in Cambodia. UNTAC had both positive and negative effects in this regard.

The 1993 election in Cambodia represented the first time that the UN had "assumed responsibility for directly conducting an election."[105] The election was widely recognized as being the most significant accomplishment of the mission. Michael Doyle traces UNTAC's success in carrying

---

[103] Human Rights Watch, "Hun Sen Systematically Silences Critics," January 4, 2006, accessed November 21, 2007, at http://www.hrw.org/english/docs/2006/01/04/cambod12360.htm; LICADHO, *Threats to Human Rights Defenders in Cambodia, 2005*, p. 12.

[104] The political heritage of postcolonial states, where many of the faux democracies can be found, should not be discounted as a form of international – if not always transnational – intervention. A recent study by Alberto Alesina, Janina Matuszeski, and William Easterly shows that states with artificial boundaries (typically imposed by European colonizers, and often combining or splitting ethnic groups) fare worse than states with "natural borders" such as rivers and mountains when it comes to political and economic quality of life. See Austan Goolsbee, "Count Ethnic Divisions, Not Bombs, to Tell If a Nation Will Recover from War," *New York Times*, July 20, 2006, p. C3.

[105] Brown and Zasloff, p. 130.

out the election process and distributing information to the population during the campaign to the fact that UNTAC did not need the cooperation of the four factions to the Paris Agreements in order to make the election happen: UNTAC took this aspect of the mission directly to the Cambodian people, who welcomed it enthusiastically.[106]

Although UNTAC itself was not accountable in any meaningful way to the Cambodian voting population, the intention of the election process that UNTAC organized was to give people a way to exercise their voices in a process aimed at establishing an accountable regime. Regarding the "true objectives" of UNTAC, the mission's electoral director, Reginald Austin, suggested that UNTAC was not so much about ending the armed conflict in Cambodia by any means necessary, but rather featured a "wider objective: to implant democracy, change values, and establish a new pattern of governance based on...free and fair elections."[107] In other words, because UNTAC failed at the demobilization part of its mission, it would make an all-out effort to establish some accountability between Cambodian citizens and their government.

One way to evaluate the accountability of peacekeeping operations to the local community is through a gendered lens.[108] Examining UNTAC in Cambodia in this light presents a mixed portrait of the UN mission. On one hand, measures were taken during preparation for the elections to try to ensure that women's participation in the vote would be extensive, although women's participation in UNTAC itself was a poor model to follow in that regard: "There were so few women appointed to UNTAC...that a UN Division for the Advancement of Women study on women's involvement in peacekeeping missions registers their presence, in statistical terms, as 'zero.'"[109] The election process, however, was in part intended to establish a government that would be responsible to female as well as male citizens. The United Nations Development Fund for Women (UNIFEM) exerted efforts to reach the female public, exhorting women to vote and urging women to work together politically to resolve issues affecting them. UNIFEM also sponsored a four-day Women's Summit at which women from across the country gathered to discuss their priorities, so that

---

[106] Doyle, *UN Peacekeeping in Cambodia,* p. 70.

[107] Quoted in ibid., p. 86.

[108] Goetz and Jenkins adopt a gender lens to explore accountability relationships and to highlight the structural obstacles ("gendered capture and bias") in the path of getting domestic state institutions to behave accountably toward marginalized groups, including women. See Goetz and Jenkins, especially pp. 158–79.

[109] Whitworth, p. 59.

they would in turn be prepared to lobby Cambodia's political parties both before and after the election.[110]

These combined efforts worked to create a government that would be – at least on paper – more accountable to women. Funding directed to Cambodian women's NGOs enabled them successfully to push the Cambodian government to include "important equality rights provisions" in the Constitution written after the elections. These efforts legitimated women's participation in politics and helped empower Cambodian women to press their new government for action on issues ranging from domestic violence to equality in the government and labor force and on changing inequitable divorce laws.[111] UNTAC therefore helped to establish a political situation where the notion of accountability to women was discussed overtly and embodied in the form of a rhetorically and materially supported women's movement, at least temporarily.

In short, "UNTAC and the ordinary Cambodian entered into a unique partnership" where the population gave UNTAC their trust and actually came out to vote, despite their fear, and UNTAC provided the chance for Cambodians to have an "authentic voice in their future." Reflecting on Cambodians' opportunity to "participate in the struggle for power" in 1993, Doyle comments: "The most lasting effect of UNTAC will likely be the population's sense that it can demand accountability from those who govern."[112]

Thirteen years later, Gottesman was not confident in the accuracy of Doyle's prediction:

I think as the years go by there's less and less of a sense that the population can demand accountability....You can *demand* accountability – the question is whether you're going to *get* accountability. And even human rights organizations, to the extent that they are capable of operating without intimidation, which is definitely not always the case; even if they submit reports, even if international journalists are allowed to operate in Cambodia and publish stories about human rights abuses and corruption, what good does it do if nothing changes? It's this problem whereby relative levels of openness turn out not to produce accountability. Just because you can identify human rights violations or systematic corruption or some other abuse of power, just because you can publish it, put it in a newspaper, put it in some report that gets sent off to the IMF or the World Bank or whomever, doesn't mean that things change.[113]

---

[110] Ibid., p. 66.
[111] Ibid., pp. 66–67.
[112] Doyle, *UN Peacekeeping in Cambodia* pp. 51, 57.
[113] Gottesman, phone interview, July 3, 2006.

Doyle, too, had expressed concern about Cambodia's political future. Although UNTAC provided the initial opportunity for citizens to take part in their own governance through voting in 1993, he feared that power would be ethereal "unless there is an institutional mechanism to translate democratic authority into bureaucratic practice," and noted that UNTAC did not institutionalize a political system (including a national bureaucracy, army, and police) that would have protected Cambodians from their continued "[vulnerability] to the armies, police, and corruption that have dominated since the votes were tallied."[114]

Even if elections did not produce an accountable regime in Cambodia, however, the very presence of human rights organizations, whose task is also to hold governments accountable for their actions, is another outcome at least partially attributable to the UN mission. Although such groups were forbidden in the pre-UNTAC period, discussions of human rights did take place among Cambodia's top political leaders in the years between the exodus of the Khmer Rouge from power and the UNTAC intervention in 1991.[115] In the post-UNTAC period, however, discussions of "human rights and democratic freedoms" became commonplace, and local and international organizations alike did a good job of fostering awareness of human rights among Cambodians. Yet, Gottesman sadly informs us, "Cambodian democracy often seems like an abstraction. The government ignores reports of corruption and human rights abuses. The courts remain corrupt.... Soldiers and police are never prosecuted for abuses, prompting nongovernmental organizations to write lengthy reports on the problem of impunity – reports that are themselves ignored." The state's leadership may tolerate these activities, "but they only do so to the extent that it does not jeopardize their power," making such discussions a sign of the leaders' "patience and indulgence," and not the hallmark of incipient democracy.[116]

Even if democracy is not incipient, efforts to foster discourse and action in support of human rights are necessary for the long-term development of accountability if it is to occur eventually. In Cambodia's case, UNTAC provided crucial soil in which such efforts could take root. In that sense, the human rights "component" of the UNTAC mandate was reasonably successful – although woefully understaffed – managing to develop and teach an "extensive information program" on human rights awareness in Cambodian schools and universities. The human rights staff of the UNTAC mission was also "instrumental in the founding of Cambodian

[114] Doyle, *UN Peacekeeping in Cambodia*, p. 88.
[115] Gottesman, pp. xiii, 239, 245, 267.
[116] Ibid., pp. 355–6.

human rights groups...[leaving] behind an important institutional legacy, the UN Human Rights Center, headed by a special envoy with a continuing responsibility to monitor Cambodia's progress in implementing 'liberal democracy,'" as the Paris Agreements required.[117] Among its other responsibilities, the Center, staffed by foreign and local employees, conducted investigations into human rights abuses, sending their "complaints to various state institutions," which produced little response.[118] The UN Center for Human Rights, intended to be the "immediate successor" to UNTAC's Human Rights Office, opened after a three-month delay, in December 1993, and was "the first UN field office for human rights anywhere in the world."[119]

With the establishment of the UN Center for Human Rights, UNTAC laid a foundation for grassroots activists (a "fledgling civil society") who could try to hold their future rulers accountable on human rights issues.[120] The UN resisted pressure both from Ranariddh and Hun Sen to remove the Human Rights Center in 1995, as well as refusing to replace the Center's staff after Hun Sen requested it in July 1997, embarrassed by the Center's public revelation that CPP military forces had "executed at least forty supporters of Prince Ranariddh" in the course of the 1997 coup.[121] The Center's documentation of these extrajudicial killings, combined with the loss of Cambodia's UN seat and cuts in donor aid, acted as a restraint on Hun Sen in 1997, forestalling a devastating slide into further violence on the part of Hun Sen's government. The UN Center for Human Rights thus acted as a means to force a bare modicum of accountability on Hun Sen's government, even in the midst of the 1997 coup, and probably helped keep the next elections on the agenda for 1998. In 1997, the UN Center for Human Rights underwent an "upgrade," becoming the UN High Commission for Human Rights, and has continued to operate under that title.[122]

While working for the American Bar Association's Law and Democracy project in Cambodia, Gottesman observed firsthand the value of the UN Center for Human Rights:

I think it was an important institution. Because it was the UN, because it was run by foreigners, it had protection that indigenous human rights organizations did

---

[117] Doyle, *UN Peacekeeping in Cambodia*, p. 46.
[118] Gottesman, p. 355.
[119] Adams, phone interview, July 26, 2006.
[120] Doyle, *UN Peacekeeping in Cambodia*, p. 86.
[121] Brown and Zasloff, pp. 229–30.
[122] Adams, phone interview, July 26, 2006. On the Cambodia Office of the High Commissioner for Human Rights, see: http://www.unhchr.ch/html/menu2/5/cambodia.htm.

not. It certainly was annoying enough to the government that they tried to shut it down. And obviously...although local organizations are more important for the development of a local, indigenous human rights community for long-term democratic accountability, as a *protector* of human rights, the concept of human rights, the UN Human Rights Center was extremely important and helped push forward the cultural concept that human rights investigation is part of a democracy, and helped protect to a certain extent the more indigenous human rights efforts that were going on, like ADHOC or LICADHO or the efforts of Kem Sokha at the human rights commission of the National Assembly, which also had UN support.[123]

The human rights component of the UNTAC mission left a widely agreed upon positive legacy, not only as a protector of human rights but also as a promoter of extensive human rights training for the leaders of new NGOs, as well as within the Cambodian population at large. Although UNTAC's efforts to neutralize Hun Sen's government, demobilize Cambodia's armed factions, and help elect an accountable government may have faltered, the Human Rights Office of UNTAC and the institutions that succeeded it were highly effective in human rights training, enabling grassroots activists to gain the skills that they would need to attempt to defend their rights and hold the government accountable for its behavior in the future. "That's the baseline of what we were trying to accomplish," affirmed Brad Adams, who worked as chief of the Legal Assistance Unit of the High Commission for Human Rights from May 1995 to September 1998. Currently working as the director of Human Rights Watch's Asia Division, Adams regarded UNTAC's "most enduring legacy" as the "development of civil society."[124]

Grassroots human rights groups in Cambodia have been busily developing since the UNTAC period began. A variety of organizations actively publish reports and conduct human rights training and other programs with the aim of promoting democratic reform. Many of the activists in such groups originally experienced human rights advocacy training at the UN Center for Human Rights:

A large number of Cambodians cycled through the Human Rights Center and would get not only training but also on-the-job experience conducting human rights investigations, writing reports, conducting analysis, petitioning the government, and so

[123] Gottesman, phone interview, July 3, 2006. Kem Sokha is the president of an NGO, the Cambodian Center for Human Rights (CCHR). In 2007, he founded the Human Rights Party, aiming to participate in Cambodia's July 2008 elections. See "Cambodian Human Rights Activist Launches His Own Political Party," July 31, 2007, accessed December 2, 2008, at http://khmer.org/doc/o,article,74,584,0,1443,0.htm.

[124] Adams, phone interview, July 26, 2006.

on. I would imagine that a significant number of those people have remained in the human rights community and went on to work for various indigenous human rights organizations. And...helping to develop that community of Cambodians may be [the Human Rights Center's] biggest legacy.[125]

Human rights trainings in mid-1990s Cambodia were ubiquitous. "Thousands of people" received training, according to Adams, including the activists who now staff Cambodia's human rights groups and the heads of Cambodia's major NGOs: "Basically, everybody was trained by either UNTAC's human rights component, or the UN Center for Human Rights, or the Asia Foundation, or various ad hoc trainings done by the American Bar Association; there were just an incredible number of trainings – all of [the activists] would have attended." Adams himself carried out human rights trainings, both for the general public and also for narrower audiences interested in learning about more specific topics, such as advocacy strategy. Describing his work with the leaders of Cambodia's new human rights groups in 1995, Adams found them "inexperienced" in advocacy work, but eager to learn. He also witnessed the empowering potential of human rights trainings: "I saw people who came into the classroom afraid to say anything, but leaving sometimes much more confident – especially if it was an entire course, not just a single training session." Specialized trainings for lawyers had a lasting effect as well, recalled Adams: "Certainly a lot of the lawyers who went through the trainings became significant members of the legal community in Cambodia. I think it was very liberating."[126] In addition to training activists, the UN Center for Human Rights also carried out human rights education programs in high schools and universities following UNTAC's departure.[127]

To inspire sufficient protest to alter the practices of an authoritarian government, human rights groups require a considerable constituency. Human rights trainings in Cambodia may have facilitated the development of a base for such protest. Based on his work in Cambodia, Gottesman

---

[125] Gottesman, phone interview, July 3, 2006.
[126] Adams, phone interview, July 26, 2006.
[127] Although its successor organization, the Cambodia Office of the High Commissioner for Human Rights, no longer carries out human rights education programs in high schools or universities, it did help to develop a human rights course in collaboration with the Law Faculty of the Royal University of Phnom Penh in 2001–2002 and continues to conduct trainings for NGOs and government officials from time to time. Two Cambodian groups, LICADHO and ADHOC, both currently carry out human rights education programs in schools. Margo Picken, Director, OHCHR/Cambodia, email communication with author, July 30, 2006.

thought human rights trainings had produced a mixture of idealism and cynicism:

I do not believe that human rights is considered a foreign or a Western concept in Cambodia. I don't think Cambodians consider it an import.... I think the Cambodians understand very well all the theories of human rights. They've had a bunch of elections and all kinds of human rights trainings, domestic human rights trainings and international organizations doing trainings on human rights, and I haven't seen polls on it, but I imagine while for some Cambodians it prompts a certain amount of idealism that might involve political activism, I think probably for a lot of Cambodians that seeing the distinction between these theories and what is actually allowed to happen results in a lot of cynicism. And also remember that Cambodia is an impoverished country with serious, serious problems – environmental problems, health problems – and human rights is not necessarily at the forefront of people's minds.[128]

Gottesman also noted that the people who have the "time and interest for human rights groups" are often middle class, which in Cambodia is extremely limited, narrowing the mass constituency for such organizations.[129] Nevertheless, Adams believed the Cambodian government was not "completely immune to pressure," and that the advocacy, public education, and protest work by Cambodia's human rights groups paid off. For instance, when Kem Sokha, president of the Cambodian Center for Human Rights, was arrested on December 31, 2005, public protests followed:

And there [you can consider] what role the trainings have in raising people's awareness so that they become activists and show up in large numbers...making clear to the government and to the diplomats that Kem Sokha wasn't just some isolated figure. That made it much harder for them to keep him in prison.[130]

On January 14, 2006, more than 150 people, including representatives of human rights organizations and unions, protested in front of the prison where Sokha and several other political detainees were being held.[131] Sokha was released three days later.

Despite repression, Cambodia's human rights community has secured some space for public criticism of the government, such as the Voice of Democracy radio program produced by the Cambodian Center for Human Rights. Such public fora can act as a force for political accountability as

[128] Gottesman, phone interview, July 3, 2006.
[129] Gottesman, phone interview, July 3, 2006.
[130] Adams, phone interview, July 26, 2006.
[131] LICADHO, "Civil Society Members Show Support for Detainees," January 16, 2006, accessed July 27, 2006, at http://www.licadho.org/articles/20060116/34/index.html; idem, *Threats to Human Rights Defenders in Cambodia, 2005*, p. 12.

well. In the context of a "pseudodemocratic" regime such as Cambodia's, Gottesman stressed:

Press freedom is always good; and media freedom is even better, especially in a country where a lot of people can't read newspapers. And certainly the government has been sufficiently annoyed at those radio programs and stations to close them down periodically. At least the government thinks they have an effect! Talking about human rights is a step towards accountability, it's just far, far, far from sufficient. Certainly nothing can happen unless you can talk about it.[132]

Cambodia's judicial system, although perhaps less affected by UNTAC than was the community of human rights groups, is also important as a potential site of political accountability. In retrospect, the UNTAC special prosecutor recommended that such missions in the future include a "justice package" designed to build judicial institutions and train the staff to run them – a feature critical to establishing accountability relations between the citizens and the state after a UN mission ends.[133] Cambodia's legal system in the late 1980s was beset by corruption and certainly could have used a far more extensive "package." According to Gottesman, the "courts were ineffectual, subject to political pressure, and often themselves corrupt. The police were prohibited from arresting a state cadre on charges of corruption (or any other malfeasance) without first clearing the arrest with a minister, a requirement that only encouraged state officials to deliver protection money to powerful patrons."[134]

Corruption was characteristic of Cambodia's government in the period of Vietnamese military occupation and afterward. In 1990, as the leadership considered economic reforms, Hun Sen downplayed the importance of ideology as a motivator for public officials, emphasizing instead the value of allowing officials at the local level "to benefit directly and personally from local economic activity," lending top-level government support to a thoroughgoing system of patronage and state corruption. Gottesman points out the wisdom of this approach, from Hun Sen's and other top officials' perspective: "It created networks of happy officials whose loyalty the regime could count on, even after the Vietnamese withdrew and Sihanouk returned."[135] The prospect of Vietnamese withdrawal was certain; by entrenching a patronage system, Hun Sen was ensuring his continuance

---

[132] Gottesman, phone interview, July 3, 2006.
[133] Doyle, *UN Peacekeeping in Cambodia*, p. 49.
[134] Gottesman, p. 321.
[135] Ibid., pp. 299–300.

in power, irrespective of whatever political transition might be imposed superficially later on.

The Cambodian political system continues to depend on patronage. State employees are compensated for their pitifully low salaries by "pocket[ing] a percentage of any fines, taxes, fees, or bribes that they impose on the citizenry. The rest of the money is handed up, sometimes for state or party coffers but generally to individual patrons....Powerful patrons have little incentive to punish their own loyalists. As long as the money flows, officials act with impunity – engaging in theft, extortion, or worse."[136] Continued corruption within the state, including the open sale of official positions, undermines faith in the leadership and accountability to the population. "A national survey showed that people view the Ministry of Justice as the most corrupt government agency," which does not bode well for the judicial system as a check on the executive branch's observance of accountability.[137]

UNTAC faced tremendous obstacles in trying to address Cambodia's thoroughly politicized and corrupt court system. A UN Cambodia Office of the High Commissioner for Human Rights report in 2005 explained that given the lack of an independent judiciary, a Special Prosecutor's Office was established within the context of UNTAC in January 1993:

> Initially UNTAC hoped that if the Office operated within the existing court structure this might, by the public nature of such prosecutions, play a role in altering the legal and official "culture" of the courts. The Office had the power, inter alia, to prosecute criminal offences involving officials, police or military officers in Cambodian courts. But this proved to be impossible when the Minister of Justice instructed the President of the Phnom Penh Municipal Court that he would be "punished" for a violation of the law if he were to hear cases brought by the Special Prosecutor. UNTAC was thus forced to recognise that it would be impossible to conduct cases with political overtones in the Cambodian courts. ...[Also, the] authorities opposed the limitations on their own power that would necessarily follow the establishment of an independent judiciary, and were unwilling to co-operate in the investigation, arrest and prosecution of serious human rights violators. Elements of the Cambodian administration, particularly the security forces, were complicit in politically motivated violence. Both meant that the courts were not allowed to operate independently or impartially. The law, and the courts in particular, was still regarded as a tool of the governing political parties – to be paid lip service on occasion but ignored when inconvenient. Further, during the election period, judges in many provinces were obliged to campaign for the Cambodian People's Party during working hours.[138]

[136] Gottesman, p. 335.
[137] McCargo, p. 102.
[138] COHCHR, "Continuing Patterns of Impunity in Cambodia."

Stressing the need for a judiciary that could support the rule of law, during the UNTAC period one of the officials with the Human Rights Component of UNTAC claimed that Cambodia's legal system was so corrupt that in order to attain judicial independence, "it would be necessary to abolish the judiciary as it exists now, completely."[139]

The corruption of Cambodia's judiciary, combined with the decades-long delay in beginning judicial proceedings against Khmer Rouge leaders for their crimes during the genocide, may together explain what Duncan McCargo calls the "culture of legal impunity which...pervades Cambodian life."[140] After years of discussion about the potential composition of a tribunal and who the subjects of the judicial process should be, agreement was finally reached, and in July 2006, a group of seventeen foreign (UN-appointed) and Cambodian judges designated to preside over the planned trials of the remaining high-level Khmer Rouge was sworn in.[141] The trials will focus only on top Khmer Rouge leaders, so as to leave King Sihanouk and Hun Sen untouched by the proceedings.[142] By the end of November 2007, the five people targeted for prosecution had been arrested. These included Ieng Sary, former foreign minister for the Khmer Rouge; Ieng Thirith, former minister of social affairs; Nuon Chea, the Khmer Rouge's leading ideologist; Kaing Guek Eav (Duch), the director of the famous Tuol Sleng prison; and Khieu Samphan, the former head of state.[143]

Holding a tribunal for a handful of Khmer Rouge leaders while excluding from its purview the Khmer Rouge who defected to Hun Sen's government (not to mention Hun Sen himself) may help improve the population's perception of their government's accountability while highlighting the current Cambodian leadership's impunity for its own abuses. "Accountability for Khmer Rouge genocidal leaders is a good thing – and that basic fact is what has driven the international community to support

---

[139] Quoted in Brown and Zasloff, p. 207.

[140] McCargo, p. 104. Although the fact that the Paris Agreements did not include an agreement to prosecute the Khmer Rouge's top officials for the mass killing or genocide that they implemented may suggest a considerable flaw in the UN's mandate (because one thing that an accountable government could do would be to bring to justice its genocidal predecessors), the Khmer Rouge would clearly not have agreed to such a clause, and the peace agreement would have been further delayed. Doyle, *UN Peacekeeping in Cambodia*, p. 46.

[141] "Judges Sworn in for Khmer Rouge," BBC News, July 3, 2006, accessed July 5, 2006, at http://news.bbc.co.uk/2/hi/asia-pacific/5140032.stm.

[142] "Khmer Rouge Trials Ready to Start," BBC News, June 13, 2007, accessed October 17, 2007, at http://news.bbc.co.uk/1/hi/world/asia-pacific/6747143.stm; McCargo, p. 104.

[143] Seth Mydans, "Killing Fields of Cambodia Now in Court," *New York Times*, November 21, 2007, pp. A1, A6.

the idea of trials, despite serious procedural limitations negotiated by Hun Sen's government," explains Gottesman.

> But I don't think you'd find anybody in the human rights community who's satisfied with the way things have gone, with the scope of the trial and the ability of the government to control the process.... I would guess that Cambodians understand perfectly well that something of this importance would not be held unless Hun Sen felt that nothing about it could jeopardize him and his party. Nobody is under the illusion that this thing is going to get out of control.[144]

Hun Sen's pattern of retaining control in Cambodia has been consistent and, in hindsight, predictable, from the consolidation of his power base in the 1980s through the present.[145] Described as "ruthless, violent, and intoxicated with power," Hun Sen exhibited a dedicated resistance to power sharing that undermined a significant part of UNTAC's mission.[146] The 1993 election "clearly flunked a key test of democracy, for FUNCINPEC won the vote but the CPP continued to rule. In this fundamental sense, it was not a democratic election. Whatever transition the UN Transitional Authority may have overseen, it was not a transition to democracy."[147] Given the situation of overweening CPP power before 1993, perhaps holding elections was guaranteed to fail as a means of redistributing power. And despite further rounds of elections, control remains in the hands of "most of the same people who gained power in 1979." In this sense, McCargo argues, the outcome of the UNTAC-sponsored elections, as well as the limited reach of the Khmer Rouge trials, "illustrate the ways in which substantial international interventions may be manipulated so that they do more to legitimize authoritarianism than to support democracy."[148]

BOSNIA

The international community's role in Bosnia, following the genocidal war there in the first half of the 1990s, presents another instance of large-scale transnational political intervention. As in Cambodia, the Bosnian intervention raises questions about the accountability of post-intervention governance. In Cambodia, UNTAC's brief mission was not able to do

[144] Gottesman, phone interview, July 3, 2006.
[145] On Hun Sen's construction of a power base within the People's Republic of Kampuchea (PRK) bureaucracy, see Gottesman, pp. 205–22.
[146] Adams, phone interview, July 26, 2006.
[147] McCargo, p. 107.
[148] Ibid., pp. 109–10.

enough on the ground to establish a neutral political environment in advance of the 1993 elections, and gave its implicit support to a post-election government still dominated by an unaccountable leadership. In the Bosnian case, transnational political organizations may have gone too far in trying to create a "representative" government, paradoxically undermining the mechanisms of democratic accountability in the process. Both instances highlight the complexity of transnational attempts to promote domestic accountability.

The civil war in Bosnia that gave way to international administration starting in 1995 had transformed an outwardly peaceable multi-ethnic territory into a nightmare of violence. As the communist party dictatorships across Eastern Europe collapsed, domino-style, at the end of the 1980s, the politicians of Yugoslavia's ruling communist party shed their allegiance to state socialism and began making appeals to ethnic nationalism as a means to mobilize political support. The federal state of Yugoslavia rapidly disintegrated into a series of independent countries, as its former constituent republics seceded. Croatia declared independence in 1991, followed by war when local Serbs took up arms against Croatia's nationalist government. Violence soon broke out in Bosnia as well, after a March 1992 referendum on independence registered 99 percent of non-Serb votes in favor of secession (Serbs, who constituted nearly one-third of Bosnia's population, boycotted the vote).[149] Paramilitary forces fielded by all three of Bosnia's main ethnic groups – Serbs, Croats, and Bosniaks (Bosnian Muslims) – then began fighting over territory, while Bosnian Serb militias conducted "ethnic cleansing" campaigns, forcing Bosnian Muslims and Croats to flee and murdering others outright. The Bosnian Serbs fought with the backing of Serbia's ultranationalist government, headed by Slobodan Milosevic, who sought to appropriate parts of Bosnian territory in pursuit of his vision of a "Greater Serbia." After several years of inter-ethnic violence punctuated by cease fires and internationally sponsored attempts to resolve the conflict, the Dayton Accords were signed in November 1995 and a fragile peace on Bosnia's bloodied territory was established.[150]

[149] Paris, pp. 97–8.
[150] Ibid., pp. 97–8. Also see Laura Silber and Allan Little, *Yugoslavia: Death of a Nation* (New York: T.V. Books, 1996). More than one hundred thousand people perished during the war in Bosnia. See Vince Crawley, "U.S. 'Disappointed' by Defeat of Bosnian Constitutional Reforms," Washington File, U.S. Department of State, April 28, 2006, accessed October 17, 2007, at http://usinfo.state.gov/xarchives/display.html?p=washfile-english&y=2006&m=April&x=20060428134331MVyelwarCo.9095423&t=is/is-latest.html.

How would this devastated region now be governed? Ethnic enmity seemed to pose the chief obstacle to peace, and hence the desire arose to arrange a new government that would promote cooperation between the ethnic groups, eliminating the political sphere as a generator of ethnic divisiveness. A political system was carefully constructed to meet this goal. The first step was to specify the electoral rules governing the new Bosnian state, Bosnia-Herzegovina, to be headed by a three-person presidency featuring one Serb, one Croat, and one Bosnian Muslim. Second, Bosnia-Herzegovina would include two political subregions or "entities": the Serb Republic (Republika Srpska) and the Federation of Bosnia-Herzegovina, also referred to as the Croat-Muslim Federation.[151] New governments would be elected across the territory, and the entire process would be overseen by the international community, with the hope of ensuring a successful transition to an accountable, rather than a murderous, government.

Technically, the United Nations was not the main transnational force involved in the civilian governing of postwar Bosnia. Rather, the Dayton Peace Accords provided for a multi-year period of international administration over Bosnia, involving a wide variety of other states and international organizations. A month after the Dayton Accords were signed, a Peace Implementation Conference took place in London, establishing the Peace Implementation Council (PIC) with fifty-five members, including states and international organizations.[152] The PIC's Steering Board would select a High Representative whose nomination was then endorsed by the UN Security Council, making the High Representative nominally accountable to both the PIC and the UN.[153]

---

[151] In addition to the two major "entities," the multi-ethnic town of Brcko was governed separately by an international supervisor. Brcko's status was determined by an Arbitration tribunal in 1999; in theory, its territory is held "in condominium" by the two "entities." See Office of the High Representative (OHR), "History and Mandate of the OHR North/Brcko," August 28, 2001, accessed November 21, 2007, at http://www.ohr.int/ohr-offices/brcko/history/default.asp?content_id=5531.

[152] For a list of the PIC's members, see Office of the High Representative (OHR), "The Peace Implementation Council and Its Steering Board," accessed December 12, 2008, at http://www.ohr.int/ohr-info/gen-info/#6.

[153] Office of the High Representative (OHR), "General Information," accessed December 12, 2008, at http://www.ohr.int/ohr-info/gen-info/#1. The UN Mission in Bosnia and Herzegovina lasted from 1995 to 2002, working closely with the Office of the High Representative for the Implementation of the Peace Agreement, which continued to oversee Bosnia's civilian administration. See United Nations Mission in Bosnia and Herzegovina, "Bosnia and Herzegovina – UNMIBH – Mandate," accessed November 17, 2007, at http://www.un.org/Depts/dpko/missions/unmibh/mandate.html.

Initially, the international administration of Bosnia was to end with elections in September 1996, but was extended indefinitely in December 1997.[154] The civilian aspects of that administration became embodied in the office of the international community's High Representative – an institution whose purview grew over time, eventually coming to encompass the power to fire elected officials and "unilaterally impose disputed legislation" on everything from citizenship laws to the design of Bosnia's new flag, leaving the locally elected bodies essentially to rubber-stamp legislation that had been handed down from international organizations.[155] Under this administrative system, at all levels, from the apex of the Bosnian state and the two "entities" within it, down to Bosnia's cities and municipalities, "elected Bosnian institutions of government...had a largely formal existence with little capacity to develop or implement policy independently of the international community."[156] These elected institutions were "required" to pass legislation composed by international institutions by particular deadlines; the legislation ranged across measures on "housing, education, the legal system, citizenship, travel, the constitution, refugee return, policing, the media, electoral regulation, economic reconstruction, and regional relations," including even "requirements for the Bosnian sports teams at the [1998] Winter Olympics in Nagano, Japan."[157]

Elections and Ethnicity

The extent of international administrative control over Bosnia by transnational institutions, including the Office of the High Representative (OHR), the European Union (EU), and the Organization for Security and Cooperation in Europe (OSCE), has produced questions about accountability relationships within Bosnia's domestic political system. Accountability issues have arisen most sharply in relation to the international institutions' role in Bosnian elections. The protection of ethnic minorities was a key principle behind re-creating Bosnia as a state, and electoral laws were established with the laudable aim of ensuring multi-ethnic representation in local elections. Yet, the main parties running for office across the country continued to define themselves along ethnic lines, and their exclusivist ethnic nationalism would prove disappointingly popular in the

---

[154] David Chandler, *Bosnia: Faking Democracy After Dayton* (London: Pluto Press, 1999), p. 51.
[155] Ibid., pp. 64, 74, 87. Information about the OHR can be found at http://www.ohr.int/.
[156] Chandler, *Bosnia*, p. 155.
[157] Ibid., p. 157.

elections to come. This created a number of undesirable electoral outcomes, provoking further transnational administrative "solutions." In the divided city of Mostar, for instance, the European Union Administration Mostar (EUAM) ran the June 1996 elections, specifying in advance precisely how the city council's seats would be divided among the three major ethnic groups: Bosnian Muslims, Croats, and Serbs.[158] Because the Bosnian Muslims' coalition gained more votes than the main Croatian party, five of the Serbs on the Bosnian Muslims' party list won seats, in effect giving control of the city council to the Bosnian Muslims and leading the Croats to complain that the council was "illegitimate." The EU solution was to "re-fix the elections" by reaching an agreement to form a town administration, with a mayor and deputy mayor elected by the city council – such that the mayor would be a Croat.[159] Much like the post-election fix in Cambodia, an international organization gave in to pressure from the losing party (the Croatian nationalist HDZ, in this case). This external regulation of the electoral process "marginalized the Mostari voters and elected representatives and imposed co-operation from above as opposed to increasing local accountability for policy-making," as well as removing the need for the parties to come to a negotiated solution among themselves.[160] Similarly, in the capital, Sarajevo, rather than conducting elections, the international community simply allocated city council seats according to ethnicity and political party and then wrote an article into the city constitution to govern future elections, stating: "A minimum of 20 per cent of seats in the City Council...shall be guaranteed to Bosniaks, Croats and the group of Others, regardless of the election results...."[161]

The international community, embodied in the High Representative, imposed policies that would create multi-ethnic administrations at the local level in various ways. Until December 1997, the OHR would threaten localities with the withdrawal of reconstruction funds if they did not comply with the mandate to "agree on new interim municipal assemblies." After that point, the powers of the High Representative were enhanced, giving him the power to "dismiss obstructive officials" – a power that the OHR used, firing two city mayors in 1998.[162] Similarly, following the September 1997 elections, in ten different towns, the OSCE – which, according to the Dayton Accords, held the power to run Bosnia's electoral processes – "chose

[158] Ibid., p. 79.
[159] Ibid., p. 80.
[160] Ibid., p. 82.
[161] Quoted in ibid., p. 84.
[162] Ibid., p. 87.

the mayors itself and disregarded local election results to create multi-ethnic administrations with greater parity."[163] Such power-sharing solutions, imposed from above, "challenged the hold that the three leading national parties had over local government, but this was not a reflection of the wishes of the local communities or the voters in Bosnia as a whole, who gave overwhelming support to the leading national parties."[164] Despite all the shifting of electoral results in order to protect minority voices' power in the policy-making process, political power had "not been decentralized to give minority groups a stake in government but rather transferred to the international institutions responsible for democratization and recentralized in the hands of the...High Representative." This process fostered neither accountability to the voters nor autonomy for those elected.[165]

The international community's desire to promote multi-ethnic government fostered attempts to support multi-ethnic parties (although they had minimal public support), while challenging the nationalist parties' legitimacy and controlling the media in order to minimize displays of nationalist rhetoric. The OSCE and OHR cooperated closely on this front. Like UNTAC in advance of the Cambodian elections, the OSCE was tasked in part with creating a "politically neutral environment." To that end, the OSCE and OHR strove to "[restrict] the capacities of the nationalist parties to take advantage of their control over Bosnian institutions to influence the political climate," as UNTAC had unsuccessfully tried to do when faced with CPP control over Cambodia's state bureaucracy.[166] One manifestation of this policy was the OSCE's tendency to blame the nationalist parties for outbreaks of unrest inspired by the return of refugees and to remove candidates unilaterally from the nationalist parties' lists as the OSCE saw fit. Fifty candidates were removed in the run-up to municipal elections in 1997, although no direct relationship between the unrest and the political parties was established.[167]

Similar political interventions were repeated when, in 1998, national elections again brought to power the hard-line nationalist political parties, resulting in the High Representative's decision to remove the victor in the presidential race within the Serb entity, Nikola Poplasen. The Croat member of the tripartite Bosnian state presidency, Ante Jelavic, was likewise removed from his position in 2001 for fostering ethnic divisiveness

---

[163] Ibid., pp. 46, 88.
[164] Ibid., p. 125.
[165] Ibid., p. 89.
[166] Ibid., pp. 113–14.
[167] Ibid., p. 123.

and instability.[168] Among other things, Jelavic had led a rally calling for the creation of a new, ethnically exclusive, governing body for Bosnian Croats – a "Croat National Assembly." This was the last straw for the High Representative, who argued that Jelavic's actions and speeches were "sowing hate and fear" and undermining the Dayton Peace Accords.[169] Such moves may have prevented the further exacerbation of ethnic tensions, but leave unresolved the question of whether Bosnian politicians are primarily accountable to a domestic or a transnational constituency.

It is ironic that the very rules instituted to protect minority rights and ultimately promote (it was hoped) multi-ethnic parties instead reified ethnicity further. The electoral rules for the Bosnian tripartite presidency, for example, which divided the voting population into three ethnic groups, allowed each group to vote "only for the presidential seat that corresponded to their individual ethnic affiliation" rather than establishing a system whereby presidential candidates would have to appeal to citizens of multiple ethnic groups in order to win.[170] Such rules have undercut the incentives to create multi-ethnic political parties that could foster a more inclusive civic identity. As of 2006, there were no multi-ethnic parties in Bosnia. Although one nonnationalist party, the social-democratic SDP, does exist, its supporters are overwhelmingly Bosniak.[171] Such parties are disadvantaged by the Bosnian political system, which "primarily allocates elected offices on the basis of [ethnic] group membership," thereby effectively punishing nonnational parties.[172] The transnational effort to prevent ethnic exclusivity has instead enshrined it within the political system.[173]

---

[168] Paris, pp. 105–6.

[169] Wolfgang Petritsch, "Decision Removing Ante Jelavic from His Position as the Croat Member of the BiH Presidency," March 7, 2001, accessed October 18, 2007, at http://www.ohr.int/decisions/removalssdec/default.asp?content_id=328.

[170] Paris, pp. 192, 194.

[171] Florian Bieber, *Post-War Bosnia: Ethnicity, Inequality and Public Sector Governance* (New York: Palgrave Macmillan, 2006), p. 104.

[172] Ibid., p. 107.

[173] Ibid., p. 4. Various means can be found to promote multi-ethnic parties, including establishing electoral rules that mandate multi-ethnic party lists (alternating the positions on the list according to ethnicity, for example). Donald Horowitz suggests institutionalizing "cross-cutting cleavages" by use of electoral rules that reward parties that win votes from more than one ethnic group. Jack Snyder, however, argues that such techniques do not protect against nationalist violence in the absence of professionalized, ethnic-blind bureaucracies, judicial institutions to protect individual rights, and a media that will help to depoliticize ethnicity and build a statewide civic identity. See Donald Horowitz, "Ethnic Conflict Management for Policymakers," in Joseph Montville, ed., *Conflict and Peacemaking in Multiethnic Societies* (Lexington, MA: Lexington, 1990), pp. 115–30;

Accountability and the OHR

Transnational administration by the OHR has had a significant impact on accountability within the Bosnian political system. The OHR itself functions "without transparency and accountability towards the country's population (or political elite)."[174] This lack of accountability is exacerbated by the extent of the OHR's reach: "Equipped with both legislative and executive powers [after 1997], the High Representative (HR) has emerged as the most influential institution in Bosnia – and the only one not governed by power-sharing or democratic principles." These powers are extensive, and have been used in significant ways: to enact about one hundred laws, levy fines on political parties, ban particular politicians from official party service, and remove over 180 public servants from their positions, including the two aforementioned occupants of Bosnia's highest elected offices.[175]

Although the removal of extreme nationalist politicians could be construed as a positive use of administrative power, some scholars think that the presence of the High Representative gives nationalist politicians no incentive to try to negotiate compromises with their counterparts, in effect deleting the *raison d'etre* from the political process.[176] The removal of elected officials, however provocative their politics, "has disempowered the voters and reduced the importance of votes, possibly benefiting more nationalist forces." In other words, nationalist parties have no incentive to tone down their rhetoric. In fact, inflammatory rhetoric may well garner them protest votes against international intervention in Bosnian politics.[177]

All this is not to say that the solution to Bosnia's political morass is an end to transnational control in the electoral arena. Sociologist and Balkans expert Eric Gordy explains:

Independence from international oversight is a goal, but on the ground it is usually clear that the alternative to oversight right now is letting the country be controlled by fascists. On the other hand, OHR's role also encourages people to vote for the fascists, by letting them stand as a protest option without allowing them to pose

---

Jack Snyder, *From Voting to Violence: Democratization and Nationalist Conflict* (New York: W. W. Norton, 2000), pp. 331–2.

[174] Bieber, p. 146. Although Bosnians have occupied more of the staff positions within the OHR over time, "Key decision-making positions...remain with the international staff" (ibid., p. 84).

[175] Ibid., pp. 84–5.

[176] Ibid., p. 85.

[177] Ibid., p. 146.

any real danger since they can be removed if they actually try anything. It is a real dilemma, without any obvious solutions.[178]

Nor did Bosnia's political parties appear motivated to cooperate before the OHR's powers were increased in 1997, suggesting that removal of the OHR would not necessarily lead to a well-functioning multi-ethnic democracy.[179]

David Chandler's systematic critique of transnational control over "democratization" in Bosnia highlights the ironic effects of granting such extensive control over politics to transnational organizations at the expense of domestic political institutions. Given the OHR's powers, Bosnia's political process became the province of international actors, to the growing exclusion of domestic ones. This rendered the powers of elected officials in Bosnia merely formulaic, undermining the institutionalization of accountability between voters and elected politicians.[180] The definition of democracy was thereby turned on its head. Because the international community views Bosnians as incapable of ruling themselves without deteriorating anew into nationalist civil war, rule by international institutions is legitimated: "the implication of this approach is the end of formal democracy, of legitimacy through accountability to the electorate. Democracy is redefined as its opposite, adherence to outside standards not autonomy and accountability."[181]

The powers of the ongoing institution of the OHR have produced discomfort about accountability relationships within transnational institutions as well. In 2000, the PIC began transferring responsibility for Bosnia to the EU, itself under pressure to reform the way that Bosnia has been administered. Specifically, the Council of Europe objected to the extensive powers of the Office of the High Representative, "arguing in the Venice Commission report of March 2005 that the powers of the OHR were 'fundamentally incompatible with the democratic character of the state and the sovereignty' of Bosnia," and that the prolongation of such extensive powers could lead to a "dependency culture," putting Bosnia's political future at risk.[182] Indeed, even the first occupant of the High Representative's

---

[178] Eric Gordy, email communication with author, April 23, 2006.

[179] Bieber, p. 85.

[180] Bieber reaches similar conclusions. Ibid., pp. 4, 145.

[181] Chandler, *Bosnia*, p. 162. According to Gordy, renewed civil war in Bosnia is unlikely. The territory has been effectively redistributed on an ethnic basis, and interethnic tension is relatively low at the daily level. Although protests and provocations occur, they are largely spurred by the nationalist parties. Gordy, email communication, May 8, 2006.

[182] David Chandler, "Ten Years On: Who's Running Bosnia?" November 23, 2005, accessed November 21, 2007, at http://www.spiked-online.com/Articles/0000000CAE83.htm.

position in Bosnia, Carl Bildt, asserted in 2005 that it was "now high time to close down [the OHR] and hand full powers and full responsibilities to the elected representatives of Bosnia and Herzegovina."[183]

In February 2006, the High Representative in Bosnia, Christian Schwarz-Schilling, assumed the additional title of EU Special Representative (EUSR), passing both titles to his successor, Miroslav Lajcak, in July 2007. The office of the EU Special Representative was intended to lack the depth and breadth of the OHR's power.[184] In early 2007, the PIC announced that the OHR as an institution should "aim to close" at the end of June 2008, although the EU Special Representative office ("co-located with the OHR") would remain in place.[185] Despite EU anxieties about appearances, however, the fact of international control over Bosnia is not poised to change. Instead, Bosnia has nearly been subsumed by the EU:

The EU provides its government; the international High Representative is an EU employee and the EU's Special Representative in Bosnia. This EU administrator has the power to directly impose legislation and to dismiss elected government officials and civil servants. The EU also runs the police force, taking over from the United Nations at the end of 2002, and the military, taking over from NATO at the end of 2004. The EU also manages Bosnia's negotiations with the World Bank....However, the EU has distanced itself from any responsibility for the power it exercises over Bosnia; formally Bosnia is an independent state and member of the United Nations....[186]

This divorce between accountability and power leaves the Bosnian state in a problematic position, because state-building "can only be done in relationship to social demands and pressures."[187] The OHR or EU cannot be held accountable for the choices that it makes in Bosnia, at least not by Bosnian citizens. At the same time, Bosnian elected representatives' power is limited by transnationally run institutions such as the OHR and its designated successor, the EUSR. An accountability gap in Bosnia's

---

[183] Quoted in ibid.

[184] Edith M. Lederer, "Bosnia Administrator Calls for Normality," *Associated Press*, April 18, 2006, accessed April 20, 2006, at http://www.washingtonpost.com/wp-dyn/content/article/2006/04/18/AR2006041801475.html.

[185] OHR, "Introduction," February 28, 2007, accessed November 21, 2007, at http://www.ohr.int/ohr-info/gen-info/default.asp?content_id=38519.

[186] David Chandler, "How State-Building Weakens States," October 24, 2005, accessed November 21, 2007, at http://www.spiked-online.com/Articles/0000000CADDB.htm. Also see idem, ed., *Peace Without Politics?: Ten Years of State-Building in Bosnia* (New York: Routledge, 2005).

[187] Chandler, "How State-Building Weakens States."

political process thus persists, despite the intention of transnational political institutions to close it for good.

CONCLUSION: POLITICAL GLOBALIZATION AND ACCOUNTABILITY

In the years following World War II, a wave of decolonization began, accelerating in the 1960s, enabling dozens of postcolonial countries to hold elections. In many cases, the state leaders elected soon used their positions to amass power in their own hands, cutting their opposition out of a meaningful role in the political process. Given the worldwide political record, transnational forces can certainly not be blamed for the unaccountable political outcomes in Cambodia, Bosnia, and elsewhere. Indeed, Cambodia and Bosnia constitute hard cases, as evidenced by the fact that the UN (or the "international community" in the case of Bosnia's near protectorate) steps in so extensively only in dire circumstances. Still, these two cases leave us to ponder: How might transnational involvement in the state-building process undermine or facilitate the establishment of accountability between the new government and the population?

At a fundamental level, transnational operations such as those in Bosnia and Cambodia provide cause for optimism about intervention. After all, the argument runs, "even a low-grade, purely procedural democracy" is better than dictatorship, because it starts the ball rolling in the direction of continued improvement. Aiming too high during a transition from dictatorship may lead to backlash and the collapse of the entire process.[188] A similarly optimistic take on UN peacekeeping intervention in general finds that peacekeeping missions can have a positive effect on accountability in the long run, merely by virtue of the fact that they bring conflicts to an end, even if imperfectly.[189] From that perspective, the UN-brokered agreement in Cambodia and the OHR-run system in Bosnia, although they did not reflect the value of vertical accountability adequately, may have been the best way to end the bloodshed and initiate a democratic process.

Beyond that optimism, however, transnational political intervention can support undesirable and puzzling outcomes for accountability in various ways. "Temporary" state-building projects such as UNTAC's relatively short mission may fail to unseat the powerful, leaving an unaccountable

---

[188] Phillippe Schmitter, "The Ambiguous Virtues of Accountability," *Journal of Democracy*, Vol. 15, No. 4 (October 2004), p. 52.

[189] T. David Mason, *Caught in the Crossfire: Revolutions, Repression, and the Rational Peasant* (Lanham, MD: Rowman & Littlefield, 2004), pp. 279–82.

government behind. Yet prolonged international presence or control over a state's administration may paradoxically have the same "protective" effect (witness the ongoing popularity of nationalist parties in Bosnia) while undermining the local government's capacity to be accountable to the population.

One goal of such intervention is to jump-start an accountability relationship by holding "free and fair" elections. It is not unreasonable that transnational political institutions such as the UN, EU, and OSCE, composed of member states, would plan to repair broken political systems by creating new ones through elections – a process recognized worldwide (and observed in varying degrees of authenticity) as the means to constitute new governments. The Bosnian and Cambodian cases show, however, that elections may prolong or entrench the political problems that they had intended to solve, even when they take place in the context of extensive transnational control. It is thus worthwhile to explore the debate over the practice of transnational involvement in elections in some detail.

Promoting Accountability from Above

Elections, as the optimists point out, may be flawed, but their positive results outweigh the negative ones. Cambodian National Election Commission (NEC) vice-chair Kassie Neou, for instance, saw immediate and long-term benefits to Cambodia's elections in 1993 and 1998. Neou argued that Cambodia's 1993 election process constituted a "crucial learning process" that considerably strengthened civil society.[190] Over twenty thousand domestic election observers took part in the process, as did eighty thousand poll workers and countless NGO-based participants. The elections themselves served as a dramatic means of activating civil society. Thus, even if elections fail to generate accountable government, they may generate a citizenry increasingly dedicated to *living* under an accountable government. Cambodia's post-coup election in 1998 also placed Cambodia back into the circle of international aid recipients, even if it did little to diminish Hun Sen's power.[191]

Neou's assessment of Cambodia's 1998 election was not entirely rosy. The CPP's domination of the state – and of the NEC – meant that the NEC could not be completely independent and impartial, so the election results could not be taken as seriously. Moreover, elections alone do not solve the

[190] Neou, p. 163.
[191] Ibid., pp. 163–4.

"underlying political conflicts" and "can even make things worse."[192] Both the 1993 and 1998 elections created something for the parties to fight over, literally, especially given Cambodia's recent political history of war and violence (a history likely to be echoed in many countries where the transnational organization of elections is deemed necessary).

The initial elections that follow a conflict are a source of particular concern. Paradoxically, the attempt to create accountability by holding elections can delay the advent of an accountable system if those political organizations already in power become entrenched in their positions, as occurred in both Cambodia and Bosnia.[193] Transnational institutions overseeing elections should thus be cautious about legitimating preexisting power dynamics by way of elections.

Postconflict elections held too soon also run the risk of reifying ethnicity and entrenching nationalism rather than providing civic alternatives to them. The overwhelming victory by nationalist parties in Bosnia's elections "consolidated the outcome of the war and relegitimized the national parties" across the state, making it "a textbook example of the warnings against premature post-conflict elections noted in the literature."[194] Elections held too early can serve to entrench ethnic-nationalist positions, ending in violence. Arranging power-sharing systems of government (as was done in Bosnia) similarly reifies ethnicity and "runs the risk of unnecessarily politicizing and locking in inimical cultural distinctions," whereas organizing the political system to protect individual, civic rights (rather than group rights) instead would be a safer choice.[195]

How can the risks inherent in early elections be avoided? Although some scholars balk at the idea of prolonged transnational administration of a postconflict state, seeing in such missions the potential to undermine democratization, others draw the opposite conclusion. In his study of peacebuilding missions from 1989 to 1999, Roland Paris finds that international organizations (such as the UN, the OSCE, and others) need to stay longer in postconflict states, taking over state regulatory and administrative functions more extensively, so as to ensure the building of state institutions before introducing the frequently destabilizing processes of democratization (including elections) and economic liberalization (market reforms). This would include literally "staffing governmental institutions

---

[192] Ibid., p. 163.
[193] Massing, "In Failed States, Can Democracy Come Too Soon?"
[194] Bieber, p. 86. Bieber concluded in 2005 that ethnicity would "continue to dictate the political agenda throughout the country." Ibid., p. 151.
[195] Snyder, *From Voting to Violence*, p. 40.

with international personnel, and then gradually replacing these officials with adequately trained and politically nonpartisan locals....In circumstances where local judges are nonexistent, incompetent, corrupt, or lacking independence, courts should be operated by international jurists and lawyers while a new cadre of local judges is being trained."[196] Delaying political and economic contestation in the wake of violent civil conflict until the state is institutionalized enough to regulate the political and economic contention that is part and parcel of democracy and marketization may make sense as a way to avoid revitalizing the conditions that fed into civil war originally.

Paris labels his proposed peacebuilding strategy "institutionalization before liberalization," and envisions transnational involvement in the democratization process as going well beyond even that of the OHR in Bosnia.[197] The strategy requires the international community's promotion of "good" civil society and political parties (e.g., the kinds of groups that organize along crosscutting cleavages rather than along exclusivist lines) and delaying elections until such parties have won the favor of a majority of citizens. In accordance with this model, elections should also be delayed until the institutions that underlie the rule of law – such as courts, judges, and lawyers, functioning in an independent and neutral fashion – can be trained and established.[198] It is not clear whether a higher level of engagement would promote domestic accountability, as evidenced by Bosnia, where transnational democratization forces have been extensively involved in Bosnian political processes for over a decade. The intervention in Bosnia, however, was accompanied by early elections, which allowed antidemocratic, nationalist elements to become more entrenched, perhaps taking Bosnia out of the running as a test case for the "institutionalization before liberalization" strategy.[199]

Even if transnational political interventions on the scale of those in Bosnia and Cambodia are rare, the puzzling intersection between national elections and the international community is increasingly populated by

[196] Paris, p. 206.
[197] Ibid., p. 7. The six points of the strategy are as follows: delaying elections until moderate political parties can be created and supported; using electoral rules to advantage inclusive parties rather than exclusive ones; banning exclusivist civil society groups and promoting organizations that support crosscutting cleavages; intervening to limit "hate speech" in politics and the media; avoiding economic reforms that worsen societal divisions; and building "effective security institutions and a professional, neutral bureaucracy." Ibid., p. 188.
[198] Ibid., pp. 189–90.
[199] Ibid., p. 153.

election observers, monitors, and mediators from outside the state in question.[200] Does external participation in the election process promote its accountability?

There is a place for the international community in political elections – but the international community should occupy that space in an accountable way. Specifically, writes Robert Pastor, "[t]he international community can be helpful in mediating the rules of an election, provided it (1) is welcome, (2) understands the problems associated with each stage, and (3) is sensitive to the principal cleavages that divide a country."[201] Transnational participation in domestic electoral processes can contribute a "third dimension of accountability: enhancing vertical accountability by making sure elections are successful and strengthening the horizontal axis by calling encroaching institutions to account for their actions."[202] Yet transnational participation could in some cases have the unexpected effect of decreasing vertical accountability by legitimating a process or outcome that was not, in fact, "fairly" conducted or achieved.

Such legitimation occurs more frequently than one might expect. According to historian Mark Almond, who observed dozens of elections between 1990 and 2002, the election observation process is highly politicized, and approbation from international observers does not mean that elections were free and fair on the ground. Arguing that elections sanctioned by international observers such as the OSCE gain much for a country by conferring legitimacy on the government and opening doors for international aid and loans from multilaterals, Almond quips: "A popular mandate is good, but a majority among the observers is better." But international observers are no guarantee of an election's validity. Almond sarcastically muses that in 1996, the OSCE in Bosnia "enabled a full 107 per cent of the possible voting age population listed in the 1991 census to vote – as if no one had died of natural causes, let alone violent ones, since then."[203] When a transnational body endorses or legitimizes an illegitimate electoral process or outcome, the standard for political accountability to voters is lowered, undermining democracy.

The rising number of "home-grown" election monitoring groups springing up in the 1990s may provide a more useful means than the OSCE (with its accountability to the major powers rather than to local citizens)

[200] Pastor, "The Third Dimension of Accountability."
[201] Ibid., p. 132.
[202] Ibid., p. 124.
[203] Mark Almond, "How the West Helps the Vote-Riggers," *New Statesman* (March 11, 2002), pp. 29–30.

of helping to hold "fledgling" electoral governments accountable to their populations. Groups such as the National Movement for Free Elections in the Philippines (NAMFREL), having helped "launch democracy" at home, send their members abroad to help found similar grassroots election-monitoring groups in other states. The Fair Election Monitoring Alliance in Bangladesh, having been trained by NAMFREL representatives, brought its knowledge abroad, carrying out electoral monitoring and training in Kenya and Indonesia. The leader of Guyana's Electoral Assistance Bureau similarly traveled to the West Bank, Sri Lanka, and Cambodia, to help monitor elections and train local citizens as poll watchers. In numerous cases, the election observer groups remain in the wake of the election, "transforming themselves into good-government watchdog organizations."[204] By virtue of its local investment in the outcomes, a transnational grassroots force may be more capable of holding governments accountable than a transnational intergovernmental one.

Promoting Accountability from Below

At the very least, it seems that there are difficulties with "foreign inspired and organized" elections as a means to promote accountable government.[205] Although elections empower individuals to choose their government, they center on the apex of politics – the arena that is most likely to be contested by actors seeking to bolster their own power. While transnational organizations encourage accountability from above, what other roles might they play in laying the groundwork for accountable politics from below?

One area in which UNTAC succeeded in its attempt to construct a basis for accountability was civic education. This took the form of grassroots teaching of accountability practices, through the establishment of UNTAC's human rights office, Radio UNTAC, and, later, the UN Center for Human Rights. Down the line, perhaps the most effective way for transnational political institutions to build the foundation for accountable government is to support civil society initiatives from the grassroots, particularly in the field of human rights, along with human rights education to build a constituency for those ideas. In addition to (or perhaps in place of) elections, postconflict states need grassroots "coursework" on

---

204 Seth Mydans, "Nurturing Democracy from the Grass Roots," *New York Times*, June 13, 1999, p. 5.
205 Curtis, p. 154.

the politics of accountability, efforts "to teach the traumatized population how to organize for democracy and demand it for themselves."[206]

Although the extent of international involvement in Paris's "institutionalization before liberalization" scheme may be overly ambitious, directing resources to educate the population in the skills needed to hold governments accountable could be a practical supplement to transnational attempts to introduce accountability from above. Neou, reflecting on Cambodia's experience, believes that resources could have been well spent on thoroughgoing educational efforts to promote reconciliation between the parties.[207] He also noted that one byproduct of the 1993 election was the flourishing of local civil society, including election monitoring groups. An attempt to promote accountability from above had simultaneously promoted accountability from below.

If elections are no guarantee of accountable government, human rights education might be a means of adding to the *constituency* for accountability. This should, over time, have a transformative effect on politics. The international community does not always assert its power in support of such goals, however. An example comes from the multi-ethnic Bosnian town of Brcko. There, an international supervisor appointed members of the legislature until October 2004 when elections were introduced.[208] Despite this level of intervention, "the strongest votes still [went] to national parties."[209] Schools in Brcko were integrated (as of 2001, by the international supervisor's order), but "pupils still attend separate classes for language and 'national' subjects, such as history and culture."[210] The same is true in the rest of the country; according to a Bosnian journalist speaking at a conference in 2005, children "attend three different school systems, learn from three different sets of school books, and are taught three different versions of the 1992–95 conflict."[211] This suggests that even the international supervisor's office and OHR have not tried to depoliticize ethnicity and undermine nationalism from below through education, as Neou might recommend. Such efforts could be critical to reducing the apparent need for continued transnational supervision of and intervention in the Bosnian political system.

---

[206] Sam Diener, personal communication with author, July 17, 2006.
[207] Neou, p. 164.
[208] Bieber, pp. 135–6.
[209] Ibid., p. 137.
[210] Ibid., p. 141.
[211] Patrick Moore, "Bosnia-Herzegovina: What Future for Bosnia?" Radio Free Europe(RFE)/ Radio Liberty (RL), July 18, 2005, accessed August 3, 2006, at http://www.rferl.org/ featuresarticle/2005/07/601fffd2–75d7–4e00–9659–4c93defa6194.html.

Similarly, in Cambodia, Gottesman saw continued support for grassroots political organizing as an important aspect of international pressure for democratization:

Support for human rights organizations, women's rights organizations, the labor movement, environmental organizations – monetary support, training... but *engaged* support. Because everything is capable of going awry. You support some civil society organization and these organizations are quite capable of being corrupted like anything else. So you need constant, ongoing, engaged support to make sure that the support is accomplishing what you need it to accomplish.

Also, on the theory that decreasing poverty fosters an increase in middle class formation and hence in potential constituents' mobilizing for democratization, Gottesman favored direct humanitarian assistance as well: "to the education system, or the health system – everything that makes society less poor, less economically devastated, less devastated by HIV/ AIDS, is good in and of itself, and also indirectly good for steps toward democratization."[212]

In her book on peacekeeping and armed interventions, Kimberly Zisk concludes, "Nowhere have the liberal democratic military peacekeeping operations of the 1990s created liberal democratic societies. They did not even create much forward momentum in that direction in any of the countries where they were deployed."[213] Recognizing the unfortunate tendency of states in conflict to lapse back into conflict or to fail to develop stable and democratic systems of governance even after UN intervention, the UN inaugurated a new Peacebuilding Commission in June 2006, tasked with developing "integrated strategies for post-conflict recovery" and helping states "make the transition from war to lasting peace" by analyzing particular cases and coordinating the efforts of the many institutions and actors involved in peacebuilding.[214] This Commission may begin to address some of the accountability troubles entailed in UN-led election processes. Particularly if the Commission works with local civic groups to develop reconstruction plans (as is part of their mandate), it may become a useful transnational institution in the service of political accountability.

---

[212] Gottesman, phone interview, July 3, 2006.
[213] Kimberly Marten Zisk, *Enforcing the Peace: Learning from the Imperial Past* (New York: Columbia University Press, 2004), p. 13.
[214] See the UN Peacebuilding Commission: http://www.un.org/peace/peacebuilding/questions. htm.

This chapter has explored two approaches to accountability available to transnational political institutions. Introducing accountability from above has had mixed results at best. In Bosnia, international oversight and control over politics unintentionally helped entrench a politics of exclusivist nationalism and created an accountability gap – albeit with the laudable aim of eventually training politicians to become accountable to all Bosnia's citizens, not just the ones specific to a politician's ethnic community. So far, that tactic has not borne the desired fruit. In Cambodia, focusing on elections that ended with an unjust power-sharing agreement and the perpetuation of a single party's dominance did little to devolve political control from the ruling party's grasp. However, attention to human rights initiatives and promoting accountability from below has led to visible successes at Cambodia's political margins. In short, perhaps more than elections, human rights education gives people the skills both to fight intolerance and to help close the accountability gap that defines authoritarianism. Just as political accountability is horizontal and vertical, so must be the skills to establish it and keep it in place.

4

Army for Hire

Transnational Military Forces

In his essay "Politics as a Vocation," German sociologist Max Weber defined the state as "a human community that (successfully) claims the *monopoly of the legitimate use of physical force* within a given territory."[1] Central to a state's task, then, is controlling its territory, and promoting the impression that it is the only entity entitled to wield coercive power within its borders. But what happens when control over that territory is threatened? Under such circumstances, a state has several options. Often, these entail asking for help from other states, whether by calling on a powerful and well-armed ally or patron or by requesting assistance from a regional or transnational defensive body such as the United Nations. Alternatively, a state may choose to hire military forces from beyond its borders, voluntarily giving up its monopoly over the legitimate use of force, and extending that right to private individuals or corporations, known today as private military companies (PMCs).[2]

Several types of private military companies coexist in the modern world.[3] Some engage primarily in combat operations as a supplemental or substitute

---

[1] Max Weber, "Politics as a Vocation," in H. H. Gerth and C. Wright Mills, eds., *From Max Weber: Essays in Sociology* (New York: Oxford University Press, 1958), p. 78; emphasis in the original.

[2] P. W. Singer also notes that the Weberian definition of statehood is tested by the growth in the PMC industry, which "deprivileges" the state in the realm of security. P. W. Singer, *Corporate Warriors: The Rise of the Privatized Military Industry* (Ithaca: Cornell University Press, 2003), p. 18.

[3] Deborah Avant gives a short history of the acronyms used to describe such companies; David Shearer originated the widespread term "PMC." Avant uses private security company (PSC), and Singer uses privatized military firm (PMF). See Deborah D. Avant, *The Market for Force: The Consequences of Privatizing Security* (New York: Cambridge University Press, 2005), p. 1.

military force. These might operate against recalcitrant rebels, providing "better" or more high-tech weaponry than is available on the ground in the client state. Combat-oriented PMCs may also be hired to secure and protect mining or other valuable state-owned or commercial industries, and even by rebel groups in search of more effective military tactics.[4]

More common are noncombat PMCs hired to train other states' armed forces, or to provide "policing" and "security" services, although these latter functions can quickly shade over into combat. As is evident from the early twenty-first century war in Iraq, security provision often means engaging in combat with insurgents. The Blackwater PMC personnel hired by the U.S.-led Coalition Provisional Authority in Iraq, for example, "had their own helicopters and fought off insurgents in ways that were hard to distinguish from combat."[5] Noncombat PMCs also recruit and train staff for peacekeeping missions. Finally, PMCs frequently provide "operational support" for ever more technically complicated weapons systems, and logistical support (building military bases, doing laundry, and providing food) to a state's army in the field or at home.[6]

Private military companies serve a multiplicity of functions, giving rise to questions about their impact on accountability relationships in democratic and nondemocratic states alike. PMCs may stabilize or end a military conflict and raise the level of political accountability in a nondemocratic state by enabling elections to occur. Yet PMCs can also train corrupt military forces that attack civilians and government opponents, permitting an unaccountable political regime to remain in power. The availability of private military companies may lead politicians in nondemocratic states to avoid building accountable military institutions at home; it also enables those in democratic states to circumvent domestic political accountability mechanisms that are usually activated when a state's military forces are officially involved abroad. Accountability to local populations may also suffer when private military contractors are used abroad to supplement regular troops on military missions or as part of peacekeeping operations.

This chapter investigates several concrete situations in which accountability relationships changed as a result of the use of private and transnational sources of force. First, a case study from the embattled country of Sierra Leone illustrates the ambiguous impact of combat PMCs on political

---

[4] Singer, *Corporate Warriors*, p. 10.

[5] Avant, pp. 21–2; see also Jeremy Scahill, *Blackwater: The Rise of the World's Most Powerful Mercenary Army* (New York: Nation, 2007).

[6] Avant, pp. 19–20. For a useful classificatory scheme for private military companies (military provider firms, military consultant firms, and military support firms), see Singer, *Corporate Warriors*, pp. 88–100.

accountability in weak states. The chapter then explores the troubling accountability ramifications of U.S.-licensed, noncombat PMCs working for states abroad, sometimes upholding unaccountable governments, and evading accountability within the U.S. political process. Third, I describe how employing U.S.-based PMCs both in military operations and on peace-keeping missions has had negative implications for accountability to local populations. The use of U.S.-based PMCs in Iraq – particularly at Abu Ghraib – and as part of the peacekeeping mission in Bosnia has allowed contractors to violate human rights with impunity, even as it has spurred changes to U.S. legislation in an effort to increase contractor accountability to local citizens. Finally, I discuss the ways in which the United Nations has been challenged to address accountability issues in peacekeeping operations over the past fifteen years, exploring UN responses to allegations of sexual exploitation and abuse of women by peacekeepers from Cambodia to the Congo. The cases examined in this chapter thus illustrate the problematic relationship between transnational military forces and accountability. Although the use of transnational (and even private) military force can stabilize frail states, PMCs are more likely to undercut than to strengthen the ties of political accountability between citizens and their governments, and transnational military forces in general lack accountability to the populations with whom they interact.

TRANSNATIONAL COMBAT PMCS AT A GLANCE

Most often, military combat and training PMCs operate outside of their country of origin, sending their staff abroad on contracts. The use of foreign or private military forces has a long history, perhaps starting in the thirteenth century BCE, when Egyptian pharaoh Ramses II relied on foreign mercenaries in battle. In Europe, Persian kings hired Greek fighters in the fifth century BCE, first to help invade Greece and later to resist the attack by Alexander the Great. Centuries later, the use of mercenaries in Europe was widespread. By the end of the fourteenth century CE, the city-state of Venice, which had typically called upon local nobles for military service, was "hiring mercenary captains, *condottieri*, who recruited their own troops and fought the city-state's wars for a handsome price. Since a *condotta* was a contract to make war for a particular sovereign, *condottiere* meant, essentially, contractor."[7] The use of mercenaries became standard procedure in Europe from the fifteenth to seventeenth centuries; by the

---

[7] Charles Tilly, *Coercion, Capital, and European States, AD 990–1990* (Cambridge, MA: Basil Blackwell, 1990), p. 80.

1470s, the Swiss in particular had developed a reputation for supplying mercenaries to the European powers of the day. The mercenary system did not last, however, having invited its own troubles: "when pay came too slowly or not at all, mercenaries commonly mutinied, lived off the land, became bandits, or all three at once."[8] The modern version of the *condottiere* is the contractor working for a private military company.[9]

Relatively few PMCs claim to engage in combat directly, in effect fighting alongside or even replacing a state's own troops. In his exhaustive study of PMCs, *Corporate Warriors,* P. W. Singer lists only a handful of firms that rent forces to states for combat. Two of these, Executive Outcomes and Sandline, are "defunct."[10] Others include Strategic Consulting International (SCI), founded by Tim Spicer, previously Sandline's director, and NFD, an Executive Outcomes spin-off.[11] This relatively small category of PMCs has engaged in combat operations in numerous states, including Angola, Indonesia, Papua New Guinea, and Sierra Leone. Singer also includes in this category, alongside the combat PMCs, the U.S.-based corporation Airscan (because of its military reconnaissance capacity) and the Russian firm Sukhoi (which rented out fighter aircraft and pilots to Ethiopia).[12]

States hiring combat PMCs may have reason to do so. Governments using private contractors to provide security abroad or to train foreign military forces can avoid some of the political costs of incurring casualties among their own troops.[13] Utilizing a PMC in the short term may also be

---

[8] Ibid., pp. 80, 83.

[9] For a history of private military and mercenary activity, see Singer, *Corporate Warriors,* pp. 19–39.

[10] Avant, p. 17. Although EO closed its doors in 1999, its employees continued to operate through a variety of other corporations carrying out similar tasks. See Jakkie Cilliers and Richard Cornwell, "Africa – From the Privatisation of Security to the Privatisation of War?" in Jakkie Cilliers and Peggy Mason, eds., *Peace, Profit or Plunder: The Privatization of Security in War-Torn African Societies* (Institute for Security Studies, 1999), p. 239.

[11] Singer, *Corporate Warriors,* pp. 93, 105. SCI was renamed Trident Maritime and then merged with Hudson, forming Hudson Trident, and then spun off a new PMC, Aegis, which lists Hudson Trident and SCI as subdivisions; SCI is listed as the one that provides defense assistance. Nick van den Bergh, a former operations manager for EO, founded NFD in South Africa. See Khareen Pech, "Executive Outcomes: A Corporate Conquest," in Cilliers and Mason, eds., *Peace, Profit or Plunder,* p. 96. NFD may also have contracted with the Sudanese government to protect their oil fields. See http://www.focusweb.org/peace/html/.

[12] Singer, *Corporate Warriors,* p. 93. For a brief summary of the activities of various private military firms around the globe, ranging from participation in combat to logistical support, see ibid., pp. 9–17. Avant also provides an extensive list of private military companies organized by geographical base and types of services. See Avant, pp. 10–15.

[13] Herbert M. Howe, *Ambiguous Order: Military Forces in African States* (Boulder: Lynne Rienner, 2001), p. 193.

a relatively light burden on state coffers compared to funding an adequate army, because PMC troops arrive trained; the state, in effect, merely leases a PMC's equipment and only pays for its services when its troops are actually engaged, none of which is the case with a standing military. PMCs can also deploy "faster than multinational (and even some national) forces," and can take steps from which UN peacekeeping forces are typically forbidden or that they avoid because of the risk involved, namely, to "take sides, deploy overwhelming force, and fire 'preemptively' on [the] contractually designated enemy."[14]

Even if sensible on the surface, the use of combat PMCs by states presents a significant challenge to the state from a Weberian point of view. PMCs in this role perform what is typically designated as a central function of the state: protecting a territory and attempting to monopolize the use of legitimate force there. States thereby undermine their own function: "By agreeing to 'delegate' the maintenance of public order, a government endangers the very essence of public authority."[15] Yet public authority may be a secondary concern for state leaders when confronted with territorial breach, constricted access to natural resources and other sources of income, and imminent state collapse, all of which have occasioned the hiring of combat PMCs.

TRANSNATIONAL COMBAT PMCS AND
ACCOUNTABILITY IN SIERRA LEONE

Of the several types of PMCs, combat PMCs have generated the highest levels of scholarly and popular interest in the past decade. The best known of these in the 1990s was a South African firm, Executive Outcomes. In 1995, Executive Outcomes was hired by the government of Sierra Leone and won a stunning victory against a vicious rebel movement, the Revolutionary United Front (RUF). Sierra Leone's experience with Executive Outcomes is one of the clearest cases of a state's leadership turning to a combat PMC to supplant its own military. This case highlights the positive and negative changes in accountability relationships engendered by the use of combat PMCs. Does the use of private military companies help a weak state move toward democracy or does it reinforce the ruling regime's detachment from

---

[14] Ibid., p. 193; Elizabeth Rubin, "An Army of Their Own," *Harper's* (February 1997), p. 45, quoted in Howe, p. 192.

[15] Yves Sandoz, "Private Security and International Law," in Cilliers and Mason, eds., *Peace, Profit or Plunder*, p. 221.

society? What impact might borrowing a military force from abroad have on accountability at home?

The roots of the civil war that enveloped Sierra Leone from 1991 to 2001 included long-standing governmental corruption, the presence of plentiful diamonds, and the country's unfortunate proximity to Liberia's civil war. There, a rebel movement led by Charles Taylor sought to expand the zone of conflict and to profit by illegally exporting gems from Sierra Leone, Liberia's diamond-rich neighbor. Ten years of civil war, starting in March 1991, killed seventy-five thousand people in Sierra Leone and maimed many more. Sierra Leone's army (the SLA, also known as the Republic of Sierra Leone Armed Forces, or RSLAF), supplied with few resources, proved incapable of fighting RUF forces. By 1995, with rebels approaching the capital, Freetown, the state's control over its territory had evaporated. In this context, Sierra Leone's government hired Executive Outcomes. Understanding how the SLA had reached a state of disrepair meriting the hiring of outside forces requires a brief foray into Sierra Leone's political history.

Political Accountability and Civil War in Sierra Leone

A former center of the British slave trade, Sierra Leone won its independence from Britain in 1961. Three years later, the country's prime minister, Milton Margai, died and was succeeded by his brother Albert. Rich in diamonds but poor in political leadership, Sierra Leone's government was soon mired in corruption. Albert Margai became the first in a string of political leaders who regarded ruling the state as an opportunity for self-enrichment, not as a position from which to pursue the common good.[16] A patronage network spread, based on Margai's political network, the Sierra Leone People's Party (SLPP).

Elections held in 1967 generated a change in political leadership with the victory of Siaka Stevens and the All People's Congress (APC). A period of uncertainty ensued when Margai sponsored a coup, followed by a countercoup; Stevens was sworn in as president in 1968.[17] Upon taking power, Stevens' distrust of the regular army led him to rely instead on a patronage-based paramilitary force of his own creation, the Internal Security Unit (ISU), for his personal support.[18] Despite an existing (unarmed) police force

---

[16] John Hirsch, *Sierra Leone: Diamonds and the Struggle for Democracy* (Boulder: Lynne Rienner, 2001), p. 28.

[17] Ibid., p. 29.

[18] Lansana Gberie, *A Dirty War in West Africa: The RUF and the Destruction of Sierra Leone* (Bloomington: Indiana University Press, 2005), p. 29. This paramilitary force

in Sierra Leone, the ISU was granted police powers, and ISU officers were issued AK-47s, which they flaunted at "checkpoints" on Sierra Leone's road-ways in order to extort bribes from drivers.[19] The ISU, "accountable only to Siaka Stevens and the APC," was intended explicitly as a counterbalance to the state's military forces, which were "deliberately starved... of supplies. An under-equipped Army would be no match for the generous firepower of the ISU in case of any attempt by the soldiers to once again take over the running of the state."[20] Thus began the slighting of the SLA, a trend with disastrous consequences for the country over the following two decades.[21]

With the ISU "ruthless[ly] suppressing" his political opponents, Stevens consolidated power and in 1978 declared Sierra Leone a one-party state.[22] This single-party dictatorship presided over significant infrastructure development, using inflated contracts for patronage. Stevens' rule "destroyed and corrupted every institution of the state": the parliament was "gutted of significance"; the legal system devolved into a farce of bribery and intimidation; army "professionalism" declined; and opponents of the regime were forcibly suppressed.[23]

In 1985, Stevens retired, handing the presidency to Major General Joseph Momoh in a "staged election."[24] Momoh's APC continued to run the single-party regime, while reforms were delayed. Widely regarded as less charismatic and more inept than his predecessor, Momoh presided over an accelerating economic collapse. Corruption ran unchecked, and the government found itself bankrupt. Civil servants looted their offices, teachers went unpaid, the school system ground to a halt, and professionals fled into emigration.[25] Soon, Sierra Leone's economy, reliant on the export of agricultural and mineral raw materials (cocoa, coffee, palm oil, diamonds,

---

was unpopular with Freetown residents, who initially referred to the ISU as the "I Shoot You's." When the force's name was later changed to the Special Security Department (SSD), they were labeled "Siaka Stevens' Devils." See Stephen Riley, "Review: Sierra Leone Politics: Some Recent Assessments," *Africa: Journal of the International African Institute*, Vol. 52, No. 2 (1982), p. 109.

[19] Augustine Kposowa, "Erosion of the Rule of Law as a Contributing Factor in Civil Conflict: The Case of Sierra Leone," *Police Practice and Research*, Vol. 7, No. 1 (March 2006), p. 39.

[20] *The Final Report of the Truth & Reconciliation Commission of Sierra Leone (2002–2007)*, accessed March 9, 2007, at http://trcsierraleone.org/drwebsite/publish/v3a-c2.shtml?page=5.

[21] The ISU's formation, and the fact that it was "better armed than the regular army," left Sierra Leone's police force and the SLA "demoralized and alienated" (Kposowa, pp. 35, 40).

[22] *The Final Report of the Truth & Reconciliation Commission of Sierra Leone.*

[23] Hirsch, p. 29.

[24] William Reno, "Privatizing War in Sierra Leone," *Current History* (May 1997), p. 228.

[25] Hirsch, p. 30.

iron ore, bauxite, and rutile), neared a state of collapse. The oil crisis of the 1970s, followed by the accumulation of foreign debt, had led to the intensive participation of international financial institutions in Sierra Leone's economy. Starting in 1979, the World Bank and IMF engaged in "almost permanent participation" in Sierra Leone's economic planning. Structural Adjustment Programs were introduced, which devalued the local currency and eliminated subsidies on the most essential goods (fuel and the staple food, rice). Sierra Leone's political leaders exhibited only superficial compliance with the SAPs, hoping to avoid a popular reaction against their rule. The IMF suspended its programs and withdrew credit in 1988.[26] The state could no longer pay salaries, provide jobs, or supply basic welfare services such as health and education.

When rebel forces crossed the border from Liberia into Sierra Leone in March 1991, they found a population of rural, undereducated, unemployed youth from which to recruit.[27] The Revolutionary United Front's (RUF) incursion was led by Foday Sankoh, a former member of the Sierra Leone Army who had trained in Libya with Charles Taylor (the leader of Liberia's rebel movement). Momoh had arrested Sankoh in 1971. Twenty years later to the day, Sankoh led one hundred rebels into Sierra Leone to "open the country to multiparty elections." Sankoh's "anti-corruption" message was empty, however. The RUF proceeded to attack the rural population, lacking any evident ideological or programmatic agenda.[28]

The main cause of Sierra Leone's civil war lay just beneath the surface of the country's alluvial diamond fields. After independence, government ministers controlling mining and natural resources had profited enormously from bribes given by foreigners for mining contracts, as well as from their support of diamond smuggling (rather than taxing legally exported diamonds and generating revenue for the state).[29] By 1988, official diamond exports from Sierra Leone were worth only $22,000, while $250 million worth of diamonds were being smuggled out of the country.[30] A variety of West African states "laundered Sierra Leone's diamonds and sent them

---

[26] Max Sesay, "Security and State-Society Crises in Sierra Leone and Liberia," in Caroline Thomas and Peter Wilkin, eds., *Globalization, Human Security and the African Experience* (Boulder: Lynne Rienner), pp. 155–8.

[27] Hirsch, p. 30. By 1990, Sierra Leone's economy was at a standstill: "average annual growth in [GNP] per capita between 1965 and 1990 was 0%," and in the last few years preceding the invasion, the "average combined [primary and secondary] school enrollment" was a mere 34 percent. Kposowa, p. 42.

[28] Hirsch, p. 31.

[29] Ibid., p. 25.

[30] William Reno, *Warlord Politics in African States* (Boulder: Lynne Rienner), p. 120.

to the world's cutters and polishers, who claimed ignorance of their likely origins." Despite being devoid of diamond mines, Gambia, for instance, exported over $100 million in diamonds to Belgium between 1996 and 1999, "the height of RUF mining activity in Sierra Leone. Likewise, Liberia exported an annual average of six million carats to Belgium between 1994 and 1998, when its own modest mines were capable of producing a mere 200,000 carats annually."[31]

The SLA proved inadequate against the RUF.[32] Under Stevens, the army had become "largely ceremonial, completely unprofessional, and recruited from among the same alienated youths as the RUF," and was nearly useless as a counterforce to the rebels. Confronted by an invasion, the state's frantic attempts to reinvigorate the army amounted to recruiting criminals and street youths, sending them into the fray without military training, motivated by "daily ration[s] of marijuana and rum," while officers sold the army's rice rations instead of feeding the troops.[33] Soldiers were treated so poorly that when conscripted by the SLA, recruits often became "sobels" – soldiers by day and rebels by night – joining the rebel forces and engaging in illegal diamond mining.[34] Momoh had attempted to bolster the army in response to the RUF's attack, expanding its ranks from three thousand to fourteen thousand troops. But without the IMF and World Bank loans that had been withdrawn a few years earlier, Momoh could not afford to support his forces: "Soldiers went unpaid and commanders, many inherited from the Stevens era, 'led' from the rear, leaving young noncommissioned officers in charge of actual battle operations."[35]

In April 1992, junior officers in the SLA revolted against the government's failure to provide sufficient pay, food, and medical care for those wounded in fighting the RUF. Their rebellion brought down Momoh's regime, installing military rule.[36] Thus began the period of government by junta in Sierra Leone. The National Provisional Ruling Council (NPRC), under a twenty-six-year-old army officer, Valentine Strasser, promised an all-around improvement in living standards and an end to corruption and the RUF.[37] Such improvements would be impossible while the RUF held

---

[31] Greg Campbell, "Blood Diamonds," *Amnesty Now* (Fall 2002), pp. 4–7, p. 6.
[32] Kposowa (p. 46) sees the creation of the ISU and Stevens' concomitant disarmament of the SLA as the root cause of the SLA's ineffectiveness against RUF forces.
[33] Hirsch, p. 36; Singer, *Corporate Warriors*, p. 111.
[34] Hirsch, p. 32.
[35] Reno, "Privatizing War," p. 228.
[36] Hirsch, p. 32.
[37] Ibid., p. 37. In an interesting side note, Strasser reportedly undertook his coup against Momoh "after a rebel attack had disrupted his unit's illicit mining operation." Reno,

much of the diamond mining territory, and in January 1995 the RUF took control of Sierra Leone's aluminum and rutile mines as well. These losses were devastating for the state's already collapsed economy, depriving the leadership of its sources of foreign exchange.[38] Strasser's new government "could not finance an effective army, much less provide social services to the population from which soldiers were recruited."[39]

Enter Executive Outcomes

Under rebel pressure, the SLA rapidly became a force for looting rather than protecting civilians and the common good.[40] By April 1995, RUF forces, in addition to rampaging through the countryside and taking over the diamond fields, had come within twenty miles of Freetown. Recognizing the army's failure to stall the RUF's attacks, the NPRC under Strasser bought assistance from a combat PMC, Executive Outcomes (EO).

Who were these modern mercenaries? Executive Outcomes' troops were drawn from the former South African Defense Forces, some from assassination and torture squads whose job had been to hunt down anti-apartheid activists before the white South African regime fell in 1994.[41] Despite this unsavory background, EO claimed to accept contracts exclusively from "legitimate governments recognized by the United Nations or businesses incorporated on the stock exchange," and one of its directors cheerily labeled EO's employees as "privatized peacekeepers."[42] The Executive Outcomes forces arriving in Sierra Leone numbered roughly two hundred soldiers, with ten Afrikaner officers, and had at their disposal military equipment including MIG-23 fighter bomber aircraft and helicopter gunships.[43] It was no contest. Within two weeks, Executive Outcomes had restored the ruling government's security and reestablished control over the diamond mining areas within two months, inflicting serious damage on the rebel forces.[44]

Warlord Politics, p. 123. Not only was the army insufficiently recompensed for its efforts against the rebels, but its soldiers' moonlighting in the diamond fields was also disrupted by the war.

[38] Hirsch, p. 37.

[39] Reno, *Warlord Politics*, p. 126.

[40] Singer, *Corporate Warriors*, pp. 111–12.

[41] Hirsch, p. 38.

[42] Christopher Coker, "Outsourcing War," in Daphné Josselin and William Wallace, eds., *Non-State Actors in World Politics* (Basingstoke: Palgrave), pp. 189, 196.

[43] Ibid., p. 196; Hirsch, p. 39; Singer, *Corporate Warriors*, p. 113.

[44] Reno, *Warlord Politics*, p. 224.

Like the SLA, Executive Outcomes had no interest in fighting for free. The Strasser government's contract with EO "stipulated that EO would provide 150–200 soldiers (fully equipped with helicopter support) to support, train, and aid the [SLA] in their war against the RUF."[45] In exchange, EO would be paid $35 million. For the first eight months of EO's presence, however, the government paid nothing, and in total EO received only $15.7 million of the agreed-upon fee.[46] In reality, the means of compensating EO were more complex. Executive Outcomes was to be paid $1.8 million a month or to receive by some means the equivalent in profit sharing with Branch Energy Corporation, which had negotiated EO's contract with the government and had acquired diamond concessions in Sierra Leone.[47] For this payment method to be effective, EO would first find it necessary to secure the diamond mining sites. In the end, "Sierra Leone reportedly awarded significant mining concessions to the Branch Group when the government could not pay EO's monthly fee."[48]

Given the foreseeable disadvantages to mortgaging a state's national resources, the government's earlier decisions to cast its own military forces aside seem puzzling. From the perspective of the ruler in a one-party state, however, the decision is rational. Rulers "debilitate" their armed forces on purpose so that they can preserve their own political power and decrease the risk of a military coup.[49] Relying on a private army (foreign or domestic) appears safer than building up a state military force that could later be used against the ruling regime. Kings in early Europe similarly preferred foreign mercenaries to domestic forces, seeking "to limit the independent armed force at the disposition of townsmen, for the very good reason that townsmen were quite likely to use force in their own interest, including resistance to royal demands." Other armed persons similarly contributed to rulers' thinking on this topic, including "bandits (who were often

---

[45] Avant, p. 86.

[46] Howe, p. 206.

[47] Hirsch, pp. 38–9; Howe, p. 206. For the complex web of financial relationships between EO and Branch Energy, see Singer, *Corporate Warriors*, pp. 104–5.

[48] Howe, p. 205. After EO's departure in January 1997, the companies in control of mining operations then hired EO personnel to stay behind and provide security (through Lifeguard, a sister company to EO). See Singer, *Corporate Warriors*, p. 117.

[49] Howe, p. 23. In the late 1940s, Costa Rican president Jose Figueres abolished his country's military, not to preserve his power indefinitely, but to avoid military coups and more permanently demilitarize Costa Rican politics. See Eric Pace, "Jose Figueres Ferrer Is Dead at 83, Led Costa Ricans to Democracy," *New York Times*, June 9, 1990, accessed August 8, 2008, at http://query.nytimes.com/gst/fullpage.html?res=9C0CEFD81639F93A A35755C0A966958260.

demobilized soldiers, continuing their plunder without royal assent)."[50] The phenomenon of sobels in Sierra Leone's army in a centuries-later echo proves the point: A domestic army could not be trusted.

Even under Executive Outcomes' tutelage, the SLA's decline appeared irreversible. EO initially worked alongside the SLA and succeeded in pushing the rebels out of the Freetown area, but discovered upon moving their operations further east into the countryside (to retake the diamond mines in Kono district) that the SLA became exceedingly unreliable, fleeing from RUF attacks even when the RUF was considerably less prepared for a fight.[51] At that point, EO teamed up with local militias of Mende ethnicity, known as Kamajors (*Kamajoisia*, or "hunters" in the Mende language), training and equipping them and working together to retake the area from the RUF.[52]

Against this background, grassroots agitation for elections began within Sierra Leone's civil society.[53] But the political system was fragile. In January 1996, Strasser was ousted by other members of the NPRC junta. Replacing Strasser was Julius Maada Bio, who had been Strasser's liaison to EO, and whose military units had been trained by the PMC.[54] Once in charge, Bio persuaded Sankoh to start talking peace, promising the rebel leader some measure of political power in return.[55]

The RUF was undeterred by the promise of elections. In January 1996, a vicious RUF campaign ensued against the upcoming vote, scheduled for late February. The tactic employed was the deliberate amputation of civilians' hands and arms, among men, women, children, and the elderly. The symbolism was graphic and direct: lose an arm if you dare to vote.[56] Approximately twenty thousand people suffered the mutilating attacks of the RUF, losing arms, legs, lips, and ears to rebel machetes and axes.[57] Commenting on the war's enormous brutality, Sankoh remarked in a 1996 interview: "When two lions or elephants are fighting, who is going to suffer? The grass, of course. I cannot deny it."[58]

Despite the violence, Sierra Leone's first multiparty elections in decades were held in late February 1996, and in a second round in March, Ahmed

---

[50] Tilly, *Coercion, Capital, and European States*, p. 55.

[51] Avant, p. 87.

[52] Ibid., p. 88; Singer, *Corporate Warriors*, p. 113.

[53] Hirsch, p. 41.

[54] Reno, *Warlord Politics*, pp. 130–1.

[55] Hirsch, p. 43.

[56] Ibid., pp. 43, 45.

[57] Campbell, p. 5.

[58] Quoted in Somini Sengupta, "African Held for War Crimes Dies in Custody of a Tribunal," *New York Times*, July 31, 2003, p. A6.

Tejan Kabbah, a lawyer and United Nations Development Program (UNDP) administrator, was elected president. Power changed hands and attempts at a peace process began anew. In April 1996, Kabbah began meetings with Sankoh, whose main demand was that foreign armed forces – namely, Executive Outcomes – leave the country, given their military successes in collaboration with the Kamajors against the RUF. By fall 1996, the combined efforts of EO and the Kamajors had pushed Sankoh and the RUF into an unfavorable position; the Abidjan Accords were signed in November 1996, allowing for a ceasefire and broad-based amnesty.

Exit Executive Outcomes

Two months later, short on funding, Kabbah asked EO to cease its operations; its forces exited Sierra Leone at the end of January.[59] In the wake of EO's departure, the Kabbah regime found itself pressed from all sides. In early 1997, the IMF pushed Kabbah to cut rice rations to the army. Faced anew with state betrayal, junior army officers in the SLA carried out a coup against Kabbah in May, frustrated by the continued lack of attention to the army under civilian rule and by Kabbah's support of the Kamajors at the army's expense. Kabbah fled to Guinea as the plotters formed a new junta, the Armed Forces Revolutionary Council (AFRC), which proceeded to ally itself with its ostensible nemesis, the RUF.[60]

Although Kabbah returned to Sierra Leone in March 1998, he found himself secluded in his Freetown offices.[61] The RUF renewed its military campaign, terrorizing the countryside. Amputations increased, as the AFRC/RUF junta pursued those they suspected of supporting Kabbah, as well as "men of voting and fighting age." This continued after Kabbah's return to power, "reportedly to discourage citizens from giving political or military help to the restored government."[62] In January 1999, the armed RUF/AFRC coalition attacked Freetown and was turned back only after several days of amputations and destruction.[63]

In July 1999, the undefeated RUF acceded to peace accords signed in Lome, Togo. The accords made significant concessions to RUF interests. Foday Sankoh became chair of Sierra Leone's Strategic Resources

---

[59] Hirsch, pp. 40, 118.
[60] Ibid., pp. 57–8.
[61] Ibid., pp. 76–7.
[62] William Reno, "The Failure of Peacekeeping in Sierra Leone," *Current History* (May 2001), p. 220.
[63] Hirsch, p. 71.

Commission, placing him in charge of the state's diamond trade and thereby exponentially expanding his opportunities for bribery and smuggling. A no doubt delighted Sankoh announced that "[a]nyone wishing to mine diamonds had to go through his Commission to obtain a license – with any evaders being treated with 'the full consequences of the law.'"[64] The peace agreement also gave the RUF/AFRC four cabinet positions and four deputy minister positions, as well as a blanket amnesty and permission to become a political party.[65] Six months later, RUF control over the diamond fields continued and the rebels resisted disarmament.

The turning point came in May 2000, when the RUF kidnapped hundreds of United Nations peacekeepers present in Sierra Leone as per the Lome agreement. British troops then intervened in the ongoing civil conflict on the side of Kabbah's government, alongside the UN forces.[66] This intervention decisively tipped the balance, and by November 2000, the Sierra Leonean government and the RUF had signed a new ceasefire agreement, which led, this time, to the cessation of most of the fighting. Among the factors pressuring the RUF into signing were likely the work of the British forces; the government's acquisition of two helicopter gunships in April 1999, which helped identify the RUF bases; and the fact that the RUF was getting less money and fewer guns for their diamond smuggling because of an international corporate agreement not to sell "conflict" diamonds (this grossly limited the number of diamonds that could now successfully be smuggled into Liberia in exchange for RUF weapons).[67] In early May 2001, the RUF and the Kabbah government signed an agreement to end all hostilities, after which the UN peacekeeping forces set about disarming the RUF, a task declared accomplished on January 13, 2002.[68]

[64] "Diamonds: A Rebel's Best Friend," BBC News, May 15, 2000, accessed September 28, 2006, at http://news.bbc.co.uk/1/hi/world/africa/745194.stm.

[65] Hirsch, p. 82.

[66] Mark Doyle, "Bringing Justice to Sierra Leone," BBC News, January 17, 2002, accessed November 22, 2007, at http://news.bbc.co.uk/1/hi/world/africa/1765611.stm; Hirsch, p. 87.

[67] Sierra Leone Web, "News Archives: July 26, 2002," accessed September 28, 2006, at http://www.sierra-leone.org/slnews0702.html. The "conflict diamonds" agreement brought together diamond importers who pledged (under pressure from NGOs) to buy only diamonds state certified by the exporter, as a means to cut down on the smuggling of diamonds from war zones.

[68] "Last Sierra Leone Rebels Disarm," BBC News, January 13, 2002, accessed September 28, 2006, at http://news.bbc.co.uk/1/hi/world/africa/1757912.stm. Also reinforcing the peace in May 2001 were sanctions placed on Liberia for continuing to supply weapons to the RUF, as well as a ban on Liberia's export of rough diamonds (which were assumed to have been smuggled from Sierra Leone). In July 2002, the British forces that had intervened in May 2000 left Sierra Leone, leaving behind one hundred advisers to train the SLA. Sierra Leone Web, "News Archives: July 28, 2002," accessed September 28, 2006, at

Sierra Leone's ten-year civil war left economic wreckage in its wake. Of 173 countries ranked in 2002 on "human development," Sierra Leone occupied last place.[69] By contrast, the political aftermath of the civil war was encouraging. In May 2002, elections for president and parliament were held. People whose hands had been hacked off by rebels voted with their ink-stained big toes.[70] Kabbah was reelected as president with 70 percent of the vote.[71] Stressing the importance of maintaining the fragile peace, Kabbah asked crowds to forgive the former rebel fighters: "All ex-combatants who have come forward begging for forgiveness, ... let us receive them as brothers and sisters."[72] Simultaneously, a joint UN-Sierra Leone tribunal was established to prosecute those who bore the greatest responsibility for the war crimes in Sierra Leone after November 30, 1996, when the Abidjan accords were signed.[73] Nine years after Executive Outcomes appeared on

http://www.sierra-leone.org/slnews0702.html. The UN's peacekeeping mission in Sierra Leone (UNAMSIL) ended in December 2005, replaced by a UN peacebuilding mission, the UN Integrated Office for Sierra Leone, and an international military training group, led by the British, to train the local Sierra Leonean army. United Nations Department of Public Information, "Sierra Leone: Consolidating a Hard-Won Peace," 2005, accessed November 22, 2007, at http://www.un.org/events/tenstories/story.asp?storyID=1400; UNAMSIL, "United Nations Mission in Sierra Leone," accessed November 22, 2007, at http://www.un.org/Depts/dpko/unamsil/body_unamsil.htm.

[69] Sierra Leone Web, "News Archives, July 26, 2002." Indeed, a visiting journalist reported that Sierra Leonean villagers welcomed British military advisors in late 2001, lining up and singing, "Welcome British, welcome British." The population had tired of state corruption and an inept army. The journalist reported that in a poll, a majority of Freetown's residents said "they would welcome recolonisation," suggesting the deplorable conditions in place before the UN and British interventions a few years earlier. See Mark Doyle, "UK Backs Sierra Leone Border Force," BBC News, January 16, 2002, accessed February 10, 2006, at http://news.bbc.co.uk/1/hi/world/africa/1763030.stm.

[70] Norimitsu Onishi, "Where Battered People Find Wholeness in a Ballot," *New York Times*, May 15, 2002, p. A4; Matthew Tostevin, "Votes Cast in Sierra Leone," *Boston Globe*, May 15, 2002, p. A10.

[71] Reuters, "President of Sierra Leone Wins Re-Election by a Wide Margin," *New York Times*, May 20, 2002, p. A8.

[72] Norimitsu Onishi, "For Sierra Leone Ballot, Hope Trumps Despair," *New York Times*, May 13, 2002, p. 3. Sierra Leone survived its first postwar turnover of power in August 2007, when the SLPP lost to the APC in peaceful national elections; the APC won 59 seats in the 112-seat parliament, the SLPP won 43 seats, and a new party that split from the SLPP won 10. A presidential run-off election preceded by relatively minor clashes between the two main parties in September 2007 similarly ended with an APC victory. The losing SLPP candidate was Kabbah's former vice-president.

[73] Prosecutions are likely to be few. Foday Sankoh was intended to be the main defendant, but died while in the custody of the war crimes tribunal on July 29, 2003. Sengupta, "African Held for War Crimes Dies in Custody of a Tribunal." Charles Taylor, a former Liberian rebel turned president, living in Nigerian exile, was transferred to Sierra Leone in March 2006 and imprisoned at the Special Court for Sierra Leone on war crimes

the scene in Sierra Leone, significant steps had been taken toward establishing an accountable government, including two rounds of national elections and the start of local elections in 2004.[74] Can Executive Outcomes' intervention be credited with these improvements in political accountability?

Executive Outcomes and Accountability in Sierra Leone

According to political scientist Deborah Avant, state capacity can affect whether privatization increases or decreases a state's control of force. In weak states, the value added of a private security force may range from protecting the territory so that the state does not completely collapse, returning natural resources to state control, or defeating rebels in order to enable the state to "centraliz[e] power over coercion so as to perform a more state-like function – potentially laying the functional foundation for a rational legal authority claim" and a more accountable state thereby.[75] To what extent did Executive Outcomes serve these functions for the government of Sierra Leone?

Executive Outcomes indisputably achieved military successes against the rebels, helping to regain control over Freetown and the diamond fields and other mines that had been taken over by the RUF in early 1995.[76] Accountable government relies on resource control; states unable to access their resources cannot tax them and therefore cannot provide public goods.[77] Executive Outcomes' military victories against the RUF also provided sufficient stability for elections to be held in February and March 1996, bringing Kabbah to the presidency and renewing the flow of foreign aid.[78] They also prompted the RUF to sign the Abidjan Accords in November 1996. EO's efforts toward stabilization of the territory thus enabled elections to occur, bringing a modicum of political accountability to the population.

charges; his trial was later moved to the Hague and was plagued by delays (the trial resumed in January 2008). See Marlise Simons, "Trial of Liberia's Ex-Leader Languishes Amid Delays, Bureaucracy, and Costs," *New York Times*, August 27, 2007, p. A6. Three AFRC members were convicted in July 2007; two members of the CDF were convicted in October 2007; and the trial of three RUF leaders was ongoing in November 2007 (see http://www.sc-sl.org).

[74] Bureau of African Affairs, U.S. Department of State, "Background Note: Sierra Leone," October 2007, accessed November 24, 2007, at http://www.state.gov/r/pa/ei/bgn/5475.htm.

[75] Avant, p. 59.

[76] Reno, "Privatizing War," p. 228.

[77] Cilliers and Cornwell, p. 229.

[78] Reno, "Privatizing War," p. 229.

Yet direct evidence linking EO's presence in Sierra Leone to the initiation of the election process is ambiguous. Two of EO's top officials (Eebon Barlow and Lafras Luitingh) claimed that their contract with the Strasser government was contingent upon that government's initiation of a "democratization process." According to Barlow, "When Strasser started reneging, we threatened to withdraw. We insisted on a timetable for democracy – within one to one and a half years. We kept on pushing, pushing...ten months later the (election) occurred."[79] Yet a U.S. diplomat who had been based in Sierra Leone believed that EO's pressure for elections was inconsistent once the military operation in Sierra Leone actually began.[80] In any case, whatever pressure EO may have placed on the junta to hold elections was likely outweighed by grassroots pressure to do so.[81] By mid-1995, civil society, led by women's organizations, pressed the government to make good on its "half-hearted" commitment to elections and a return to civilian rule.[82]

Although EO can be credited with quelling the RUF sufficiently to be able to conduct the 1996 elections, laying the groundwork for a democratically elected and potentially accountable political leadership, the security that EO provided was short-lived, as was the elected government that held office for a little over a year. Although EO did serve an initially stabilizing function, it also contributed to the state's declining control over the military and to the government's loss of power several times during and following EO's mission.

Specifically, EO's decision to strengthen a paramilitary force, the Kamajors, would prove fateful for accountability relations in the longer term. As the strength and prestige of the Kamajors grew, the discouragement and frustration of the SLA increased, provoking the January 1996 coup. EO's intervention, combined with the arming of the Kamajors, had alarmed elements of the army, who "feared the CDF [Kamajors] would replace them. This encouraged some soldiers to collaborate more closely with the RUF."[83] After the elections, Sierra Leone's new president was unable or unwilling to address the concerns of the SLA, and, fearing a coup, "purged the army and cut its budget in half" in September 1996, again raising tensions between the Kamajors and SLA.[84]

---

[79] Quoted in Howe, p. 201.
[80] Ibid., p. 234, ft. 65.
[81] Avant, p. 88, ft. 39.
[82] Yasmin Jusu-Sheriff, "Sierra Leonean Women and the Peace Process," Conciliation Resources, September 2000, accessed September 20, 2006, at http://www.c-r.org/our-work/accord/sierra-leone/women-peace.php.
[83] Reno, "The Failure of Peacekeeping," p. 220.
[84] Avant, p. 89.

Following EO's withdrawal in January 1997, Kabbah's security strategy was to elevate the Kamajors further, making their nominal leader, Chief Hinga Norman (a retired army officer), his deputy defense minister and charging him with the formation of a new force, the CDF (Civil Defense Force), bringing together several different militias. This affront to the army, exacerbated by Norman's "public disrespect" for the SLA, provoked the May 1997 coup led by Major Johnny Paul Koroma: "The plotters justified their actions by referring to Kabbah's marginalization of the army."[85] After all, the government had "paid large sums to Executive Outcomes and other forces [the EO-assisted Kamajors], rather than improving and paying the army."[86] The chain of events beginning with EO's empowerment of the Kamajors had led to senior RUF figures merging with the SLA in a junta "government," which proceeded to terrorize the country further and prolonged the civil war.[87]

EO's record on promoting accountability in Sierra Leone is therefore mixed. Beyond the military destabilization aggravated by EO's support for the Kamajors, one must also question EO's contribution to political accountability. As a private military force, the company's central motivation was profit, not democracy, and its leadership was accountable to shareholders, not citizens. In general, such a company thrives on instability rather than seeking to promote stable and accountable government.[88] Finally, the payment arrangement between Sierra Leone's government and EO could contribute to accountability conflicts later on. Such deals mortgage state resources to foreigners under conditions advantageous to them, which may decrease state access to taxable resources (and the provision of public goods) in the future, thereby "potentially creating generations of debt burdens for the populace as a whole."[89]

COMBAT PMCS AND ACCOUNTABILITY

The best form of counterinsurgency is good government.

– Donald Snow[90]

State rulers opting to "bypass" national military institutions by using PMCs have undermined accountability relationships outside of Sierra Leone as

[85] Ibid., pp. 92–3.
[86] Howe, p. 236, ft. 106.
[87] Avant, p. 93.
[88] Reno, "Privatizing War," p. 230.
[89] Cilliers and Cornwell, p. 229; Singer, *Corporate Warriors*, p. 167.
[90] Quoted in Howe, p. 14.

well.[91] In January 1997, Sandline, a combat PMC closely affiliated with EO, contracted with the government of Papua New Guinea to defeat a long-standing rebel movement on the territory of Bougainville – the site of the country's main source of export income, an enormous copper mine. The revelation of this lucrative contract, which, at $36 million, amounted to 150 percent of the Papua New Guinea armed forces' annual budget, provoked an army rebellion, ultimately forcing the resignation of the civilian leadership. The contract had been approved by Papua New Guinea's executive branch, but parliament had not been informed and there was no public debate, signifying a breach in political accountability.[92]

For various reasons, the Papua New Guinea mission itself was left incomplete.[93] But even in the wake of Sandline's departure, the cost of the contract continued to eat into the funding for other government services, including the national military, which was still "so short of funds that it was having trouble feeding its troops." As in Sierra Leone, the choice to hire an outside force rather than building up state forces resulted in embitterment of the army, provoking a loss of control that the state had been seeking to avoid in the first place.[94]

Additional accountability issues are raised by the secrecy of combat PMCs' contracts and the impunity that they confer. PMCs including EO "have confidentiality clauses written into their contracts with both client governments and their hired forces."[95] In the Papua New Guinea case, the contract stated, "all Sandline personnel will be furnished with the necessary multiple entry visas without passport stamps and authorization to enter and leave the country free from hindrance at any time." In the event of human rights abuse, it would be impossible to hold Sandline's employees accountable.[96] Although EO was not found to be particularly problematic in terms of human rights abuses in Sierra Leone, civilian casualties did occur at the hands of EO personnel, and the NGO Human Rights Watch believed EO was responsible for numerous abuses during its Angolan operations.[97] In general, combat PMCs raise an accountability gap in the event of human rights abuses or the repression of civilians: "The UN special rapporteur on mercenaries asks, 'Who will be responsible for

[91] Ibid., p. 194.
[92] Singer, *Corporate Warriors*, pp. 192–5.
[93] For a fuller account, see ibid., pp. 195–6.
[94] Ibid., pp. 198–9.
[95] Pech, p. 98.
[96] Cited in Howe, p. 213.
[97] Ibid., p. 234, ft. 75.

any repressive excesses that the security companies may commit against the civilian population....Who will take responsibility for any violations of international humanitarian law and of human rights that they may commit?'"[98]

Accountability to the local population is not at the forefront of combat PMCs' concern. Instead, by contract, they are accountable to their employers, who may seek the perpetuation of their own rule above all else.[99] Even an abusive government with sufficient resources or funds could conceivably stay in power by hiring PMCs.[100] PMCs thus may not distinguish between the best interests of a state's population and the preservation of the power of its ruling elite. Because the international community of states tends to back the notion of state sovereignty, even when authoritarian governments hold power, PMCs can back nondemocratic leaders with impunity – and profit by so doing.[101]

This problem of "personal rule" is particularly acute in postcolonial sub-Saharan Africa, where the lines between civilian and military spheres are blurred and often broken, detracting from the strength and legitimacy of both. One substitute for what Herbert Howe describes as an appalling lack of "military professionalism" is the hiring of private security companies to enhance the security of a state or, more likely, of a regime.[102] Such privatization of force expanded dramatically in the wake of the Cold War. In 1997, ninety private armies were operating in Africa alone.[103]

Not only foreign but also local PMCs can enable governments to continue their unaccountable relationships to the population because local PMCs are similarly unaccountable to civilians in their "leadership, funding, composition and mission." They also receive government financing at the expense of other social priorities and of national militaries' material and moral support.[104] The "privatization" of national military forces by undemocratic rulers – whether by hiring private security forces or by "privatizing" elements of their national military forces (ensuring a force loyal to the ruler in power) – allows for unaccountable uses of the military. In the first case, the PMC is enabling the autocratic regime to maintain its power. In both cases, because the regime is undemocratic and the military privatized, the

---

[98] Ibid., p. 194.
[99] Ibid., pp. 19, 194.
[100] Ibid., p. 210.
[101] Cilliers and Cornwell, p. 230; also Sandoz, p. 221.
[102] Howe, p. 2. For a thorough discussion of the security dilemmas facing African states, and various options for addressing them, see Howe, *Ambiguous Order*.
[103] Reno, "Privatizing War," p. 230.
[104] Howe, pp. 224–5.

ruler will be able to make use of the military (and divert funds to it) in ways for which the ruler will not have to account to the population. Indeed, the "privatized" sections of a national military, paramilitary forces, presidential guards, and other kinds of "parallel" forces loyal to a particular ruler are likely to be "even less accountable than the national militaries." Unaccountable armed forces, driven by profit, "may well encourage human rights abuses and perhaps even the perpetuation of conflict."[105]

Not only might private military forces be less accountable than national militaries, but their use enables rulers to avoid political accountability to the population by changing the reciprocity relationship between rulers and citizens such that the former need not rely on the latter for support. Charles Tilly, examining the state-building process in Europe, found a significant relationship between war and popular pressure for political voice. As armies expanded, state rulers supported their military machines with large extractive bureaucracies, which themselves grew powerful enough to contain the military, while the population that staffed the military resisted and bargained with the state to meet nonmilitary needs. The state's functions acquired during wars continued and expanded afterward, while popular claims on the state increased as well.[106] This negotiation process resulted in large part from the fact that the state relied on its domestic population to serve the war machine.

In Sierra Leone, by contrast, the pursuit of war and the resources to pay for it did not correlate with an increasingly open political process.[107] Instead, the "option of incorporating foreign financiers and fighters into a new political alliance offered Sierra Leone's rulers…an alternative arrangement" that favors transnational political alliances based on commerce in natural resources at the expense of "liberal democracy."[108] Sierra Leone's leaders were free to rule without popular accountability, relying instead on foreign commercial ties and foreign military forces to protect their interests.[109] Given the availability of such foreign support, weak state rulers have even less reason to try and gain domestic support by appealing to the population with public goods or to a rising middle class with rule of law. Nor need they go to the trouble of building an institutionalized army loyal to any civilian commander rather than a personalized army loyal to the present occupant of the ruling office.

---

[105] Ibid., p. 13.
[106] Tilly, *Coercion, Capital, and European States*, p. 206.
[107] Reno, *Warlord Politics*, p. 140.
[108] Ibid., p. 140–1.
[109] Ibid., p. 219.

In short, writes Howe, combat PMCs "can perform a valuable service...if they help to stabilize relatively accountable governments, especially against such extreme violators of human rights as Sierra Leone's RUF."[110] They may also foster economic development by securing natural resources and can train local military forces to behave in ways more compatible with democratization (exhibiting loyalty to a state rather than to a particular government in power).[111] But combat PMCs can also be used by governments to evade accountability to the population and to national military forces, as well as to support a corrupt regime depriving the population of needed resources.

NONCOMBAT PMCS: FACILITATING THE EVASION OF ACCOUNTABILITY

Noncombat PMCs may similarly contribute to the erosion of accountability, both in the countries where they operate and in the states that license them. The process of exporting private security is handled differently by different states. The United States and Great Britain are the two most significant democracies exporting military training and services.[112] I focus here on U.S.-based noncombat PMCs because the process by which their services are licensed is considerably more formal than the process in Great Britain, and thus would appear more likely to preserve both state and PMC accountability.[113] Even so, licensing noncombat PMCs for work in nondemocratic states abroad can result not only in support for repressive regimes but can also be detrimental to accountability within the U.S. political process.

Various U.S. companies, such as DynCorp and Vinnell, function as noncombat PMCs. The largest of these is Military Professional Resources International (MPRI).[114] Typically, noncombat PMCs are tasked with training or developing other states' military or police forces and, depending on the contract, are paid for their services either by U.S. tax dollars or by the state in which the training or work takes place. In either case, the contracts require approval from the U.S. State Department. MPRI's work in Croatia and Equatorial Guinea highlights the risks of using U.S.-based PMCs in support of authoritarian regimes.

[110] Howe, p. 225.
[111] Ibid., p. 226.
[112] Avant, p. 145.
[113] Ibid., p. 170.
[114] See MPRI's website, accessed November 24, 2007, at http://www.mpri.com/channels/home.html.

Noncombat PMCs Supporting Authoritarian Governments: MPRI in Croatia and Equatorial Guinea

In 1994, in the midst of the violent breakup of the former Yugoslavia, the government of the newly independent Croatian state, seeking to improve its military capacity, signed a contract with MPRI. At the time that the U.S.-based PMC was hired to educate and train Croatia's military forces, Croatia was embroiled in the war in Bosnia (early 1992 through mid-1995), chafing under both a UN-sponsored ceasefire in its own civil war against Serbs in the Krajina region of Croatia and a UN embargo on arms and military training.[115] In September 1994, two contracts between the Croatian government and MPRI, licensed by the U.S. State Department, were signed. One concerned the restructuring of Croatia's defense department; the second was designed to facilitate Croatia's democratic transition by retraining and democratizing the army as a step toward preparing Croatia for entry into NATO's Partnership for Peace program. During the period of training, alleged by MPRI to be unrelated to battlefield activities, the Croatian army managed to conduct two intensive military operations. The second of these, Operation Storm, culminated in the expulsion of Serb forces from Krajina, using "a series of lightning quick movements" reminiscent of NATO operations.[116] The retaking of Krajina was followed by the largest ethnic cleansing campaign of the war in Yugoslavia up until that time. MPRI denied participation in the planning or execution of Operation Storm and "expressed regret" about the ethnic cleansing, but did not cease its training operations.[117] Lieutenant General Harry E. Soyster, spokesperson for MPRI, claimed that "No MPRI employee played a role in planning, monitoring or assisting in Operation Storm," but acknowledged that some of the Croatians who took part in the operation had graduated from MPRI's training course.[118]

The ramifications for accountability in this case are several. First, by signing the contracts, MPRI lent international legitimacy to (and may have thereby helped to maintain in office) the right-wing nationalist Croatian government intent on expelling Serbs from its territory. Second, despite a Croatian law requiring the support of both the government and parliament for international agreements, MPRI's contract was not shared with

---

[115] Avant, p. 101; Singer, *Corporate Warriors*, p. 125.
[116] Avant, pp. 102–3.
[117] Ibid., p. 106.
[118] Leslie Wayne, "America's For-Profit Secret Army," *New York Times*, October 13, 2002, Section 3, p. 10.

parliament, and was categorized as "intellectual services" rather than as defense-related.[119] Political control over the use of force thus shifted away from the hypothetically more accountable parliament to the relatively insulated executive branch controlled by Franjo Tudjman's extreme nationalist party. Avant notes the ironic fact that MPRI was trying to teach the Croatian military about the importance of accountability and transparency while itself operating in Croatia under neither condition.[120] Later criticism of the contracts by "Croatian military experts" focused on the fact that Croatia had purchased MPRI's training program without any competitive bids, and that "the private alternative allowed the US to influence events in Croatia on Croatia's dime."[121]

Due to its work in Croatia, MPRI has the dubious distinction of being the only PMC that had (as of 2002) been "mentioned in a war crimes tribunal."[122] The Croatian commanders of the Operation Storm offensive – whether or not they were trained or assisted by MPRI – were indicted by the International War Crimes Tribunal for the many human rights violations accompanying those operations.[123] The MPRI training may have led indirectly to violations of human rights. The contract did not facilitate accountable behavior either on the battlefield or within the political system.

Another example of support for an authoritarian regime by a U.S.-based noncombat PMC arose when MPRI sought to gain a license to "evaluate Equatorial Guinea's defense department and need for a coastguard in 1998."[124] The probable reason for such a force was protection of the "oil-rich waters being explored by Exxon Mobil off the coast."[125] The State Department initially rejected MPRI's request on the basis of Equatorial Guinea's "poor human rights record."[126] MPRI's employees then paid visits to relevant U.S. government officials, asserting that it would be better for MPRI to "engage" with such a country and attempt to improve its human rights record than to deny the contract and allow another company the opportunity to forge ties with Equatorial Guinea (and its oil resources). Two years later, the U.S. government granted MPRI's request.[127] In so doing, it had given its seal of approval for military support of a country

[119] Avant, p. 106.
[120] Ibid., pp. 110–11.
[121] Ibid., p. 109, ft. 148.
[122] Singer, *Corporate Warriors*, p. 122.
[123] Ibid., p. 126.
[124] Avant, p. 154.
[125] Wayne, p. 11.
[126] Avant, p. 154.
[127] Ibid., p. 155.

whose human rights record was abysmal. In 2000, Equatorial Guinea was "one of the most tightly closed and repressive societies still remaining after the end of the Cold War,...a strict military dictatorship," whose leadership presided over a polity where a "gathering of ten or more people...is considered illegal and citizens have been jailed and tortured for violations as minimal as possessing photocopies of foreign news paper articles."[128] Even the State Department, which eventually approved the MPRI contract, had characterized Equatorial Guinea's president since 1979, Teodoro Obiang Nguema Mbasogo, as retaining power by means of "torture, fraud, and a 98 percent election mandate."[129]

A variety of noncombat PMCs back the regimes of U.S. allies with authoritarian political systems, including Saudi Arabia and Kuwait. A roughly fourteen-hundred-person force working for Vinnell Corporation "trains and advises the Saudi National Guard, which functions like a praetorian guard to the regime, protecting important strategic sites." Other PMCs train and advise the Saudi army and air force, provide personal security for the royal family, and train locals in urban warfare.[130] There may be as many as forty thousand employees of private American military companies in Saudi Arabia, "equipping, training, and managing virtually all branches of the Saudi Arabian armed forces."[131] Many such military skills are transferable and could easily be used against a domestic opposition.

When U.S.-licensed PMCs offer support to authoritarian regimes, the PMCs in question are in effect legitimating and strengthening those regimes against potential opposition, obstructing the development of political accountability. However, in such cases, the licensing of PMCs affects accountability not only in the recipient states, but also can detract from political accountability in the United States.

PMCs and the Degeneration of Accountability in the U.S. Political Process

The licensing of noncombat PMCs' contracts enables the U.S. government to pursue military options abroad, even when the use of national military

---

[128] Singer, *Corporate Warriors*, p. 132.
[129] Wayne, p. 11.
[130] Singer, *Corporate Warriors*, p. 13.
[131] Jonathon Wells, Jack Meyers, Maggie Mulvihill, "U.S. Ties to Saudi Elite May Be Hurting War on Terrorism: Businesses Weave Tangled Web with Saudis," *Boston Herald*, December 10, 2001, p. 6.

forces is "prohibited."[132] MPRI's training contract in Croatia constitutes one such example, because Croatia was under a UN embargo on training. Similarly, in 1996, MPRI received a license from the State Department to train the Sri Lankan army's special forces, although the U.S. military was at the time forbidden from providing such assistance due to the Sri Lankan army's dismal record on human rights (Sri Lanka's government "backed out of the negotiations for causes unknown" and the contract was never signed).[133] The use of PMCs allows for the pursuit of foreign policy below the accountability radar of the U.S. political process. In several cases, such as Croatia, the use of MPRI enabled U.S. foreign policy to be carried out when U.S. troops were not allowed to participate, and did so in a way that evaded the "public oversight or debate" that would have accompanied such moves if they had taken place through a public process.[134]

The use of U.S.-based PMCs to support counterinsurgency efforts in Colombia presents a similar case. Because of the egregious human rights records of some of the units of the Colombian armed forces, U.S. troops can – in theory – work only with units "proven free of human rights violators," and even then can only assist in counterdrug operations, but not counterinsurgency (despite the porous line between the two, because the insurgents engage in narcotics trade).[135] The U.S.-based PMC DynCorp has been central to the prosecution of the antidrug program "Plan Colombia," and provides a variety of services, from training pilots and police working in drug crop eradication to "aerial reconnaissance and combat advisory roles for the Colombian military" and possibly even combat roles fighting Revolutionary Armed Forces of Colombia (FARC) rebels.[136] As a PMC, DynCorp is not "bound by the same rules" as U.S. troops would be, and apparently, in February 2001, DynCorp flew helicopter gunships and sent in ground troops to rescue the personnel on a Colombian military

---

[132] Singer, *Corporate Warriors*, p. 119.

[133] Ibid., pp. 130–1.

[134] Ibid., p. 133.

[135] Ibid., p. 207. Despite U.S. legislation passed in 1997, the ban on cooperation was not upheld, and U.S. military aid continued to flow to rights-violating Columbian military units. See Human Rights Watch, "The 'Sixth Division': Military-Paramilitary Ties and U.S. Policy in Colombia," 2001, accessed November 1, 2007, at http://www.hrw.org/reports/2001/colombia/1.htm.

[136] Singer, *Corporate Warriors*, p. 208. "In Colombia, a US company flies the planes destroying the coca plantations and the helicopter gunships protecting them, in what some would characterize as a small undeclared war." Ian Traynor, "The Privatisation of War," *Guardian*, December 10, 2003, accessed on February 9, 2006, at www.guardian.co.uk/print/0,3858,4815701–103681,00.html.

helicopter attacked by rebels. Remarked one congressional staff person, "This is what we call outsourcing a war."[137]

Such contracts can create an accountability gap within the U.S. political system. The U.S. State Department is not required to notify Congress of a PMC contract unless the contract is for $50 million or more.[138] Thus DynCorp's involvement in the war in Colombia "has been entirely without Congressional notification, oversight, or approval."[139] Army Colonel Bruce Grant summed up the problem: "Consequently, a private firm can train another nation's army without congressional notification, much less congressional approval. Thus, significant foreign policy actions related to foreign security assistance do not receive the benefit of the checks and balances system inherent in our system of government."[140] Singer concurs that using PMCs in this way "may permit operations to occur that maybe should not. If an operation cannot deploy without privatized assistance because it lacks both public and congressional support for the proper troop numbers, then perhaps the original rationale deserves further debate."[141]

Vinnell Corporation's contract with Saudi Arabia in 1975 (to train Saudi forces to protect local oil fields) represented the first time a U.S.-based PMC sold military training directly to a foreign government. Since that time, the industry has expanded enormously, with noncombat PMCs providing roughly the same range of services to the U.S. and foreign governments.[142] Under ITAR (International Transfer of Arms Regulations, which comes under the Arms Export Control Act), PMC contracts are licensed by the Department of State's Office of Defense Trade Controls, which solicits opinions from various State Department offices relevant to each contract.[143]

Beyond its licensing requirements, the military export process appears to be light on accountability relations. Once licensing has taken place, ITAR requires "no formal reporting or oversight process...by which to insure that what was licensed was really what was delivered," although the State Department can "freeze contracts" in the event of "egregious acts" undertaken by a country with such a contract. Yet "those nominally responsible for overseeing the behavior of [PMCs] in the State Department

[137] Singer, *Corporate Warriors*, p. 208.
[138] Lora Lumpe, "U.S. Foreign Military Training," *Foreign Policy in Focus Special Report* (May 2002), pp. 12–13.
[139] Singer, *Corporate Warriors*, p. 209.
[140] Ibid., p. 210.
[141] Ibid., p. 213.
[142] Avant, p. 148.
[143] See ibid., pp. 149–50, for a more thorough explanation of the licensing process.

often do not see themselves as overseers."[144] Following an incident where employees of the U.S.-based PMC AirScan organized deadly air strikes in Colombia against civilians, a State Department official said, "Our job is to protect Americans, not investigate Americans."[145]

By involving Congress only when contracts exceed $50 million worth of services, the regulation of private military exports privileges the executive branch. Congressional scrutiny is easily evaded:

The first Vinnell contract with Saudi Arabia was for over $50 million, required congressional notification, and generated a lot of controversy. Since that time contracts have often been written for less than $50 million. There is nothing to prevent a company from selling several separate contracts for services to avoid the $50 million bar.[146]

Nor is the State Department required to publish a list of which PMCs have received authorization (export licenses) to provide military/security training, and where such training will be provided. When a foreign country purchases training, there is no requirement to investigate the recipient's human rights record; this is necessary only when the program is paid for by U.S. taxes.[147]

The accountability gap is illuminated by contrasting the degree of oversight for PMC missions with that for official military engagement (whether in the form of direct combat or training). When a democratic state's foreign policy entails the use of a national military abroad, that policy is subject to the scrutiny of multiple branches of government. By contrast, PMCs "allow leaders to short-circuit democracy by turning over important foreign policy tasks to outside, unaccountable companies" in order to avoid the involvement of branches of government beyond the executive – which licenses PMCs in a "process outside public view."[148] Similarly problematic is the fact that "the State Department office [that licenses PMC contracts] cannot provide information on [PMC] contracts to the public, due to the claimed need to protect proprietary information." Neither must private military companies respond to questions from the press or from Congress, although the Defense Department is "required by law" to do so when U.S. military power is applied abroad.[149] As Ken Silverstein observes, "By adding a new layer of secre[cy] and

[144] Ibid., p. 151.
[145] Quoted in Singer, *Corporate Warriors*, p. 239.
[146] Avant, p. 151.
[147] Lumpe, p. 13.
[148] Singer, *Corporate Warriors*, p. 214.
[149] Ibid. p. 214.

unaccountability, the use of private contractors offers the government even greater opportunities to conduct covert foreign policy."[150] In short, executive branch control over licensing and the contracting out of security functions is destructive of accountability because it distances the public further from critical decision-making opportunities.[151] This sort of "accountability once removed" – especially regarding the use of force – is problematic for a democratic polity.

The executive branch also uses PMCs to sidestep restrictions on the use of U.S. military forces. On many occasions "when Congress institutes stipulations on the numbers of U.S. troops, the executive has used contractors to go above this number."[152] In Bosnia, for instance, two thousand contractors were used in order to circumvent the congressionally imposed limit of twenty thousand troops.[153]

Similarly, when PMCs sell their training programs directly to foreign governments (rather than working abroad on contract to the U.S. government), it "opens the way for an even greater role for the executive branch relative to Congress and even less transparency over foreign policy." It was thus only a limited number of people in the executive branch who licensed MPRI to train the Croatian army while the embargo was in place and the United States could not technically get involved.[154] By contrast, using U.S. troops to provide security or training abroad would involve more government decision makers than does using PMCs:

> The use of [PMCs] is often regarded as a lower political commitment that reduces the need to mobilize public support for foreign engagement activities. Indeed, congressional leaders and the public appear to be less aware, interested, and concerned about sending [PMCs] than US forces. The use of [PMCs] to conduct foreign military training makes decisions to use this kind of force abroad less visible and less transparent. It thus enhances the authority of individual decision makers in the executive branch and reduces the processes of inter-agency cooperation and institutional wrangling.[155]

Avant suggests that using PMCs can also enable a "more adventurous [foreign] policy than would otherwise be the case," because decreasing "the process of political mobilization required for action opens the way for

---

[150] Ken Silverstein, "Mercenary, Inc.?" *Washington Business Forward*, April 26, 2001, quoted in Singer, *Corporate Warriors*, p. 214.
[151] Singer, *Corporate Warriors*, p. 215.
[152] Avant, p. 128.
[153] Wayne, p. 10.
[154] Avant, p. 129.
[155] Ibid., p. 133.

leaders to take action more readily."[156] The more closed political process also gives PMCs an informational advantage: "[PMCs] can report information that encourages training programs that are not worth their cost, [PMCs] can encourage relationships with governments that do not support US interests, can encourage investment in areas that do not serve US interests, etc."[157] The danger to horizontal accountability inherent in leaving Congress out of the decision-making process is evident.

Another fundamental accountability problem surfaces when PMCs are used, given that their employees are accountable to the company (whose leadership decides whether to reward or fire them) and not to government officials or the public, and because the firms are fundamentally motivated by profit.[158] Although retired army Lieutenant General Harry E. Soyster of MPRI maintains that profits would not lead MPRI to work against U.S. government interests, he acknowledged the power of the profit motive: "We go someplace because we are either sent there by the U.S. government or we're contracted by another government. We do it for the money, I'm not ashamed to say. But we do it right."[159] MPRI has profited handsomely in recent years. The stock of L3 Communications (which owns MPRI) has doubled in price since September 11, 2001, given the increased demand for its services abroad.[160] However, the profit motive provokes PMCs to staff their missions inexpensively when they can; DynCorp, for example, was alleged to have hired "waitresses, security guards, cooks, and cashiers" to maintain U.S. combat aircraft, with disastrous results.[161] The profit motive can also lead to fraud. As a logistical contractor for the war in Iraq, Halliburton allegedly defrauded the U.S. government on multiple accounts, from overcharging for fuel brought in from Kuwait and billing the army "for three times as many meals as it actually served to U.S. troops at several of its dining halls," to being "unable to account" for billions of dollars in reconstruction funds, "renting luxury vehicles," and purchasing monogrammed towels.[162]

---

[156] Ibid., p. 135.

[157] Ibid., p. 135.

[158] Singer, *Corporate Warriors*, pp. 154–5.

[159] Esther Schrader, "U.S. Companies Hired to Train Foreign Armies," *Los Angeles Times*, April 14, 2002, p. A1, accessed August 24, 2006, at http://www.globalpolicy.org/security/peacekpg/training/pmc.htm.

[160] Ibid.

[161] Singer, *Corporate Warriors*, p. 156.

[162] William D. Hartung, "Soldiers vs. Contractors: Emerging Budget Reality?" World Policy Institute, February 10, 2006, accessed on March 10, 2006, at http://www.worldpolicy.org/projects/arms/reports/soldiers.html. For more on misuse of reconstruction funds by contractors in Iraq, see Committee on Government Reform (Minority Office), "Iraq

Occasionally, governments hire private military contractors to supplement or substitute for their own military forces in armed conflicts or as part of peacekeeping missions abroad. The next section explores the ramifications for accountability in two cases where U.S.-based PMCs were hired by the U.S. government: to provide various types of security and logistical support during the war in Iraq starting in 2003, and to comprise a peacekeeping contingent in the Balkans following the 1995 Dayton Peace Accords.

NONCOMBAT PMCS: ACCOUNTABILITY AND THE PRIVATIZATION OF SECURITY AND PEACEKEEPING

The use of noncombat PMCs in war zones and in "recent war zones" as peacekeepers raises accountability issues beyond those that arise when U.S.-based PMCs train the military forces of foreign governments or when such PMCs are hired by foreign governments directly. The use of U.S.-based noncombat PMCs in Iraq and Bosnia has highlighted in particular the potential lack of PMC accountability to local populations in the event of human rights abuses.

Private Military Companies in Iraq

The influx of private contractors providing security in Iraq raised the salience of private military companies for American audiences. Grisly descriptions of Blackwater security workers killed in a March 2004 grenade attack, their burned corpses hung from a bridge and otherwise publicly mocked, brought to national attention the question of civilian deaths in a military operation – when the civilians in question were not locals, but seemed more or less indistinguishable from the U.S. soldiers operating in Iraq.[163] Such contractors constitute the second largest "contributor" to the so-called Coalition of the Willing, leading P. W. Singer to quip that a more apt moniker might be the "Coalition of the Billing."[164] Upwards of twenty

---

Reconstruction: All Investigations," accessed November 23, 2007, at http://web.archive.org/web/20060210170146/http://www.democrats.reform.house.gov/investigations.asp?Issue=Iraq+Reconstruction. Also see T. Christian Miller, *Blood Money: Wasted Billions, Lost Lives, and Corporate Greed in Iraq* (Boston: Little, Brown, 2006) on the waste and abuse of reconstruction funds in Iraq.

[163] CNN, "U.S. Expects More Attacks in Iraq," May 6, 2004, accessed November 23, 2007, at http://www.cnn.com/2004/WORLD/meast/03/31/iraq.main/.

[164] Cited in Tim Rogers, "Private Military Firms Find Golden Goose," *Z Magazine*, Vol. 18, No. 3 (March 2005), accessed November 27, 2007, at http://zmagsite.zmag.org/Mar2005/rogerspro305.html.

thousand people employed by at least sixty private security companies were operating in Iraq in 2004, hired to carry out a broad spectrum of jobs from providing security for journalists and oil fields to training the Iraqi police and army.[165] DynCorp held the contract to train the Iraqi police force, and Vinnell won a $48 million one-year contract to train nine thousand men for the post-Baathist Iraqi army.[166] By the end of 2006, some estimated that there were one hundred thousand employees of private military companies operating in Iraq – a number roughly equivalent to that of U.S. soldiers in the field.[167] Even before the most recent war in Iraq, the private military industry was growing: "Between 1994 and 2002 US-based [PMCs] received more than 3,000 contracts worth over $300 billion from the US Department of Defense."[168]

The widespread use of private contractors raises a range of account-ability issues. Some politicians in the United States, for instance, have questioned whether contractors in Iraq have been used so extensively as a means of minimizing body counts and limiting public objection to the con-tinuing war. Said Representative Janice Schakowsky (D-Illinois), "We talk a lot in Congress about how many U.S. troops are there and for how long, but not at all about the contractors....They don't have to follow the same chain of command, the military code of conduct may or may not apply, the accountability is absent and the transparency is absent – but the money keeps flowing."[169]

If the Blackwater incident led Americans to wonder about the extent of the use of private security contractors in Iraq, the revelations of torture used during interrogations at the Abu Ghraib prison in Iraq in 2003 raised a different question: How might private security contractors accompany-ing U.S. forces on military missions such as the Iraq war be held account-able when abuses occur?

Contractors figured prominently in the Abu Ghraib scandal.[170] The February 2004 Taguba report investigating the allegations of torture

---

[165] Avant, p. 2.
[166] Ibid., p. 8, ft. 20, p. 124.
[167] Jeremy Scahill, "Bush's Shadow Army," *The Nation*, April 2, 2007, accessed March 21, 2007, at http://www.thenation.com/doc/20070402/scahill.
[168] Avant, p. 8.
[169] Dan Baum, "Nation Builders for Hire," *New York Times Magazine*, June 22, 2003, p. 36.
[170] On contractor involvement at Abu Ghraib, see Joel Brinkley and James Glanz, "Contrac-tors in Sensitive Roles, Unchecked," *New York Times*, May 7, 2004, p. A12; Seymour M. Hersh, "Torture at Abu Ghraib," *New Yorker*, May 10, 2004, accessed on February 3, 2006, at http://www.newyorker.com/printables/fact/040510fa_fact; James Risen, "Command Errors Aided Iraq Abuse, Army Has Found," *New York Times*, May 3, 2004, pp. A1, A11.

and abuse of detainees at Abu Ghraib prison found that military intelligence officers and "interrogation specialists" hired by private contractors "actively requested that MP [military police] guards set physical and mental conditions for favorable interrogation of witnesses" (in other words – that the prison guards "break the will" of detainees in advance of interrogations).[171] Specifically, Taguba fingered Steven Stefanowicz and John Israel, both private contractors working for CACI International, as well as Lieutenant Colonel Steven Jordan, who had headed the Joint Interrogation and Debriefing Center, and Colonel Thomas Pappas, commander of a military intelligence brigade.[172]

Stefanowicz, a former Navy reserve intelligence specialist who was directly implicated in the actions of several U.S. soldiers later indicted for their behavior at Abu Ghraib, was hired through CACI to work as an interrogator at Abu Ghraib. The defense at both Sergeant Michael Smith's and Corporal Charles A. Graner's courts-martial presented testimony arguing that Stefanowicz "directed" the various abuses, from using unmuzzled dogs to petrify prisoners to imposing sleep deprivation and sexual humiliation. The Taguba and Fay reports (both investigations by the U.S. army) pointed to Stefanowicz as "a perpetrator of abuse"; the Fay report in August 2004 suggested that several CACI and Titan employees, including Stefanowicz, be prosecuted by the U.S. Department of Justice. By March 2006, the Justice Department had not brought charges, nor would it comment on its lack of action against what Susan Burke, a lawyer prosecuting a civil case against Stefanowicz, called "corporate torturers."[173]

Despite the army's recommending "immediate disciplinary action" for four contractors, as of May 2004 CACI denied receiving any "formal communication" to that effect from the army, and none of the four contractors noted in the Taguba report on Abu Ghraib faced criminal charges.[174]

---

[171] Quoted in Hersh, "Torture at Abu Ghraib."

[172] Hersh, "Torture at Abu Ghraib." Other accounts state that John Israel worked for a subcontractor to Titan, not for CACI. See Leon Worden, "Iraqis Sue SCV Translator," The-Signal.com, accessed November 23, 2007, at http://www.scvhistory.com/scvhistory/signal/iraq/sg061004a.htm. Jordan was eventually acquitted on the charges of responsibility for the maltreatment of detainees; he was convicted only of violating an order not to discuss Abu Ghraib and was reprimanded. See Paul von Zielbauer, "Marines' Trials in Iraq Killings Are Withering," *New York Times*, August 30, 2007, pp. A1, A10.

[173] Mark Benjamin and Michael Scherer, "'Big Steve' and Abu Ghraib," Salon.com, March 31, 2006, accessed March 31, 2006, at http://www.salon.com/news/feature/2006/03/31/big_steve/print.html.

[174] Hersh, "Torture at Abu Ghraib"; Taguba Report/Hearing Article 15–6 Investigation of the 800th Military Police Brigade, accessed November 23, 2007, at http://www.globalsecurity.org/intell/library/reports/2004/800-mp-bde.htm.

Allowing private contractors in effect to control military guards had led to abuses and to a failure to hold the civilian perpetrators accountable for their actions.[175]

The private civilian contractors implicated in the Abu Ghraib violations were not prosecuted for their abuses because of an accountability loophole in U.S. law at the time. In 2000, Congress had passed the Military Extraterritorial Jurisdiction Act (MEJA), a law intended to hold contractors accountable in U.S. courts in the event of their allegedly committing felonies while under contract to the Department of Defense (DOD). The rationale for Congress adopting MEJA in 2000 was to prevent military contractors and other civilians serving with the U.S. military abroad from being able to avoid accountability for crimes committed while overseas.[176] So far, MEJA has not served this purpose effectively.

Holding Contractors Accountable Abroad: MEJA

MEJA constituted an attempt to resolve the confusion over accountability for contractors' actions while in the field. Although official state military forces are not known worldwide for their stellar treatment of civilians, provisions for prosecution exist when members of the U.S. armed services commit crimes. The actions of private contractors, by contrast, were not governed by the Uniform Code of Military Justice (UCMJ) unless the United States had officially declared war.[177] Until MEJA was passed, contractors could be prosecuted only under the legal system of the host country whose laws were violated. "However, in situations where the local government is not functioning effectively, this may lead to less than satisfactory outcomes," and was rarely encountered as an option.[178] In its initial form, MEJA closed the

---

[175] As of October 2005, new rules were put in place by the Pentagon, designed in part to prevent incidents like Abu Ghraib. "The new rules mandate background checks and permission from the military before a contractor can carry a weapon." However, the rules apply only to new contracts; the Pentagon would have to "reopen" extant contracts in order to carry out the regulations fully. P. W. Singer, cited in Tony Capaccio, "U.S. Military Tightens Rules for Contractors in Combat Zones," Bloomberg.com, October 27, 2005.

[176] Lance Cpl. Lukas J. Blom, "U.S. Criminal Justice System Travels Overseas," Marine Corps Air Station Iwakuni, Japan, April 22, 2005, accessed February 9, 2006 at: www.usmc.mil/marinelink/mcn2000.nsf/0/1A9407432D9D802D85256FE900247928?opendocument.

[177] P. W. Singer, "The Law Catches Up to Private Militaries, Embeds," DefenseTech.org, January 3, 2007, accessed March 7, 2007, at http://www.defensetech.org/archives/003123.html.

[178] Avant, p. 234. The contractor "escape route" may have been eliminated in 2007, when the Department of Defense's budget legislation (H.R. 5122) altered a phrase of the

contractor loophole only for PMCs working for the Defense Department. In 2004, MEJA was amended, extending its coverage to all U.S. government contractors working toward Defense Department missions abroad, a status sometimes phrased as contracts "with a nexus to the Department of Defense."[179] These amendments meant that not only would employees of any DOD contractor (or subcontractor) be subject to the provisions of MEJA, but so would "Civilian employees, contractors (including subcontractor(s) at any tier), and civilian employees of a contractor (or subcontractor(s) at any tier) of any other Federal Agency, or any provisional authority, to the extent such employment relates to supporting the mission of the Department of Defense overseas," effectively extending MEJA to all contractors operating abroad in the context of military missions.[180] As of the end of 2006, MEJA had only been used once – to "prosecute a woman who killed her servicemember husband" on a U.S. military base in Turkey.[181]

The civilian contractors at Abu Ghraib could not technically be held liable under MEJA, because in 2003 the Act allowed for the prosecution only of those contractors hired through the Department of Defense, whereas the CACI and Titan contractors had been hired by the Central Intelligence Agency (CIA) and Department of the Interior.[182] Although MEJA in its amended form would have covered the Abu Ghraib contractors, it could not be applied retroactively to prosecute them. Nor could the Abu Ghraib contractors be prosecuted under the PATRIOT Act, a little-known section of which "covers crimes committed by U.S. citizens at military facilities abroad," because Abu Ghraib was not a military facility.[183]

UCMJ, potentially bringing contractors under the UCMJ's jurisdiction. Previously, the UCMJ had applied to contractors only if the United States had declared war; the adjusted phrase (in Paragraph (10) of section 802(a) of title 10, United States Code (article 2(a) of the Uniform Code of Military Justice) now reads "declared war or a contingency operation." See Singer, "The Law Catches Up To Private Militaries, Embeds."

[179] Avant, p. 234, ft. 55. The Abu Ghraib incident was followed by a criminal investigation under MEJA by the Justice Department. Ibid., p. 234. No contractors were indicted under MEJA, however; the Justice Department found it did not have jurisdiction because the contractors were not DOD contractors. Martina Vandenberg, attorney, phone conversation with author, July 28, 2006.

[180] U.S. Department of Defense, Instruction Number 5525.11, March 3, 2005, accessed February 3, 2006, at http://www.ipoaonline.org/uploads/05–03–03%20MEJA%20Instructions%2015525l%201x=DoD.pdf. In March 2005, the Department of Defense issued an "instruction" implementing MEJA's new amendments (the Military Extraterritorial Jurisdiction Act of 2000, as amended by Section 1088 of the Ronald W. Reagan National Defense Authorization Act for Fiscal Year 2005).

[181] Vandenberg, phone conversation with author, July 28, 2006.

[182] Vandenberg, phone conversation with author, September 10, 2005.

[183] Benjamin and Scherer, "'Big Steve' and Abu Ghraib."

Absent the opportunity for a criminal lawsuit against the contractors, in June 2004 the New York–based Center for Constitutional Rights (CCR) teamed up with a Philadelphia law firm to file a class action (civil) law suit in federal court on behalf of those tortured and abused in the Abu Ghraib prison. The suit charged Titan Corporation and CACI International with violation of the Racketeer Influenced and Corrupt Organizations (RICO) Act, contending that these companies "engaged in a wide range of heinous and illegal acts in order to demonstrate their abilities to obtain intelligence from detainees, and thereby obtain more contracts from the government." The suit also entails claims under the Alien Tort Claims Act, among other U.S. and international laws, and was filed in U.S. District Court in San Diego.[184] Under pressure from the lawsuit, CACI announced it would no longer retain staff in Iraq once its DOD contract expired in September 2005.[185] On September 12, 2005, CCR submitted an amended class action complaint against CACI and Titan.[186] In November 2007, U.S. District Court Judge James Robertson dismissed the case against Titan, but ordered a jury trial against CACI.[187] As the lawsuit moves forward, according to Robertson, "the next step must be to determine whether the defendants' employees "'were essentially acting as soldiers.'"[188] This is one of several lawsuits that may have decisive ramifications for the accountability of the private military industry in the United States.

National military forces are not immune from violating local citizens' human rights, and are perhaps only marginally more accountable than their private and transnational military counterparts. The NGO Human

---

[184] Center for Constitutional Rights, "CCR Files Lawsuit Against Private Contractors for Torture Conspiracy," Press Release, June 9, 2004, accessed November 23, 2007, at http://ccrjustice.org/newsroom/press-releases/ccr-files-lawsuit-against-private-contractors-torture-conspiracy.

[185] Center for Constitutional Rights, "The Center for Constitutional Rights Credits Pressure from Advocacy Group and Public with CACI International Withdrawal from Iraq," accessed November 23, 2007, at http://web.archive.org/web/20051130080938/http://www.ccr-ny.org/v2/reports/report.asp?ObjID=5Ar4fA7mMX&Content=633.

[186] *Saleh v. Titan Corporation*, Third Amended Class Action Complaint, accessed November 23, 2007, at http://ccrjustice.org/files/Saleh_3rdamendedcomplaint.pdf. CACI and Titan filed a motion to dismiss the case in April 2006, which was denied in June 2006. Jennifer Green, staff attorney at the Center for Constitutional Rights, phone interview by author, March 31, 2006; see also http://www.burkepyle.com/saleh.html.

[187] Center for Constitutional Rights, "Saleh v. Titan: Timeline," accessed November 23, 2007, at http://ccrjustice.org/ourcases/current-cases/saleh-v.-titan.

[188] James Robertson (United States District Judge), "Saleh, et al., Plaintiffs, v. Titan Corporation, et al., Defendants," Memorandum Order, United States District Court for the District of Columbia, June 29, 2006, accessed March 21, 2007, at http://www.burkepyle.com/Saleh/June-29-2006-order-on-motion-to-dismiss.pdf.

Rights First, analyzing thirty-four cases where Iraqi detainees died as a result of torture, found that in only twelve of those instances was anyone punished, and in almost half of the ninety-eight detainee deaths since 2002, "the cause of death was never announced or was reported as undetermined," creating a vacuum of responsibility within the U.S. military. A dramatic example is provided by the case of an Iraqi general who died in detention in 2003 after a U.S. army interrogator "covered him in a sleeping bag, sat on his chest and put his hand over his mouth." Although the interrogator was initially charged with murder and convicted of negligent homicide, he received a mere reprimand and no jail time.[189]

Accountability is often limited by the way in which national military forces handle abuses carried out by their troops. The U.S. military's response to the Abu Ghraib abuses has been to prosecute low-ranking soldiers, leaving higher-ranking officers (not to mention civilian officials such as Donald Rumsfeld, who was secretary of defense at the time that the abuses occurred) largely untouched. One reason for the short chain of prosecution is the lack of a "district attorney's office" within the military judicial system that could pursue cases: "There is no central prosecution office run by commanders. So you don't have a D.A. thinking, 'I'm going to follow this wherever it leads'."[190] Military judges did not permit Lynndie England and Charles Graner, famously convicted in 2005 of abusing inmates at Abu Ghraib, to bring in Defense Secretary Rumsfeld or Lieutenant General Ricardo Sanchez, the former top U.S. commander in Iraq, to testify.

In total, between October 2001 and March 2006, over six hundred "accusations of detainee abuse in Iraq and Afghanistan...had been investigated," resulting in the punishment of 251 U.S. officers and enlisted soldiers. An army captain convicted in March 2005 of kicking detainees and "staging the mock execution of a prisoner" was the highest-ranking officer sentenced, receiving forty-five days in jail and a $12,000 fine.[191] A dog-handler, Sergeant Michael J. Smith, convicted in March 2006 of detainee abuse, received a sentence of 179 days, far from the maximum sentence of eight and a half years. He was demoted, fined, and would be discharged from the army upon completion of his jail term. "Several generals and colonels have received career-ending reprimands and have

---

[189] Associated Press, "Abusive G.I.'s Not Pursued, Survey Finds," *New York Times*, February 23, 2006, p. A8.
[190] Quoted in Eric Schmitt, "Iraq Abuse Trial Is Again Limited to Lower Ranks," *New York Times*, March 23, 2006, pp. A1, A20.
[191] Ibid., p. A20.

been stripped of their commands, but there is no indication that other senior-level officers and civilian officials will ever be held accountable for the detainee abuses that took place in Iraq and Afghanistan," because Congress has made no serious effort to hold such officials accountable.[192] The highest-ranking military officer to be punished was Brigadier General Janis Karpinski, the former commander of Abu Ghraib, who was demoted and relieved of her job as a result of the scandal.[193] However insufficient the accountability process has been within the U.S. military, that process has been successfully used to call at least some soldiers to account for their actions under the Uniform Code of Military Justice. By contrast, contractors working with PMCs and subject to MEJA have thus far escaped prosecution.

The use of PMCs as accompaniment to military forces raises broad human rights accountability issues. In 2006, already some years beyond the Abu Ghraib scandal, Amnesty International issued a report lambasting U.S. use of military contractors in Iraq for security, intelligence, and detention. Labeling the use of contractors as "war outsourcing," Amnesty USA's executive director expressed concern that such use of military contractors was "creating the corporate equivalent of Guantanamo Bay – a virtual rules-free zone in which perpetrators are not likely to be held accountable for breaking the law."[194] Although the expansion of MEJA technically enables the U.S. Department of Justice to hold contractors accountable for crimes, Amnesty International contends that MEJA has not solved the problem, because contractors are "exempt from Iraqi law per a Coalition Provisional Authority order and they fall outside the military chain of command."[195] Private military contracts themselves fail to consider any accountability relationship between the contractors and the local population, including the obligation to observe human rights. A study published by the *Yale Journal of International Law* analyzed sixty such contracts in use during the Iraq war, finding that "none contains specific provisions

[192] Ibid, p. A20.
[193] As of May 2006, U.S. government sources claimed that 103 U.S. service members and intelligence officers had been court-martialed for detainee abuse since 2001, resulting in 19 convictions entailing jail terms of at least a year. See Tom Wright, "U.S. Defends Itself on Inmate Abuse," *New York Times*, May 9, 2006, p. A11.
[194] Alan Cowell, "Rights Group Criticizes U.S. over 'Outsourcing' in Iraq," *New York Times*, May 24, 2006, p. A12.
[195] Amnesty International, "Governments Worldwide Attack Human Rights in the Name of Fighting Terror with Deadly Consequences, Amnesty International to Assert During 2006 Annual Report Release," May 23, 2006, accessed November 23, 2007, at http://www.amnestyusa.org/annualreport/.

requiring contractors to obey human rights, anticorruption or transparency norms."[196]

The prospect of holding contractors accountable in Iraq is complicated by private security companies that hire personnel from outside the United States, particularly from "militaries known for human rights abuses or paramilitaries with ties to narcotrafficking." Blackwater, one of the PMCs operating in Iraq, hired "a group of soldiers who once served for Chilean dictator Augusto Pinochet," and Halliburton employs former soldiers from Colombia to guard Iraqi oil sites.[197] A subcontractor for Erinys, a British security company hired by the Coalition Provisional Authority in 2003, apparently hired as guards four former members of the apartheid-era South African security forces, one of whom had "admitted to crimes in an amnesty application to the Truth and Reconciliation Commission there" (this was discovered upon the guards' deaths in January 2004).[198] The founder of Southern Cross Security company (a former employee of Executive Outcomes) suggested in 2004 that the United States was moving toward hiring PMCs along the "cowboy" model – those perceived as being "less accountable" and more willing to apply "dirty tricks."[199] In May 2004, the Coalition Provisional Authority hired a UK-based security firm called Aegis Defense Services (run by the former chief of Sandline, Tim Spicer) to field armed bodyguards for some of its employees, and to coordinate the activities of the thousands of private contractors working in Iraq, rather than hiring DynCorp, which "protested" the contract to no avail.[200]

Private military companies operating in Iraq have also engaged in questionable labor practices. For instance, Kellogg, Brown & Root (KBR), a Halliburton subsidiary and the largest private provider of logistical support to the U.S. military in Iraq, works with over two hundred subcontractors

[196] Cited in Amnesty International, "Annual Report: Outsourcing Facilitating Human Rights Violations," 2006, accessed November 23, 2007, at http://www.amnestyusa.org/annualreport/2006/overview.html.

[197] Scahill, *Blackwater*, p. 199; Foreign Policy Editors, "The Top Ten Stories You Missed in 2005: The New Coalition of the Willing," ForeignPolicy.com, December 2005, accessed February 9, 2006, at http://www.foreignpolicy.com/story/cms.php?story_id=3315.

[198] David Barstow et al., "Security Companies: Shadow Soldiers in Iraq, " *New York Times*, April 19, 2004, pp. A1, A11; Erinys, "Oil Protection Force Article,"accessed November 23, 2007, at http://www.erinysinternational.com/NewsInformation-Articles.asp.

[199] See Avant, pp. 226–8.

[200] Ibid., p. 227; P. W. Singer, "Nation Builders and Low Bidders in Iraq," *New York Times*, June 15, 2004, p. A23; SourceWatch, "Aegis Defence Services," accessed November 23, 2007, at http://www.sourcewatch.org/index.php?title=Aegis_Defence_Services; the Aegis website can be found at http://web.archive.org/web/20030812031345/http://www.aegisdef.com/.

who hire foreign workers – sometimes illegally – from South and Southeast Asia. Subcontractors draw workers in with fraudulent job descriptions and promises of high pay, neglecting to mention that the jobs are located on a military base in a war zone.[201] Two Indian men recruited by one such subcontractor in India to work as butchers on a U.S. base in Kuwait reported that they were unexpectedly rerouted to northern Iraq, where they were kept for six months on a U.S. base, cleaning toilets and washing dishes and receiving only half the pay the recruiter had promised.[202]

Foreign employees hired by subcontractors are in a highly disadvantageous position from the standpoint of accountability. After a dozen Nepali workers were kidnapped and killed while on their way to a U.S. military base in Iraq, it was revealed that neither the U.S. military nor Halliburton/KBR screens workers hired through subcontractors to see whether they come from countries whose nationals are prohibited from working in Iraq, and both pass the buck when it comes to the mistreatment of such employees in Iraq. KBR denied responsibility for monitoring their subcontractors, saying that questions "regarding the recruitment practices of subcontractors should be directed to the subcontractor." Despite U.S. army control over the KBR contract, army officials echoed KBR's position: "Questions involving alleged misconduct towards employees by subcontractor firms should be addressed to those firms, as these are not army issues." Even the deaths of subcontracted employees in Iraq may not be publicly recorded. "Halliburton would not say whether it includes such laborers in its public tallies of contractor casualties in Iraq," but estimates suggest that up to 100 of the approximately 270 contractors killed in Iraq between the start of the war and October 2005 were "third-country nationals" – neither from Iraq nor from the coalition-member countries.[203] The deaths of contractors from outside the United States are "even less likely...to make the news" than the deaths of U.S. contractors or soldiers.[204]

Contractors' use of deadly force against civilians in Iraq presents another accountability issue, namely, the ability of Iraqis to investigate such killings or be compensated when they occur. Employees of private military

[201] Cam Simpson and Aamer Madhani, "Iraq: War Fuels Human Labor Trade," *Chicago Tribune*, October 13, 2005, accessed February 8, 2006, at www.corpwatch.org/article.php?id=12688.
[202] David Rohde, "Indian Contract Workers in Iraq Complain of Exploitation," *New York Times*, May 7, 2004, p. A14.
[203] Simpson and Madhani, "Iraq: War Fuels Human Labor Trade."
[204] P. W. Singer, quoted in Foreign Policy Editors, "The Top Ten Stories You Missed in 2005."

contractors in Iraq are under considerably less scrutiny than regular military forces and bear immunity from prosecution under Iraqi laws if their use of fatal force took place in connection with the contractors' official duties. The frequency of such shootings – and the fact that Iraqi insurgents often retaliate against U.S. military units, which appear largely indistinguishable from contractors – provoked Brigadier General Karl Horst, whose infantry division provides security in the Baghdad region, to keep a count of such incidents. Horst recorded "at least a dozen shootings of civilians by contractors" between May and July of 2005 alone. "These guys run loose in this country and do stupid stuff," Horst was quoted as saying. "There's no authority over them, so you can't come down on them hard when they escalate force...They shoot people, and someone else has to deal with the aftermath. It happens all over the place."[205] As of late 2007, none of the thousands of private military contractors in Iraq had been prosecuted for any acts of violence; legal experts in the U.S. believed prosecutors would be reluctant to bring cases under MEJA because of the difficulties inherent in collecting evidence from a possible crime scene in a war zone thousands of miles distant.[206] A much-publicized incident in September 2007, where Blackwater guards in Baghdad killed and wounded several dozen civilians in Baghdad's Nisour Square, highlighted this problem and led to fresh calls for contractor accountability.[207] Fourteen months later, the U.S. Department

---

[205] Jonathan Finer, "Security Contractors in Iraq Under Scrutiny After Shootings," *Washington Post Foreign Service*, September 10, 2005, p. A1, accessed February 9, 2005, at http://www.washingtonpost.com/wp-dyn/content/article/2005/09/09/AR2005090902136.html.

[206] Alissa J. Rubin and Paul von Zielbauer, "The Judgment Gap," *New York Times*, October 11, 2007, pp. A1, A12; John M. Broder and James Risen, "Armed Guards in Iraq Occupy a Legal Limbo," NYTimes.com, September 20, 2007, accessed December 13, 2008, at http://www.nytimes.com/2007/09/20/world/middleeast/20blackwater.html?_r=1&scp=1&sq=Armed%20Guards%20in%20Iraq%20Occupy%20a%20Legal%20Limbo&st=cse.

[207] James Glanz and Alissa J. Rubin, "From Errand to Fatal Shot to Hail of Fire to 17 Deaths," NYTimes.com, October 3, 2007, accessed December 3, 2008, at http://www.nytimes.com/2007/10/03/world/middleeast/03firefight.html?scp=1&sq=From%20Errand%20to%20Fatal%20Shot%20to%20Hail%20of%20Fire&st=cse. In this case, the guards were contracted to the State Department, whose investigators argued that MEJA did not apply to any non-DOD contractors. See David Johnston, "Immunity Deals Offered to Blackwater Guards," NYTimes.com, October 29, 2007, accessed December 12, 2008, at http://www.nytimes.com/2007/10/30/washington/30blackwater.html?scp=1&sq=immunity%20deals%20offered%20to%20Blackwater%20guards&st=cse. In yet another attempt to close the contractor loophole, in October 2007 a bill passed the U.S. House of Representatives extending MEJA "to all contractors operating in war zones." David Johnston and John M. Broder, "F.B.I. Says Guards Killed 14 Iraqis Without Cause," NYTimes.com, November 14, 2007, accessed December 13,

of Justice indicted five of the guards involved in the Nisour Square killings under MEJA, relying on the 2004 amendment that extended MEJA to cover all contractors working to support Department of Defense missions abroad. No charges were brought against Blackwater itself, however.[208]

Just as private contractors on the ground in Iraq have constituted a problem for accountability to locals and others, so too have contractors (and even peacekeepers) working with peacekeeping missions.

Peacekeepers and PMCs in Bosnia

Peacekeeping missions provide fertile ground for exploring the nexus between transnational military forces and accountability.[209] One means to explore accountability and private military contractors in peacekeeping missions is to examine the accountability relationships among peacekeepers, contractors, and women living in areas where the missions are located. Accountability problems surface in regard to the trafficking, prostitution, and exploitation of women and girls – by UN military peacekeepers, civilian UN personnel, and civilian contractors (including those hired as military support and those accompanying the mission as civilian police). Transnational military/peacekeeping forces' engagement with sex trafficking during the UN Mission in Bosnia-Herzegovina (UNMIBH) between 1995 and 2002 sheds light on these accountability issues.

Trafficking in the Balkans
Sex-trafficking networks had grown dense in Bosnia and Herzegovina by 1999, several years after the UN Mission in Bosnia and Herzegovina (UNMIBH) began its work as mandated by the 1995 Dayton Accords.[210]

2008, at http://www.nytimes.com/2007/11/14/world/middleeast/14blackwater.html?scp= 1&sq=Guards%20Killed%2014%20iraqis%20without%20cause&st=cse. Despite the Nisour Square episode, Blackwater's contract with the State Department was renewed in May 2008. See James Risen, "Iraq Contractor in Shooting Case Makes Comeback," *New York Times*, May 10, 2008, p. A1, A9.

[208] Ginger Thompson and James Risen, "Plea by Blackwater Guard Helps Indict Others," NYTimes.com, December 8, 2008, accessed December 15, 2008, at http://www.nytimes.com/2008/12/09/washington/09blackwater.html?_r=1&hp.

[209] Sarah Mendelson, *Barracks and Brothels: Peacekeepers and Human Trafficking in the Balkans* (Washington: CSIS Press, 2005), p. 2.

[210] A detailed analysis of sex trafficking in Bosnia and Herzegovina after the signing of the Dayton Accords is provided by Martina Vandenberg, *Hopes Betrayed: Trafficking of Women and Girls to Bosnia and Herzegovina for Forced Prostitution*, Human Rights Watch, November 2002, accessed November 23, 2007, at http://www.hrw.org/reports/2002/bosnia/Bosnia1102.pdf; also see idem, "Peacekeeping, Alphabet Soup, and

As of autumn 2002, UNMIBH believed 227 of Bosnia's nightclubs and bars were engaged in trafficking-related activity. A UN source in 2001 substantiated the widespread nature of sex trafficking in Bosnia, noting that roughly a quarter of the women and girls employed in these establishments had been trafficked.[211] Despite the fact that "purchasing sex is illegal in Bosnia" – to say nothing of trafficking – brothels featuring trafficked women proliferated in part to "service" the influx of peacekeepers and others affiliated with the mission.[212]

Among the personnel accompanying UNMIBH was an International Police Task Force (IPTF) composed of IPTF "monitors" (civilian police), intended to support the development of rule of law in postwar Bosnia by supervising local police forces. Ironically, some IPTF personnel engaged in the trafficking-related activities that they should have been working to eradicate – such as purchasing sex in brothels enslaving trafficked women, and even purchasing the women themselves.[213] Promoting democracy – one aspect of the UN's mission – was thus accompanied by violations of human rights and a striking absence of accountability for such violations, because IPTF monitors enjoy immunity from criminal prosecution while serving on UN missions.[214]

The UNMIBH chose not to request that the UN secretary general waive IPTF employees' immunity in cases where IPTF monitors were allegedly involved in activities related to trafficking. Instead, eighteen monitors were merely repatriated for "incidents of sexual misconduct" over the course of the mission and, as of November 2002, none had been prosecuted upon return to their home countries.[215] In one case from November 2000, IPTF monitors ostensibly from Spain, France, the United States, and elsewhere raided three brothels in Prijedor and then transported some of the trafficked women to Sarajevo for assistance under an International Organization for Migration program. There, the women's testimony revealed that at least nine IPTF monitors, including those who had conducted the raids, were among their clients.[216] In at least one case, a U.S. IPTF monitor purchased a trafficked woman from a brothel in Sarajevo, ostensibly to pay

Violence Against Women in the Balkans," in Dyan Mazurana, Angela Raven-Roberts, and Jane Parpart, eds., *Gender, Conflict and Peacekeeping* (Lanham, MD: Rowman & Littlefield, 2005), pp. 150–67.
[211] Vandenberg, *Hopes Betrayed*, p. 4.
[212] Mendelson, p. 9; Vandenberg, *Hopes Betrayed*, p. 11.
[213] Vandenberg, *Hopes Betrayed*, p. 5.
[214] Ibid., pp. 14, 47.
[215] Ibid., pp. 5, 51.
[216] Ibid., pp. 49–50.

off her "contract." He was repatriated but not prosecuted.[217] At that time, U.S. courts lacked jurisdiction in the event that civilian police monitors from the United States were to commit such crimes while on foreign missions, and none have been prosecuted.[218]

The repatriation of IPTF monitors to their home states made it impossible for them to appear as witnesses to convict the brothel owners and traffickers; they were not even interrogated before repatriation, rendering accountability impossible. The UN addressed the investigation of the IPTF monitors only cursorily; one investigating officer was told by his supervisor that he should "only scratch the surface."[219] Local officials in Bosnia were dismayed by the immunity enjoyed by IPTF officers. One state prosecutor interviewed for a Human Rights Watch report stated, "The allegations are not in the competence of the national prosecutor's office – they have immunity. It cannot be a case in this office. But I would welcome it if some kind of procedure would be brought against those people in their home countries....I don't know of a single case where someone was charged at home. I am not entitled to bring charges."[220]

IPTF monitors are typically mobilized from national police forces to serve on such missions. The United States has no national police force, so private military contractors recruit IPTF monitors from among local and state police forces nationwide. For the Bosnian mission, the U.S. IPTF personnel were hired by the PMC DynCorp. Because of this decentralized recruiting practice, "information on disciplinary actions against particular officers rarely makes it back to a U.S. police officer's home force," and accountability suffers.[221]

Also participating in the Bosnian mission was a NATO-led stabilization force (SFOR), along with its own contractors – civilians providing logistical support to the troops in the area. Along with IPTF monitors, SFOR contractors also reportedly participated in sex trafficking during the Bosnian mission. Such contractors have immunity only for actions taken in relation to their official duties, but, like IPTF monitors, were not prosecuted locally for their alleged trafficking-related crimes, in part because they were repatriated before investigations could get off the ground.[222] Like their

[217] Ibid., p. 53.
[218] Vandenberg, "Peacekeeping, Alphabet Soup, and Violence Against Women in the Balkans," p. 159.
[219] Vandenberg, *Hopes Betrayed*, p. 59.
[220] Ibid., p. 61.
[221] Ibid., p. 48, ft. 250.
[222] Ibid., pp. 5–6.

IPTF counterparts, U.S. SFOR contractors in Bosnia were hired through DynCorp under a Department of Defense contract. Although there was no evidence that SFOR soldiers participated in trafficking-related activities in Bosnia, U.S. civilian contractors faced fewer restrictions on their freedom of movement and were able to visit nightclub/brothels as a result. The SFOR contractors in question "faced allegations of buying women, transporting trafficked women, and violence against trafficked women."[223]

U.S. contractor involvement in sex-trafficking–related activities in Bosnia has been closely scrutinized. A report based on an investigation by the U.S. army's Criminal Investigation Division stated that approximately five DynCorp staff (contracted to SFOR) had been "involved in white slavery," purchasing women from brothels and selling them back "when tired of the women."[224] One such contractor "purchased a trafficked Moldovan woman and an automatic weapon in a package deal from a brothel owner" for the price of $740, according to his confession to U.S. army investigators, but was never prosecuted upon return to the United States. Other cases of contractors purchasing trafficked women have been documented, as have been instances of trafficking facilitated by contractors in Bosnia. Between 1999 and 2002, Human Rights Watch documented "at least eight cases of U.S. contractors who allegedly purchased trafficked women and girls as chattel" – half of them were private contractors with the Department of Defense, and half were on contract to the State Department as police officers in the UN Mission in Bosnia and Herzegovina.[225] Yet "no U.S. contractor has ever faced criminal prosecution in U.S. courts or abroad for trafficking or for purchase of a human being as chattel. In most instances, once the purchase was discovered overseas, the contractor simply fled back to the United States on the next flight out," making prosecution impossible.[226] When an American SFOR contractor was caught during a March 2001 raid of a local nightclub/brothel, and a local judge sought to interview him the following day as a potential witness against the owner of the club, the American had already left the country.[227] In one case from the Balkans, "a U.S. contractor country manager made *ad hoc* arrangements with local police to ensure that any of his personnel caught conducting illegal

[223] Ibid., p. 62.
[224] Ibid., p. 62.
[225] Martina E. Vandenberg, "Out of Bondage," *Legal Times*, February 14, 2005, accessed December 1, 2008, at http://www.jenner.com/files/tbl_s20Publications/RelatedDocuments PDFs1252/889/Legal_Times_Vandenberg_021405.pdf.
[226] Ibid.
[227] Vandenberg, *Hopes Betrayed*, p. 67.

activities in the host nation would be immediately placed in his custody," from whence they would be swiftly repatriated to the United States.[228]

A former DynCorp employee, Ben Johnston, similarly testified (to the U.S. Congress) to contractors' engagement with the sex-trafficking system, explaining that DynCorp employees could bring trafficked women onto "locked-down military installations because the [UN] vans will not get searched if you drive them on post." His testimony also described a pornographic videotape made in Bosnia in which his boss, the DynCorp contract manager, "appeared to rape a female." Johnston testified: "There is my supervisor, the biggest guy there [in Bosnia] with DynCorp, videotaping having sex with these girls, girls saying no, but that guy now, to my knowledge, he is in America doing fine. There was no repercussion for raping the girl."[229]

Contractors in such a system face no accountability for their actions, although they are part of a U.S. mission. Despite the passage of MEJA in 2000, which made Department of Defense contractors subject to U.S. felony law while working abroad, "right up until the U.S. pull-out from Bosnia and Herzegovina in November 2004, the purchases of women by U.S. contractors continued."[230] As of April 2006, there had been no prosecutions of any peacekeepers from the United States for trafficking offenses.[231]

Although MEJA could have been used to prosecute U.S. contractors hired through the Department of Defense (such as those working for SFOR in Bosnia), MEJA would not have allowed for the prosecution of U.S. contractors working as IPTF monitors, because they had no connection to the Department of Defense but rather were hired on a DynCorp contract to the State Department. In 2005, this loophole for contractors was closed by the Trafficking Victims Protection Reauthorization Act (TVPRA). Section 103 of the TVPRA in essence amended MEJA, making prosecutable in the United States any trafficking-related felony offense committed by anyone employed by or contracted to the agencies of the U.S. government not covered under MEJA (the contractors' dependents are also covered under the TVPRA). Under the TVPRA, U.S. police officers hired by

---

[228] Martina Vandenberg and Sarah Mendelson, "Comments on DFARS Case 2004-D017, Defense Federal Acquisition Regulation Supplement; Combating Trafficking in Persons," August 22, 2005, on file with author; also see Mendelson, p. 43.
[229] Quoted in Mendelson, p. 36.
[230] Vandenberg, "Out of Bondage."
[231] Martina Vandenberg, speaking at Harvard University following the film *The Peacekeepers and the Women*, April 18, 2006.

DynCorp to serve in a U.S. IPTF contingent are in effect under contract to the State Department and could now be prosecuted if they were to commit a trafficking-related offense.[232]

Rapid repatriation, however, serves as a significant obstacle to prosecuting U.S. contractors under either MEJA or the TVPRA. Prosecution in the U.S. is plausible only if significant evidence in the case has been collected. Gathering such evidence after repatriation is impractical. When trafficking cases occur involving peacekeepers, the UN typically collects little data. Once a U.S.-contracted peacekeeper is repatriated, it would take enormous effort and expense for a U.S. prosecutor in the Criminal Division of the Department of Justice to investigate the case abroad, to find the woman (or women) in question, and to convince her to testify in order to build a prosecutable case.[233]

Compared to U.S. military personnel, contractors enjoy relative impunity in cases of alleged sex trafficking. A Department of Defense report from December 2003 concluded that there was "negligible evidence" of U.S. armed forces in the Balkans having engaged in prostitution or supporting sex trafficking, particularly because U.S. military personnel could leave their bases only under limited conditions. By contrast, Department of Defense contractors working for SFOR were not "subject to the same restrictions that are placed on U.S. Service members" and are allowed to "circulate in host country communities" in some cases; military personnel from other countries were also found to be more likely to be involved in such activities.[234] In contradiction to the DOD report's findings, however, a special forces officer who served in Bosnia and a lieutenant colonel billeted to NATO in Kosovo both confirmed that U.S. military forces frequented prostitutes and trafficked women there. The finding of only "negligible evidence" of U.S. military involvement with trafficking and prostitution was perhaps not surprising, given the fact that the inspectors failed to "interview local police near the base in Bosnia, brothel owners near the bases in Bosnia or Kosovo, shelter directors, or victims," who would have

[232] MEJA is Chapter 212 of the US Code of Laws; the TVPRA adds Chapter 212A. See Trafficking Victims Protection Reauthorization Act of 2005 (TVPRA), accessed November 23, 2007, at http://www.state.gov/g/tip/rls/61106.htm; US Code, Title 18 Crimes and Criminal Procedure, Chapter 212, Military Extraterritorial Jurisdiction (MEJA), accessed November 23, 2007, at http://www.access.gpo.gov/uscode/title18/partii_chapter212_.html.

[233] Vandenberg, speaking at Harvard University, April 18, 2006.

[234] U.S. Department of Defense Inspector General's Office, "Assessment of DOD Efforts to Combat Trafficking in Persons: Phase II: Bosnia-Herzegovina and Kosovo," December 8, 2003, on file with author, p. 26.

been most likely to provide relevant evidence; instead, the inspectors relied almost entirely on witnesses from the U.S. military.[235]

Transnational support for building accountability and rule of law locally is grossly undermined when peacekeeping forces violate local and international laws, such as those on trafficking. In a detailed report on peacekeeping and trafficking in the Balkans, political scientist Sarah Mendelson notes that when uniformed peacekeepers or civilian contractors "get away with purchasing women or girls as chattel, that sends a strong message that criminality is condoned." Just as problematic is the material support that men provide to traffickers when they purchase sex – money that traffickers then use to bribe local police, allowing the lucrative flow of trafficked women to continue, and undermining attempts to establish an accountable legal system.[236] The Norwegian NATO ambassador summarized the problem of peacekeepers' (even unwitting) support for trafficking:

> [N]ot only do we destroy the reputation of our country and our organization and the operation, we violate fundamentally [the] human rights of women and children. And we do harm to the objectives of our mission, which is to establish rule of law, establish the foundation for democracy and for a decent economy. Not to tear down rule of law, not to create gray economies [and] stimulate corruption.[237]

The UN's lack of response to peacekeepers' involvement in sexual abuse and trafficking reflects the fact that the UN has two conflicting agendas: one to support, at least rhetorically, human rights (including women's human rights); and the other to avoid taking steps that could limit troop contributions, such as punishing peacekeepers who engaged in trafficking or sexual abuse. As a result, the UN's ability to support the construction of local accountability structures and the rule of law has suffered – and this is not even to mention the human cost when the UN turns a blind eye to the sexual slavery of women.[238]

UN complicity in protecting peacekeepers who engage in prostitution and trafficking goes beyond the failure to waive immunity in individual cases. When UNMIBH closed up shop at the end of 2002, it was replaced by the European Union Police Mission (EUPM), which discovered that UN personnel had taken with them "hundreds of files" on trafficking incidents during the mission. EUPM officials were told that "the files had either been archived in New York or burned" – quite possibly because "the information

[235] Mendelson, pp. 34, 44.
[236] Ibid., p. 17.
[237] Quoted in ibid., p. 18.
[238] Ibid., p. 51.

contained in the files implicated IPTF officers" and the UN did not want that information released.[239] According to the International Organization on Migration's May 2004 report on Balkan trafficking, the UN's action meant that

no intelligence information collected by the UN/IPTF [on trafficking] was transferred to the national police. Databases containing thousands of details acquired in several years of work and related to criminals and victims of trafficking were never handed to the national police or to the monitoring EUPM mission...[including] details [for] approximately 1,500 potential victims and hundreds of potential traffickers, locations, etc.[240]

Rapid repatriation from Bosnia, in combination with other choices – such as the failure to transfer the UN's collected data on trafficking incidents – meant that the Bosnian peacekeeping mission's accountability to the local population could not be enforced. The intentional "loss" of information also undermined the goal of rebuilding a local judicial system. The Bosnian government was thus left less accountable to the population because it was deprived of a means to punish the alleged violators.

Two years after the UN peacekeeping mission in Bosnia withdrew, an internal UN report referring to sexual abuse by peacekeepers in the Congo criticized the UN's culture of impunity, summarizing the situation as "zero compliance with [the UN policy of] zero tolerance."[241] The accumulated experience with these issues in Bosnia, as well as in other peacekeeping missions that preceded and followed it, led the UN to take additional steps to address the accountability problems that arise at the intersection of peacekeeping and sexual exploitation.

Beyond Bosnia: Peacekeepers and Accountability

Although private contractors were the focus of much attention in connection with trafficking in Bosnia, it is not only contractors accompanying peacekeeping missions, but peacekeepers more generally who may engage in sexual exploitation, defined by the UN as "any actual or attempted abuse of a position of vulnerability, differential power, or trust, for sexual purposes."[242] UN peacekeeping missions, however well intentioned,

---

[239] Ibid., pp. 63–4.
[240] Cited in ibid., p. 64.
[241] Quoted in ibid., p. 68.
[242] Sexual abuse is defined as "actual or threatened physical intrusion of a sexual nature, whether by force or under unequal or coercive conditions." See Jehan Khaleeli and Sarah Martin, "Addressing the Sexual Misconduct of Peacekeepers," Refugees International,

can be undermined because of peacekeepers' lack of accountability to the local population, made visible when exploitation of local women occurs. Examples of such violations have included the rampant use of prostitutes by UN peacekeepers in Cambodia; peacekeepers in the Democratic Republic of Congo, Liberia, and Sierra Leone demanding sex from children and women in exchange for food; and European peacekeepers in Eritrea having sex with local minors and making pornographic films.[243] A brief treatment of sexual exploitation and peacekeeping in the UN's Cambodian and Liberian missions provides some illustration of the issue.

Cambodia and Liberia

Although the United Nations Transitional Authority in Cambodia (UNTAC) supported accountability to women in the electoral process that the mission oversaw from 1991 to 1993 (see Chapter 3 of this book), UNTAC personnel engaged in some of the abuse of women that would later be echoed in peacekeeping missions in West Africa and elsewhere. Under UNTAC, prostitution, including child prostitution, flourished. A local women's NGO "estimated that the number of prostitutes in Cambodia grew from about 6,000 prostitutes in 1992 to more than 25,000 at the height of the mission."[244] The expansion of this industry was so dramatic that it appeared to become permanently fused with the UNTAC mission in popular memory. A wax museum exhibiting "scenes from Cambodia's history and culture" captured the UNTAC period with two life-size

September 23, 2004, accessed February 2, 2006, at http://www.refugeesinternational. org/content/article/detail/4047/. See also Sarah Martin, "Must Boys Be Boys? Ending Sexual Exploitation and Abuse in UN Peacekeeping Missions," Refugees International, October 2005, accessed February 22, 2007, at http://www.refugeesinternational.org/ content/publication/detail/6976/.

[243] Sarah Lyall, "Aid Workers Are Said to Abuse Girls," *New York Times*, May 9, 2006, p. A8; Colum Lynch, "U.N. Faces More Accusations of Sexual Misconduct," *Washington Post*, March 13, 2005, p. A22, accessed February 2, 2006, at http://www.washingtonpost. com/wp-dyn/articles/A30286-2005Mar12.html; Martin, "Must Boys Be Boys?" pp. 4–5; United Nations High Commissioner for Refugees (UNHCR) and Save the Children–UK, "Sexual Violence and Exploitation: The Experience of Refugee Children in Guinea, Liberia and Sierra Leone," February 2002, accessed February 22, 2007, at http://www. savethechildren.org.uk/scuk_cache/scuk/cache/cmsattach/1550_unhcr-scuk_wafrica_ report.pdf. On reports of the sexual exploitation of women in Congo in 2005, see Nile Gardiner, "The UN Peacekeeping Scandal in the Congo: How Congress Should Respond," Heritage Foundation, March 22, 2005, accessed February 22, 2007, at http://www. heritage.org/Research/InternationalOrganizations/hl868.cfm; see also Khaleeli and Martin, "Addressing the Sexual Misconduct of Peacekeepers."

[244] Sandra Whitworth, *Men, Militarism and UN Peacekeeping: A Gendered Analysis* (Boulder: Lynne Rienner), p. 67.

figurines – a UN peacekeeper, complete with beret, holding a female prostitute in his arms. The UNTAC mission brought not only an expansion of commercial sex but also complaints of sexual abuse at the hands of peacekeepers, ranging from street harassment by UNTAC personnel, to rape, to "fake marriages" that terminated upon a peacekeeper's departure to his home country.[245]

Yasushi Akashi, the head of UNTAC, when confronted by NGOs on the subject of such "sexual misconduct," shocked his audience by stating, "boys will be boys," and noting that he thought it "natural for [the soldiers] ... to chase 'young beautiful beings of the opposite sex.'"[246] His comments were met with a letter of protest from 165 Cambodian citizens and expatriates objecting to violent behavior on the part of some of UNTAC's employees, whom they also held "responsible for the dramatic rise of prostitution and HIV/AIDS. The letter described how women felt restricted in their movements and powerless as a result of UNTAC's presence in Cambodia."[247] Although Akashi responded more appropriately to the letter, putting an officer in place to hear community complaints, the complaints themselves suggest that as UNTAC was trying to create conditions for the establishment of an accountable Cambodian government, UNTAC itself had behaved unaccountably and left parts of the population feeling powerless and without a means to hold peacekeepers accountable for their actions (including rape, the impregnation of local women, and so forth).

A decade later, in 2002, UN operations in West Africa were wracked by scandal when peacekeepers, other UN staff, and NGO workers were allegedly found to be exchanging "scarce relief supplies for sex."[248] Sexual exploitation continued within the United Nations Mission in Liberia (UNMIL), established in 2003, where peacekeepers reportedly "routinely engage[d] in sex" with young girls, according to an "internal U.N. letter" penned by a UNICEF employee. The letter accused peacekeepers of visiting a club where "girls as young as 12 years of age are engaged in prostitution, forced into sex acts and sometimes photographed by U.N. peacekeepers in exchange for $10 or food or other commodities."[249] In the wake of these revelations, the UN mission in Liberia placed several known

---

[245] Ibid., pp. 69–70.
[246] Ibid., pp. 13, 71.
[247] Ibid., p. 71.
[248] Refugees International, "Sexual Exploitation in Liberia: Are the conditions ripe for another scandal?" April 20, 2004, accessed February 22, 2007, at http://www.refugeesinternational. org/content/article/detail/957.
[249] Quoted in Lynch, "UN Faces More Accusations of Sexual Misconduct."

brothels off-limits to UN personnel, but civilians working for the UN could still purchase women and set them up in houses to evade the sanctions on nightclubs: "What I'd heard from different staff people I interviewed was men just buy a house or rent a house and put women in there," explained Sarah Martin, a senior advocate at the NGO Refugees International.[250]

In May 2006, a report by Save the Children (UK) found that sexual abuse of girls (aged eight to eighteen) by aid workers and peacekeepers had continued in Liberia, particularly in displaced persons' camps and in communities to which displaced people were now returning. A UN statement revealed that its workers had been involved in eight cases of sexual abuse and exploitation in the first four months of the year, and that one staff person had been suspended as a result. The Save the Children report called on the UN to prosecute the abusers, and if they were found guilty, to prevent them from being redeployed as peacekeepers elsewhere. At the time, no system to prevent such redeployment existed.[251]

Immunity, Impunity, and Accountability

Although the UN Department of Peacekeeping Operations (DPKO) now expresses a "zero tolerance" policy on the issues of sexual exploitation and abuse, it is not observed uniformly in the field. Acknowledging its failure to address the problem of accountability to local populations in the wake of repeated violations, the UN's zero tolerance policy was supplemented in 2002 by a Peacekeeper Code of Conduct, printed on cards handed out to peacekeepers in the field, titled *We Are United Nations Peacekeepers* and *Ten Rules – Code of Personal Conduct for Blue Helmets*.[252] The fourth of the *Ten Rules* states, "[d]o not indulge in immoral acts of sexual, physical or psychological abuse or exploitation of the local population or United Nations staff; especially women and children." Similarly, *We Are United Nations Peacekeepers* states, "[w]e will never…commit any act that could result in physical, sexual or psychological harm or suffering to members of the local population, especially women and children; become involved in sexual liaisons which could affect our impartiality, or the well being

---

[250] Quoted in Nick Wadhams, "Civilian Employees, Not Soldiers, Will Be Big Problem as United Nations Tackles Sex Abuse, Official Says," Associated Press, March 15, 2005, accessed February 22, 2007, at http://www.refugeesinternational.org/content/article/detail/6356.

[251] Lyall, "Aid Workers Are Said to Abuse Girls."

[252] Kate Holt and Sarah Hughes, "Sex and Death in the Heart of Africa," Refugees International, May 25, 2004, accessed February 22, 2007, at http://www.refugeesinternational.org/content/article/detail/1093.

of others."[253] According to DPKO, "Eradicating sexual exploitation and abuse became a major priority for DPKO in 2005," when the department implemented a "comprehensive strategy to eliminate sexual exploitation and abuse in its peacekeeping missions, including the establishment of Peacekeeping Conduct and Discipline Units at UN Headquarters and in the field."[254] These efforts were spurred by an investigation within the UN in late 2004 exposing the fact that "dozens of peacekeepers serving on a mission to the Congo had committed sex abuse crimes against refugees, including many minors." In an attempt to stop the continuing abuses, the UN's Code of Conduct incorporated a ban on purchasing sex from prostitutes and instituted a curfew for DPKO personnel.[255]

In October 2005, when asked about the UN's response to ongoing reports of sexual abuse by peacekeepers, a DPKO official asserted that "tremendous progress has been made over the past year to drive home the U.N.'s message of zero tolerance and zero impunity," represented by a dramatic increase in the number of repatriations in the previous twenty months (88 troops had been repatriated and 10 civilian employees fired as the result of investigations into the conduct of 221 peacekeepers). The official admitted, however, that despite such progress, the "message had still not taken hold."[256] Over the course of 2005, according to DPKO statistics, there were 340 allegations of sexual exploitation and abuse (SEA) against peacekeepers worldwide, 193 of which involved military personnel, 24 involved civilian police, and 123 involved civilian staff on the peacekeeping mission.[257] From January 2004 through November 2006, investigations into 319 SEA cases involving peacekeeping personnel worldwide generated

---

[253] Quoted in Khaleeli and Martin, "Addressing the Sexual Misconduct of Peacekeepers." On the history of DPKO's policy regarding sexual exploitation and abuse (SEA), see Anna Shotton, "A Strategy to Address Sexual Exploitation and Abuse by United Nations Peacekeeping Personnel," *Cornell International Law Journal*, Vol. 39, No. 1 (Winter 2006), pp. 97–107.

[254] Department of Peacekeeping Operations (DPKO) Fact Sheet, February 2008, accessed December 2, 2008, at http://www.un.org/Depts/dpko/factsheet.pdf.

[255] Office to Monitor and Combat Trafficking in Persons, U.S. Department of State, "Trafficking in Persons Report," June 3, 2005, accessed February 22, 2007, at http://www.state.gov/g/tip/rls/tiprpt/2005/46606.htm.

[256] Quoted in Warren Hoge, "Report Finds U.N. Isn't Moving to End Sex Abuse by Peacekeepers," *New York Times*, October 19, 2005, p. A5.

[257] Secretary General of the United Nations, "Special Measures for Protection from Sexual Exploitation and Sexual Abuse," May 24, 2006, accessed December 13, 2008, at http://documents-dds-ny.un.org/doc/UNDOC/GEN/N06/360/40/pdf/N0636040. pdf?OpenElement, p. 10. There were 357 allegations against DPKO personnel in 2006, although the frequency of reported SEA declined over the course of the year. See Secretary General of the United Nations, "Special Measures for Protection from Sexual

18 dismissals (of UN civilian staff) and the repatriation of 144 troops and 17 civilian police; 56 percent of the cases deemed worthy of investigation resulted in termination of the person's participation in the mission.[258]

There exists a range of obstacles to peacekeeper accountability in the area of sexual exploitation and abuse. These include the immunity agreements between troop-donating countries and host countries (the Status of Mission or Forces Agreements, or SOMA/SOFA), the weakness of the legal systems in most states where UN peacekeepers operate, and the "cumbersome bureaucratic procedures" in place for pursuing allegations against peacekeepers. These agreements "reserve full jurisdiction over misconduct by military troops serving as peacekeepers to the country of origin of the peacekeeper," leaving the UN mission leaders with the sole option of sending offenders home if their "misconduct" is discovered.[259] In the end, punishment upon repatriation varies according to the practices of the peacekeepers' states of origin; the UN has limited ability to follow up to see what (if anything) happens to repatriated troops. Jacques Paul Klein, the special representative to the UN secretary general for Liberia, complained, "I don't have direct chain of command to contingents [of peacekeepers]. I send recommendations to DPKO but I don't know what happens when soldiers are sent home. It's very frustrating."[260] The chain of accountability between the UN mission and the local population thus breaks down almost as soon as the abuse has occurred.[261]

In an attempt to address the accountability loopholes occurring in cases of SEA, in 2006 the UN Secretariat issued a new "draft model memorandum of understanding" (MOU) – an agreement signed between the UN and countries contributing troops to peacekeeping operations – to be debated during the sixty-first session of the UN General Assembly (which

Exploitation and Sexual Abuse," June 15, 2007, accessed November 1, 2007, at http://www.un.org/Depts/dpko/CDT/A.61.957%20Eng.pdf.
[258] Maya Dollarhide, "Sexual Abuse: The UN Under Fire," *Voices-Unabridged: the E-Magazine on Women and Human Rights Worldwide*, No. 11 (February–April, 2007), accessed April 25, 2007, at http://www.voices-unabridged.org/article.php?id_article=169&numero=11.
[259] Khaleeli and Martin, "Addressing the Sexual Misconduct of Peacekeepers."
[260] See Refugees International, "Sexual Exploitation in Liberia."
[261] One proposal for ameliorating the existing accountability gap is to change the SOFA such that a contributor state would retain "primary jurisdiction" over its peacekeeping troops in the event of crimes committed, but the host state would have jurisdiction in the event that the contributor state chose not to prosecute. This is similar to the SOFA under which NATO troops operate within NATO member states. See Barbara Bedont, "The Renewed Popularity of Rule of Law: Implications for Women, Impunity, and Peacekeeping," in Mazurana et al., eds., pp. 89–92.

opened in September 2006). If approved by the General Assembly, the revised MOU would include a section explicitly stating that all troop contingents and commanders would be obligated to abide by the UN's codes of conduct, including the prohibitions on SEA, and that troop-contributing countries would not only familiarize their troops with those standards and prohibitions, but that those states would "issue or promulgate the United Nations standards of conduct in a form or manner that makes them binding under their laws or relevant disciplinary code upon all members of its national contingent."[262]

In addition to requiring troops, peacekeeping missions also involve military observers, civilian UN staff, and civilian police (CIVPOL). Unlike soldiers, they hold the status of "experts performing missions," and enjoy "functional immunity applicable under official functions." If they break local laws while doing something that is not regarded as part of their official mission, then they can be tried under local civil and criminal law. Local law enforcement bodies, however, are unlikely to serve as a reliable accountability mechanism, because peacekeeping missions are typically found in states that lack functional judicial systems. As a result, "very few military observers or civilian police/staff have been tried by a host country."[263]

Less attention has been paid to abuses by civilian personnel on UN peacekeeping missions, although civilians may be responsible for a greater share of the problem of sexual exploitation in the field. Sarah Martin of Refugees International argues:

In reality, it is easier to discipline military personnel in peacekeeping missions than civilians. While there are command structures in place in the military, the multiplicity of civilian agencies and personnel in these missions makes investigating and punishing their abusive behavior more difficult.[264]

Civilian personnel working for UN missions are technically employed not by the UN but by a private contractor, which makes follow-up in the event of violations difficult. According to a peacekeeping expert interviewed by Refugees International, "Not only are we unsure if they are punished, we

---

[262] Note by the Secretary General, "Revised Draft Model Memorandum of Understanding Between the United Nations and [Participating State] Contributing Resources to [the United Nations Peacekeeping Operation]," October 3, 2006, p. 3, accessed April 19, 2007, at http://daccessdds.un.org/doc/UNDOC/GEN/N06/553/30/PDF/N0655330.pdf?OpenElement. I thank Yewande Odia, Chief of the Conduct and Discipline Team (DPKO) for pointing me to this information.

[263] Khaleeli and Martin, "Addressing the Sexual Misconduct of Peacekeepers."

[264] Martin, "Must Boys Be Boys?" p. ii.

suspect that they are sometimes just rotated to another mission," and the appropriate follow-up with victims is nearly impossible.[265]

A first step toward improving the external accountability of UN peace-keeping missions might lie in providing a procedure for complaints that would be transparent to the local community.[266] Confusion over the proper route for complaints was a significant issue for UNMIL. In December 2003, DPKO asked the Liberian mission to select a "community focal point" – a person to whom community complaints about sexual exploitation could be reported.[267] An investigation by Refugees International in 2004 revealed that the management of the UN mission in Liberia could not identify an appropriate person to receive complaints about such violations – and found that local women who had been abused would have neither the means of reporting such a problem nor a person to whom to report.[268] Two years later, the UNMIL Conduct and Discipline Unit website listed a hotline number that could presumably be used to report cases of sexual abuse and exploitation, but this would be of little use if community members were not aware of it or lacked telephone access, as is the case in rural areas.[269] According to a researcher who visited Liberia in March 2007, UNMIL's hotline was "up and running," and a handful of people affiliated with the UN and Liberia's national police made mention of it. "However, no one seemed to know whether and to what extent it was actually being used."[270]

The accountability principle would be further ensured by a process informing victims of the outcome of any investigation or legal proceeding that takes place as a result of the complaint:

Currently peacekeeping troops report to their home country commanders. If a soldier is found guilty, that person is sent back to his country for discipline. It is very difficult, if not impossible, for victims and their families to determine what, if any, actions have been taken. In order for local communities and victims to trust the UN enough to begin reporting violations, victims must know they will be protected and treated with respect when they report and that there will be action taken against the perpetrator.[271]

[265] Quoted in ibid., p. 22.
[266] Ibid., p. iii.
[267] See Refugees International, "Sexual Exploitation in Liberia."
[268] Sarah Martin, "'Must Boys Be Boys? Confronting Sexual Exploitation and Abuse in UN Peacekeeping Operations," Lecture at Fletcher School, Tufts University, February 1, 2006.
[269] United Nations Mission in Liberia (UNMIL), "Conduct and Discipline Unit," accessed November 23, 2007, at http://unmil.org/content.asp?ccat=cdu; Sarah Martin, Senior Advocate, Refugees International, phone interview by author, March 29, 2007.
[270] Asal Esfahani, email communication with author, April 4, 2007.
[271] Martin, "Must Boys Be Boys?" p. iii.

In July 2004, at the behest of UN Secretary General Kofi Annan, former civilian peacekeeper and Jordanian ambassador to the UN, Prince Zeid Ra'ad Zeid al-Hussein, produced a report on eradicating sexual abuse and exploitation in peacekeeping missions. Among other things, the Zeid report called for troop-contributing countries to create "on-site courts martial for guilty parties and [to] adopt formal memoranda of understanding in advance of deployment so that the cases of sexual exploitation and abuse [would be] forwarded to their competent national or military authorities."[272] The Zeid report further recommended that victims of sexual exploitation by peacekeepers be compensated monetarily (from those peacekeepers' wages) and that in cases where paternity is established, peacekeepers should be held financially responsible. Individual UN peacekeepers could thus more easily and transparently be held accountable for their actions in the local community.[273]

Following the Zeid report, Refugees International's own report on this issue suggested that the UN raise the importance of eliminating peacekeepers' sexual abuse and exploitation of women by making compliance with UN policy on the issue an explicit criterion of job performance for UN managers, and to fire senior UN officials who do not carry out the policies to eliminate such abuses.[274] This would help to hold mission commanders and managers accountable for any failures to disrupt a mission culture that tolerates sexual exploitation.[275]

Finally, to cut down on abuses, Refugees International recommended advance training for peacekeeping troops, as well as careful "follow-up" and that "troop-contributing countries work more closely with local women's groups to incorporate culturally appropriate curriculum into their military training," and hence improve accountability.[276] One interesting development along these lines is the Indian government's creation of an all-women peacekeeping police force (CIVPOL), which deployed to Liberia in October 2006. The gender adviser to the UN Mission in Liberia believed that sexual exploitation (in the form of sex

---

[272] Ibid., pp. iii–iv. Jordan is a major contributor of troops to peacekeeping operations.
[273] Ibid., pp. 1, 23.
[274] Ibid., p. 16.
[275] Ibid., p. 1. The leadership of the UN Mission in Haiti was more devoted to expressing a clear policy on prostitution than was the one in Liberia; peacekeepers in Haiti (MINUSTAH) understood that sex with prostitutes was forbidden. Martin, "Must Boys Be Boys?" p. 16. Even so, 108 peacekeepers were expelled from Haiti in November 2007 after accusations of sexual exploitation surfaced. See "U.N. Ousts Peacekeepers in Sex Case," *New York Times*, November 3, 2007, p. A10.
[276] Martin, "Must Boys Be Boys?" p. iii.

exchanged for food) declined in the face of increased numbers of female peacekeepers: "It limits the sexual exploitation that our people get involved in. In the groups that have a lot more women we get very little reporting of sexual exploitation."[277] In combination, such actions would improve the accountability of UN peacekeepers to the populations they are protecting, and would enhance the ability of peacekeeping missions to transform postconflict zones into locales with stable and accountable governments.

According to the Conduct and Discipline Unit (CDU) of the UN Mission in Liberia, the concerns expressed in the Zeid and Refugees International reports have been addressed, at least on paper. As of March 2007, the CDU's website alerted UNMIL personnel to the fact that sex with people under eighteen violates the Code of Conduct and is "strictly prohibited," as is the "exchange of money, employment, goods, assistance or services for sex." Peacekeepers are warned that such violations "will result in administrative and/or disciplinary action and ineligibility to participate in future peacekeeping operations or [have] access to any employment within the UN system once listed in the DPKO database for serious misconduct" in addition to possible punishment upon repatriation.[278] Martin expressed skepticism about the utility of the database: "They've been saying that there was a database all along, but the database has never functioned." Instead, the UN relies on troop-contributing countries to screen peacekeepers, but they fail to do so because it would further draw out the process of providing troops to missions.[279] Regarding accountability for paternity, the CDU also alerted "military contingent members" to the possibility of "paternity payments if pregnancy is confirmed to have occurred as a result of sexual exploitation or abuse."[280] It is not clear how such a claim could be proven, however.[281]

The frequency of sexual exploitation and abuse by transnational military or civilian peacekeeping forces pales by comparison to that perpetrated by government soldiers and rebel forces in many of the states to

[277] Joanna Foster, quoted in Will Ross, "Liberia Gets All-Female Peacekeeping Force," BBC News, Liberia, January 31, 2007, accessed March 1, 2007, at http://news.bbc.co.uk/2/hi/africa/6316387.stm.

[278] UNMIL, "Conduct and Discipline Unit."

[279] Sarah Martin, phone interview by author, March 29, 2007. According to the DPKO, a "global database on misconduct allegations and cases covering all missions" will be established in 2007. See "DPKO's Comprehensive Strategy on Sexual Exploitation and Abuse," accessed April 19, 2007, at http://www.un.org/Depts/dpko/CDT/strategy.html.

[280] UNMIL, "Conduct and Discipline Unit."

[281] Sarah Martin, phone interview, March 29, 2007.

which UN peacekeeping missions deploy. The probable percentage of Liberian women raped during the fourteen-year-long civil war approaches 40 percent, for instance, compared to a total of seventy-five complaints of reported rape lodged against UN personnel in Liberia in 2005 and 2006 combined (according to UNMIL).[282] Similarly, the practice of girls exchanging sex for food, money, or protection from government soldiers in displaced persons' camps is common (as is sexual violence more generally). A September 2005 Human Rights Watch report documented the widespread sex-for-protection racket (as well as flat-out rape) in such camps in northern Uganda. Government soldiers ostensibly guarding against rebel attacks are often the perpetrators; a Ugandan expatriate working for the UN commented on the frequency of rape by government soldiers, saying, "There is a complete culture of impunity.... The soldiers feel that they own the women in the camps; that they can do anything with them." Like the UN's failure to appropriately sanction peacekeepers who sexually abuse and exploit the women and girls under their care, government soldiers enjoy a lack of accountability and are rarely disciplined by the military. According to the report, "Even when a victim identifies her violator... in many cases, nothing happens to him or he is transferred elsewhere."[283]

Even bearing in mind the backdrop of women's sexual exploitation that pervades conflict and postconflict situations, for peacekeepers to contribute to the exploitation of the local population – even in a small way – contravenes the purpose of peacekeeping as a means of building accountability. As one expert in the field of peacekeeping summed it up: "the United Nations' mission is not to undermine rule of law but rather to strengthen it. When they blatantly disregard local laws about prostitution and encourage the cover-up of violations within the mission, they are poisoning the mission and corrupting the mandate."[284] Integrating accountability to women across peacekeeping missions would not only improve the effectiveness of UN missions but could also set an example for postconflict governments, encouraging them to take seriously issues of accountability within their own military and security forces.

---

[282] Tristan McConnell, "All-Female Unit Keeps Peace in Liberia," *Christian Science Monitor*, March 21, 2007, accessed April 20, 2007, at http://peacejournalism.com/ReadArticle.asp?ArticleID=17876.

[283] Rachel Scheier, "Soldier Verdict Spotlights Rape in Ugandan Camps," Women's E-news, May 29, 2006, accessed June 2, 2006, at http://www.womensenews.org/article.cfm?aid=2756.

[284] Quoted in Martin, "Must Boys Be Boys?" p. 4.

PRIVATE MILITARY FORCES AND PEACEKEEPERS: CONCLUSIONS
ABOUT ACCOUNTABILITY

In what ways does the use of transnational military forces compromise or
promote political accountability? The impact of transnational PMCs and
peacekeeping forces on accountability relationships is mixed and occasionally paradoxical. Although PMCs and peacekeeping forces – themselves
nearly always including employees of PMCs[285] – can help stabilize conflicts
and pave the way to elections and the possibility of establishing politically
accountable government, states can also avoid accountability through the
use of PMCs. And, in some cases, military contractors and others serving
on transnational peacekeeping missions may commit human rights violations with impunity, highlighting the absence of accountability to local
populations and undermining both the development of and confidence in
local justice systems.

In postconflict states hosting peacekeeping missions, political accountability has often been reduced to near nil. External, transnational (sometimes private) military forces are introduced in such cases as a prior step to
the establishment or reestablishment of accountable government. But the
use of private military force is not without ramifications.

Analyzing the increasingly widespread use of PMCs, Deborah Avant
suggests that the use of private security matters because it changes – or
can change – the ways in which violence is controlled.[286] To determine
whether state control over violence is undermined or promoted by the use
of private security forces, the concept of control must be disaggregated
into three components: political control (who decides how force is used),
functional control (whether military effectiveness is served when a state
adds private forces to the equation), and social control (whether or not private forces support and encourage the profusion of rhetorically supported
international values such as the rule of law, civilian control, and support
for human rights in military behavior).[287]

Although the use of private security forces may have varied effects on
functional and social control, it always diffuses political control over the
use of force:

Though states retain budgetary control and can select between contractors, screening and selection of individuals and the organizational incentives for individuals

---

[285] Since 1990, each of the UN's multilateral peacekeeping missions has involved private
military contractors. Avant, p. 7.
[286] Ibid., p. 3.
[287] Ibid., pp. 5–7, 81–2, and Chapter 2, "Private Security and the Control of Force."

are left in the hands of firms. In and of itself, this is a political change because the control over individuals authorized to use violence slips into the hands of a firm rather than being in the hands of the state.[288]

Allowing the market to play this expanded role in security provision permits "the responsibilities of government [to be] transferred to corporate hands."[289] Private businesses are considerably less accountable to the public than are government institutions, at least in democratic states. Moreover, once service provision is relocated to the private sphere (even if it is typically regarded as a public service, such as defense), it is removed to some degree from public scrutiny and discussion. The use of PMCs thus shifts the locus of political control.

Private military companies' effect on the social control of force is also important from the accountability standpoint.[290] If human rights and legal protections decline when institutions or functions are transferred from the public to the private sphere, social control over violence decays. If private or transnational institutions do not uphold the rule of law (as is the case when PMCs or UN peacekeeping missions too rapidly repatriate people accused of violating human rights), then social control and accountability both suffer. The behavior of private military contractors (and personnel on UN peacekeeping missions) must therefore be examined under the rubric of the social control of force, inasmuch as that behavior affects the human rights of "host country" populations. Like the private contractors who violated detainees' rights at the Abu Ghraib prison and committed acts of violence against civilians with impunity elsewhere in Iraq, transnational peacekeeping forces (both civilian and military) are held accountable to local populations for human rights abuses in only a limited way, if at all. The sexual exploitation of women by peacekeepers and the rapid repatriation of the latter are inimical to accountability and to increasing the social control of force, whether in Bosnia, Cambodia, or Liberia. Yet law is not applied the same way in the private sector as it is in the public sector, making it even more difficult to prosecute private contractors than to prosecute national military forces who violate human rights abroad.[291]

PMC supporters argue that the market enforces a certain kind of accountability on PMCs – namely, accountability to shareholders. This accountability should lead to PMC support for social control, as it provides

[288] Ibid., p. 6, p. 59.
[289] Ken Silverstein, *Private Warriors* (New York: Verso, 2000), cited in Avant, p. 4.
[290] Ibid., p. 6.
[291] Alfred Aman, *The Democracy Deficit: Taming Globalization Through Law Reform* (New York: New York University Press, 2004), p. 102.

an incentive for military contractors to behave professionally, abide by international law, and avoid human rights violations, so as to preserve a good reputation and future contracts.[292] It is also reasonable to suggest, however, that the desire for future profits creates incentives for PMCs to cover up crimes committed by their employees, who may then be hired anew by other PMCs.[293] The case of DynCorp is instructive; after several of its employees violated women's rights in Bosnia through trafficking and other types of sexual exploitation, the company dismissed "whistleblowers" who sought to make management aware of the problem.[294] DynCorp was then hired for the lucrative contract to train the Iraqi police force a few years later.[295]

Another means to explore whether the use of PMCs increases social control over violence is in the support for human rights evidenced in military behavior. In weak states, social control (and, down the line, accountability to the population) could be improved as the result of a state's forces receiving military training from a PMC – especially if professional norms and human rights are emphasized in the process of training.[296] Yet, the human rights effects of PMC activity are not uniform. In some cases, PMCs fail to train foreign forces in lawful military conduct. MPRI personnel working to train the Bosnian military after the 1995 Dayton Accords, for example, found that "their teaching on the military code of conduct and laws of land warfare in the Bosnian program was kept minimal, as the clients/students were uncomfortable with the subject."[297]

Nor is the record clear concerning PMCs' effects on military forces' violation of human rights. Although in some cases PMCs can save civilian lives (protecting Sierra Leone's citizens from the RUF rebel forces, for instance), PMCs can also facilitate governments' attacks on civilians. Although PMC training could increase an army's professional standards of behavior and enthusiasm for democracy, evidence of PMCs assisting military forces that attack civilians – particularly civilians opposed

---

[292] Singer, *Corporate Warriors*, p. 217.
[293] Ibid., p. 222.
[294] Tod Robberson, "Employees Not Convinced Whistle-Blowers Are Safe," *Dallas Morning News*, February 9, 2007, accessed August 13, 2008, at http://www.contractormisconduct. org/ass/contractors/59/cases/690/761/veritas-capital-dyncorp-in-bosnia_dmn.pdf.
[295] "Dyncorp should never have been awarded the Iraqi police contract," according to the chief UN human rights officer in Sarajevo, Madeleine Rees. Traynor, "The Privatisation of War."
[296] Avant, p. 61.
[297] Singer, *Corporate Warriors*, p. 218.

to the current regime – suggests that the picture is not one-sided.[298] For example, under a 1997 contract, Defense Systems Limited (DSL) – a PMC that worked for British Petroleum (BP) in Colombia – apparently trained the Colombian Fourteenth Army Brigade (a unit with a record of massacring civilians) "in counterinsurgency techniques."[299] DSL provided the brigade with information about local activists "who opposed BP's project. Provided with this information from private sources, the Colombian military would then deal with the local leaders directly, that is by kidnappings, torture, and murder, or indirectly through associated paramilitary groups." The DSL employees were not "held accountable or punished for their actions."[300] Such cases show that national military forces – in this case, working with corporations – can use PMCs to help them *suppress* the very people who are demanding governmental or corporate accountability to local populations.

PMCs, then, can enable a lack of political accountability to continue in nondemocratic states, as governments interested mainly in preserving their own power "may benefit from the status quo and use contracts to maintain their rule and privilege rather than increase governance."[301] When the PMCs in question are transnational, and the task of "public" security is privatized to them, ruling regimes may be led "further away from strategies that enlist the support of their populations," such as providing food, health care, education, and jobs.[302] States reliant on external private forces for their security have less incentive to meet popular needs or install institutions of political accountability.

The use of PMCs detracts from accountability even in rule-of-law states. The act of privatizing military functions removes them from public purview because contracts "are protected under proprietary law" and cannot be exposed, for example, through a Freedom of Information Act (FOIA) request.[303] Although PMC contracts are paid for with taxpayer money, the details of the contracts (such as salaries for PMC employees doing the jobs that would otherwise be done by U.S. military forces) are not public information.[304] Turning a "public good," such as providing for the common defense, over to the private sector transfers information into a relatively

[298] Ibid., p. 217.
[299] Ibid., p. 221.
[300] Ibid., p. 221.
[301] Avant, p. 63, citing Reno, *Warlord Politics in African States*.
[302] Avant, pp. 63–4.
[303] Singer, *Corporate Warriors*, p. x.
[304] Baum, p. 36.

inaccessible realm – limiting the potential for vertical accountability. And, because the use of PMCs rather than national military forces concentrates decision-making power in the executive branch, horizontal accountability suffers as well.[305]

In a variety of ways, then, PMCs can sidestep accountability to local populations, while their use enables a lack of political accountability to continue in weak states, and an evasion of political accountability in stronger, rule-of-law–based states. Naturally, it is not only by licensing and hiring PMCs that governments avoid accountability. States may also directly violate their citizens' human rights and refuse to uphold their own laws. In nondemocratic states, the judicial branch may be in thrall to the executive, and hence not suitable as a horizontal accountability mechanism. In such cases, transnational judicial institutions may come in handy. The next chapter explores citizens' attempts to use a transnational court, the European Court of Human Rights (ECHR), as a means to render Russia's law enforcement system more accountable to the population. Like the provision of state security, the practice of justice is becoming transnational.

[305] Avant, p. 60.

5

Trials and Tribulations

Transnational Judicial Institutions

The global political system has become increasingly permeated by transnational judicial institutions and legal instruments. As more and more states subject themselves to elements of this transborder legal system, it is worth exploring the ways in which transnational judicial bodies hinder or promote state accountability and the rule of law. Although individual citizens may see in transnational judicial forums an immediate and practical way to pursue justice previously unavailable to them, nongovernmental organizations (NGOs) also regard such institutions as having a more long-term transformative potential, hoping to use them as a means to press for political change at home.

This chapter focuses on Russia as a nondemocratic state subject to the rulings of the European Court of Human Rights (ECHR), a transnational court located in Strasbourg, France. The ECHR rules on the basis of the 1953 European Convention on Human Rights and its protocols, holding signatory states accountable for violating the rights of their citizens. The increasing number of cases brought to the ECHR in recent years suggests that when national courts fail to protect human rights, people invest their hopes for accountability in transnational judicial institutions. Although claimants must exhaust their options for recourse within their domestic legal systems before turning to the ECHR, the growing use of this transnational court by Russian citizens indicates reliance on an external actor to redress domestic accountability failures.[1]

---

[1] Making claims through "external institutional channels" such as the ECHR represents an instance of what political scientist Sidney Tarrow calls "externalizing contention." Sidney Tarrow, *The New Transnational Activism* (New York: Cambridge University Press, 2005), pp. 151–4.

Historically, in Western Europe, citizens' rights such as press freedom, the right to freedom of assembly, and the right to property – all of which find defense in the European Convention on Human Rights – were recognized and enforced (or ignored and violated) by local actors rather than at the national or transnational level. The "control over justice," for instance, had been previously the province of "manorial lords, churches and communities."[2] Over time, the power to adjudicate such rights came to be located in the state as the result of its "abridging, destroying or absorbing rights previously lodged in other [more local] political units."[3] As a result of this "public-ization" of formerly private or local rights, tasks such as the management of justice became the job of the state. As the twenty-first century began, however, that particular task was becoming less exclusively the job of the state and was increasingly shared with transnational judicial entities aiming to hold states accountable for observing human rights at home.

In what ways has participation in the ECHR affected the Russian state's protection of human rights? In brief, Russia's experience with the ECHR to date has produced an ambivalent response from the Russian political leadership and judicial system. Although the government continues to enforce citizens' rights only selectively and has not changed course on some of the major issues raised in ECHR decisions, there are signs that Russia has taken steps toward remedying some of the human rights violations most frequently raised at the ECHR by its citizens. Russian judges, too, are paying attention to the ECHR's rulings to varying degrees, which may in the long run improve the state's legal accountability mechanisms. But over the decade during which Russia has been subject to ECHR rulings, the Russian government has become more authoritarian, not less. Although transnational legal institutions such as the ECHR give the aggrieved citizens of non–rule-of-law states such as Russia a chance for a fair hearing, their ability to force more than marginal improvements in governmental accountability is highly constrained.

THE POWER OF TRANSNATIONAL COURTS

Even in democratic states, courts appear distinctly undemocratic. But such nonelected courts are "undemocratic" by design. Their occupants

[2] Charles Tilly, "Reflections on the History of European State-Making," in Charles Tilly, ed., *The Formation of National States in Western Europe* (Princeton: Princeton University Press, 1975), pp. 36–7.
[3] Ibid., p. 37.

are protected from sanction by the public, and hence from democratic accountability, so that they will be able to protect the rights of the minority or to back individual claims against a government's abuse of power. Despite their unaccountable design, courts – particularly transnational courts, for citizens living in less-than-democratic states – can enhance democracy by providing new avenues for citizens' political participation and empowerment[4] and by trying to hold member states accountable to the human rights agreements to which they are party. The European Court of Human Rights (ECHR) commands "great legitimacy despite [a] near total lack of direct democratic legitimacy."[5]

There exist a handful of regional human rights charters and courts to uphold them, including the European Court of Human Rights, the Inter-American Court of Human Rights, and the Banjul (African) Charter on Human and Peoples' Rights of the Organization of African Unity (OAU).[6] Regional human rights agreements such as the European Convention on Human Rights or the Inter-American Convention on Human Rights are designed not to regulate inter-state relations, but "to hold governments accountable for purely internal activities."[7] When brought to transnational court, a state may find itself in a position where its domestic law is ruled in violation of an international convention even if the law in question was "enacted and enforced through fully democratic procedures."[8] Transnational human rights courts would thus appear to present a "challenge…to liberal ideals of direct democratic legitimacy and self-determination."[9] However,

---

[4] Rachel A. Cichowski, "Courts, Rights, and Democratic Participation," *Comparative Political Studies*, Vol. 39, No. 1 (2006), p. 53.

[5] Moravcsik, "Is There a 'Democratic Deficit' in World Politics?" A Framework for Analysis," *Government and Opposition*, Vol. 39, No. 2 (April 2000), p. 360.

[6] The latter lacked a court of human rights as an enforcement mechanism until 1998, unlike the European and American charters. For an overview of transnational courts, see Mary L. Volcansek, "Supranational Courts in a Political Context," in Mary L. Volcansek, ed., *Law Above Nations: Supranational Courts and the Legalization of Politics* (Gainesville: University Press of Florida, 1997), pp. 1–19; Burns H. Weston, Robin Ann Lukes, and Kelly M. Hnatt, "Regional Human Rights Regimes: A Comparison and Appraisal," in Richard Pierre Claude and Burns H. Weston, eds., *Human Rights in the World Community*, 2nd edition (Philadelphia: University of Pennsylvania Press, 1992), pp. 244–55. On the Inter-American Court, see John F. Stack, Jr., "Human Rights in the Inter-American System," in Volcansek, ed., *Law Above Nations*, pp. 99–117; on the establishment of the African court, see Project on International Courts and Tribunals, "African Court of Human and Peoples' Rights," accessed November 23, 2007, at http://www.pict-pcti.org/courts/ACHPR.html.

[7] Andrew Moravcsik, "The Origins of Human Rights Regimes: Democratic Delegation in Postwar Europe," *International Organization*, Vol. 54, No. 2 (Spring 2000), p. 217.

[8] Ibid., pp. 217–18.

[9] Ibid., p. 218.

the fact that the European Convention on Human Rights has been given the status of national law in many European states would seem to attenuate the criticism of transnational courts as flouting democratic legitimacy.[10]

Transnational (sometimes called "supranational") courts can have dramatic effects within the states subject to their rulings. In 2000, Tanja Kreil, a twenty-three-year-old German engineer, won a significant victory at the European Court of Justice (ECJ), leading to the elimination of Germany's prior ban on women in combat positions.[11] In January 2001, 244 women entered the German military forces, no longer restricted to "medical and musical units."[12] Court rulings about the rights of gay, lesbian, and transgender people have similarly shaken European societies.[13] The ECHR, for instance, ruled in 1999 that lesbians and gay men in the United Kingdom could not be discharged from the military on the basis of their sexual orientation; the Court held that this was a violation of privacy rights. As a result, the British government changed the offending policy.[14] In Portugal, a gay man who had been denied custody of his daughter brought suit to the ECHR, where his claim was supported on the basis that he had been discriminated against due to his sexual orientation (an issue "undoubtedly covered" by Article 14 of the European Convention, which states that the rights and freedoms guaranteed by the Convention apply independent of a person's social, political, ethnic or "other status") and that the state had interfered with his family life, violating Article 8 (which addresses the "right to respect for [a person's] private and family life").[15]

---

[10] Ibid., p. 218.

[11] Roger Cohen, "Germany: Arms for Women," *New York Times,* January 12, 2000. The Strasbourg-based ECHR should be distinguished from the European Court of Justice (ECJ) in Luxembourg, which interprets the European Union (EU) treaties and applies EU law across its member states. The ECJ allows cases to be brought by EU-country citizens, who can sue for damages against member states that fail to uphold EU laws. The ECJ is an effective institution of political accountability, helping to ensure that EU law is applied consistently across member states. See Rachel A. Cichowski, *The European Court and Civil Society: Litigation, Mobilization and Governance* (Cambridge, UK: Cambridge University Press, 2007); CURIA, "The Court of Justice of the European Communities," accessed June 25, 2008, at http://curia.europa.eu/en/instit/presentationfr/index_cje.htm.

[12] Peter Finn, "German Women Gain Job Parity in Military," *Washington Post,* January 3, 2001, accessed March 23, 2006, at http://www.globalpolicy.org/socecon/inequal/2001/0103pf.htm.

[13] Kristen Walker, "Moving Gaily Forward? Lesbian, Gay and Transgender Human Rights in Europe," *Melbourne Journal of International Law,* Vol. 2, No. 1 (June 2001), pp. 122–43.

[14] Ibid.

[15] Ibid. See also European Convention on Human Rights at http://www.hri.org/docs/ECHR50.html#C.Art14.

The European Court of Human Rights (ECHR)

The European Court of Human Rights was founded in 1959 as an institution of the Council of Europe (COE), and has as many presiding judges as there are states in the COE having ratified the European Convention on Human Rights and Fundamental Freedoms (forty-five out of forty-six states, as of June 2006). Judges are elected by the Parliamentary Assembly of the Council of Europe for six-year terms and serve as individuals rather than "representing" their country of origin (at any given time, more than one judge may serve from the same COE country).[16]

States joining the Council of Europe are required to "ratify the Human Rights Convention, as well as Protocol 6 on abolishing the death penalty," and to implement the Convention across their territory.[17] The Convention protects numerous rights and freedoms, including "the right to life; prohibition of torture, slavery and forced labor; right to a fair trial; freedom of expression, thought, assembly, conscience, and religion; and right to privacy." The Convention's thirteen protocols further "promote the right to property ownership, education, free elections, freedom of movement, and the general outlawing of discrimination," as well as banning capital punishment.[18] The Court's purpose is to ensure that states, having ratified the European Convention, abide by it. The ECHR may consider cases brought by member states against other states allegedly violating the European Convention, but in the main, cases are brought by citizens of member states who complain that their rights under the European Convention have been violated by their own governments. The ECHR will take cases only if the complainant has pursued the issue in the domestic legal system to the furthest extent possible. Council of Europe member states found to have violated the European Convention are expected to change their laws and practices to bring them into line with the Convention and are obligated to carry out the decisions made by the ECHR.[19] Countries entering

---

[16] European Court of Human Rights, "Organization of the Court," accessed November 23, 2007, at http://www.echr.coe.int/ECHR/EN/Header/The+Court/The+Court/Organisation+of+the+Court/. Not to be confused with the European Union, the Council of Europe is a more expansive group of European nations that a state must join before being considered for EU membership. See Pamela A. Jordan, "Russia's Accession to the Council of Europe and Compliance with European Human Rights Norms," *Demokratizatsiya* (Spring 2003), p. 282.

[17] Jordan, "Russia's Accession to the Council of Europe," p. 282.

[18] Ibid., p. 283. The text of the Convention and its protocols is available in English at http://www.hri.org/docs/ECHR50.html#C.Art14.

[19] Jordan, "Russia's Accession to the Council of Europe," p. 283.

the Council of Europe and ratifying the European Convention therefore relinquish some degree of sovereignty.

In 1998, the ECHR's challenge to state sovereignty increased when two previously optional Articles of the Convention were made obligatory: Article 25, which enables individuals to submit claims directly to the ECHR; and Article 46, which obligates states to accept the Court as final arbiter.[20] Rachel Cichowski, analyzing ECHR decisions through 2004, found that the European Convention and the ECHR "have served as an expanding opportunity for rights claims above and beyond the domestic legal system," particularly given the right of individuals to file complaints against their governments.[21] It is also clear that the ECHR does not hesitate to rule against member states, and does so in an "overwhelming majority" (71 percent) of cases.[22]

Within Cichowski's dataset, 72 percent of cases judged by the ECHR to be violations referred to Article 6 – the right to a fair trial – suggesting that claimants find it useful and necessary to seek the enforcement of their legal rights from beyond the judicial systems in their own countries. The desire for individual access to the ECHR, met in 1998, reflects "a continued demand for better access to justice within the domestic legal system," as indicated by the large number of cases where the right to a fair trial was violated.[23] In short, individuals use the ECHR to try and make their domestic legal systems more accountable and observant of citizens' rights.

Decisions made by the European Court of Human Rights are carried out through the Council of Europe's Committee of Ministers. This body, composed of the foreign ministers of each of the forty-six member states of the Council of Europe, is responsible for ensuring that a member state that loses a case at the ECHR compensates the applicant materially and/ or takes further measures, such as changing a domestic law to make it compatible with the Convention. For example, as the result of ECHR judgments, the United Kingdom had to forbid corporal punishment in schools, and Turkey was made to "[reduce] the maximum duration of police custody."[24] Judgments by the court "imply an obligation on the part of the

---

[20] Cichowski, "Courts, Rights, and Democratic Participation," pp. 58–9.
[21] Ibid., pp. 57–8.
[22] Ibid., pp. 62–3.
[23] Ibid., pp. 63–4.
[24] Council of Europe, "About the Committee of Ministers," accessed November 23, 2007, at http://www.coe.int/T/CM/aboutCM_en.asp; idem, "The ECHR in Practice," accessed November 23, 2007, at http://www.coe.int/T/E/Com/About_Coe/Brochures/fiche_dhc.asp.

states concerned to avoid any similar violations in future," and states are monitored by the Committee of Ministers to verify whether or not they are making progress toward rectifying the conditions that gave rise to a particular case in the first place (especially if similar cases continue to come to the Court from that state).[25] As part of the monitoring process, the Committee meets six times per year to "supervise the execution of judgments of the European Court of Human Rights." The Committee retains cases on its agenda until its members are satisfied that a judgment has been fully carried out, at which point they adopt a "final resolution."[26] The Council of Europe's Committee of Ministers is empowered to expel states from the Council of Europe if they fail to "remedy proven violations," but has never done so.[27] Although the Committee's unwillingness to use its ultimate power may limit its ability to induce dramatic change in member states persistently violating human rights, expelling a member state could deprive the Council of Europe of its influence altogether.

States may delay altering national laws to take the rulings of transnational courts into account (Cyprus, for instance, took six years to repeal its antisodomy laws after being found in violation of the Convention in 1993), but EU states typically comply with ECHR rulings.[28] By 2000, compliance with ECHR rulings was so thorough that its rulings were seen to be "as effective as those of any domestic court."[29] Because conformity with the Convention is crucial for states planning accession to the EU or Council of Europe, activists can use their governments' desire to join those institutions as leverage toward improving national human rights policies by bringing domestic law into line with the ECHR.[30] Such pressure uses membership (or desired membership) in a transnational economic institution as a means to try to expand the equal treatment of citizens and operates in the service of political accountability and observance of human rights.

Whether a state changes its rules or behavior as the result of the decision of a transnational court or other international legal entity depends on the will of the state in question – conditioned perhaps by pressure on the part

[25] Council of Europe, "The ECHR in Practice."
[26] Council of Europe, "About the Committee of Ministers."
[27] Weston, Lukes, and Hnatt, p. 246.
[28] Walker, "Moving Gaily Forward?"
[29] Moravcsik, "The Origins of Human Rights Regimes," p. 218, quoting Lawrence Helfer and Anne-Marie Slaughter, "Toward a Theory of Effective Supranational Adjudication," *Yale Law Journal*, Vol. 107, No. 2 (1997), pp. 273–391.
[30] Walker, "Moving Gaily Forward?"

of citizens. As Robert O. Keohane, Andrew Moravcsik, and Anne-Marie Slaughter explain:

...states are bound by international law to comply with judgments of international courts or tribunals, but no domestic legal mechanism assures legal implementation. If national executives and legislatures fail to take action because of domestic political opposition or simply inertia, states simply incur a further international legal obligation to repair the damage...This is not to say that individuals and groups have no impact on compliance....Even if governments do not ultimately comply, a negative legal judgment may increase the salience of an issue and undermine the legitimacy of the national position in the eyes of domestic constituents.[31]

Even if a state fails to act on a transnational court's judgment, decisions by such courts can be empowering: "Individuals and groups can zero in on international court decisions as focal points around which to mobilize, creating a further intersection between transnational litigation and democratic politics."[32] For these reasons, having an institution to which individuals can bring claims against a rights-violating state is crucial for accountability. In the words of a judge at the ECHR, that institution is the "last resort protector of oppressed individuals."[33] The fact that the Court typically finds for the individual against the state testifies to that protective function.[34]

Citizens who turn to the European Court of Human Rights obviously constitute a self-selecting group. Taking into account the fact that transnational judicial appeals can only be admissible if the applicant has first exhausted all domestic remedies, the most likely litigants in transnational courts will be those who

perceive some use in resorting to the courts at all, suggesting a correlation between the most successful transnational tribunals and those presiding over countries with at least a minimum tradition of the rule of law. Alternatively, litigants in countries with a once-functioning legal system that has been corrupted or otherwise damaged may be quicker to resort to an international tribunal as a substitute or corrective for ineffective or blatantly politicized domestic adjudication.[35]

Although it is difficult to construe Russia's domestic legal system as having featured even a "minimum tradition" of the rule of law, the long era of

[31] Robert O. Keohane, Andrew Moravcsik, and Anne-Marie Slaughter, "Legalized Dispute Resolution: Interstate and Transnational," *International Organization*, Vol. 54, No. 3 (June 2000), pp. 466–7.
[32] Ibid., p. 478.
[33] Quoted in ibid., p. 482.
[34] Ibid., p. 482.
[35] Ibid., p. 484.

communist party rule undoubtedly featured a corrupted judiciary. Indeed, in the years following the collapse of communist party rule, Russia's judicial system remained both "blatantly politicized" as well as "ineffective."

In 1996, Russia was admitted to the Council of Europe and ratified the European Convention in May 1998, giving it the status of Russian domestic law.[36] The path to transnational justice was open. Russia's troubled judicial system, in combination with systematic violations of a number of human rights protected in the European Convention, soon provoked great interest among Russia's citizenry in addressing the ECHR.

THE NON-DEMOCRATIC RUSSIAN STATE

Although Russia shares with more democratic countries some of the trappings of a liberal-democratic state, often, Russian democracy is a matter of form rather than content. In that sense, Russia's "democratization" has been a disappointment in the years following the Soviet Union's collapse in 1991. Writing in 2005, fifteen years after the Soviet dictatorship had come to an end, M. Steven Fish argued that "democratization [had] failed in Russia," and labeled the state an oligarchy, where meaningful political participation was limited to "a circumscribed elite."[37] Holding Russian political realities in the mid-2000s up to Robert Dahl's oft-cited criteria for modern political democracy, Fish found Russia lacking on all but Dahl's first criterion, namely, that "Control over government is constitutionally vested in *elected* officials."[38] On Dahl's other criteria, which include free and fair elections in which "practically all" adults can both vote and run for office, as well as freedom of speech and association, Russia failed. Fish rooted Russia's democratic failures partially in the "superpresidential" system, which privileges the executive over the legislative branch, with dismaying effects for democracy, particularly "the reduction of [political] parties to supplicants for presidential favor."[39] In Fish's view, the other two main sources of Russia's retreat from democracy were its overreliance on natural resources (which fosters corruption, patronage, and economic statism) and, in turn, insufficient economic liberalization, leaving the economy too much in the hands of the state and restricting the dispersion of power thereby. By retaining extensive state control through "predatory"

[36] Jordan, "Russia's Accession to the Council of Europe," p. 283.
[37] M. Steven Fish, *Democracy Derailed in Russia* (New York: Cambridge University Press, 2005), pp. 26–7, 81.
[38] Ibid., p. 30.
[39] Ibid., p. 268.

regulation and patronage, economic statism had reduced the incentives to form representative political parties and interest groups, rendering Russian society "underorganized, inarticulate, and incapable of holding rulers accountable."[40]

"Guilty Until Proven Guilty": Courts in Russia

A young judge in Russia asks an older judge for advice: "One side gave me $1000, and the other gave me $1,020. What should I do?" The older judge responds, "Take another $20 from the first side, and rule according to the law." – Russian anecdote heard in 2006

Another facet of Russia's political infrastructure that hampers democracy is a weak court system. Courts can serve as a crucial means of restraining a powerful executive branch, but only if they are free to act independently of it. Russia's courts, however, largely enhance rather than counterbalance executive power. For instance, the courts have failed to counteract extensive election fraud: "… the executive branch's control of the courts, combined with the nature of the prosecutorial process, virtually excludes the courts as agencies of redress in electoral affairs."[41] In 2002, when a prosecutor in Samara *oblast'* took the rare step of pursuing an election fraud case in the wake of an election to the regional legislature, the prosecutor "acknowledged that for someone in his position to take up such a case was virtually unheard of," because political pressure dictated against it and the resources of the prosecutor's office were extremely limited.[42] Russia's courts under Vladimir Putin's presidency (2000–2008) exhibited subservience to executive branch officials in a variety of cases concerning local elections. This political influence is most evident when courts (and electoral commissions) disqualify candidates not viewed favorably by the Kremlin.[43]

[40] Ibid., p. 248. Other scholars, politicians, and well-informed journalists have reached similarly despairing conclusions about the demise of Russia's fledgling democracy. See Andrew Jack, *Inside Putin's Russia: Can There Be Reform Without Democracy?* (New York: Oxford University Press, 2006); Joel M. Ostrow, Georgiy A. Satarov, Irina M. Khakamada, *The Consolidation of Dictatorship in Russia: An Inside View of the Demise of Democracy* (Westport, CT: Praeger, 2007); Anna Politkovskaya, *A Russian Diary* (New York: Random House, 2007). For analysis of the obstacles to establishing liberal democracy and political accountability in the early post-Yeltsin era, see Marcia Weigle, *Russia's Liberal Project* (University Park: Pennsylvania State University Press, 2000).

[41] Fish, p. 45.

[42] Ibid., pp. 45–6.

[43] See ibid., pp. 61–6, for representative cases.

Russian courts typically support state officials' criminal charges against journalists, especially when journalists write articles critical of the executive branch or the prosecutor's office in a given region.[44] Such cases include criminal "libel" (Article 129 of Russia's Criminal Code) and "insult" (Article 130), as well as "insulting a government official" (Article 319). Between 2000 and 2006, more than three hundred such criminal cases against journalists were launched in Russia, creating a situation that the Russian Union of Journalists described as "legal terror."[45] After an annual address in which Putin drew attention to Russia's declining birthrate and proposed incentives to reverse it, Vladimir Rakhmankov, the editor of an Internet-based independent news website, published a satirical article referring to Putin as "Russia's phallic symbol" and proposing that souvenirs be produced portraying "the president's head as the head of a penis."[46] Rakhmankov, who had also published several pieces critical of the local governor, was charged under Article 319, tried in September 2006, and sentenced to pay a 20,000 ruble fine (roughly $750) the following month.[47]

Courts' suppression of press freedom detracts from a key component of political accountability: the public availability of information. According to the nonprofit organization Freedom House, between 1994 and 2004 press freedom in Russia deteriorated from "partially free" to "not free."[48] Russian courts also suppress freedom of speech through prosecutions of human rights groups. In October 2006, the Russian-Chechen Friendship Society – one of the few human rights groups monitoring Russian military abuses in the breakaway province of Chechnya – was dissolved by court order in the city court of Nizhnii Novgorod, where the group is based.[49] Freedom of information in Russia is limited by more than a

[44] Ibid., pp. 68–70.

[45] Interfax, "Journalists' Organizations Call for Criminal Liability for Libel to Be Abolished," June 20, 2006, accessed August 8, 2006, at http://feeds.moscownews.net/?rid=1 c30d14da74c31ac&cat=871e5a31f6912bb3&f=1. I thank Pamela Jordan for bringing this article to my attention.

[46] "Journalist goes on trial for calling Putin 'Russia's Phallic Symbol," RFE/RL Newsline, September 22, 2006; C. J. Chivers, "Putin Urges Plan to Reverse Slide in the Birthrate," *New York Times*, May 11, 2006, p. A6.

[47] Committee to Protect Journalists, "Russia: Journalist Goes on Trial for Satirizing Putin," September 21, 2006, accessed September 28, 2006, at http://www.cpj.org/news/2006/europe/russia21sept06na.html; Reporters Without Borders, "In 'Grotesque' Sentence Court Fines Website Editor for Insulting Putin," October 27, 2006, accessed November 9, 2006, at http://www.rsf.org/article.php3?id_article=19473.

[48] Fish, pp. 74–5.

[49] Committee to Protect Journalists, "CPJ fears silencing of critical Web site on Chechnya," October 13, 2006, accessed November 9, 2006, at http://www.cpj.org/news/2006/europe/russia13oct06na.html.

toadying court system. In 2006, the assassination of Anna Politkovskaya – a well-known critic of the Putin administration and of the conduct of the war in Chechnya – highlighted the severity of constraints on independent journalism in Russia. Between 2000 and 2006, thirteen journalists in Russia perished in such "contract-style" killings, while none of the murders was solved.[50] Not surprisingly, Russia ranked 147th out of 168 states on the 2006 index of World Press Freedom compiled by the NGO Reporters Without Borders.[51]

Russia's judicial system not only contributes to electoral illegitimacy and the violation of press freedom but is additionally riddled by problems that often prevent it from upholding individual human rights within court proceedings themselves. Before the introduction of a new Criminal Procedure Code in 2002, Russia's judicial system was characterized by a bias toward the prosecution and by an overwhelming conviction rate (approaching 100 percent). A scholar studying a Siberian district court in 1999–2000 repeatedly observed these tendencies. Judges feared to acquit defendants, because regional courts reversed "practically all" acquittals, and judges who did acquit found their careers at risk.[52] Rather than pronouncing defendants "not guilty" in cases where evidence of guilt was lacking, judges routinely turned the case back to the prosecution for further investigation.[53] During such processes of repeated "further investigation," defendants would remain in jail.[54] Nor were coerced confessions forbidden as evidence. Defense attorneys were a rarity in court.[55]

Post-Soviet Russia also lacked jury trials until 1993, at which point Russia's new Constitution mandated their reintroduction. The experimental initiation of jury trials in nine regions in 1993 was beset by difficulties, ranging from finding funds to cover payments to jurors and renovate courtrooms to training judges to operate under the jury trial system. Districts using jury trials were quickly overwhelmed. Once they were able to choose, up to 43 percent of eligible defendants opted for jury

[50] Committee to Protect Journalists, "Russia: Thirteen Murders, No Justice," accessed November 9, 2006, at http://www.cpj.org/Briefings/2005/russia_murders/russia_murders. html.

[51] Reporters Without Borders, "Worldwide Press Freedom Index: 2006," accessed November 23, 2007, at http://www.rsf.org/article.php3?id_article=19384.

[52] Stanislaw Pomorski, "In a Siberian Criminal Court," *East European Constitutional Review*, Vol. 11, Nos. 1/2 (Winter/Spring 2002), p. 112.

[53] Ibid., p. 113.

[54] Mark Kramer, "Rights and Restraints in Russia's Criminal Justice System," Program on New Approaches to Russian Security (PONARS) Policy Memo No. 289, May 2003, p. 5.

[55] Pomorski, pp. 114–15.

trials, given acquittal rates of less than one-half of 1 percent in traditional Russian "bench trials," producing many more cases than could be handled in a timely fashion.[56] By 2003, jury trials were available in all of Russia's eighty-nine regions except the war-torn province of Chechnya, where jury trials were slated to be introduced only in 2007.[57] In late 2006, the Duma passed legislation delaying the implementation of jury trials in Chechnya until 2010.[58]

To some extent, reforms in the 1990s brought positive changes to Russia's legal system regarding judicial independence from the executive branch and the upholding of human rights within the courts.[59] As of 1993, courts would be financed from the federal budget, rather than being beholden financially (and hence politically) to local officials. By 2003, some judges saw improvements in their salaries, which could reduce the prevalence of bribery.[60] But the perceived impact of Russia's legal reforms overall has been unimpressive. A survey on human rights violations in Russia in February 2003 found that 87 percent of respondents believed that "the rights and interests of average Russians are often violated by their employers, public officials, and the police as well as by judges and doctors," and that only 5 percent would be likely to seek the assistance of a court first "to remedy a violation of their legal rights."[61]

Citizens polled in Russia felt overwhelmingly in the late 1990s and early 2000s that attempting to use their court system was fruitless; 72 percent thought it not only costly, but corrupt, and 78 percent agreed that people did not take grievances to court "because they do not expect to find justice there."[62] In May 2005, Russians polled about the judiciary's independence of the executive branch seemed skeptical, with only 6 percent

[56] Irina Dline and Olga Schwartz, "The Jury Is Still Out on the Future of Jury Trials in Russia," *East European Constitutional Review*, Vol. 11, Nos. 1/2 (Winter/Spring 2002), p. 106.

[57] Peter Finn, "In Russia, Trying Times for Trial by Jury," *Washington Post*, October 31, 2005, p. A12, accessed March 27, 2006, at http://www.washingtonpost.com/wp-dyn/content/article/2005/10/30/AR2005103001026_pf.html; Kramer, p. 7.

[58] RIA Novosti, "State Duma Backs Delay in Introducing Jury Trials in Chechnya," November 15, 2006, accessed November 23, 2006, at http://en.rian.ru/russia/20061115/55674530.html. On jury trials and other reforms, particularly concerning the role of defense attorneys *(advokaty)* in Russia's legal system, see Pamela A. Jordan, *Defending Rights in Russia: Lawyers, the State, and Legal Reform in the Post-Soviet Era* (Vancouver: University of British Columbia Press, 2006).

[59] Ibid., p. 146.

[60] Ibid., pp. 146–7.

[61] Ibid., p. 200.

[62] Mikhail Krasnov, "Is the 'Concept of Judicial Reform' Timely?" *East European Constitutional Review*, Vol. 11, Nos. 1/2 (Winter/Spring 2002), pp. 92–4.

saying they did not think that the authorities "use the law enforcement agencies for political purposes," and nearly 50 percent believing that "the authorities use the police and courts for political ends 'constantly'…or 'frequently.'"[63] Highly placed judges have questioned the courts' independence as well, with direct consequences. A Moscow Municipal Court judge, Olga Kudeshkina, was fired in May 2004 after a radio interview during which she "accused the Prosecutor-General's office of pressuring Moscow Municipal Court judges in connection with a number of criminal cases." Kudeshkina appealed her dismissal to Russia's Supreme Court, but was denied.[64]

In July 2002, a new Criminal Procedure Code came into effect in Russia, outlawing many of the previous system's violations of defendants' rights. But the effects of the changes were slow to create "a criminal justice system appropriate for a democratic polity," and even after the new Code entered into effect, some of the Soviet system's flaws remained.[65] Although the new Code reversed the assumption that defendants were guilty, in practice acquittals remained low and were frequently reversed; in 2002, 40 percent of acquittals were overturned by higher courts.[66] According to the new Code, each suspect is guaranteed a defense lawyer, who is supposed to be present during interrogation (to decrease the number of physically forced confessions).[67] Yet indigent suspects often lack lawyers due to a paucity of public defenders (who, in turn, often go unpaid by local governments). Despite being prohibited, coerced testimony is still obtained and used in court.

Importantly, the new Code prohibits returning weak cases to the prosecution for additional investigation and mandates acquittal in such cases. In practice, however, the "results have been disappointing."[68] For example, in a 2004 case against the Sakharov Museum's director and deputy, who curated an exhibit critical of religion in January 2003 and were then

---

[63] "Vast Majority of Russians Have No Faith in Judicial Independence," RFE/RL Newsline, June 3, 2005.

[64] Kudeshkina voiced her intention to appeal to the ECHR. "Supreme Court Upholds Dismissal of Judge for Criticizing Prosecutors," RFE/RL Newsline, January 20, 2005. For more details on the Kudeshkina story, see Guy Chazan, "Benched in Russia's Courts, a Judge Speaks Up – and Gets Fired," *Wall Street Journal*, August 5, 2004, p. A1, accessed November 23, 2007, at http://courses.wcupa.edu/rbove/eco343/040Compecon/Soviet/Russia/040805legal.txt.

[65] Kramer, p. 2.

[66] Ibid.

[67] Ibid., p. 4.

[68] Ibid., p. 5.

charged with inciting ethnic hatred, the prosecution presented a case so weak that the judge "gave the prosecutors more time to refine the charges" rather than dismissing the case, as the 2002 reforms mandate.[69] A year later, the museum director and deputy were convicted and fined $3,300 apiece, while vandalism charges against half a dozen Orthodox believers who had destroyed artwork at the exhibition were dismissed.[70]

Although the new Criminal Procedure Code prohibits double jeopardy, acquitted defendants can still be brought back to trial on similar charges.[71] Moreover, as of 2005, acquittals in jury trials were still subject to appeal by higher courts. Indeed, "almost all jury acquittals are appealed," many on highly technical grounds. Between 2000 and 2005, Russia's Supreme Court overturned between 25 and 50 percent of not-guilty verdicts rendered by juries. In one case from the southern Russian city of Krasnodar, Vladislav Kozachenko had been acquitted by three different juries, but the prosecutor was prepared to appeal to Russia's Supreme Court on the basis of information revealed after the trial – not about the defendant, but about the jurors. Explained the prosecutor, some of the jurors had "concealed certain information about themselves, criminal records and previous service in the police" – providing a basis for appeal. Many prosecutors keep such a "card up their sleeve" according to a Krasnodar regional court judge.[72] Even so, defendants whose alleged crimes make them eligible for a jury trial far prefer such a trial rather than a bench trial.

The differences between jury and non-jury trials continue to be stark. In 2005, the acquittal rate for jury trials was 18 percent, whereas non-jury trials produced only a 3 percent acquittal rate, and 43 percent of acquittals were overturned by higher courts. The chair of Russia's Supreme Court judged the acquittal rate in jury trials as being too high, stating that not only were prosecutors conducting flawed investigations, breaking the law in various ways as they collected evidence, but that the majority of jurors were not qualified to serve, resulting in the high acquittal rates.[73]

---

[69] Steven Lee Myers, "Verdict in Russian Courts: Guilty Until Proven Guilty," *New York Times*, June 20, 2004, Week in Review, p. 3.

[70] "Museum Director Convicted of Inciting Religious Hatred," RFE/RL Newsline, March 29, 2005.

[71] Kramer, p. 6.

[72] Finn, "In Russia, Trying Times for Trial by Jury."

[73] Interfax, "Juries Are Too Lenient – Russian Supreme Court Head," April 9, 2006, accessed August 7, 2006, at http://www.interfax.ru/e/B/politics/28.html?id_issue=11494330; RIA Novosti, "Trial by Jury Provides Too Many Acquittals – Supreme Court Head," April 7, 2006, accessed April 12, 2006, at http://en.rian.ru/russia/20060407/45428737.html.

Public opinion about jury trials in Russia remains mixed. An April 2006 poll conducted across Russia found that 30 percent of citizens surveyed thought jury trials superior to trials where a judge ruled on a defendant's guilt or innocence, while 21 percent thought jury trials less reliable than the traditional bench trials (19 percent thought both methods were equally trustworthy, and 30 percent found it difficult to say one way or the other). The majority of those who preferred jury trials believed that such trials left less room for corruption, and hence were more honest, objective, and independent. A full 78 percent of respondents, however, had no desire to serve on a jury.[74]

Russia's judicial system, despite reform in recent years, faces numerous constraints on its capacity to act as an institution of horizontal accountability (checking the power of the executive branch) as well as its ability to protect Russian citizens' rights. Its limitations stem from the historical legacies of abuse by the state and the communist party, economic constraints, and inadequate provision of legal aid to low-income defendants. The legal system puts defendants at a tremendous disadvantage in many ways and provides average citizens "little hope of using legal instruments reliably to protect their own interests, especially against the powerful."[75] Because Russia's legal system is not yet fully capable of serving as a bulwark against executive power or as a consistent source of protection of Russian citizens' human rights, it is all the more important to explore whether the transnational court now available to the population will have an impact on Russia's domestic courts and law enforcement bodies.

RUSSIA AND THE ECHR

Russia's accession to the Council of Europe and subsequent ratification of the European Convention meant that individual citizens could now bring Russia to the European Court of Human Rights. This opened up a new method for holding the Russian government accountable for human rights violations both inside and outside of the Russian court system. Since 1998, Russia has been the subject of many such complaints. Most of these are never actually heard by the ECHR; like cases originating from other countries, those from Russia are routinely dismissed as inadmissible by

[74] Anna Petrova, "Sud prisiazhnykh" [Trial by Jury], *Fond 'Obshchestvennoe mnenie,'* April 6, 2006, accessed April 12, 2006, at http://bd.fom.ru/report/map/projects/dominant/domo614/ domto614_4/do61423, translation mine.
[75] Stephen Holmes, "Introduction: Reforming Russia's Courts," *East European Constitutional Review*, Vol. 11, Nos. 1/2 (Winter/Spring 2002), p. 90.

the Court.[76] Admissible or not, the thousands of complaints filed yearly by Russian citizens indicate a certain enthusiasm for holding their government accountable for violations of human rights. Thwarted at home by an overly powerful executive branch, a weak court system, and the pervasive violation of human rights, Russia's citizens, now entitled to appeal to the ECHR, began reaching out transnationally to hold their rulers accountable from abroad. The Russian state soon found itself struck by the business end of the ECHR's gavel, losing case after case at the Court.

Popular awareness of the ECHR expanded rapidly, and with it the number of applications to the court skyrocketed. Over the course of 1999, the Court had "taken up more cases from Russia...than from any other country."[77] By the end of 2004, of the states with over two thousand applications pending, Russia and Poland were tied for first place, each with 14 percent of the total number of applications pending at the ECHR.[78] One year later, there were 13,945 cases pending against Russia at the ECHR, and citizens of Russia had submitted more complaints than from any other country (a total of 8,500 over the course of that year alone).[79] In March 2006, the ECHR had reportedly received a total of 28,000 complaints from Russian citizens since 1998.[80] On January 1, 2007, there were 19,300 Russian cases pending at the ECHR, equaling 21.5 percent of the total number of pending cases (far more than from any other state).[81]

The terms describing the progress of a case at the ECHR can be confusing. Citizens seeking redress at the ECHR submit "applications," which are then logged and reviewed to determine whether they are "manifestly inadmissible" (if, for instance, the applicant failed to exhaust his or her

---

[76] In 2006, the ECHR registered 50,500 applications, declared 28,160 "inadmissible or struck off," and found only 1,634 admissible. In 2006, Russian citizens lodged 10,569 applications, and 151 were declared admissible (note that admissibility is not necessarily determined during the year in which the complaint is brought to the ECHR). See European Court of Human Rights, "Survey of Activities: 2006," pp. 38, 40, accessed November 8, 2007, at http://www.echr.coe.int/NR/rdonlyres/69564084–9825-430B-9150-A9137DD22737/0/Survey_2006.pdf.

[77] "Russian Cases Most Numerous at European Human Rights Court," RFE/RL Newsline, January 25, 2000.

[78] European Court of Human Rights, "European Court of Human Rights Statistics 2004," April 2005, p. 11, accessed March 27, 2006, at http://www.echr.coe.int/NR/rdonlyres/F2B964EE-57C5–4C86-8B8F-8B4B6095D89C/0/MicrosoftWordstatistical_charts_2004__internet_.pdf.

[79] Guy Chazan, "In Russia, Grim Case Spotlights Distress of Justice Denied," *Wall Street Journal*, April 26, 2006, p.A1.

[80] "European Court Says Police Mistreated Russian Woman," RFE/RL Newsline, March 10, 2006.

[81] European Court of Human Rights, "Survey of Activities: 2006," p. 51.

domestic remedies, or if the claim was filed more than six months after a final Russian court decision). Claims that raise genuine issues under the European Convention and are not deemed manifestly inadmissible are then "communicated" to the government of the state in question (e.g., the government is notified of the application and its contents), which is asked to present its side of the story in writing. The applicant can then respond to the government's submission. Only after these steps does the Court make a decision on the admissibility or inadmissibility of the case. Those few cases that scale this hurdle and are labeled admissible will then be addressed by the ECHR. Applications located at any stage of the procedure are labeled "pending." Only a small fraction of the cases submitted are eventually taken up by the Court, resulting in a judgment on the "merits" or substance of the complaint. Because of the enormous number of cases and the scrutiny that they undergo, it can take several years for a case to proceed all the way from the application to the final judgment phase.[82]

Applicants are encouraged to engage professional assistance in preparing and submitting their claims. In Russia, human rights lawyers and a handful of nongovernmental organizations (NGOs) focusing on legal consultation provide this service. One such NGO is the Urals-based group Sutiazhnik (Sutyajnik), which provides free legal advice to Russian citizens in Ekaterinburg and the surrounding region, as well as advice by phone and on-line, allowing for a broader geographic range of citizen access. According to Sutiazhnik's 2005 annual report, the organization gave 856 free consultations in 2005, around 40 percent of which were to people who wanted to prepare an appeal to the European Court of Human Rights. Sutiazhnik's analysis of citizens' requests between 2004 and 2005 showed a growing "awareness and understanding" of both the Russian legal system and the ECHR, suggesting an increase not only in the number of people seeking redress from abroad, but also in their legal sophistication.[83]

The fact that the ECHR is available to Russian citizens now approaches common knowledge. Some Russian NGOs (such as the Urals Center for Constitutional and International Protection of Human Rights, a project of Sutiazhnik) provide instructions on their websites about how to submit a case to the ECHR and offer extensive documentation and analysis of ECHR activities as well as critiques of the Russian legal system's failings. Diederik Lohman, a senior researcher at Human Rights Watch, notes that

---

[82] I am grateful to Diederik Lohman for clarifying this process for me. Diederik Lohman, Senior Researcher, Human Rights Watch, phone interview by author, July 20, 2006.

[83] Sutyajnik, "2005 Annual Report," accessed November 24, 2007, at http://www.sutyajnik. ru/rus/reports/2005/eng/cons.htm.

familiarity with the existence of the Court should not be mistaken for an understanding of its procedures or its function:

> Most people will have heard of the European Court. But the real knowledge about how to pursue a case is absent. People have a vague notion that the Court is there, but the fact that you have to exhaust your domestic remedies – very few people are aware of that, and of the fact that you can only complain about your rights in the Convention's articles – that's something that most people are not aware of.[84]

Of the cases proceeding all the way to a judgment, the percentage of cases where the ECHR has found violations is consistently high across states. In 2005, the ECHR reached judgments on a total of 994 cases where at least one violation was found and 48 where no violations were found – an overall violation rate of 95 percent.[85] Russia's violation rate exceeds this only slightly. Looking cumulatively from 1998, when Russia ratified the European Convention, through the end of 2005, the total number of judgments involving Russia was 105; 101 of them were violations (four were nonviolations), or 96 percent (see Table 1).[86]

The human rights violations brought to the ECHR from Russian citizens tend to cluster around particular articles of the European Convention. According to Anatolii Kovler, a Russian judge serving on the ECHR in 2005, "a plurality of complaints involve the failure to enforce Russian court decisions" (covered under Article 6, the right to a fair trial), as well as complaints by journalists accused of crimes by local political

TABLE 1. *Number of Russian cases in which ECHR judgments were rendered, by year, 2002–2005*

Year	Judgments	Violations	Nonviolations
2005	83	81	2
2004	15	13	2
2003	5	5	0
2002	2	2	0

[84] Lohman, phone interview, July 20, 2006.
[85] European Court of Human Rights, "Survey of Activities: 2005," p. 31, accessed November 8, 2007, at http://www.echr.coe.int/NR/rdonlyres/4753F3E8-3ADo-42C5-B294-0-F2A68507FCo/o/2005_SURVEY__COURT_.pdf.
[86] Compiled from Council of Europe/European Court of Human Rights, "Yearly Surveys of Activities, 1998–2005," accessed March 27, 2006, from Reports at http://www.echr.coe.int/ECHR.

authorities (covered by Article 10, freedom of expression), and also those stemming from "the state of Russia's remand prisons" (covered under Article 3, which prohibits degrading treatment).[87] Other subjects warranting significant numbers of claims to the ECHR include the violation of the right to free assembly (Article 11) and complaints under Article 2 (the state's obligation to protect life), particularly concerning the state's failure to conduct a sufficient investigation into the cause of a person's death.[88] Acknowledging the failures of Russia's state bureaucracies and courts alike that generated such overwhelming numbers of complaints to the ECHR, Kovler stated, "It is very important that we educate bureaucrats and jurists so that they know exactly what the European-style human rights are that Russia is striving for."[89]

Russia Goes to Court: Losing Cases at the ECHR

Russia's initial losses at the ECHR demonstrated that the state's "bureaucrats and jurists" routinely violated the European Convention at home. The first completed case at the ECHR featuring Russia, *Burdov v. Russia*, was declared partly admissible by the Court in June 2001. The Burdov case concerned a retiree who had not received compensation promised him from the Soviet government after he participated in the cleanup following the accident at the Chernobyl nuclear power station in 1986. Despite proving in a Russian court that his health had suffered as a direct result of his efforts to contain the effects of the nuclear disaster, and winning the right to claim benefits on that basis, Burdov was unable to compel the social security service to make the payments due him. The Russian court decision had legal force, but no practical consequences. In May 2002, the ECHR found that Russia was in violation of Article 6 (the right to a fair trial) and Article 1 of Protocol 1 (the protection of property), and awarded Burdov 3,000 euros to be paid by the Russian government.[90]

In Russia's second case at the ECHR, Valery Kalashnikov, president of a small Siberian bank from which he was accused of embezzling, was jailed in

---

[87] "Russians Have 22,000 Complaints Pending in Strasbourg," RFE/RL Newsline, April 21, 2005.

[88] See http://www.humanrights.by.ru/sutjazhnik/otch2002.shtml.

[89] Quoted in "Russians Have 22,000 Complaints Pending in Strasbourg."

[90] Jordan, "Russia's Accession to the Council of Europe," p. 284. For details of the case, see European Court of Human Rights, "Case of Burdov v. Russia," Judgment, May 7, 2002, accessed December 13, 2008, at http://cmiskp.echr.coe.int/tkp197/view.asp?action=html&documentId=698326&portal=hbkm&source=externalbydocnumber&table=F69A27FD8FB86142BF01C1166DEA398649.

pretrial detention for four years, during which he was beaten and held with twenty-four other prisoners in a 17-square-meter cell intended to hold eight people. In July 2002, Kalashnikov won what was to be a significant victory. The ECHR found that his rights under Article 3 (prohibiting torture and degrading treatment), Article 5 (the right to liberty), and Article 6 (the right to a fair trial) were violated. Kalashnikov was awarded 5,000 euros in non-pecuniary damages as well as 3,000 euros to cover legal costs. Russia's representative to the Court, Pavel Laptev, voiced disagreement with the ruling itself, while acknowledging that "the conditions of Kalashnikov's custody did not meet the requirements set for penal institutions in other Council of Europe member countries."[91] Ella Pamfilova, at the time serving as Russia's human rights commissioner, noted that the ECHR decision constituted a "precedent" and sounded "a very serious [warning] bell" for Russian courts and law enforcement.[92] Both the Burdov and Kalashnikov cases highlighted serious problems in Russia's observance of the Convention, and would be followed by many other applications to the Court in the same vein.

In January 2006, in an even more striking application of the European Convention's Article 3, the ECHR ordered the Russian government to pay over U.S.$300,000 in compensation to Aleksei Mikheyev, who became paralyzed from the waist down after jumping out of a window in a police station where he was being tortured as part of a criminal investigation in 1998. Mikheyev, a former traffic police officer, remarked that the ECHR's verdict "would not have been possible in Russia."[93] During his interrogation, Mikheyev was accused of raping and murdering a teenager (who showed up alive and well some days later, having gone to visit friends without informing her parents). When he denied having committed the crime, his interrogators "attached metal clamps to his earlobes" and applied powerfully painful electric shocks. In desperation, after several such shocks, Mikheyev broke away, smashed a window, and jumped.[94]

In March 2006, the ECHR similarly ruled for Russian citizen Olga Menesheva, who was, after being arrested in 1999, "allegedly bundled into

[91] "European Court Of Human Rights Finds Against Russia...," RFE/RL Newsline, July 16, 2002; "... In Case Called Precedent-Setting," RFE/RL Newsline, July 16, 2002. Also see European Court of Human Rights, "Case of Kalashnikov v. Russia," Judgment, July 15, 2002, accessed December 13, 2008, at http://cmiskp.echr.coe.int/tkp197/view.asp?action=html&documentId=698483&portal=hbkm&source=externalbydocnumber&table=F69A27FD8FB86142BF01C1166DEA398649.

[92] Quoted in "... In Case Called Precedent-Setting."

[93] "European Court Tells Russia to Pay Torture Victim," RFE/RL Newsline, February 1, 2006.

[94] Guy Chazan, "In Russia, Grim Case Spotlights Distress of Justice Denied."

a car and taken to a police station, where she was beaten up and threatened with rape and violence against her family." She then received a sentence of five days in jail for "resisting arrest." The failure of the Russian government to investigate her claims about the abuse, as well as the abuse itself (covered by the prohibition on torture in Article 3), as well as adverse findings under several other articles, resulted in the ECHR's ruling to award Menesheva U.S.$42,000 in damages.[95] The ECHR judgment found that Menesheva's complaints about ill treatment were not effectively investigated, and that the "investigation was only opened almost four years after the events complained of, when the matter was brought to the attention of the domestic authorities in connection with the applicant's proceedings before the Court." Even then, continued the judgment, there was no follow-up, and "the Court could not but conclude that in the past three years the authorities had not remedied the shortfalls of which they had been acutely aware." The ECHR judgment also pointed explicitly to the lack of the domestic court's independence from the prosecutor: "The domestic civil courts did not make an independent assessment of the facts and simply endorsed the prosecutor's opinion that the applicant's claim was unmeritorious." The Russian government's response was to accept "that the proceedings at issue had been defective both under domestic law and the Convention."[96]

Delays at trial constitute a significant portion of cases brought against Russia at the ECHR. In 2005, the ECHR found against Russia in the case of Tamara Rokhlina, who was accused, in a somewhat sensational case, of murdering her politician husband, General Lev Rokhlin, in 1998. Rokhlina was initially convicted for the killing in 2000, but the verdict was reversed in 2001 by Russia's Supreme Court, which ordered a new trial. Four years later, however, no retrial had been convened, and she remained in jail. The ECHR ruled that this considerable delay violated Rokhlina's right to a "speedy trial" as well as her right to "remain at liberty" while on trial, and ordered the Russian government to pay her U.S.$10,300.[97] The Russian government then began Rokhlina's new trial and appealed the ECHR's verdict, but the ECHR upheld it in November 2005.[98] Rokhlina

---

[95] "European Court Says Police Mistreated Russian Woman"; ECHR Registrar "Chamber Judgment Menesheva v. Russia," Press Release, March 9, 2006, accessed March 29, 2006, at http://www.echr.coe.int/Eng/Press/2006/March/ChamberjudgmentMeneshevavRussia090306.htm.

[96] Ibid.

[97] "Russia Suffers Another Loss at European Court of Human Rights," RFE/RL Newsline, April 8, 2005.

[98] "European Court of Human Rights Upholds Verdict Against Russia," RFE/RL Newsline, November 2, 2005.

was convicted anew of the same crime by a court in the Moscow region in November 2005.[99]

Cases arising from political repression have also found a hearing at the ECHR. In particular, the Russian state has found itself the subject of attention from the Court as a result of jailing its critics on false charges. Grigory Pasko, a military journalist and whistleblower (about the dumping of nuclear waste), was sentenced to hard labor for alleged espionage in 2001. Freed in 2003, Pasko appealed to the ECHR on the basis that he had not had a fair trial and about various other violations of his rights. His case was communicated to the Russian government in May 2005, but as of the end of September 2005 the state had failed to respond to the Court.[100] In a similar case, Igor Sutyagin, a political scientist jailed since 1999 for alleged espionage, took his case to the ECHR, where it was pending as of 2004, after Russia's Supreme Court upheld his fifteen-year sentence.[101] In another espionage case, this time against a physicist, Valentin Danilov, the defendant was acquitted by a jury and then jailed after a 2004 appeal to the Supreme Court by his prosecutors.[102] Political influence over the judges was evident; it was clear that the "guilty" verdict had been prepared in advance, since the Court presented its written ruling "only minutes after hearing arguments."[103] Danilov appealed to the ECHR in January 2006.[104] In another case involving the political opponents of Russia's government, in March 2006 the ECHR supported the claim of an alleged member of Russia's National Bolshevik Party who took part in a sit-in at the reception area of President Putin's office in December 2004. She was subsequently jailed for nearly a year "on remand," then found guilty in December 2005 and given a three-year (suspended) sentence.

---

[99] "Widow of Slain Duma Deputy Convicted in Retrial," RFE/RL Newsline, November 29, 2005.

[100] Jon Gauslaa, "European Court Takes Action," September 30, 2005, accessed August 10, 2006, at http://www.bellona.org/english_import_area/international/russia/envirorights/pasko/40027.

[101] "Sutyagin Loses Another Appeal...as Attorneys Pin Hopes on European Court," RFE/RL Newsline, August 18, 2004; see also Bellona, "Sutyagin Case," accessed August 10, 2006, at http://www.bellona.org/subjects/Sutyagin_case. In May 2006, the ECHR communicated twenty questions about the Sutyagin case to the Russian government. U.S. Department of State, Bureau of Democracy, Human Rights, and Labor, *Country Reports on Human Rights Practices: Russia* (2006), March 6, 2007, accessed November 8, 2007, at http://www.state.gov/g/drl/rls/hrrpt/2006/78835.htm.

[102] Myers, p. 3.

[103] Ibid., p. 3.

[104] "Jailed Nuclear Scientist Appeals to European Court of Human Rights," RFE/RL Newsline, January 6, 2006.

Valentina Dolgova (twenty years old in 2006) appealed to the ECHR, which found a violation on the basis of Article 5 section 3 (the right to be tried within a reasonable amount of time or to be released from custody pending trial).[105]

The ECHR has also ruled in favor of some of Russia's most famous "oligarchs." In May 2004, the ECHR held that Vladimir Gusinskii (the former head of a once-powerful company called Media-MOST) had been illegally arrested in June 2000, when "Russian officials pressured him to transfer his assets to the state in exchange for his release from jail" (specifically, Gusinskii was forced to sign an agreement that he would sell Media-MOST to the Russian state's natural gas monopoly, Gazprom). The Court found that the Russian state should pay Gusinskii U.S.$105,000 to cover the cost of his trial.[106] In another case involving an oligarch, Mikhail Khodorkovskii (CEO of the now-bankrupt oil company Yukos), was jailed on fraud and tax evasion charges in a penal colony in Siberia; his arrest was widely viewed as payback for his financial support of political parties opposing the executive branch. Khodorkovskii announced in December 2005 that he had appealed to the ECHR about his transfer to the penal colony, and perhaps would appeal the trial as well.[107] In April 2006, the ECHR took Khodorkovskii's appeal under consideration.[108]

Occasionally, the ECHR's judgments identify areas of domestic law incompatible with the European Convention. In such cases, the state in question is required to change the law. In one such judgment, *Rakevich v. Russia*, the ECHR found in October 2003 that Russia's Law on Psychiatric Treatment and the system of involuntary psychiatric hospitalization was

---

[105] "European Court of Human Rights Rules in Favor of a Russian National Bolshevik Party Member," *In Their Own Voices: Eurasian Human Rights Digest*, No. 11 (February 27–March 6, 2006), citing the ECHR press release of March 2, 2006. According to Dolgova's claim, she was not a member of the National Bolshevik Party, but was swept into the action at the President's office unwittingly by the crowd, while taking a walk in central Moscow. See European Court of Human Rights, "Case of Dolgova v. Russia," Judgment, March 2, 2006, accessed December 14, 2008, at http://cmiskp.echr.coe.int/tkp197/view.asp?action=html&documentId=793001&portal=hbkm&source=externalb ydocnumber&table=F69A27FD8FB86142BF01C1166DEA398649.

[106] "Oligarch Wins Suit Against Russia at European Court," RFE/RL Newsline, May 20, 2004. See also European Court of Human Rights, "Case of Gusinskiy v. Russia," Judgment, May 19, 2004, accessed December 13, 2008 at http://cmiskp.echr.coe.int/tkp197/view.asp?action=html&documentId=699643&portal=hbkm&source=externalbydocnu mber&table=F69A27FD8FB86142BF01C1166DEA398649.

[107] "Embattled Oligarch Sent to Pack Boxes," RFE/RL Newsline, April 4, 2006; "Khodorkovskii Appeals to European Court of Human Rights...as Lawyer Assails Prison Conditions," RFE/RL Newsline, December 5, 2005.

[108] U.S. Department of State, *Country Reports on Human Rights Practices: Russia (2006)*.

inconsistent with the European Convention. The applicant in this case was involuntarily confined in a psychiatric hospital for thirty-nine days before a local court determined that her detention had been medically necessary, violating the five-day time limit for such decisions specified in Russian law. The ECHR also found a section of the Russian law on psychiatric treatment to be in violation of Article 5 (freedom from unlawful detention) and thus that Russia's law should be changed to allow a person in a psychiatric hospital to appeal to a court on their own behalf (to challenge the legality of their detention) rather than through a representative of the hospital – something Rakevich had been unable to do.[109] The law in question had not been changed as of July 2008.[110]

This diverse collection of findings illustrates that a transnational judicial institution has repeatedly held the Russian government accountable to some of its citizens, at the very least, by ordering it to provide monetary compensation to claimants when it violates the human rights convention to which it is party. It is, however, easier to pay what are to the Russian government minor amounts of compensation to individuals than to overhaul the political system, judicial system, and state bureaucracies, which together generate the bulk of human rights violations. Such broad-based changes would render the state more proactively accountable to its citizens across the board rather than the post-hoc individual redress accessible only to those who have lawyers capable of submitting a case to the ECHR.

---

[109] See News Agency Sutyajnik-Press, "Rakevich v. Russia," October 28, 2003, accessed March 25, 2006, at http://www.sutyajnik.ru/eng/news/2004/r_v_r.html; for more explanation, see Anton Burkov and Anna Demeneva, "Probable Legal Consequences of Rakevich v. Russia," *Human Rights Law Review Student Supplement*, Human Rights Law Center, School of Law, University of Nottingham, August 2004, pp. 7–11, accessed August 10, 2006, at http://www.sutyajnik.ru/eng/news/2004/HRLR_Student_Supplement_2004.pdf; see also Anton Leonidovich Burkov, "Detention of Mentally Ill Persons in the Russian Federation under Article 5 of the European Convention on Human Rights," in A. Umland, ed., *The Implementation of the European Convention on Human Rights in Russia: Philosophical, Legal, and Empirical Studies (Soviet and Post-Soviet Politics & Society)*, Vol. 1, 2004, pp. 121–43, accessed August 10, 2006, at http://www.sutyajnik.ru/cgi-bin/articles.php?pub_id=11. See also European Court for Human Rights, "Case of Rakevich v. Russia," Judgment, October 28, 2003, accessed December 13, 2008, at http://cmiskp.echr.coe.int/tkp197/view.asp?action=html&documentId=699291&portal=hbkm&source=externalbydocnumber&table=F69A27FD8FB86142BF01C1166DEA398649. The text of Article 5 (4) states, "Everyone who is deprived of his liberty by arrest or detention shall be entitled to take proceedings by which the lawfulness of his detention shall be decided speedily by a court and his release ordered if the detention is not lawful."
[110] Anton Burkov, attorney, Urals Center for Constitutional and International Protection of Human Rights (Russia), email communication with author, July 26, 2008.

Beyond the superficial band-aid of monetary compensation, what changes has the ECHR inspired within Russia's judicial institutions and law enforcement bodies, and at the policy level, to prevent the violation of Russian citizens' human rights? This section explores the responses of the Russian government to ECHR decisions regarding the area riddled with the most severe human rights violations – the military conflict in Chechnya. The chapter then turns to signs of the ECHR's impact on Russian government policy regarding reform of the law enforcement and judicial systems and then takes up the impact of the ECHR on Russian judges themselves.

The ECHR's Impact on Human Rights Violations: Chechyna

A mountainous region located in southern Russia, Chechnya has been the site of an extended, devastating war between the Russian military and ethnic Chechen rebels seeking independence for their territory. The first phase of the war in Chechnya began in 1994 and lasted until Russian forces were routed in 1996. The war's second phase began in 1999, under the leadership of Russia's then–prime minister Vladimir Putin, who pledged to rub out the Chechen rebels after cornering them "in the shithouse."[111] Over the course of the war, Russian military forces razed Chechnya's capital city, Grozny; massacred Chechen villagers; and attacked Chechen civilians. For their part, Chechen rebels sponsored terrorist acts in Russian cities as far off as Moscow.[112] After Russia's ratification of the European Convention in 1998, the war continued against the backdrop of a subtle difference: Chechens victimized by the conflict could now turn to the ECHR, complaining of human rights violations.

By November 2000, the failure of Russia's law enforcement system to properly investigate attacks on Chechen civilians by Russian troops had provoked sixteen applications to the ECHR from civilian victims of the war. A few months later, close to one hundred applications from Chechnya had been sent to the Court.[113] The Chechnya cases slowly wended their way through the Court procedures. Finally, in February

---

[111] Quoted in Anna Politkovskaya, *A Dirty War: A Russian Reporter in Chechnya* (London: Harvill Press, 1999), p. 91.

[112] See Matthew Evangelista, *The Chechen Wars* (Washington: Brookings Institution Press, 2002).

[113] John Crowfoot, "Postscript" to Politkovskaya, *A Dirty War*, p. 322.

2005, the ECHR ruled in three separate cases that Russia had to pay damages to the families of Chechen residents "whose relatives died at the hands of Russian troops or who suffered as a result of Russian military action in 1999 and 2000." The ECHR's decision found that Russia had violated the complainants' human rights and that Russian soldiers had "killed innocent Chechen civilians" without having been held accountable.[114] When the Russian government appealed the decision, the appeal was denied, leaving Russia to pay $228,000 in damages to the affected families.[115] Well over one hundred complaints about human right violations associated with the Chechen conflict were pending at the ECHR as of mid-2006.

Such cases come to the attention of the ECHR with the aid of human rights NGOs. Initial assistance was provided by the Russian human rights organization Memorial, which was soon joined by other organizations hoping to hold the Russian government accountable for its atrocities.[116] One such group, the Stichting Russian Justice Initiative (SRJI), founded in 2001, had its origins in the work of a transnational NGO, Human Rights Watch. Diederik Lohman, one of SRJI's initiators, explained:

Human Rights Watch doesn't normally do litigation work. It started because we had done research on abuses in Chechnya. At some point, we decided to do some research on accountability to see whether the Russians were actually acting on the information that we and others were filing with them, on executions, and so forth. We reinterviewed people we had spoken to earlier, to see: Had anything happened? Had the prosecutor's office contacted or questioned any of them? Had the prosecutor's office requested that an exhumation be done for forensic examination? It was quickly clear that there was none of that. And we found that a lot of the victims really wanted to see justice done, and it was clear that it wasn't going to happen in Russia, and that people didn't have the knowledge to be able to bring a case themselves to the ECHR, and yet at the same time, there was such strong evidence. We were even getting evidence from the civilian prosecutor's office; they would say, "We can establish that the person was taken to a military base, so it's not in our jurisdiction; we handed it over to the military prosecutor – and then the case died." That's very good evidence – it establishes that the person was indeed detained and taken to a military base! It seemed criminal not to act on such good evidence.[117]

[114] "European Court Rules Against Russia in Chechnya Cases," RFE/RL Newsline, February 25, 2005.
[115] "European Court for Human Rights Rejects Russian Appeal," RFE/RL Newsline, July 19, 2005.
[116] Crowfoot, p. 322. On the origins of Memorial, see Kathleen E. Smith, *Remembering Stalin's Victims* (Ithaca: Cornell University Press, 1996).
[117] Lohman, phone interview, July 20, 2006. The website for the Stichting Russian Justice Initiative, an NGO based in the Netherlands with an office in Russia, is www.srji.org.

The overwhelming majority of cases handled by the Russian Justice Initiative involve "disappearances," the ramifications of which can fall under several articles of the European Convention, including the state's obligation not only to protect life, but also to investigate cases of suspicious death properly. By and large, such cases occur when a Chechen man is unlawfully detained by Russian military forces and never returns. Relatives of the missing person typically appeal to the local prosecutor's office to demand an investigation into the person's disappearance, to no avail.[118]

The prosecutors' offices clearly constituted a sticking point within Russia's legal system. Numerous victims of the conflict were able to submit admissible "disappearance" cases to the ECHR even though many of them technically had not pursued their cases to the top of Russia's judicial hierarchy:

At some point, these [disappearance] cases are admissible because you *can't* exhaust your domestic remedies. A case is opened [at the prosecutor's office], and they don't close the investigation, and you're kind of stuck; you're in a holding pattern. So the Court looks at what reasonable expectations are in terms of the exhaustion of domestic remedies. Its view on this is somewhat lenient. If you filed your complaint with the prosecutor, and the criminal investigation is not making progress, the Court doesn't require you to take further steps.[119]

Recognizing that these applicants had been thwarted by Russian prosecutors' offices, the ECHR did not reject their cases.

Chechen applicants ultimately turned to the ECHR because their attempts to use the legal system to hold the Russian government and military accountable had failed. Indeed, disappearance cases typically stall within the prosecutor's office despite abundant evidence, even when the identity of the perpetrators would not be difficult to establish. In cases where the prosecutor's office pursues the case, "as soon as it gets close to identifying the actual perpetrators, it dies."[120] In the end, "the military intelligence service doesn't want to sacrifice someone who's responsible for a disappearance, and a lid is put on the whole thing. ...When an investigation goes on and then stops, it must be political."[121] The notable lack of

[118] Lohman, phone interview, July 20, 2006.
[119] Lohman, phone interview, July 20, 2006.
[120] Lohman, phone interview, July 20, 2006.
[121] Lohman, phone interview, July 20, 2006. Lohman's point about military intelligence being the likely source of responsibility for the disappearances of detainees is confirmed by the case of *Bazorkina v. Russia*; the ECHR's judgment states that in this disappearance case, it was military intelligence and Russia's Federal Security Service (FSB) who "dealt with the detainees" (see point 58 in the *Bazorkina v. Russia* judgment). European Court of Human Rights, "Case of Bazorkina v. Russia," Judgment, July 27, 2006,

investigative effort by prosecutors' offices in Chechnya is thus rooted in a deep-seated accountability problem.

The availability of the ECHR to Russia's citizens has had a visible effect on the pattern of lackadaisical prosecutorial activity. Although investigations into disappearances tend to grind to a halt within the prosecutor's office, in cases where a complaint is not found manifestly inadmissible at the ECHR, the situation can change dramatically:

What you see is that when the European Court *communicates* a case to the Russian government, then the prosecutor's office *does* pursue the case – they start conducting all the investigative steps that they should have conducted three years earlier, when they first learned about [the disappearance]. In the course of a few months they start doing everything, from requesting exhumations for forensic examination, to interviewing witnesses, and so on.[122]

Transnational attention to a case by the ECHR thus generates an improvement in the pursuit of evidence in individual investigations.

An ECHR judgment from July 2006, *Bazorkina v. Russia*, echoed the pattern characterizing the course of typical disappearance cases in Chechnya. The case was brought by Fatima Bazorkina regarding her son, Khadzhi-Murat Yandiyev. The latter had left for Chechnya in August 1999. Some months later, in a peculiar twist of fate, Bazorkina saw her son on the Russian TV news "being interrogated by a Russian officer... [after which] the officer in charge gave instructions for the soldiers to 'finish off' and 'shoot'" Yandiyev. After Bazorkina determined that her son could not be found within any of Russia's prisons or detention centers, she attempted to have her son's disappearance case investigated, but a military prosecutor refused to open an investigation. A criminal investigation into Yandiev's "abduction by unknown persons" was begun in July 2001, but stalled. In the meantime, Bazorkina appealed to the European Court of Human Rights, which communicated her case to the Russian government in November 2003. Predictably, the investigation took off only after that point. According to the ECHR's press release on the case, the "majority of documents in the case file were dated after December 2003."[123] In

---

accessed December 13, 2008, at http://cmiskp.echr.coe.int/tkp197/view.asp?action=html &documentId=807138&portal=hbkm&source=externalbydocnumber&table=F69A27F D8FB86142BF01C1166DEA398649.

[122] Lohman, phone interview, July 20, 2006.

[123] European Court of Human Rights, Press Release by ECHR Registrar, "Chamber Judgment: Bazorkina v. Russia," July 27, 2006, accessed December 13, 2008, at http://cmiskp. echr.coe.int/tkp197/view.asp?action=html&documentId=807136&portal=hbkm&sourc e=externalbydocnumber&table=F69A27FD8FB86142BF01C1166DEA398649.

its judgment for Bazorkina, the Court found serious inadequacies in the investigative process, as well as in the state's observance of its obligation to protect life under Article 2 of the Convention.

Pressure from the ECHR regarding individual cases reaches local prosecutors' offices by way of Moscow. A case communicated to the Russian government by the ECHR will initially land at the prosecutor-general's office in Moscow. Explains Lohman:

From there it gets referred to the Department of the Prosecutor-General's Office for Southern Russia, and the Department for Southern Russia will put a special investigator on the case. And so instead of the case being supervised only at the local level, suddenly you have these bigshots from Moscow starting to ask about the case, and to demand documents about the case. What happens is that when a case concerns a prosecutor's office in Grozny, say, the top person in the prosecutor's office in Grozny gets a message from Moscow saying, 'We need all the information on this case, you need to investigate it, you need to do this, this, and this.' And I imagine what happens is that at the next working meeting with all of the colleagues in that local office, they're going to talk about it. The whole office will be aware that there's this "*Ch.P.*" (as they say in Russia), this emergency situation. And now that there are something like fifty [SRJI] cases that have been communicated, and something like twenty or thirty Memorial cases that have been communicated, every prosecutor's office in Chechnya is dealing with them. And so they become aware that this is not something that's just going to happen once or twice.[124]

Repeated ECHR judgments finding violations in Chechnya may have begun to have a salutary effect on the conduct of investigations across the board. In addition to prosecutors' offices enhancing activity on particular cases once they have been communicated by the Court, prosecutors are sometimes responding differently to initial requests for investigations:

Another thing that we're starting to see is that the prosecutor's office in some cases is starting to be more careful about how they respond. I think they're starting to understand that when they get a complaint, the individual may very well go to the ECHR. So in a number of cases, they *are acting rather than ignoring*. That's obviously something on the positive side.[125]

Use of the ECHR, therefore, has shown some limited success at holding Russian prosecutors' offices accountable for the investigation of disappearances in cases concerning Chechnya.

Although the ECHR deals with cases one at a time, accumulated cases exhibiting the same violations do draw the attention of the Council of Europe's Committee of Ministers, which is responsible for monitoring the

[124] Lohman, phone interview, July 20, 2006.
[125] Lohman, phone interview, July 20, 2006.

implementation of the Court's judgments by the state in question. Repeated cases pointing to the failings of Russia's prosecutors' offices should generate pressure on the Russian government to initiate change at the policy level, addressing the gaps in the procuracy's effectiveness in order to prevent further violations:

Once the Court has looked at an individual case and has issued a ruling, it's referred to the Committee of Ministers for supervision of implementation. And so the Committee will ask: What are the general issues that flow from this ruling, and what are the general measures that should be implemented in order to address the systemic problem? And so what is going to happen over time is that as the Court issues more and more rulings in individual cases, we'll start seeing that the prosecutor's office in each of those cases will be identified as not having done its job. Once you've seen twenty opinions by the court identifying the same failings, then the Committee of Ministers can start saying that there's clearly something wrong with the prosecutor's office, because it's constantly being identified as failing in its obligations by the Court.[126]

The degree of pressure that the Committee of Ministers is willing to exert on Russia's government to address even such egregious violations of accountability is limited, however. As Lohman frankly states, "The Committee of Ministers is a political organ. They are not keen on taking Russia to task over this. It is going to take a good amount of evidence before they say 'something's got to change here.' We're years away from that."[127]

In accordance with the Court's rules, the Russian government has responded to the Committee of Ministers with respect to the judgments on the first three cases from Chechnya (*Khashiyev and Akayeva v. Russia*; *Isayeva, Yusupova, and Bazayeva v. Russia*; and *Isayeva v. Russia*), issued by the Court in February 2005. In a draft statement describing Russia's progress toward the implementation of measures leading to compliance with the judgments in these cases, the Russian government reported that it had paid the nonpecuniary damages awarded by the ECHR to the applicants and had also reopened the relevant criminal investigations into the killings of Khashiyev and Akayeva's civilian relatives by Russian military forces. It further reported investigating the "proportionality" of the use of deadly force in "counterterrorist operations" in the Chechen villages brought to light by the court cases and pledged to "inquire into the issues of ensuring safety of civilians" (raised by the *Isayeva, Yusupova, and Bazayeva* case and by *Isayeva v. Russia*, which concerned death and injury resulting from Russian forces' aerial bombing of civilians). The Russian

---

[126] Lohman, phone interview, July 20, 2006.
[127] Lohman, phone interview, July 20, 2006.

government had also disseminated the ECHR judgments in these cases to the relevant authorities across Russia's government ministries, procurators' offices, military procurators' offices, and to Russia's Supreme Court, and asserted that commanders and servicepeople in Russia's military forces, as part of their "law-related training," were informed about the "activity" of the ECHR. As additional evidence of its commitment to preventing further such violations, the Russian government posted the three judgments in Russian translation on the Defense Ministry's website so as to "inform" its military personnel about the ECHR "and the judgments rendered by it," implying (however improbably) that rank-and-file soldiers would be likely to seek them out and read them there.[128]

In trying to convince the Russian government to enforce the European Convention proactively in the context of Chechnya, the ECHR has undertaken an enormous task, one that comes up against assertions of "national security" and the state's desire to shield its military forces from prosecution. Although the ECHR is making a good-faith effort to hold the Russian state accountable on cases related to Chechnya, its effectiveness in injecting accountability into the particularly challenging area of military policy is severely limited.

The ECHR's Impact on Russian Government Policy

Chechnya aside, the Russian state, in order to avoid future cases, has improved somewhat its treatment of citizens on issues that have gone against Russia at the ECHR. Resolutions published by the Committee of Ministers evaluate a state's progress toward fully implementing a judgment by the Court and may include government statements submitted as evidence of measures taken to comply with a judgment. According to Committee of Ministers resolutions and other sources, it is clear that the Russian government has made policy changes following upon judgments from the Court. More precisely, the Russian government has made both rhetorical and limited material commitments to change, although such changes may not have been consistently carried out. The following subsections explore the

---

[128] "Draft: Official Statement of the Permanent Representative of the Russian Federation to the Council of Europe at the Meeting of the Committee of Ministers of the Council of Europe Concerning the Action Plan as Regards Execution by the Russian Federation of the Judgments of the European Court of Human Rights in the Cases of Khashiyev and Akayeva v. Russia (nos. 57942/00 and 57945/00), Isayeva, Yusupova and Bazayeva v. Russia (nos. 57947/00, 57948/00 and 57949/00), and Isayeva v. Russia (no. 57950/00)," accessed August 8, 2006, at http://www.londonmet.ac.uk/londonmet/library/u70061_3.pdf.

extent to which the government has introduced legal and policy reforms in response to judgments and follow-up by the Committee of Ministers on several issues deemed problematic by the ECHR: the use of *nadzor* (or "supervisory review" by Russia's domestic courts); the execution of Russian court judgments; and conditions in Russia's detention centers, or SIZOs.[129]

Nadzor

Supervisory review *(nadzor)* is a feature of the Russian legal system that has been criticized by the Committee of Ministers as undermining the "principle of legal certainty," because it allows ostensibly final court decisions to be overturned. Court rulings therefore attain only a certain level of legal force, because they can still be challenged in a later "supervisory" review that goes beyond a more typical appeals process. Following two judgments critical of the *nadzor* procedure in civil cases, the Committee of Ministers issued an "interim resolution" in February 2006 strongly encouraging the Russian government to reform the judicial system comprehensively, eliminating the need for such supervisory review, and, in the meantime, to rein in the use of *nadzor* further and thereby to limit "as far as possible the risk of new violations of the Convention of the same kind" already ruled upon. The Committee of Ministers also "invited" the Russian government "to present, within one year, a plan of action for the adoption and implementation of the general measures required to prevent new violations of the requirement of legal certainty," and pledged to reconsider the issue in 2007. The Russian government had restricted the use of *nadzor* in its new Code of Civil Procedure (adopted in November 2002) in response to the ECHR's first communication on the subject (in the *Ryabykh v. Russia* case), showing that it took the ECHR's concern seriously. In an appendix to the Committee of Ministers' interim resolution, the Russian government also pledged to present a plan of action as requested, "with a view to fully meeting the requirements of the Convention and the Court's judgments."[130]

---

[129] Committee of Ministers documents on the implementation of ECHR judgments can be found on the Council of Europe's "Execution of Judgments" website: http://www.coe.int/T/E/Human_rights/execution/.

[130] "Interim Resolution ResDH(2006)1, Concerning the Violations of the Principle of Legal Certainty Through the Supervisory Review Procedure ("Nadzor") in Civil Proceedings in the Russian Federation – General Measures Adopted and Outstanding Issues," adopted by the Committee of Ministers on February 8, 2006. The Committee of Ministers' statement on *nadzor* can be found by going to http://www.coe.int/T/CM/WCD/simpleSearch_en.asp#; and searching for "nadzor."

A state's compliance with or active attention to ECHR judgments is not guaranteed. As the *nadzor* issue illustrates, multiple judgments on the same subject lead the Committee of Ministers to respond, because if the problem is not resolved, repeated judgments would be likely to occur on the same grounds, overwhelming the Court. But even repeated attention to an issue by the ECHR and Committee of Ministers does not necessarily generate immediate or thorough action to guard against further violations. The extent to which a transnational judicial institution can hold a state accountable is limited by the enforcement power it wields – or is willing to use.

The Non-Execution of Russian Court Decisions

European Court of Human Rights judgments on other issues have led to similar resolutions by the Committee of Ministers, and to likewise limited Russian government responses. In the 2002 case of *Burdov v. Russia* noted previously, the court found that Russia had violated the Convention through the "non-execution" of Russian court decisions. Burdov's inability to collect his social security payment even after receiving a Russian court verdict in his favor was viewed by the ECHR as the violation of the right to a fair trial, because inability to collect on the award made by a court constitutes an obvious breach of the legal system's purpose. Subsequent cases to the ECHR based on the non-execution of court judgments by Russian state authorities led the Committee of Ministers in 2006 to issue a Memorandum on the non-enforcement of Russian judicial decisions, reviewing the various measures that Russia had implemented to correct such problems (from better funding the Social Security Service to passing a law in December 2005 making the Federal Treasury – rather than the Ministry of Finance – the responsible authority for ensuring compliance with such court rulings). The Council of Ministers deemed Russia's measures incomplete, asking, for instance, what mechanism exists "if the Treasury fails to fulfill its duties?" Obstacles to payment, in short, continued well after the *Burdov* decision, although the Russian government attributed such problems not to budgetary shortfalls, but to "complicated budgetary procedures within the Russian Federation." The Committee's Memorandum proposed a set of recommended solutions intended to stanch the "incessant flow of new complaints before the Court." Roughly 40 percent of all the Russian complaints found admissible at the ECHR stem from such violations. The fact that Russia had attempted to solve the problem suggests a certain level of concern, but its gross failure overall to provide a simplified means of ending the enforcement-of-judgments crisis meant that the violations of the Convention on this score continued.[131]

This particular challenge to accountability was discussed at a round-table with the Sverdlovsk region's human rights ombudsperson, Tat'iana Merzliakova, in December 2005. There, Merzliakova noted that one of the most critical problems in Russia's legal system was the difficulty that Russian citizens faced in carrying the legal process through to completion. Only 34 percent of judgments in civil cases were implemented. Moreover, she added, citizens of Russia were turning to the ECHR ever more frequently, and Russia had already lost seventy-three cases there, including two from Sverdlovsk *oblast* (*Rakevich v. Russia* and *Zimenko v. Russia*). Russia's losing record at the ECHR, she believed, was inspiring more accountable behavior within Russia's state bureaucracies. "The very fact that a citizen appeals to the ECHR often rouses the state structures to settle conflicts before they go to court," Merzliakova said. "In this past year alone, twelve cases were settled in this fashion in our [region]." As examples, she noted one citizen who was finally paid wages owed to her since 1998, and another who received compensation from a local military base where a soldier was implicated in the death of his relative. The author of the article describing the roundtable commented, "But if it is so clear to the government what the European court's verdict would be, might it not make sense not to violate citizens' rights in the first place?"[132]

Pretrial Detention Centers (SIZO)

Another incomplete response to ECHR judgments concerns the conditions in Russia's pretrial detention centers (Special Isolation Facilities, or SIZOs). This issue was first raised in the case of Valery Kalashnikov, whose nearly five-year tenure in a detention center was deemed a violation under Article 3 (protection from torture and inhuman or degrading treatment), given the unsanitary and crowded conditions to which he was subjected. The Council

---

[131] See CM/Inf/DH(2006)19, "Non-enforcement of Domestic Judicial Decisions in Russia: General Measures to Comply with the European Court's Judgments," June 6, 2006. The Committee of Ministers' resolutions can be found in the Council of Europe's searchable database, HUDOC, by searching "resolutions" and entering "Russia" under "respondent state." See http://cmiskp.echr.coe.int/tkp197/search.asp?skin=hudoc-en.

[132] Roman Toporkov, "Ostrye problemy kruglogo stola," *Vechernii Tomsk*, December 6, 2005, translation mine. As noted earlier, the *Rakevich* case dealt with involuntary psychiatric hospitalization; the *Zimenko* case concerned a violation of Article 6, Section 1 (the right to a "fair and public hearing within a reasonable time"). Zimenko's attempt to contest his dismissal from a job and obtain salary compensation had taken more than six years of proceedings within Russia's legal system.

of Ministers followed up on the 2002 Kalashnikov judgment with an interim resolution in which the ministers noted Russia's progress toward improving conditions in SIZOs, but stressed that overcrowding remained a significant problem in the SIZOs of fifty-seven of Russia's eighty-nine regions. In response to the Kalashnikov judgment, the vice-chair of Russia's Supreme Court circulated an announcement to all of Russia's regional and republic-level courts, highlighting the "precedent value" of the Kalashnikov judgment and its "very serious consequences," and asking that each court be sure to observe "strict compliance with the time-limits set by the Code of Criminal Procedure for investigation and trial and to prevent unjustified delays in proceedings."[133] To some extent, the Russian government showed its intention to eradicate the violations identified by the Court, but had been unable (or had chosen not) to do so fully.

Incomplete as the Russian government's implementation may be of general measures to rectify conditions – in the procurators' offices, in SIZOs, in the court system, and otherwise – the chair of the European Court for Human Rights, Luzius Wildhaber, spoke with optimism in November 2005 about the ECHR's impact on Russia:

> The European Court for Human Rights usually awards financial compensations or the recovery of moral damages in the event the court establishes a certain violation of the Human Rights Convention. All states pay the compensations, although it may take a certain state a longer period of time to make the adequate payment. As far as I know, Russia pays this money regularly. However, the court may expose certain drawbacks of the legal system of a state, which gives an impetus to this country's government to amend its legislation. Russia has repeatedly introduced such changes following our recommendations.[134]

Despite the Russian government's repeated violations on a number of human rights issues, the Council of Europe thus far appears intent on retaining Russia as a member, banking perhaps on the potential to reform Russia through cooptation over time.

The ECHR's Impact on Russian Judges

Policy changes such as those described in the preceding section undoubtedly have an impact on the frequency and nature of human rights violations.

[133] "Interim Resolution ResDH(2003)123 Concerning the Judgment of the European Court of Human Rights of 15 July 2002, Final on 15 October 2002, in the Case of Kalashnikov Against the Russian Federation," June 4, 2003.

[134] "Russia Sets Record with Number of Lawsuits Filed at Strasbourg Court," in PRAVDA. Ru: http://english.pravda.ru/, November 5, 2005, accessed July 28, 2006, at http://www.londonmet.ac.uk/index.cfm?FADB56DF-966B-43FB-B73C-7B97CC42645F.

Also important, however, is judges' awareness of their state's commitment to observe human rights as they are specified in the European Convention and ECHR case law. Judges within Council of Europe member states take the European Convention into account in varying degrees when deciding cases. After Britain incorporated the Convention into its domestic law in 1998, conservatives and liberals alike predicted significant effects on the legal system. Yet an article from 2004 in *The Economist* argued that "just because judges now have a new standard by which to assess the claims of plaintiffs doesn't mean they will reach a different decision." Even with the incorporation of the Convention into domestic law, its precepts are "rarely invoked" in British courts.[135]

There is no legal obstacle to Russian judges using ECHR judgments and the European Convention in their own rulings. Russia, among other former Soviet states, has "adopted constitutional provisions declaring international law to be part of the law of the land....[and] proclaimed the supremacy of international treaties over contrary domestic legislation."[136] Writing in 1998, just as Russia had ratified the European Convention, Russian legal scholar Gennady Danilenko noted that domestic legal systems in member countries of the Council of Europe have been influenced significantly by ECHR decisions, and expected that "interaction" between Russian domestic courts and the ECHR would have "a particularly significant impact on the direct domestic application of human rights treaties." Moreover, according to Article 15(4) of Russia's Constitution, "it is possible not only to invoke rules of treaties before domestic courts but to rely on the interpretation of such treaties by international organs." In other words, once Russia ratified the Convention, there was no reason why the ECHR's case law (the body of decisions interpreting and applying the Convention in concrete instances) could not be "gradually transformed into Russian domestic jurisprudence."[137]

On the other hand, Danilenko observed, political context significantly influences the degree to which international law will be taken seriously in domestic courts. Nondemocratic states typically exhibit a gap between their constitutional rhetoric and its implementation in practice. The incorporation of international human rights law into the domestic law of such a state would likely have little impact within the judicial system.[138] Human

---

[135] "The Menace That Wasn't," *The Economist*, November 13, 2004, pp. 59–60, at p. 59.
[136] Gennady M. Danilenko, "Implementation of International Law in Russia and Other CIS States," 1998, p. 49, accessed March 27, 2006, at http://www.nato.int/acad/fellow/96-98/danilenk.pdf.
[137] Ibid., p. 46.
[138] Ibid., p. 41.

rights activists have made a similar point with respect to Russia. If the government is moving away from the rule of law, the impact of the ECHR on Russia's human rights violations could be quite narrow:

The big problem we face here is that if in Russia we were living in an environment where there was a real attempt to change things for the better, to become more of a law-based society, then I think the ECHR would make an important contribution over time. But what we're seeing now is that on the one hand, the ECHR is forcing a certain amount of attention to how the law should be enforced, but at the same time, you have other forces that are rapidly moving Russia away from being law-based – the amount of arbitrary decision making at the highest level of the government right now is higher than it was in the Yeltsin period.[139]

Concern about arbitrary rule and the development of a more accountable, rule-of-law–based government in Russia has been voiced within Russia's judicial branch as well. The chair of the Constitutional Court, Valery Zorkin, believes that the court system must be "very solid [and] independent," especially given the strength of the executive branch in Russia, in order to protect citizens' rights and keep a check on the power of the executive. If such strong courts were lacking, Zorkin stated, Russia would find itself moving "toward arbitrary rule, toward dictatorship of the worst kind."[140] Along these lines, Russia's Constitutional Court has used the European Convention as a guide in several decisions, signaling that it takes the document seriously as a standard for observing human rights within Russian laws.

Such citation of the European Convention may be a sign of its increasing legitimacy within the Russian court system.[141] For instance, the European Convention's effect is visible in the process by which Russia's new Criminal Procedure Code was altered by the Constitutional Court in March 2002. Before the new Criminal Procedure Code took effect, prosecutors, rather than judges, were empowered to make decisions on pretrial detention, arrest, and searches. The renovated Code, "passed with an eye to promises made when Russia signed the ECHR...now assigns that function to judges, in line with all other modern criminal procedure codes."[142] However, the Code allowed for responsibility for arrest and detention to be transferred from prosecutors to judges only in 2004, delaying the

---

[139] Lohman, phone interview, July 20, 2006.
[140] Quoted in "Chief Judge Calls for Check on Kremlin's Power," RFE/RL Newsline, January 24, 2006.
[141] Jordan, "Russia's Accession to the Council of Europe," p. 293.
[142] Jeffrey Kahn, "A Marriage of Convenience: Russia and the European Court of Human Rights," *RFE/RL Russian Political Weekly*, June 19, 2002.

change. In March 2002, Russia's Constitutional Court ruled the delay unconstitutional, "making repeated and direct citation to the European Convention on Human Rights."[143]

The Constitutional Court has shown further dedication to the European Convention, even citing ECHR case law. The Russian legal consultation NGO Sutiazhnik described a significant move on the part of the Constitutional Court in a case concerning the failure to execute judgments by Russia's domestic courts – a violation of the right to a fair trial, the ubiquitous subject of applications to the ECHR. In this "landmark case," *Ponyatovsky v. Government*, the Russian Constitutional Court ruled in July 2005 that the Federal Government Order on the Execution of Judgments (No. 666, passed in September 2002) was unconstitutional, because it had allowed for the government to avoid carrying out monetary judgments, thereby violating the right to a fair trial and the right to property. Fundamentally, the Constitutional Court "held that an important category of judgments against the Government [would now] be legally enforced."[144] Before the 2005 decision, although plaintiffs could win a court judgment against the state, they had no way, other than submitting their claims for compensation to the Ministry of Finance, to guarantee that the government would follow through. Because the bailiff system "had no authority to execute judgments against the government," an individual winning a case against the state had no alternative but to rely on the state's "good will" in executing the judgment against itself. For instance, if a person had successfully appealed a criminal conviction and was awarded damages, there was no means to compel the Ministry of Finance to follow through with the payment.[145] The government's news outlet, *Rossiiskaia gazeta*, labeled the Constitutional Court's decision "truly revolutionary" with regard to the right to a fair trial. It was also, according to Sutiazhnik, "unique, in that the Court applied four European Court of Human Rights judgments...which is rare in the legal practice of the Russian courts."[146] In line with the Constitutional Court's decision, the Russian government abolished its Order No. 666 in March 2006.[147]

---

[143] Ibid.
[144] Sutyajnik, "2005 Annual Report."
[145] Anton Burkov, phone interview by author, August 23, 2006.
[146] Sutyajnik, "2005 Annual Report."
[147] Sutyajnik, "Poniatovskii protiv Pravitel'stva," accessed July 12, 2006, at http://www.sutyajnik.ru/rus/cases/p_v_gov; for more details, see Anna Kotova, "Pravo est', a garantii otsutstvuiut," *Ezh-Iurist*, No. 25 (June 2005), accessed July 12, 2006, at www.sutyajnik.ru/rus/library/articles/2006/ezh_urist.pdf. As part of its decision, the Constitutional Court instructed Russia's parliament (the Duma) to regulate the payments process, which it did,

This particular case is significant as an instance of ECHR influence on Russia's government and legal system. As of August 2005, nearly a quarter of the ECHR's decisions relating to Russia concerned the government's failure to carry out the decision of a domestic court, thereby violating the right to a fair trial as well as property rights. This was the finding of the ECHR's first judgment against Russia *(Burdov)* and has continued to arise repeatedly. The repetition of such "clone" cases is a clear sign that the Russian government had not taken the necessary measures to prevent such violations. According to human rights lawyer Anna Demeneva, even in 2005 the Constitutional Court decision had not gone far enough. Although "formal measures" may have been adopted, Demeneva argued, governments are obliged to take effective measures to "carry out their obligations in the sphere of human rights." The Russian government was evidently prepared to pay its obligations, but only when a decision by the ECHR demanded it – along with the "traditional 3000 euros" that the ECHR often awards for nonpecuniary damages in such cases. "It remains a mystery," Demeneva concluded, "why the state is prepared to lose, time after time [at the ECHR]...in the same kinds of cases, while making no effort to reduce the number of violations by making structural changes in law and in practice."[148]

Within Russia's courts of general jurisdiction, there is evidence that some Russian judges are influenced by the existence of the ECHR and by the European Convention. In January 2006, the city court of Ioshkar-Ola (in Russia's Mari-El region) deemed illegal a prosecutor's refusal in 2002 to bring a criminal case against police officers who had beaten a suspect while he was in detention. The suspect, Dmitrii Orlov, had informed the prosecutor about the beating, and the prosecutor confirmed it but never initiated a criminal investigation. The judge, in finding the prosecutor's refusal illegal, referred to the violation of Orlov's right to legal protection under Article 13 of the European Convention on Human Rights.[149] The judge also referred to a decision *(postanovlenie)* by the Presidium

---

in a December 2005 law, but the law did not address fundamental problems with the enforcement procedure. Bailiffs still lacked the authority to enforce state compliance with judgments, and the law failed to establish a "right for claimants to use coercive enforcement mechanisms against the public authorities" in the event of non-compliance. See CM/Inf/DH(2006)19, "Non-enforcement of Domestic Judicial Decisions in Russia."

[148] A. V. Demeneva, "Ispolneniiu ne podlezhit," *Kommersant-Den'gi*, No. 37, 2005, translation mine, accessed July 13, 2006, at http://www.sutyajnik.ru/rus/library/articles/2005/ispolneniu_ne_podkezhit.htm.

[149] Article 13 of the European Convention on Human Rights reads: "Everyone whose rights and freedoms as set forth in this Convention are violated shall have an effective remedy

of Russia's Supreme Court in 2003, which mandated that Russia's trial courts and appellate courts observe the norms of international law when considering their cases, because those norms are part of Russia's judicial system.[150]

The ECHR's influence on Russian judges is far from uniform. Anecdotal evidence of its uneven impact on Russian judges comes from a group of lawyers and judges from western Siberia, visiting a U.S. university in September 2005.[151] At a seminar featuring this Russian delegation, its members were asked whether they thought the presence of the European Court of Human Rights had any impact on the Russian legal system or on individual judges as they ruled on the kinds of cases that could come to the ECHR. The question provoked a range of responses worth quoting in their entirety:

LAWYER 1: Brussels is a long way from [our city] – judges don't think a lot about the ECHR.

JUDGE 1: [Our city] is actually not so far from the European Court of Human Rights. There was already one case from [our city] that was admitted at the ECHR: the case of [F.]. He claimed that his rights were violated because he had to wait too long in custody while his case was investigated.[152] As for the

before a national authority notwithstanding that the violation has been committed by persons acting in an official capacity."

[150] Informatsionnoe agenstvo PRIMA-News, "Rossiiskii sud vynes reshenie na osnovanii Evropeiskoi konventsii o pravakh cheloveka," January 1, 2006. I am grateful to Dmitri Glinski for sending me this article. A human rights organization in Marii-El, called "Chelovek i Zakon" (Person and Law), had in late November 2005 sent a report to the UN Committee Against Torture, documenting police abuses and repeated failures by the local prosecutor's office to conduct thorough investigations when such incidents occur. "Marii El Group Protests Violations by Procurator's Office," *Russian Regional Report*, Vol. 10, No. 20 (November 23, 2005), accessed August 17, 2006, at http://www.mari.ee/eng/news/soc/2005/11/01.htm. The co-chair of Chelovek i Zakon, Sergei Poduzov, has made extensive efforts to spread knowledge of the European Convention within the legal system in the region; he argued the *Orlov* case, which is the likely source of the judge's familiarity with the Convention. For the judge's decision, see E. G. Cherednichenko, "Postanovlenie, g. Ioshkar-Ola," January 16, 2006, accessed November 24, 2007, at http://www.sutyajnik.ru/rus/echr/rus_judgments/distr/orlov_16_01_2006.pdf. I thank Anton Burkov for bringing Poduzov's role to my attention.

[151] "A Conversation with Russian Lawyers and Judges from Russia," Seminar, September 2005. Notes on file with author. Delegation responses were redacted to disguise the speakers' identities.

[152] The case in question concerned a married couple accused of fraud; they allegedly turned in false receipts from business trips for compensation from the veterinary office where the husband worked. The accused were ordered in 1996 not to leave their place of residence without permission, a condition that persisted for seven years, during which the case was investigated and brought to court several times. The ECHR ruled in October 2005 that the "length of the [criminal] proceedings was excessive and failed to meet the 'reasonable

question about whether judges take ECHR decisions into account – well, the ECHR decisions are published in our country; they are publicized in the Bulletin of the Supreme Court, and judges must consider these decisions – although our judges themselves have not yet quoted them.

JUDGE 2: I have quoted their rulings in my decisions several times, actually.

JUDGE 3: Defense attorneys often now tell us, "If we're not satisfied with your decision, we will appeal it to the ECHR!"

JUDGE 4: The Strasbourg Court is used like a scarecrow for us. Ten people were fired as a result of that case, somewhere in the Far East, that detention case, and substantial fines are imposed on the country by the ECHR, so judges do take it seriously.[153]

JUDGE 2: I study the ECHR cases – and not only the ones that come from Russia, but all of them.

From this dialogue, it is clear that some judges (at least in one city) considered ECHR judgments when ruling in their own courts.[154] Yet no standard level of knowledge or familiarity with the ECHR's judgments was observed within the group, and the delegation members appeared to have differing degrees of information and engagement. Their remarks also suggested that the state was publicizing ECHR decisions, which corresponds to the Russian government's claim in several of its informational statements to the Council of Europe's Committee of Ministers. However, the Bulletin of the Supreme Court includes ECHR judgments only sporadically,[155] and not all judges would necessarily read it, although the chair of any given

---

time' requirement, thereby breaching Article 6, s. 1 of the European Convention." See European Court of Human Rights, "Case of Fedorov and Fedorova v. Russia," Judgment, October 13, 2005, accessed December 13, 2008, at http://cmiskp.echr.coe.int/tkp197/view.asp?action=html&documentId=787923&portal=hbkm&source=externalby docnumber&table=F69A27FD8FB86142BF01C1166DEA398649.

[153] The judge was likely referring to the *Kalashnikov* case, which resulted in a verdict against Russia in 2002 and fines of a total of 8,000 euros. During the course of Kalashnikov's detention, in June 1999, "the High Qualification Board of Judges removed the president of the Magadan City Court from office, as well as the president of the Regional Court and his two deputies, due to the delay in examining [Kalashnikov's] case." See European Court of Human Rights, "Case of Kalashnikov v. Russia," Judgment, July 15, 2002.

[154] The city in question was the site of a branch of Russia's Academy of Justice, a judicial training program affiliated with the American Bar Association. The Academy's program for judges in training covered, among other things, the case law of the ECHR. There is no way of knowing which, if any, of the judges on the delegation had been through that program, however. See "The Conception of the Russian Academy of Justice," Moscow, 2000, accessed November 24, 2007, at https://www.abanet.org/ceeli/special_projects/jtc/russia_raj_concept.pdf.

[155] Burkov, phone interview, August 23, 2006.

court would be likely to do so and to bring relevant issues to the attention of other judges on the court.[156]

Some scholars' assessment of judges' mastery of the European Convention is more pessimistic. Anton Leonidovich Burkov, a staff attorney and project manager at the Ekaterinburg-based human rights organization Sutiazhnik, analyzed the implementation of the European Convention in the jurisprudence of the Russian Supreme Court, the commercial *(arbitrazh)* courts, and the district courts over a period of several years, and found sparse and largely superficial application of the Convention.[157] Examining the Russian Supreme Court's judgments from May 5, 1998, through August 1, 2004, Burkov found that only twelve judgments out of 3911 made mention of the Convention, and of those, only eight included the Supreme Court's "assessment of compliance with the Convention."[158] In the other four cases, the Court merely quoted the Convention-based arguments made by applicants. Worse, Burkov's research revealed that none of the eight judgments referred to the case law of the ECHR; the Supreme Court "merely reproduces verbatim the content of an article [or refers only to its number]" or "simply states that a particular government act does not contradict the Convention as a whole."[159] A similar situation exists in the commercial courts, which also fail to make note of ECHR case law, while making passing mention of the Convention on rare occasions.[160]

The bright spot in Russia's judicial system, according to Burkov's analysis, is Russia's district courts. There, "rare occasions of Convention implementation by the district courts were prompted by the applicants' arguments based on the ECHR case-law, rather than the courts' own initiative."[161] Burkov explains that two Russian human rights protection NGOs have undertaken "strategic litigation" projects in order to improve the courts' implementation of the Convention, and that the improvements witnessed

---

[156] Lohman, phone interview, July 20, 2006. A monthly "Bulletin of the ECHR" (a joint project of the Council of Europe and the Moscow Lawyers Club) publishes Russian-language summaries of all ECHR decisions, and the full text of decisions concerning Russia, but is only available by paid subscription: http://www.femida.ru/bulletin/.

[157] Anton Burkov, "Implementation of the Convention for the Protection of Human Rights and Fundamental Freedoms in Russian Courts," *Russian Law: Theory and Practice* 1 (2006), pp. 68–76, accessed September 8, 2006, at http://www.sutyajnik.ru/rus/library/articles/2006/russian_law_2006.pdf.

[158] Ibid., p. 70.

[159] Ibid., p. 70.

[160] Ibid., pp. 70–1.

[161] Ibid., p. 71.

stem from such grassroots efforts. The Glasnost Defense Foundation undertook a strategic litigation campaign on the basis of implementing Article 10 of the Convention (on the right to freedom of expression) "in all the defamation cases where its lawyers were involved." The Foundation discovered that when it began "submitting comprehensive memorandums as to the direct implementation of the Convention and case-law in every case," the district court judgments in turn began to feature citations to ECHR case law.[162]

Similarly, the Urals Center for Constitutional and International Protection of Human Rights undertook in 2000 to "engage the Convention in every domestic legal proceeding possible" – not as a means of increasing the number of cases later appealed to the ECHR, but rather as a means of avoiding appeals to the ECHR on the basis of noncompliance with the Convention. Following the same principle of submitting comprehensive memoranda citing ECHR case law, the Center's lawyers found that "there was not a single case where a judge engaged the Convention, let alone the ECHR case-law, on his own initiative." Rather, judges seemed to resist invoking the Convention, and typically applied it only when they had been "constantly" confronted with applicants' Convention-based arguments. In cases where judges were hearing Convention-based arguments for the first time, they avoided citing ECHR case law in their judgments, referring only to domestic law even when judges sided with the applicants. Over time, however, "those judges regularly placed by the applicant into a situation where they have to consider the Convention and the case-law, start to apply the Convention and, [what is] even more valuable, look into the case-law."[163]

Burkov's assessment of the situation is that although Russian citizens may view their right to appeal to Strasbourg as a "panacea" for human rights violations, the goal of international human rights law is to raise domestic standards for observing human rights, and that "the impact of the Convention on the Russian legal system as measured by [its] implementation in domestic courts is unsatisfactory."[164] The strategic litigation campaigns by the two previously mentioned human rights NGOs (something akin to the American Civil Liberties Union in the United States) revealed that although Russia's lower courts (unlike the Supreme Court) occasionally refer to case law when analyzing alleged violations of the

[162] Ibid., pp. 71–2.
[163] Ibid., p. 73.
[164] Ibid., p. 69.

European Convention, "it is difficult to apply the Convention and in particular its interpretation in ECHR case-law in Russian courts."[165] The few positive examples show that change in the judicial system is driven from below:

[T]he judicial practice of the district courts as a whole demonstrates that systematic and persistent arguments based on the Convention and case-law raised by the applicants are crucial for good practice. The lack of substantiated submissions by the applicants concerning the implementation of the Convention leads to an absence of analysis of the ECHR's case-law and consequently its poor application by the courts. Consistent arguments of the parties are crucial for the Convention['s] implementation in domestic courts.[166]

In August 2006, Burkov reported that judges' practice had changed little since the period of his study, which had ended two years earlier. He ruefully concluded, "It's still easier to win a case by bribing than by arguing the ECHR."[167]

Analyzing the reasons that judges show so little regard, relatively speaking, for the European Convention, Russian human rights litigators Anna Demeneva and Liudmila Churkina point out that judges have nothing to fear from the ECHR's decisions: "Not one judge has been punished for allowing a case to go to a transnational organ when it could have been resolved by applying the same standards and principles within the country." Judges are disciplined neither for failing to apply the European Convention nor for their "action or inaction" leading directly to the violation of individuals' or organizations' human rights under the Convention. This explains the "utter lack of initiative exhibited by judges in applying the international norms and precedents of the European Court [of Human Rights]." Even "conscientious" judges who do apply the Convention may doubt the utility of doing so, because higher courts tend to overturn rulings referring to the Convention on the basis of "insufficient substantiation *(obosnovannost')*."[168]

---

[165] Ibid., p. 75.

[166] Ibid., pp. 75–6.

[167] Anton Burkov, email communication with author, August 17, 2006. For a comprehensive assessment of the theory and practice of the European Convention's application in Russian courts, see Anton Burkov, *The Impact of the European Convention for the Protection of Human Rights and Fundamental Freedoms on Russian Law* (Stuttgart: ibidem-Verlag, 2007); idem, ed., *Primenenie Evropeiskoi konventsii o zashchite prav cheloveka v sudakh Rossii* (Ekaterinburg: Izdatel'stvo Ural'skogo Universiteta, 2006), accessed November 24, 2007, at http://www.sutyajnik.ru/rus/library/sborniki/echr6/.

[168] A. V. Demeneva and L. M. Churkina, "Primenenie Konventsii o zashchite prav cheloveka I osnovnykh svobod iuristami Ural'skogo tsentra konstitutsionnoi i mezhdunarodnoi

Chechyna, which represents one of the sharpest topics of legal contention over human rights violations, provides little opportunity for Russia's judges to demonstrate their knowledge of ECHR judgments and case law. Lohman could not comment on whether the ECHR's Chechnya-related rulings had had much impact on judges presiding over human rights cases there:

The reason that you don't really see much change with judges [in Chechnya] is because most of these cases never make it to a judge; they never make it to the courts because the prosecutor's office doesn't finish its investigation.... In our submissions to the ECHR, it's primarily the prosecutor's office that gets our criticism, not so much the judiciary.

This situation could change in the next few years, because the trend as of 2006 was toward fewer disappearances and more cases where individuals were being detained by Russian forces and forced to confess, under torture, to participating in an "armed formation." Such cases do proceed to Russian courts, where the defendants are sentenced on the basis of this coerced "evidence." Lohman expected that in the coming years, human rights lawyers would begin to address these illegitimate court proceedings: "My colleagues now are working on a number of cases like that, but none have been filed with the ECHR yet, and certainly none have been communicated. But in time, you may see the litigation criticizing judges for their actions, and judges might start to then pay more attention [to the ECHR, as prosecutors have done]."[169]

THE POWER OF PERSUASION? THE ECHR'S IMPACT ON ACCOUNTABILITY IN RUSSIA

Democracy is not a potato that grows wherever you plant it.
– Russian Defense Minister, Sergei Ivanov, speaking
to an international security conference in Munich,
February 5, 2006[170]

Individual judges may be influenced by the presence of the ECHR, and its various judgments may motivate systemic changes within Russia's law enforcement system to some degree. The large number of cases lodged

zashchity prav cheloveka: opyt i rekomendatsii," in Burkov, ed., *Primenenie Evropeiskoi konventsii o zashchite prav cheloveka v sudakh Rossii*, p. 85 (translation mine).
[169] Lohman, phone interview, July 20, 2006.
[170] "And Compares Democracy to Potatoes," RFE/RL Newsline, February 6, 2006.

at the ECHR based on long periods of pretrial detention and on prison conditions has pushed the Russian government to improve those aspects of the system.[171] Individual cases brought to the ECHR also seem to rouse the Russian government to at least rhetorical action. The aforementioned Mikheyev case, where a police officer was tortured during a criminal investigation and ended up as a paraplegic, having jumped out the window to escape electric shocks, provides an example. When Russian prosecutors began a criminal investigation into the circumstances surrounding Mikheyev's fall from the window, the case was rather remarkably closed after only three months, based on "lack of evidence." Between 1998 and 2004, prosecutors initiated investigations no fewer than fifteen times – sometimes in a perfunctory way, and other times with more dedication, but none of the investigations resulted in a case.[172] However, when the European Court announced in October 2004 that it would take the case, the Russian authorities moved quickly to reinvestigate the matter and convicted two of Mikheyev's interrogators in November 2005.[173] When in 2006 the ECHR ruled in favor of Mikheyev, finding that Russia had violated Article 3 of the Convention, prohibiting torture and "inhuman or degrading treatment," the Russian government's representative to the ECHR, Pavel Laptev, declared that the ruling "should be studied carefully in police stations across the country," suggesting that the government had an interest in trying to prevent such incidents of abuse in the future.[174]

It is unlikely that the monetary awards that Russia is obligated (by the ECHR) to pay successful applicants will alone provoke thoroughgoing change in the way that the Russian state treats individuals in police custody, prisoners in detention, oppositional "oligarchs" and journalists, or residents of Chechnya in the course of war. One commentator, Vadim Dubnov, noted that despite the increasing numbers of Russian cases at the ECHR, "the authorities" appear unconcerned:

They are not scared. Sure, the world has shown what it thinks of our oddities but does not intend to bankrupt our treasury. Citizen Kalashnikov asked Strasbourg for two and a half million dollars. He got eight thousand. Sixty-eight suits [filed

---

[171] Chazan, "In Russia, Grim Case...," p. A1.
[172] The explanation for this lack of appropriate action may lie in the fact that Mikheyev was (falsely) accused of raping and murdering the "relative of a local bigwig" and thus that "senior figures in local law enforcement" were involved in ordering his brutal interrogation. Ibid., p. A14.
[173] Ibid., p. A14.
[174] Quoted in ibid., p. A14.

by victims of the hostage-taking at Moscow's Dubrovka theater in 2002], and one or two hundred Chechens are in line. Pasko, Moiseyev, who else? Maybe some hundred more cases. Each for several thousand dollars. A few million dollars will not undermine the regime.[175]

This assessment is probably correct, given that Russia's federal budget in 2005 set aside 60 million rubles for that purpose (up from 10 million rubles in 2003).[176] The selective enforcement of human rights is one means by which the Russian government maintains its power. ECHR judgments and pressure from the Committee of Ministers more broadly have succeeded so far in promoting systemic change only at the margins. The fines levied by the ECHR can be understood as a transaction cost of dictatorship.[177]

The power of transnational organizations to alter the behavior of the states subject to their rulings is limited. Beyond resolutions, memoranda, and various other rhetorical pronouncements, the most significant step that the Committee of Ministers can take against states that fail to implement the rulings is to expel them from the Council of Europe – an outcome that few people expect in Russia's case.[178] In admitting Russia and other former Soviet bloc countries, the Council of Europe hoped to improve the standards of human rights observed in those states.[179] Yet, as Pamela Jordan argues, some of the countries entering the Council of Europe, including Russia, were motivated in part by the opposite goal, namely, "to legitimate their own regimes" through membership while maintaining the status quo in terms of human rights violations.[180]

Jon C. Pevehouse takes a more optimistic perspective on the role that regional organizations can play in domestic democratization processes, finding that membership in a democratic-dominated regional organization can play a "significant role in the democratization process," and thus that

---

[175] Vadim Dubnov, "The Russian Mutiny," *New Times* (June 2006), accessed July 6, 2006, at http://www.newtimes.ru/eng/detail.asp?art_id=708.

[176] Demeneva, ft. 8.

[177] By mid-November 2006, Russia had paid out more than 12.3 million rubles that year in fines (roughly U.S.$462,000). See "Russia Appeals Ruling of European Court," *Moscow Times*, November 15, 2006, p. 3.

[178] "Russia's only way out of the Council of Europe is to step out." Lohman, phone interview, July 20, 2006.

[179] Russia's new Criminal Procedure Code, entering into force in 2002, was in part an outcome of Russia's accession to the Council of Europe in 1996. Russia's entry into the Council of Europe was contingent on the latter's commitment to meet European standards of criminal procedure and observance of human rights. Dline and Schwartz, p. 110. The new Code was thus supposed to reflect the standards set out in the European Convention.

[180] Jordan, "Russia's Accession to the Council of Europe," p. 281.

international influences on democratization should not be overlooked.[181] He notes, however, that the "lack of enforcement of conditions" by regional organizations such as the Council of Europe reduces their effectiveness, which might explain Russia's slide into apparent authoritarianism despite its membership in that organization.[182] The salutary effect of Council of Europe membership on Russia's human rights policies more generally can be doubted, given that Russia assumed the rotating chair of the Council of Europe in May 2006, despite not having abolished the death penalty – an obligation for all Council of Europe states.

Russia was accepted into the Council of Europe despite concerns over the gross violations of human rights in Chechnya, in hopes that "integration" would foster change in Russia more effectively than exclusion.[183] By 2006, ten years of integration had not prevented Russia's government from becoming increasingly authoritarian. In May 2006, as Russia presided over the Council of Europe, Lohman voiced his disappointment:

Russia is definitely a whole lot less democratic than it was in 1996. Freedom of speech, freedom of the media have been restricted severely over the last 10 years. In addition to that, there is still the lingering armed conflict in Chechnya, where people continue to disappear on a very regular basis at the hands of Russian forces or pro-Moscow Chechen forces....And the Russians have not taken any effective steps to stop these abuses there or to bring the perpetrators to justice.[184]

Lohman set these violations, as well as the relatively less lethal ones, in the context of accountability failure within Russia's political system more broadly:

I don't think that [these violations necessarily stem from] lack of knowledge of the Convention. I think it's more the legal culture in Russia, where court rulings are for sale, and even where you have a court ruling it doesn't necessarily mean that it will be implemented. A lot of appeals to the ECHR are exactly about the failure to carry out court rulings – so if the pensions agency, for instance, would just pay their pensions like they're supposed to, then people wouldn't need to go to the ECHR. The ECHR is not supposed to be a court for large numbers of people. Once there's a ruling, the implementing practice is supposed to be changed so it won't happen again. Supposedly, after the first case which dealt with this issue of nonimplementation [*Burdov*], Russia was supposed to make sure it would happen that all rulings by local courts are implemented properly – but it's hard, because even going back to

[181] Jon C. Pevehouse, *Democracy from Above: Regional Organizations and Democratization* (Cambridge, UK: Cambridge University Press, 2005), pp. 12, 209.
[182] Ibid., p. 13.
[183] Jordan, "Russia's Accession to the Council of Europe," p. 285.
[184] Brian Whitmore, "Concerns Raised About Russia Chairing Council of Europe," RFE/RL Newsline, May 22, 2006.

tsarist times, there wasn't really rule of *law*, but rule of *force*. The law was a tool to be used by people in power, and that culture certainly hasn't changed, by and large. There's not a lot of respect for the law.[185]

Retaliation

Such "disrespect" for the law is disturbingly evident – not only in Russia's continued violations, but also in state-sponsored efforts to reduce the ECHR's accessibility to Russia's citizens. Although the Russian government has responded to some extent to ECHR judgments and the Committee of Ministers resolutions that follow those judgments, a sinister pattern is also emerging in Russia whereby those who facilitate citizens' appeals to the ECHR are punished in various ways.

Following the ECHR's initial judgments on Chechnya in February 2005, Russian troops in Chechnya responded on the ground to Russia's defeat at the transnational level by engaging in a "pattern of harassment of Chechen applicants to the ECHR."[186] In nearby Daghestan, Osman Boliev, the head of a human rights NGO, who had previously appealed to the ECHR in two cases (one regarding the killing of a six-year-old Chechen girl during a military "special operation" in Daghestan in summer 2005) was detained while washing his car. He was charged with illegal possession of weapons when a hand grenade was said to be found in his vehicle.[187] Boliev was acquitted by a Daghestani court in May 2006.[188] In July 2006, however, after the prosecutor's office appealed his acquittal, Boliev fled Daghestan for Ukraine, where he sought political asylum.[189] In a similar case, Metkhi Mukhaev, a Chechen whose family member had lodged a complaint at the ECHR, was arrested in late December 2005 by "unidentified armed people in camouflage uniforms," taken into custody, and tortured. The human

---

[185] Lohman, phone interview, July 20, 2006.

[186] Human Rights Watch, "Russia: World Report, 2005," accessed March 24, 2006, at http://hrw.org/english/docs/2005/01/13/russia9867.htm.

[187] "Human Rights Activist Arrested in Daghestan," RFE/RL Newsline, November 21, 2005.

[188] "Khasaviurtovskii sud Dagestana opravdal pravosashchitnika Bolieva," May 18, 2006, accessed May 22, 2006, at http://www.kavkaz.memo.ru/newstext/news/id/1002460.html.

[189] Associated Press, "Dagestani Rights Activist Seeks Asylum in Ukraine," July 30, 2006, accessed August 7, 2006, at http://groups.yahoo.com/group/chechnya-sl/message/49175; "Dagestanskii pravozashchitnik Osman Boliev uekhal iz Rossii i poprosil ubezhishcha v predstavitel'stve verkhovnogo komissara OON po bezhentsam v Kieve," July 28, 2006, accessed November 24, 2007, at http://www.echo.msk.ru/news/325065.html. I thank Dmitri Glinski for directing me to these articles.

rights organization Memorial appealed to the Russian prosecutor-general's office on behalf of Mukhaev, noting that he "is the member of the family of petitioners to the European Court for Human Rights about the kidnapping of people in the village of Zumskoi on 15–16 January 2005, which gives grounds for seeing the illegal actions directed against him as an attempt at revenge, or [as] the intimidation of witnesses by the power structures."[190]

The Russian government has also relied on the legal system as a tool of executive power, using it to retaliate against organizations that help people appeal to the ECHR. One such case concerns Sutiazhnik, the aforementioned human rights NGO based in Ekaterinburg. When the group attempted twice to comply with new Russian legislation on NGOs mandating that each NGO "reregister" by July 1999 with their regional Department of Justice, Sutiazhnik's applications for registration were denied. Sutizahnik went to court and won – in June 1999, the Sverdlovsk Regional Department of Justice was ordered to register the organization and reimburse it for its court expenses. In October 2001, when Sutiazhnik found itself still unable to register, the organization discovered that the Presidium of the Supreme Commercial Court of the Russian Federation had annulled the lower court's decision through supervisory review (nadzor) – the very policy to which the Council of Europe's Committee of Ministers had so vigorously objected. Sutiazhnik's staff attorney Anton Burkov explained: "When a state agency loses a case in…court, they prefer to use nadzor to reverse the judgment. This is a very common practice. Among human rights lawyers, we like to say that nadzor exists not for us to challenge courts' mistakes; it exists so that state officials can do what they want to do."[191]

Sutizhnik naturally registered a complaint at the ECHR. As with so many other cases, Sutiazhnik objected to the violation of its right to a fair trial. Eight years after its initial attempt to comply with the reregistration

---

[190] "Appealing in Strasbourg Comes with a Heavy Price," *Jamestown Foundation: Chechnya Weekly*, Vol. 7, No. 4 (January 26, 2006), accessed March 24, 2006, at http://www.jamestown.org/publications_details.php?volume_id=416&issue_id=3598&article_id=2370707. In another probable instance of retaliation for making an appeal to the ECHR, Chechen antiwar activist Zura Bitiyeva was "extrajudicially executed" (along with three of her relatives) at her home in May 2003. Bitiyeva had filed a complaint at the ECHR in April 2000, after having been illegally detained and held under inhuman conditions in January and February of that year. In June 2007, the ECHR ruled the Russian state responsible for Bitiyeva's death. See European Court of Human Rights, "Case of Bitiyeva and X v. Russia," Judgment, June 21, 2007, accessed December 15, 2008, at http://cmiskp.echr.coe.int/tkp197/view.asp?action=html&documentId=819060&portal=hbkm&source=externalbydocnumber&table=F69A27FD8FB86142BF01C1166DEA398649.
[191] Burkov, phone interview, August 23, 2006.

law (and, predictably, following the Russian government's receipt of queries from the ECHR about the case), Sutiazhnik finally achieved reregistration in May 2005.[192] Such refusal to register NGOs seen as "objectionable, for one reason or another," is a widespread tactic wielded by Russia's bureaucracies. Sutiazhnik's press release on the occasion of their registration summarized the government's operative principle: "No organization – no problem!"[193] Likewise, in November 2006 Russia's Federal Registration Service refused to grant registration to the Moscow office of the Stichting Russian Justice Initiative on the basis of three technicalities in its application. In the previous six months, the ECHR had decided four cases of human rights abuse in Chechnya in favor of applicants represented by the SRJI.[194]

Other human rights NGOs have been similarly targeted, as the government finds new means by which to threaten their closure. The International Protection Center (IPC), one of the foremost Russian NGOs in the field of helping Russian citizens make appeals to the ECHR, was the astonished recipient of a tax bill in July 2005, demanding U.S.$180,000 in back taxes for grants received from foreign sources between 2002 and 2005.[195] The IPC's cases at the ECHR include an attempt to appeal oligarch Mikhail Khodorkovskii's conviction, as well as cases seeking "accountability for victims of human rights violations in Chechnya and for relatives of hostages killed during the Moscow theatre siege in 2002."[196] Each month, the IPC advises roughly one thousand people seeking to appeal to the ECHR, making it an attractive target for a regime that wants to discourage citizens from making use of the transnational court.[197] Valentin Moiseyev, deputy

---

[192] Meanwhile, Sutiazhnik's case was declared admissible by the ECHR in March 2006: "the quashing of the final judgment in their favour by way of supervisory review breached the principle of 'legal certainty,' enshrined in Article 6 S. 1 of the Convention...." See ECHR, "First Section Decision as to the Admissibility of Application no. 8269/02 by Sutyazhnik Against Russia," March 2, 2006, accessed November 24, 2007, at http://www.sutyajnik.ru/rus/cases/sutyajnik_v_russia/decision.html.

[193] "Prazdnik prishel na 'ulitsu' sutiazhnikov...ili Rukovodstvo k deistviiu dlia obshchest-vennykh ob'edinenii Rossii," May 17, 2005, accessed August 23, 2006, at http://www.sutyajnik.ru/rus/news/2005/05/17-1.htm.

[194] "Russian Government Rejects Registration of Russian Justice Initiative," November 23, 2006, accessed December 7, 2006, at: http://www.srji.org/en/news/2006/11/23/.

[195] "Russian NGO Receives Tax Bill for Foreign Grants," RFE/RL Newsline, July 25, 2006.

[196] International Commission of Jurists, "Russian Federation: Tax Order Threatens Leading Human Rights Organization," Press Release, July 31, 2006, accessed November 24, 2007, at http://www.icj.org/IMG/PR_Russia_Protection_Centre.pdf.

[197] Alexey Kozenko, "Taxes Can Deal Death Blow to NGOs," *Kommersant*, August 2, 2006, accessed November 24, 2007, at http://www.kommersant.com/page.asp?idr=528&id=694490.

director of the IPC, was not alone in suspecting a political motivation for the tax authorities' unexpected action.[198] Russia's human rights activists see the tax bill as a form of punishment for groups that promote access to the ECHR. Stated Liudmila Alexseeva, of the Moscow Helsinki Group, "[the Russian] authorities are tired of the fact that every decision from Strasbourg is a slap in the face to them. Therefore, they have chosen one of the most effective human rights organizations to lynch."[199] That Russia occupied the seat of the chair of the Council of Europe while simultaneously persecuting an NGO that helps individuals apply to the ECHR constitutes further evidence of the Council of Europe's limited impact on Russian state policy. On the other hand, the fact that the Russian government reacts to the activities of NGOs that help its citizens appeal to the ECHR suggests a certain level of fear on the part of the state about the potential power that the ECHR wields.

CONCLUSION

Transnational legal action can have positive effects on accountability to individuals in states where a powerful executive overrides the rule of law. By holding Russia's government to the standards set out in the Convention, the ECHR addresses gaps in the Russian state's "performance accountability" – a type of accountability in evidence when states fully and fairly carry out the policies on which they have settled, implementing the law correctly in any given instance.[200] Regional judicial bodies such as the ECHR can also help alter the norms within a formerly authoritarian state, provided that the current government is amenable to raising the standards of human rights protection. Although this is clearly a matter decided by the vagaries of domestic politics, transnational influence on the margins of those decisions could play a supportive role to the forces within the state or society that are pushing for change in the direction of accountability.

Pressure from citizens can help form a vise on a government under scrutiny by a transnational body such as the ECHR.[201] Several NGOs operating in Russia with the aim of promoting Russia's observance of the European

---

[198] "Russian NGO Receives Tax Bill For Foreign Grants."

[199] Quoted in Kozenko, "Taxes Can Deal Death Blow to NGOs."

[200] On the distinction between "performance accountability" and "policy-making accountability," see Susan Rose-Ackerman, *From Elections to Democracy: Building Accountable Government in Hungary and Poland* (New York: Cambridge University Press, 2005), pp. 5–6.

[201] Keohane, Moravcsik, and Slaughter, "Legalized Dispute Resolution."

Convention constitute such a nascent community of pressure on the state. Lawyers working for Sutiazhnik, SRJI, the International Protection Center, and other similar organizations attend the same workshops, follow each other's legal progress, and help their clients send applications to the ECHR.[202] This small but dedicated community influences judges, informs the population of its rights, and finds various other means to use a transnational force to support change from below. In this way, these NGOs are pushing their state to approach an accountable political system, governed by rule of law, one judgment at a time.

Theoretically, transnational judicial institutions should contribute to governmental accountability and support for human rights over time. A group of international relations scholars exploring transnational legal instruments concludes that governments pursuing "legalization" – choosing to "impose international legal constraints" in various policy areas – may find their politics transformed.[203] In short, "International law can become internalized."[204] Likewise, two legal scholars in Mexico found that "increased competition from international tribunals promotes domestic judicial reform in Mexico."[205] Finally, the fact that some transnational courts, including the ECHR, allow individual claims to be addressed makes for a "de facto shift in the institutional representation for social actors," potentially changing the balance of power within the domestic political system over time.[206]

There is only hypothetical concern that progress toward accountability in domestic legal systems could be stalled as a result of using transnational legal instruments. Trying human rights violators in courts outside of their home states, for instance, could hypothetically undermine the judicial institutions in the states where the abuses occurred.[207] Use of the 1789 U.S. Alien Tort Claims Act (ATCA) to bring human rights violators to trial for crimes allegedly committed on other states' territory has

[202] Lohman, phone interview, July 20, 2006.

[203] Judith Goldstein, Miles Kahler, Robert O. Keohane, and Anne-Marie Slaughter, "Introduction: Legalization and World Politics," *International Organization*, Vol. 54, No. 3 (June 2000), p. 386.

[204] Ibid., p. 399.

[205] Ibid., p. 391, citing Hector Fix-Fierro and Sergio Lopes-Ayllon, "Communication Between Legal Cultures: The Case of NAFTA's Chapter 19 Binational Panels," Unpublished manuscript, Instituto de Investigaciones Juridicas de la Universidad Nacional Autonoma de Mexico, Mexico City, 1997.

[206] Ibid., p. 392.

[207] On the changing nature of "accountability jurisdictions" under globalization, see Anne-Marie Goetz and Rob Jenkins, *Reinventing Accountability: Making Democracy Work for Human Development* (New York: Palgrave Macmillan, 2005), pp. 110–33.

been subject to scrutiny on this basis. Some scholars note that critics of this tactic fear using the ATCA could "[risk] stunting the development of institutions of democratic accountability elsewhere in the world" as citizens of states with nonresponsive legal institutions abandon them and bring suit in U.S. courts instead.[208] In one such case, the ATCA was successfully used by a group of Bosnian Serb women who brought a suit in the New York courts against Radovan Karadzic, the former leader of the Bosnian Serbs, "for allegedly ordering [his soldiers to commit] mass rapes, forced prostitution, killings and torture."[209] Clearly, the ATCA's accountability benefits outweigh its hypothetical harms. Like the International Criminal Court (ICC), the ATCA serves to remind would-be perpetrators that they could be held accountable for their crimes, even if not in their home states.[210]

Transnational judicial bodies aim to safeguard the rights of individuals after the fact. They do so, however, with an eye toward building domestic political systems featuring strong accountability relationships that will render the transnational institutions unnecessary over time. As Ella Pamfilova, chair of the Russian Presidential Council for Assistance in the

---

[208] Ibid., p. 196; Marc F. Plattner, "Globalization and Self-Government," *Journal of Democracy*, Vol. 13, No. 3 (July 2002), p. 63. Although this concern may be germane in border-crossing lawsuits, it should not be relevant regarding regional judicial institutions such as the ECHR, because the exhaustion of domestic remedies is an obligatory hurdle to the initiation of a case.

[209] Richard J. Goldstone, "International Jurisdiction and Prosecutorial Crimes," in David Barnhizer, ed., *Effective Strategies for Protecting Human Rights: Economic Sanctions, Use of National Courts and International* Fora *and Coercive Power* (Burlington, VT: Ashgate, 2001), pp. 113–123, at p. 116.

[210] The International Criminal Court (ICC) aims to enforce accountability, but unlike the ECHR, it cannot hear complaints about states, only about individuals. Starting its activity in July 2002, and designed to rule on crimes against humanity, war crimes, genocide, and the as yet undefined "crime of aggression," the ICC is intended to have a deterrent effect on individual behavior. Similarly, it is meant to encourage government policies that would eschew the gross violation of human rights, particularly in war. Like the ECHR, the ICC cannot adopt a case unless a national court has failed (or is unwilling) to do so; in that sense, it provides a forum in which individual accountability could be achieved if national courts fail in that regard. By mid-2008, the ICC had begun investigating four situations and had issued about a dozen arrest warrants. However, because no ICC trial has been concluded at the time of this writing, the Court's capacity to hold war criminals accountable remains to be seen. For further analysis, including commentary on the Bush administration's opposition to the ICC, see Ray Murphy, "International Criminal Accountability and the International Criminal Court," Columbia International Affairs Online (CIAO), November 2004, accessed June 25, 2008, at http://se1.isn.ch:80/serviceengine/FileContent?serviceID=PublishingHouse&fileid=598B0548-DAA5-FFED-A435-D9DE8EDEEF9A&lng=en.

Development of Civil Society and Human Rights, wrote in 2006, "the main goal of international law is to 'bring human rights home.'"[211]

International financial institutions, multinational private corporations (military or otherwise), and national governments, as the preceding chapters illustrate, perpetuate accountability gaps in ways that give rise to protest, often in transnational form. Transnational bodies such as the ECHR, working with local activists, constitute a means of trying to close states' accountability gaps from above. Transnational social movements working with grassroots activists try to fill accountability gaps generated by governments, IFIs, and MNCs via pressure from below. But even as border-crossing social movements strive to hold governments and powerful transnational entities accountable for their effects on people's lives and livelihoods, they must also confront the accountability relationships within their own activist coalitions. The next chapter examines the intersection between transnational social movement activism and accountability.

[211] E. A. Pamfilova, "Predislovie" (Preface), in Burkov, ed., *Primenenie Evropeiskoi konventsii o zashchite prav cheloveka v sudakh Rossii*, accessed November 24, 2007, at http://www.sutyajnik.ru/rus/library/sborniki/echr6/foreword.htm.

6

My Country Is the Whole World

Transnational Civil Society

> "For," the outsider will say, "in fact, as a woman I have no country. As a woman I want no country. As a woman my country is the whole world."
> – Virginia Woolf[1]

Virginia Woolf penned her proclamation in the mid-1930s, at a time when letters constituted the main means of interpersonal communication across long distances. Since that time, technology has sped the flow of information and made inter-state travel far easier, with dramatic effects on politics, economics, and civic activism. As multinational corporations (offering everything from manufactured goods to military services) and institutions of global governance expand their reach, so too have civic activists been globalizing their activities. As global "distances" diminish, the obstacles to human connection and cooperation are reduced, enabling transnational social movements to flourish.

Although border-crossing social movements constitute a long-standing feature of the political landscape, transnational organizing is expanding. A study of transnational social movement organizations found 183 such groups in 1973 and 959 in 2000.[2] These groups whittle away at state sovereignty – a rhetorical mask often shrouding oppression within a country's borders – and embrace the potential for a worldwide "country" where human rights would be protected and human needs would be met. Civil

[1] Virginia Woolf, *Three Guineas* (Harvest, 1963), p. 109.
[2] Charles Tilly, *Trust and Rule* (New York: Cambridge University Press, 2005), p. 158, citing Jackie Smith and Joe Bandy, "Introduction: Cooperation and Conflict in Transnational Protest," in Joe Bandy and Jackie Smith, eds., *Coalitions Across Borders: Transnational Protests and the Neoliberal Order* (Lanham, MD: Rowman & Littlefield, 2004), p. 6.

society, traditionally understood as a set of intermediary organizations designed to check state power and hold state leaders accountable, has taken on an increasingly global purview and scale.

Yet, like the transnational economic, political, and military forces discussed in this book, transnational civic organizing is not without its perils from the accountability standpoint. On occasion, transnational advocacy coalitions and social movements enjoy success at holding transnational economic or political institutions accountable to transnationally organized civil society. But such victories do not necessarily mean that the transnational civic groups are accountable to the actual people affected by the institutions' decisions. The degree of accountability within any transnational coalition can affect its success in meeting the needs of the local community whose plight it champions. The same is true in cases where a transnational movement targets a state for policy change. If the transnational coalition is led (or dominated) by people from outside the targeted state, an authoritarian government can more easily play the nationalist card and dismiss the social movement entirely, undermining its effectiveness. Foreign support can also encourage complacency among local activists. Specifically, dependence on foreign monetary assistance can contribute to a social movement's failure to develop grassroots organizing strategies and a domestic constituency that would help hold state leaders accountable in the longer term.

This chapter explores transnational social movement organizing from several perspectives. First, I consider transnational organizing aimed at holding states accountable to marginalized sectors of their populations. By way of illustration, I draw on Margaret Keck and Kathryn Sikkink's work analyzing transnational organizing against footbinding in China and against female genital mutilation (FGM) in Kenya, and the pressure put on Latin American governments in the 1970s and 1980s to uphold human rights. I also bring in cases of transnational pro-democracy organizing from Kenya and Nigeria that exemplify the risks to democratization when local activists rely on foreign allies for support. I contrast these cases to that of a small transnational organization fighting FGM in contemporary Mali, to highlight the importance of internal accountability within transnational advocacy coalitions. The chapter then examines internal accountability within transnational civic coalitions that push international financial institutions (such as those treated in Chapter 2) to act accountably to the populations affected by their policies and decisions. Finally, I explore the "accountability dilemmas" inherent in the growing phenomenon of transnational service provision, where large nongovernmental organizations (NGOs) step in to provide social services generally regarded as the responsibility of states. Taken together, these sections suggest that although transnational civic activists can sometimes successfully pressure national governments and international institutions to observe human rights and behave accountably to those affected by their policies, it is not uncommon for those activists to have few chains of accountability tying them to their local "constituents." Civil society, both local and transnational, is thus itself increasingly a "target of accountability," and rightly so.[3]

TRANSNATIONAL CIVIL SOCIETY: HOLDING STATES ACCOUNTABLE

How might the world of transnational civic organizing affect the struggle for accountability at home? Extending human rights and rule of law to marginalized groups constitutes the core of a state's deepening democratization and popular accountability. The external world plays an important role, if not a decisive one, in this democratization process. Writes Hans Peter Schmitz, "the role of domestic actors in leading efforts to democratize is not only shaped by socioeconomic conditions, it is also influenced by the external environment that includes international institutions and transnational activists."[4] Specifically, the external world surrounds any given country's democratization process within a "normative order" ostensibly favoring democracy. Transnational activist coalitions and international organizations help to diffuse those norms and sometimes provide protection to local activists.[5] Also, incentives shift when dictators are faced with transnational civic organizing – both in the norms that transnational groups propagate and in the material or moral support that they offer to domestic movements; these may increase the leaders' "political uncertainty and pressures to democratize."[6] Transnational social movements, even if rooted outside the target state, permeate territorial borders. They cross those borders on passports of moral suasion, backed by norms of justice.

Many transnational social movement organizations aim to universalize the enjoyment of civil rights and civil liberties and to make states more

[3] Anne-Marie Goetz and Rob Jenkins, *Reinventing Accountability: Making Democracy Work for Human Development* (New York: Palgrave Macmillan, 2005), pp. 79, 102–9.
[4] Hans Peter Schmitz, "Domestic and Transnational Perspectives on Democratization," *International Studies Review*, No. 6 (2004), p. 416.
[5] Ibid., pp. 404, 408.
[6] Ibid., p. 419.

accountable to their citizens, although they apply diverse tactics toward that end. A handful of organizations, including Peace Brigades International, seek to influence government behavior in a more accountable direction by sending transnational volunteers to the targeted country to engage in "protective accompaniment" of human rights activists and opposition politicians.[7] Ideally, the presence of foreign accompaniment limits the government's options, circumscribing the use of violence against political challengers.[8] By protecting opposition figures, foreign accompaniment increases the potential for building an accountable and pluralist political system. This type of transnational organizing points to an increasingly transborder community of moral concern.

A more widespread means of bringing transnational resources to bear on states takes the form of cross-national citizen coalitions pressuring states to improve their human rights records across the board. Such coalitions are often based on the notion of transnational "shaming," with the goal of protecting human rights under an oppressive regime. The abolitionist movement, starting in the late eighteenth century, was one of the first such coalitions.[9] Transnational human rights organizations and campaigns have multiplied since that time. To provide a contemporary example, Amnesty International (AI) initiated a project in 2001 holding that domestic violence constitutes torture if a state fails to address it legally or to enforce its antiviolence laws when women are abused. In 2004, AI's campaign to raise popular consciousness on this subject was extended internationally "to raise awareness of violence against women as a human rights violation." According to the director of the Women's Human Rights Program at AI USA, the campaign furthers AI's previous work "holding governments accountable to prevent, punish and investigate violence against women by state and non-state actors."[10] Governments hoping to dismiss AI's campaigns as foreign interference in matters

[7] Patrick Coy, "Cooperative Accompaniment and Peace Brigades International in Sri Lanka," in Jackie Smith, Charles Chatfield, and Ron Pagnucco, eds., *Transnational Social Movements and Global Politics* (Syracuse: Syracuse University Press, 1997), pp. 81–100.

[8] Ibid., p. 100.

[9] Adam Hochschild, *Bury the Chains: Prophets and Rebels in the Fight to Free an Empire's Slaves* (Boston: Houghton Mifflin).

[10] Shauna Curphey, "Amnesty Pushing Nations to End Gender Violence," Women's E-News, March 19, 2004, accessed April 12, 2007, at http://www.womensenews.org/article.cfm?aid=1755; also see "It's in Our Hands: Stop Violence Against Women," London: Amnesty International Publications, 2004, accessed November 24, 2007, at http://web.amnesty.org/web/web.nsf/8bad1ff50703146980256e32003c42f0/2def35f72dfaa2f980256e320038f366/$FILE/SVAW%20report%20ENGLISH.pdf.

of national sovereignty are confronted by the organization's grassroots credentials. AI has 1.8 million members based in roughly 150 countries, and uses (among other tactics) grassroots organizing campaigns, thus wielding significant democratic legitimacy.[11]

In their pathbreaking book *Activists Beyond Borders: Advocacy Networks in International Politics*, Margaret Keck and Kathryn Sikkink offer an extended analysis of a particular form of transborder coalition promoting social change: the transnational advocacy network (TAN).[12] TANs comprise "actors working internationally on an issue, who are bound together by shared values, a common discourse, and dense exchanges of information and services" and aim to shape the policy choices of states and international organizations.[13] The most successful TANs typically organize around issues that involve "bodily harm to vulnerable individuals, especially when there is a short and clear causal chain...assigning responsibility," and/or "issues involving legal equality of opportunity."[14] Their methods echo those of domestic social movements; TANs frame their chosen issue, utilize symbolic events, make available information that the target state (or transnational institution) has not released, and use various types of economic or rhetorical pressure in an attempt to hold states and transnational institutions accountable to their own agreements, or to induce those entities to alter the offending policies or practices.[15]

When confronting recalcitrant states in particular, TANs exert their effect through the "boomerang pattern," whereby "domestic NGOs bypass their state and directly search out international allies to try to bring pressure on their states from outside."[16] These international networks enable local activists ignored or repressed by their own states to voice their concerns abroad, "which in turn can echo back into their own countries."[17] In states that violate group or individual rights, where popular mobilization is

---

[11] Amnesty International USA, "About Amnesty International," accessed November 24, 2007, at http://www.amnestyusa.org/About_Us/page.do?id=1101195&n1=2; Amnesty International USA, "Annual Report 2007: The State of the World's Human Rights," accessed November 24, 2007, at http://thereport.amnesty.org/eng/Facts-and-Figures; Schmitz, "Domestic and Transnational Perspectives on Democratization," p. 420.

[12] Margaret E. Keck and Kathryn Sikkink, *Activists Beyond Borders: Advocacy Networks in International Politics* (Ithaca: Cornell University Press, 1998).

[13] Ibid., p. 2.

[14] Ibid., p. 27.

[15] Ibid., pp. 2–3, 23–4.

[16] Ibid., p. 12. For a nuanced view of the boomerang effect, building on Keck and Sikkink's model, see Sidney Tarrow, *The New Transnational Activism* (New York: Cambridge University Press, 2005), pp. 143–60.

[17] Keck and Sikkink, p. x.

dampened by fear of violent repression, recourse may appear to come only from outside the domestic political and legal system.[18] A TAN's success at the state level, however, turns on domestic considerations: A government indifferent to its international reputation will be swayed neither by local nor transnational activism.[19]

Transnational feminist networks (TFNs) constitute a subset of TANs, organizing around a variety of issues, including "women's human rights, reproductive health and rights, violence against women, peace and anti-militarism, or feminist economics."[20] The activist network mobilized by Women Living Under Muslim Laws (WLUML), for instance, organizes campaigns to increase state recognition of women's human rights in Muslim-majority countries. Such campaigns encourage the repeal of laws discriminating against women and seek to overturn cases of individual rights violations, such as forced marriage.[21] Like other TANs, TFNs are seeking accountability – specifically to women – at both the national and transnational levels, addressing international institutions such as the United Nations and the World Bank as well as transnational corporations, and aiming to shape public opinion in the process.

Keck and Sikkink consider several transnational advocacy networks on feminist issues, including early attempts at eradicating footbinding in China (1874–1911) and FGM among the Kikuyu in Kenya (1920–31).[22] These cases illustrate both the importance of framing an issue, especially when cultural borders are crossed, and the fact that a successful TAN campaign to pressure a state to change its policies necessitates close cooperation with local activist groups.[23] In the anti-footbinding campaign, efforts from all sides, including state elites, missionaries, the wives of Western merchants, and local Chinese activists, achieved their goal.[24] Footbinding was framed by this early TAN as a limitation on China's modernization and ability to compete internationally.[25] Similar arguments by Western missionaries failed in the Kenyan case, where local nationalists in the 1920s pitched FGM as a tradition that set Kenya apart from its exploitative colonizers, and where local activist opposition to the practice was not in evidence

---

[18] Ibid., p. 12.
[19] Ibid., p. 29.
[20] Valentine M. Moghadam, *Globalizing Women: Transnational Feminist Networks* (Baltimore: Johns Hopkins University Press, 2005), p. 4.
[21] Ibid., p. 149.
[22] Keck and Sikkink, p. 39.
[23] Ibid., p. 73.
[24] Ibid., p, 62.
[25] Ibid., p. 65.

(outside of the missionary context), making the sorts of local-transnational alliances present in the Chinese case impossible.[26]

More recent instances of TANs organizing to defend human rights in Mexico and Argentina illustrate the success of the boomerang pattern in the former case, and the importance of local activists' provision of legitimate information to their foreign allies in the latter. The Mexican government's willingness to address its breaches of human rights began "only after the [transnational human rights advocacy] network concentrated international attention on Mexico after 1987."[27] The Mexican state's desire to improve its international image led in the 1990s to the creation of a human rights commission to investigate the killings and disappearances under Mexico's single-party government in the late 1960s and 1970s.[28] Testifying to the importance of transnational reputation, the Mexican human rights commission's reports were published in Spanish and English and shipped "via international express mail to representatives of key human rights organizations in the United States."[29] Similarly, the junta that had been torturing, arresting, and "disappearing" its ostensible opponents in Argentina ceased its habit of disappearances after several years of transnational pressure in the late 1970s, including cutoffs in military and economic aid by foreign governments turned critics of the Argentine regime.[30] That pressure, however, was made possible by local organizations' supply of information on their government's human rights violations – and by a strong and visible domestic constituency for regime change, spearheaded by the Mothers and Grandmothers of the Plaza de Mayo and other local human rights groups.[31]

Both campaigns point to the successful accountability relationship between local activists and their transnational partners, who were able to convince foreign governments to pressure the target states to change their policies, given those states' vulnerability to pressure from outside.[32] These cases highlight the dramatic ways in which transnational advocacy networks have "transform[ed] understandings about the nature of a state's sovereign authority over its citizens,"[33] making national governments – in

[26] Ibid., pp. 67–70.
[27] Ibid., p. 80.
[28] Ibid., p. 110.
[29] Ibid., p. 114.
[30] Ibid., p. 107.
[31] Ibid., p. 107.
[32] Ibid., pp. 116–17.
[33] Ibid., p. 116.

limited circumstances – accountable to a transnational constituency rather than retaining the "right" to treat – or mistreat – their populations as they please. In some cases, when states are held accountable to transnational institutions, particularly international financial institutions (IFIs), such "upward accountability" detracts from governments' "downward accountability" to the population, as discussed earlier in this book. By contrast, states' accountability to transnational civic institutions (such as TANs) in effect increases state accountability to the population when that transnational human rights "constituency" is closely linked to a domestic constituency. Keck and Sikkink also point out that the most successful TANs are the ones with multiple nodes (a high "density" of information exchange) that include strong domestic groups.[34] Both the internal accountability of the transnational network and its effectiveness in changing state policy likely turns on the degree to which the involvement of those local activists remains central.

The activity of TANs and other forms of transnational civic collaboration point to the existence of a transnational or global civil society, albeit at a somewhat elite level. There exists a stratum of concerned citizens the world over who have sufficient leisure time and energy to take up problems that do not constitute an immediate threat to their own lives, and who mobilize on a variety of issues that once may have been thought relevant only at the local level. The extent of local activists' access to that "enlightened" transnational community varies, however. The very phrase "*global* civil society" glosses over the inequalities of access to aid and international awareness that local groups across the world enjoy – or do not enjoy:

There are huge rents in this society, with whole regions and vast populations absent or underrepresented. Even in regions where transnational interactions are thick, pockets remain outside the charmed circle. Needy groups unlucky enough to be located there have far less hope of making their causes known to audiences abroad than those from other places.[35]

These power disparities shape "global" civic action considerably.

---

[34] Ibid., pp. 28–9.
[35] Clifford Bob, *The Marketing of Rebellion: Insurgents, Media, and International Activism* (New York: Cambridge University Press, 2005), p. 193. Activists from different "worlds" also rest on a grossly unequal footing when it comes to attending the transnational conferences where consensus is reached about the content and language of international human rights documents. See Sally Engle Merry, *Human Rights and Gender Violence: Translating International Law into Local Justice* (Chicago: University of Chicago Press, 2005), p. 224.

Reliance on Foreigners, or "Looking Up": Donor-Driven Political Organizing

Although innumerable civic groups around the world would be hard pressed to conduct their struggles for justice without aid from foreign "partners in the struggle" abroad, not every form or instance of transnational political organizing accomplishes its goals. Linkage with foreign funders or with transnational NGOs headquartered abroad may even be detrimental to the effectiveness of domestic human rights and democracy-promotion NGOs if they rely too heavily on foreign contacts rather than building a domestic base of constituent support. Dictators may try to undermine such domestic opponents by linking them to transnational activists and organizations, claiming that local opponents are mere dupes of outsiders seeking to undermine state sovereignty.[36]

Equally problematic for domestic pro-democracy activists financed from abroad is the "isolat[ion] from the local community" that may result from the relationship between the foreign donor and the domestic NGO.[37] The donor-driven agenda that can take over domestic groups reliant on foreign aid can further distance local groups from potential mass constituencies.[38] When local democracy activists rely too heavily on foreign resources, "they may become distracted and lose their ability to build networks at home," undermining their contribution to democratization and their power to influence their government to become more accountable.[39] To put this in terms of social movement theory, activists now have to

[36] Schmitz, "Domestic and Transnational Perspectives on Democratization," pp. 411–12; also see Hans Peter Schmitz, "When Networks Blind: Human Rights and Politics in Kenya," in Thomas Callaghy, Ronald Kassimir, and Robert Latham, eds., *Intervention and Transnationalism in Africa: Global-Local Networks of Power* (Cambridge, UK: Cambridge University Press, 2001), pp. 149–72.

[37] Schmitz, "Domestic and Transnational Perspectives on Democratization," p. 412, citing Sarah E. Mendelson and John K. Glenn, eds., *The Power and Limits of NGOs: A Critical Look at Building Democracy in Eastern Europe and Eurasia* (New York: Columbia University Press, 2002), p. 23.

[38] Schmitz, "Domestic and Transnational Perspectives on Democratization," p. 412, citing Sarah Henderson, "Selling Civil Society: Western Aid and the NGO Sector in Russia," *Comparative Political Studies*, Vol. 35, No. 2 (2002): 139–67. The Russian women's movement, largely reliant in the mid-1990s on foreign support, focused on fundable activities such as policy analysis and political advocacy rather than on popular outreach, cultural change, or mass mobilization to protest against social, economic, and political discrimination against women, and lost an opportunity for constituency building. See Valerie Sperling, *Organizing Women in Contemporary Russia* (Cambridge, UK: Cambridge University Press, 1999), p. 265.

[39] Schmitz, "Domestic and Transnational Perspectives on Democratization," p. 420, citing Henderson, "Selling Civil Society."

contend with both a domestic opportunity structure (the range of political, economic, and cultural opportunities and obstacles to social movement success) as well as an international opportunity structure. Because
the potential resources available through transnational networks are significant, the incentives offered by foreign partners can skew local activists'
priorities in ways that are ultimately detrimental to building accountability
at home.[40]

Kenya

Using the case of Kenya's pro-democracy movement in the 1980s and 1990s,
Schmitz illustrates how the reliance of local NGOs on transnational (e.g.,
Northern-based) NGOs can undermine the strength and power of civil
society in the longer term, although such alliances can be extremely helpful in the short run. During the 1980s, local human rights NGOs opposing
Daniel arap Moi's repressive rule depended heavily on foreign partners,
desperately needing that source of support to ensure their "survival."[41]
After the advent of multiparty politics in 1991, however, Kenyan civil society groups were unable to mobilize enough domestic support to entrench a
more democratic order.

Blaming this outcome largely on the authoritarian Moi regime's intran-
sigence, Schmitz suggests that opposition groups' reliance on "vertical networking" with international organizations also "constrained actors in the
domestic...struggle for political reforms."[42] Initially, the opposition, with its
foreign backers, had seemed to enjoy some success. Although the December
1992 elections produced a Moi victory and a weakened opposition within
parliament, by 1996, civil society organizations had begun to organize in
earnest in favor of constitutional reforms, and in 1997 they formed a coalition
(the National Convention for Constitutional Reform) including internationally networked NGOs, churches, and political opposition parties. The coalition's executive committee (the National Convention Executive Council,
or NCEC) proceeded to organize protests, bringing thousands of Kenyan
citizens into the streets in favor of constitutional reforms. Moi was able

[40] Sperling, *Organizing Women*, pp. 49–53.
[41] Schmitz, "When Networks Blind," p. 150.
[42] Ibid., p. 150. International actors undermined the democratization process in Kenya in
other ways as well. Donor states (including the UK, the United States, France, and Canada)
endorsed Moi's election victories in 1992 and 1997 despite election campaigns held under
grossly unfree and unfair conditions. See Stephen Brown, "Authoritarian Leaders and
Multiparty Elections in Africa: How Foreign Donors Help to Keep Kenya's Daniel arap
Moi in Power," *Third World Quarterly*, Vol. 22, No. 5 (October 2001), pp. 725–39.

to use the human rights groups' foreign contacts against them, however, blaming "'foreign-funded NGOs' for the street chaos," and painting them as politically meddlesome foreigners.[43]

A few months later, Moi agreed to meet with religious leaders to discuss reform. This provoked a split in the coalition when the parliamentary opposition parties deserted it, hoping to join in the negotiations with Moi. The remaining civil society leaders on the coalition's executive committee called for a general strike to protest the exclusion of their groups from the talks, but "without the support of many popular opposition leaders [who had deserted the coalition], the call for a general strike found little resonance in the population," enabling Moi to continue his nationalist attacks on the domestic NGOs.[44] Further calls for demonstrations met with similar levels of popular disinterest. Without a broad coalition, the NCEC was no longer capable of mobilizing large numbers of people: "The leading representatives of the NCEC themselves had no significant domestic constituency as they had mainly used vertical networking strategies and outside support to establish their authority on the domestic level."[45]

In the aftermath of the December 1997 elections, which again produced a Moi victory, the NCEC called for protests, but turnout was low. Moi's repeated injunction to citizens was to join proper political parties rather than foreign-influenced NGOs if they wished to participate in politics.[46] In short, reliance on international connections in the 1980s constituted an adaptive strategy for human rights groups in an authoritarian regime, but under a somewhat more contested political order, these groups were unable to translate their international legitimacy into domestic legitimacy and thereby hold the Moi government accountable to domestic desires for constitutional reform.[47] Without a domestic constituency, externally funded groups cannot serve as a capable opposition. Democracy-promotion groups distanced from domestic mass constituencies are thus unlikely to succeed in exerting pressure for regime change.

Nigeria
Domestic opponents of authoritarian regimes seek external support for understandable reasons. They do so, however, in a global, competitive

[43] Ibid., pp. 160–2.
[44] Ibid., p. 162.
[45] Schmitz, "When Networks Blind," p. 163.
[46] Ibid., p. 167.
[47] Ibid., pp. 169–70.

context that shapes not only the likelihood of their success but also the agenda that they adopt. The relationship between transnational NGOs (such as Amnesty International, Greenpeace, and Friends of the Earth) and local "challengers" is one in which challengers' marketing of their cause to major NGOs plays a central role in determining which causes get funded. NGOs and their clients bring vastly different amounts of power to what is in effect a "buyer's" market where there are many causes from which transnational NGOs can choose. As a result, the recipients of NGO aid are likely to transform themselves (in terms of their structure, their practices – violent or nonviolent – and the way that they frame their cause) to match more closely the desired characteristics of NGOs' adoptees.[48] Such transformations can result in less accountability between a "local challenger" and the group's ostensible constituency at home, as the challenger alters its agenda to meet the needs of the transnational NGO,[49] becoming more accountable to its patron than to its local constituency.

Illustrative of this phenomenon are the attempts made by activists within the ethnic Ogoni minority in the Niger Delta to attract international support for their cause – political autonomy within Nigeria's dictatorial and oppressive state. In an increasingly common pattern among movements seeking transnational assistance, a local movement will set aside its original demands (such as ethnic-based political autonomy), highlighting instead an issue that may have been of secondary importance (such as environmental despoiling) because the latter can be pitched more easily to international NGOs, especially if a multinational corporation constitutes a potential campaign target for the movement's foreign allies.[50] Transnational activists may believe that they will be more successful against a corporation or international financial institution than against an apparently well-entrenched dictator:

As one example, the World Bank's environmental and indigenous peoples policies may make the Bank more responsive to pressure than many foreign governments. Knowing this, local movements facing multiple opponents highlight the more accessible and tractable one, even if it is not necessarily the main culprit.[51]

In the Ogoni case, the Movement for the Survival of the Ogoni People (MOSOP), led by the charismatic and doomed Ken Saro-Wiwa, decided in 1993 to "deemphasize long-standing ethnic grievances [against the central

48 Bob, p. 5.
49 Ibid., pp. 6, 193.
50 Ibid., p. 32.
51 Ibid., p. 50.

Nigerian state] while highlighting important but previously secondary issues involving Shell's environmental record in the group's homeland." After making this "framing" change, they found considerably more international support for their cause.[52] In the long run, however, MOSOP's leadership was decimated by the repressive Nigerian government, and, having stressed environmental issues in order to acquire aid, the Ogoni had not won political autonomy within Nigeria. Clifford Bob roots this unsurprising outcome in the fact that the Ogoni were a nearly powerless minority with little chance of truly remaking dictatorial Nigeria's political and economic systems. He adds, however, that the international assistance that they received, while it brought their cause to light abroad, may have exacerbated the state's repression, especially as MOSOP stepped up its own mobilization:

> The Treason and Treasonable Offenses Act, announced during the early stages of NGO action, underlined the regime's sensitivity to the Ogoni's "conspir[ing]" with groups outside Nigeria. Whereas earlier the military [regime] had ignored the Ogoni Bill of Rights [which was focused on demands for Ogoni autonomy] and Saro-Wiwa's inflammatory writings, the state now began a bloody crackdown [which the transnational NGOs were unable to prevent].[53]

Donor-driven organizing can present great risks in states unconstrained by a commitment to combat their opponents nonviolently.

In the end, the Ogoni's political problems were left unsolved, as the issue that connected MOSOP to its original constituency – the demand for political freedom – was set aside in lieu of a primarily environmental agenda.[54] In MOSOP's "quest for support, "the group had departed from its initial focus: "Thus, by the time the Ogoni had won worldwide exposure, some of their friends in the indigenous rights community were shaking their heads at how the movement's original demands for political autonomy had gone understated abroad compared with environmental and human rights issues."[55]

Reliance on foreign funding may discourage NGOs – even human rights NGOs – from developing a domestic base or constituency, without which long-term social change is unlikely. Chidi Anselm Odinkalu, the senior legal officer for a London-based human rights group, argues skeptically that (with some exceptions) the majority of human rights organizations in

[52] Ibid., p. 80.
[53] Ibid., p. 115.
[54] Ibid.
[55] Ibid., pp. 184–5.

Africa are fully reliant on foreign funding and lack a concrete constituency. This renders local NGOs accountable only to their donors:

[T]he only obligations local human rights groups have are reporting requirements arising under grant contracts where these exist. The *raison d'etre* of the African human rights movement is primarily to fulfill such contracts rather than to service a social obligation or constituency.[56]

Accountability to donors rather than constituents may let states off the hook when it comes to taking seriously those NGOs' demands for accountable governance. Successful mobilizations for social justice, such as the anti-apartheid movement in South Africa and the civil rights movement in the United States, suggest that the strategy of "popular mobilization and inclusivity" – grassroots involvement rather than professionalism and elitism – is a more plausible path to successful social change.[57] States will more likely be held accountable by grassroots groups than by NGOs beholden to international donors. When a state's policies, laws, and public attitudes on human rights issues are at stake, an explicit understanding of the transnational power relationship and close ties to grassroots constituents are essential to a movement's success.

Outsiders Abroad: Transnational Organizing Against Female Genital Mutilation in Mali

Although NGOs and transnational coalitions may be tarred with the brush of unaccountability, transnational groups that maintain close ties to the grassroots and take their cues for activism locally evade such charges (and may be more effective). Aside from assuaging concerns about accountability, transnational activism that focuses on locally determined needs is more likely to provoke attitudinal change on the ground that can have important cumulative effects societywide, even when political change is limited. Transborder coalitions, to be successful, must therefore find approaches that resonate with and foreground the domestic activists concerned about a given issue. The partnership between the U.S.-based group Healthy Tomorrow, run by Massachusetts-based activist Susan McLucas, and its sister organization in Mali, Sini Sanuman ("Healthy Tomorrow," in Bambara), works to reduce the rate of FGM in contemporary Mali. Their

---

[56] Chidi Anselm Odinkalu, "Why More Africans Don't Use Human Rights Language," *Human Rights Dialogue*, Vol. 2, No. 1 (Winter 1999), accessed March 10, 2006, at http://www.cceia.org/resources/publications/dialogue/2_01/articles/602.html.

[57] Ibid.

efforts constitute a successful example of transnational cooperation aimed at affecting national policy and public opinion.

Transnational Cooperation Against Female Genital Mutilation in Mali

Mali is among the handful of states where FGM is widely practiced but has yet to be banned by law. As of 1999, roughly 94 percent of Malian women had undergone FGM, commonly referred to there as "excision." This practice of removing part or all of the clitoris and labia minora crosses educational, ethnic, and religious lines (the prevalence rate among Christians is 85 percent; that among Muslims is 94 percent) and is almost equally pervasive in rural and urban areas. Over the past decade, Mali's government, while supporting campaigns to reduce or eliminate the practice, has not criminalized it despite being among the twenty African states that have both signed and ratified the 2003 Maputo Protocol to the African Charter of Human Rights, which "specifies that harmful traditional practices, and FGM in particular, should be prohibited through legislative measures backed by sanctions."[58]

The joint project to stop excision in Mali epitomizes a grassroots public education and lobbying campaign. Sini Sanuman volunteers, in coalition with numerous partner organizations, initiated a petition drive to stop excision in 2001 – the Pledge Against Excision – which is their main organizing tool. As a corollary to the Pledge, they developed a handout on the dangers of excision, featuring quotes by religious leaders encouraging the abandonment of excision and explaining that it constitutes a harmful practice not mandated by Islam.[59] They also use graphic photos illustrating the complications of excision (such as stillbirths and women unable to complete the birthing process). This information is used not only to educate the general public, but also to persuade excisers to abandon the practice and adopt a different means of earning a livelihood. The group also pursues coverage in the Malian media, and produced both a music CD featuring anti-excision songs by Malian artists and music videos that have been aired repeatedly on West African television.

[58] Interparliamentary Union, "Legislation and Other National Provisions: Mali," accessed November 24, 2007, at http://www.ipu.org/wmn-e/fgm-prov-m.htm; Office of the Senior Coordinator for International Women's Issues, Office of the Under Secretary for Global Affairs, U.S. Department of State, "Mali: Report on Female Genital Mutilation (FGM) or Female Genital Cutting (FGC)," June 2001, accessed May 16, 2007, at http://www.state.gov/g/wi/rls/rep/crfgm/10105.htm.

[59] Mme. Kaniba Baguiya, "One Pledge at a Time: Stopping Excision in Mali," *Peacework* (April 2005), accessed May 16, 2007, at http://www.peaceworkmagazine.org.

Although firmly rooted in Malian traditions and practices, Sini Sanuman's organizing methods occasionally point to their connection with their Western partner organization. The introduction of ideas and organizing methods from outside varies in its effectiveness. One successful method was the creation of an anti-excision poster, a task McLucas took on. Before the founding of Sini Sanuman, McLucas volunteered at the Centre Djoliba, a long-standing Malian organization countering excision. In 1997, after working on a filing system for the organization's library, McLucas was motivated to design a poster critical of excision. UNICEF modified her design, producing eight thousand copies, some of which are still visible even two days travel beyond the capital city.[60]

The poster served as an inspiring tool, kicking off a new technique of grassroots organizing: the Pledge Against Excision. The Pledge idea was generated when McLucas brought copies of the poster to health clinics in Mali's capital city, Bamako, attracting the attention of Malian health center workers, several of whom wanted to volunteer their time in support of ending excision. In a brainstorming session with McLucas and two Malian colleagues, Sadio Sylla and Saly Koné, the three generated the idea of a campaign in which signatories would pledge not to have their daughters excised, and to support efforts to end the practice of excision.[61]

The signature campaign was initiated with a twofold purpose: to raise public awareness about the dangers of excision and about the amount of opposition to it, and to convince the national legislature to pass a law criminalizing the act. But the campaign had a difficult start, in part because of its transnational origins. When McLucas presented the idea at a meeting of a network of Malian NGOs opposing excision, twenty-five partner groups signed on, but the "government's committee [the National Action Committee (to promote the eradication of harmful health practices against women and children) within the Malian Ministry for the Promotion of Women] took a very dim view of it" despite the widespread support for the idea.[62] McLucas attributed the government's reluctance to endorse the

[60] Susan McLucas, Director of Healthy Tomorrow and General Secretary of Sini Sanuman, interview by author, August 31, 2006.

[61] "The Birth of the Pledge Against Excision," accessed November 24, 2007, at http://www. stopexcision.net/s10.html. The text of the Pledge reads: "I am against excision and I promise to fight against this practice in all its forms. If I have a daughter, I will not have her excised and I will do everything to protect her from those who would like to have her excised."

[62] McLucas, interview, August 31, 2006. The National Action Committee is now called the National Program of Struggle Against the Practice of Excision (PNLE – Programme National de Lutte Contre la Pratique de l'Excision). The NGO network is titled the Malian

petition campaign to the apparently alien nature of the method, and to her involvement as a foreigner: "They still said, 'this is that white lady's idea' – I think that's what it was." Just as the Pledge was getting off the ground in 2001, the head of the government's committee spoke out at a National Action Committee meeting, asking McLucas to stop the Pledge, explaining later "that it wasn't a Malian thing [to do]."[63] McLucas and her Malian partners debated whether to continue their work on the Pledge, given the lack of support from the person in Mali's government charged with coordinating efforts on the issue. After more than a year of discussion, with some of the Malian activists arguing that the head of the government committee did not have to be taken into account ("she can't stop us") and others feeling that the Pledge campaign required the government committee's support, the Malian activists created an independent organizational base that could coordinate the Pledge. They founded Sini Sanuman in 2002, registering it officially with the Malian government. McLucas became the organization's general secretary while continuing as the director of Healthy Tomorrow, Sini Sanuman's counterpart in the United States.

The Pledge Against Excision activated signatories in a classical snowball fashion. One of Sini Sanuman's core activists, Madame Kaniba Baguiya, found that after holding several informational meetings, she developed a "reputation...people come to get me at my house to convince people not to excise their daughters." The effects of neighborhood meetings were immediate: "Sometimes, at the end of a meeting, when I invite the participants to sign the Pledge Against Excision, people ask me if I can stay a while to give them time to go home and get people who weren't there for the meeting, so that they can sign, too."[64] Excisers also spread the word about the Pledge, in some instances serving as spokeswomen for the anti-FGM movement. One former exciser, Djarawélé, after signing the pledge, explained to "would-be customers that she'd stopped excising, and why," and even held an anti-FGM meeting at her home, inviting neighbors and other local women she had trained to become excisers, nearly all of whom signed the Pledge thereafter.[65]

Another successful public education technique was McLucas's production in 2000 of a CD of anti-excision songs written largely by Malians.

Network of Struggle Against Female Genital Mutilation (Reseau Malien de Lutte Contre les Mutilations Genitales Feminines).

[63] McLucas, interview, August 31, 2006.
[64] Baguiya, "One Pledge at a Time."
[65] "Djarawélé and the Fifth Person Principle," accessed November 24, 2007, at http://www.stopexcision.net/s1.html.

Boasting eight songs in five local languages, the CD achieved a great deal of airplay.[66] A follow-up music video ("Ça Fait Mal!") also resonated with the public, and was played on a West African TV station broadcasting to ten countries more than one hundred times in the space of several months. The video captured the tension between convincing people to oppose excision while not condemning women who have undergone the practice. It opens with one woman insulting the singer by calling her an "unexcised woman." The singer laughs and responds that she's happy about not being excised, while her husband flashes a thumbs-up sign. "It's hard how to figure out how to make people feel proud not to be excised, and to think it's okay to not excise their girls, without making the excised women feel diminished by it," explained McLucas. Ironically, McLucas had to pay the female singer an extra twenty dollars "for the embarrassment of saying that she was not excised" – although, in fact, she was.

Sini Sanuman built on the success of McLucas's previous use of music as a central component in the public awareness campaign. A few years into the Pledge campaign, the group produced a song written by former excisers, "I Abandon (Excision)," explaining why they had stopped performing the procedure: "the pain and misery of the girls I cut kept me up at night...." After being played on Malian radio, the song won the support of the Malian Ministry for the Promotion of Women, which offered U.S.$2,300 toward creating a music video. By May 2007, "I Abandon" had been transformed into a video; eighteen of the former excisers who had ceased their activity as a result of the Pledge campaign participated in its production. The video, as described by McLucas, "starts out with the main exciser unable to sleep, thinking of the cries of the girls. She and her husband call a big meeting of other excisers and they all decide to stop. They dance and throw their knives and razor blades in a big hole which is filled in, and then we see a few of them doing new jobs with big smiles on their faces. We list the names of the ex-excisers who appear in the video."[67] By early 2008, it had been shown on television a handful of times, and the Ministry had pledged to pay for further showings.[68]

[66] Creating the CD was McLucas's innovation. Although another anti-excision group had produced a few songs, they had not been played on the radio. McLucas, interview, August 31, 2006.

[67] Susan McLucas, "Conscientious Objection to Female Genital Mutilation in Mali," *Peacework* (May 2007), p. 11.

[68] Susan McLucas, "Report from Mali Project: January 8–March 7, 2008," distributed by email (on file with author).

The use of music as a public education technique transferred easily into the Malian anti-excision movement. In other cases, McLucas's inclination to introduce additional organizing techniques – such as a protest march – led to conflict. At an early meeting of organizations cooperating on launching the Pledge Against Excision, McLucas suggested that volunteers be offered a place on the petition "to check off how they'd like to help – might they want to talk to people, might they join a march if we had one, and so on – and just the very idea of bringing up a march somehow got back to the authorities and they didn't like it. They said 'That's an American thing, we Malians don't march.'" In 2006, a newly mobilized recruit to Sini Sanuman led a meeting where the idea of holding a march was raised anew. But Sini Sanuman's executive committee expressed reluctance, concerned that a march could "get out of hand," be perceived as "too militant," and thus provoke opposition, and also alienate a key ally in the struggle: the Malian Ministry for the Promotion of Women (which sponsors the National Program against FGM).[69] The Malian activists discussed the possibility of a march at a bimonthly meeting of the partners in the Pledge campaign, "and most people there thought it was not a good idea to march." McLucas was disappointed: "They were convinced that it was not the right time. I thought they were wrong, and I was so frustrated . . . but it's a group decision and if everybody in the group says [no] . . . ." McLucas did not push the point. A year later, after finally approaching representatives of the National Program with the idea, Sini Sanuman was surprised to discover that their interlocutors "agreed that a march designed to publicize and advocate for legislation to ban FGM could be effective. They encouraged Sini Sanuman to put together a proposal for funding and to build a coalition to organize it."[70] And in early 2008, as elected officials in Bamako's fifth district debated introducing a local ban on excision, they asked Sini Sanuman to organize an anti-excision march to city hall.[71] The idea of marching to protest FGM had caught on.

The results of Sini Sanuman's work have been impressive. By October 2007, in the six years spanning the Pledge campaign coordinated by Sini Sanuman, volunteers had collected the signatures of thirty thousand Malians promising not to excise their daughters, and had convinced 131 excisers to stop performing the procedure, "more than any other group,"

---

[69] McLucas, email communication with author, May 26, 2007.
[70] McLucas, "Conscientious Objection to Female Genital Mutilation in Mali."
[71] McLucas, "Report from Mali Project: January 8–March 7, 2008."

according to McLucas. Sini Sanuman activists had persuaded three villages (Missala, Tamala, and Konébabougou) near Bamako to abandon excision, holding festive celebrations to mark their decision, and had started a club for girls proud not to have been excised.[72] In May 2007, Mali's once-recalcitrant Women's Ministry promised to help Sini Sanuman obtain an appointment at the legislature to present the Pledge and its signatures officially. The organization's president, Siaka Traoré, also offered a draft version of potential legislation on FGM to Mali's Justice Department, providing "a concrete proposal for the law we hope the legislature will be voting on late this year."[73] On October 2, 2007, Traoré finally handed the Pledge signatures to the new president of Mali's National Assembly, who expressed his strong support for crafting legislation to outlaw FGM in Mali.[74]

Sini Sanuman has enjoyed this degree of success precisely because the organization is locally run and maintains a largely indigenous face even with a modicum of transnational support from McLucas and the U.S.-based organization she directs.[75] Like a microcosm of a transnational civic coalition, the Healthy Tomorrow/Sini Sanuman partnership confronts the power dynamics inherent in crossing the North-South border in the name of activism. This particular transnational partnership avoids some of the pitfalls experienced by other such coalitions. Here, the activist partnership takes its cues from local activists, respecting local concerns (about holding a march, for instance) and allowing the agenda to be driven locally.

Sini Sanuman's practices also foster accountability to the grassroots, despite the organization's financial support from abroad. McLucas is aware of the power relationship between herself as a Westerner and her

---

[72] McLucas, interview, August 31, 2006; McLucas, "Conscientious Objection to Female Genital Mutilation in Mali"; Sini Sanuman, "Press Release: Malian Government Gives Nod to Anti-FGM Movement: Public Discussion Begins at the Legislature to Outlaw Excision," October 4, 2007, on file with author.

[73] McLucas, "Conscientious Objection to Female Genital Mutilation in Mali."

[74] Sini Sanuman, "Press Release: Malian Government Gives Nod to Anti-FGM Movement." One study of anti-FGM efforts in neighboring Senegal found that banning FGM by law was counterproductive, at least initially; the grassroots approach, encouraging the voluntary "abandonment" of FGM, was more successful in decreasing the frequency of the practice. See Peter Easton, Karen Monkman, and Rebecca Miles, "Social Policy from the Bottom Up; Abandoning FGC in Sub-Saharan Africa," *Development in Practice*, Vol. 13, No. 5 (November 2003), p. 450.

[75] McLucas, interview, August 31, 2006. The presence of a sizeable domestic activist base on the issue of FGM in contemporary Mali clearly distinguishes the current transnational effort to eliminate FGM from that which occurred in 1920s Kenya, as described by Keck and Sikkink.

Malian partners. Moreover, because Healthy Tomorrow's resources are extremely limited, both partners' focus is necessarily on grassroots organizing rather than on building professional contacts and organizing seminars and conferences. Having less money creates an incentive to organize people who will then perhaps be prepared to hold the state accountable in a way that is rarely possible when a narrow sector of the NGO community constitutes the only force actively trying to shape state policy and behavior. The grassroots organizing methods applied by Sini Sanuman rely on volunteers – all of whom are Malian men and women – organizing their neighbors to renounce the practice of excision. The group's program staff, too, "are drawn from the community...This approach ensures that the program goals and methodologies are appropriate to the communities being served and will endure into the future."[76] Popular mobilization and inclusion, such as using the Pledge and reaching out to excisers, are more effective than (or possibly are complementary to) the elite detachment from grassroots organizing exhibited in the Kenyan case.[77]

McLucas has gleaned several lessons from experiencing the challenges of transnational civic cooperation. Foremost among these is that awareness and sensitivity promotes success for the local movement – especially as regards power relationships and the movement's perceived connection to foreigners. There are, naturally, tensions inherent in close cooperation across the North-South border:

I do try to pull back and not be playing too much of a leadership role. I would never be on TV, for instance. But then the other side of that is that when I go with some of our people to do presentations, if I intervene at all, people really like it. At one point, at the start of an event, there was some time to fill, and I was telling my Malian partner who was going to do the presentation, we have to do something to fill the time. So, I sang an anti-excision song, in Bambara ["Deni to a Cogola" (Leave Her Alone)]. They really loved it when I did that. And after that, when I didn't come along, people would ask, "Where's the white lady who sings in Bambara?"... It's really confusing to me, because I want to go on TV and sing my little song that everybody likes so much, but I haven't pushed. Some people I've worked with say: "Go ahead, people love it. We've already had eight other songs on TV and on the radio, it's not like the only song is by the white lady." But for the time being, I'm playing it safe and going along with my partners who say, "People are

---

[76] "Project Stop Excision: Collaborating Groups in Mali," accessed November 24, 2007, at http://stopexcision.net/groupsinMali.html.

[77] A similarly grassroots-driven Village Empowerment Program, developed by Tostan, a Senegalese NGO, was also implemented in Mali, where it achieved some success. Following discussions of FGM in July 2000 in three villages, no further procedures were performed there. See Easton, Monkman, and Miles, p. 452.

going to think this is all your idea if they even see you." And one kind of sad thing for me is that when we hand over our petition,...I'm not going to be there, because it's going to be televised and I don't want people thinking it was my idea....But the main thing is that it worked because a lot of people decided that they liked it. That's what's exciting.[78]

Effective transnational organizing, McLucas stresses, requires that the outsiders be led by the local activists:

Well it's obvious, but you can't do anything without working very, very closely with local people.... You might get it wrong, you'd likely get it wrong. And you'll be seen as an outsider. At first, I didn't quite have that straight in my mind enough. I knew that I should kind of keep a low profile, but I sort of assumed that people in the government would be enough behind the movement that they wouldn't be upset by my involvement. I wanted to get the Malian Health Department to be one of the partner groups in the Pledge, and went there by myself and tried to talk to the person in charge. And I can't remember just how she responded, but it was something like, "Well, I'm working on this issue. What are *you* doing here?"...It makes things complicated.

Transnational organizing aimed at pressuring a state to alter its policies is of limited effectiveness, according to McLucas's experience in Mali's anti-excision movement. Asked whether pressures from the transnational realm or the local population were more effective in pushing the government to pass legislation on FGM, McLucas concurred with political scientist Aili Mari Tripp, who writes, "Domestic actors generally have greater legitimacy than outsiders."[79] The Malian government, McLucas suspected, was more susceptible to pressure from local groups such as Sini Sanuman than from transnational human rights groups organizing on FGM:

I would guess the local groups [are more effective]. A man in Mali's Justice Department told us that they get lots and lots of letters from outside Mali – it seems that some groups run letter-writing campaigns – but they pretty much know that outsiders think that. What the government is trying to decide is whether the country is ready. So, I don't really think there's much point in outsiders pushing – from the outside. There was a big international summit [the Ninth Session of the EU-Africa Caribbean Pacific Joint Parliamentary Assembly, held in Bamako] in 2005 where they had a session on FGM, and it came down to everyone saying to Mali, "You've got to get with the program and outlaw this." And the only Malian who spoke up was a woman legislator, one of the very few, and she said that Mali was not ready.[80]

---

[78] McLucas, interview, August 31, 2006.
[79] Aili Mari Tripp, "Challenges in Transnational Feminist Mobilization," in Myra Marx Ferree and Aili Mari Tripp, eds., *Global Feminism: Transnational Women's Activism, Organizing, and Human Rights* (New York: New York University Press, 2006), p. 306.
[80] McLucas, interview, August 31, 2006.

The issue at hand is not whether the government believes that excision should be outlawed, but rather whether Malian society is ready for that change.[81] Under those circumstances, a government would more likely view activism by the local groups as having greater legitimacy and representativeness – accountability to the population – than do the transnational NGOs.

TRANSNATIONAL CIVIL SOCIETY: HOLDING TRANSNATIONAL INSTITUTIONS ACCOUNTABLE

As the reach of institutions of "global governance," such as the United Nations, International Monetary Fund (IMF), and World Bank expands, transnational civic organizing takes on an increasingly important role in trying to hold these institutions externally accountable.[82] The lines of accountability between citizens and these global governance organizations are perforated at best, because citizens are ill informed about the details of global governance institutions' actions, and within the sphere of national politics, detailed positions on such institutions are rarely the focus of political parties' platforms.[83] Transnational civil society's attention to these institutions, therefore, argues Jan Aart Scholte, may provide a better means of improving accountability to the citizens who live under the impact of global regulatory institutions than would participation in national politics alone.[84] Transnational civic groups have somewhat successfully pressured global governance institutions such as the IMF and World Bank to become more transparent and to interact more closely with civil society groups, improving the chances for the accountability of both states and transnational governance institutions to local populations. But such contacts are often limited to civil society groups in the global North, leaving a gap between the agencies and the populations that they affect most directly in the developing world.[85]

---

[81] The nominal concern is that if the practice was outlawed, women would undergo the procedure illegally, at an even greater cost to women's health. On the Joint Parliamentary Assembly, see http://www.europarl.europa.cu/intcoop/acp/60_09/default_en.htm.

[82] Jan Aart Scholte, "Civil Society and Democratically Accountable Global Governance," *Government and Opposition*, Vol. 39, No. 2 (April 2005), pp. 211–33.

[83] Ibid., pp. 211–12.

[84] Ibid., p. 212.

[85] Ibid., p. 216. For detailed descriptions of various campaigns by NGOs and transnational advocacy coalitions protesting against World Bank–supported projects and violations of World Bank reform policies, see Jonathan A. Fox and L. David Brown, eds., *The Struggle for Accountability: The World Bank, NGOs, and Grassroots Movements* (Cambridge, MA: MIT Press, 1998).

Although transnational NGOs may promote human rights norms and participation by people previously silenced, such organizations can both act and be organized in nontransparent, unaccountable ways.[86] Some international NGOs feature "insiders" closely linked to states or institutions such as the UN; they thus are far from having a concrete constituency and therefore may operate "against the most basic rule of democracy: to govern with the consent of the governed."[87] Over the past twenty years, international NGOs with "consultative status" to the United Nations have been "among the NGOs least likely to base their policies on the concerns of a well-defined constituency."[88] The more connected an NGO is to its mass (grassroots) base, "the greater its chances at promoting positive social change because it is more likely to represent a highly motivated and engaged constituency."[89]

Indeed, grassroots organizing is widely perceived (by activists, if not by some transnational NGOs) as critical to achieving social change. Along these lines, international agreements such as the UN Convention on Eliminating All Forms of Discrimination Against Women (CEDAW) will not be effective unless "women at the local level have political power to force their governments to change domestic laws and policies in accordance with the convention."[90] A study wherein grassroots women's groups evaluated the use of CEDAW across ten countries as a tool for improving women's status concluded that changing that status is "dependent upon the capacity of local women's NGOs to organize and mobilize members of their communities."[91] If few people are working locally to hold states accountable to the international agreements that they sign, success in changing women's position will be necessarily limited.

Similarly, states signing international agreements supporting women's rights (for example) may adopt the language of those agreements while failing to implement them on the ground. Organizing only at the UN level is thus a "risky" strategy for a women's movement.[92] Local organizing

---

[86] Julie Mertus, "From Legal Transplants to Transformative Justice: Human Rights and the Promise of Transnational Civil Society," *American University International Law Review*, Vol. 14. No. 5 (1999), pp. 1372–3.

[87] Ibid., p. 1373.

[88] Ibid., p. 1373.

[89] Ibid.

[90] Susan Bazilli, "Reflections of a Global Women's Activist," *Human Rights Dialogue* (Summer 2000), p. 12.

[91] Ibid., pp. 12–13.

[92] Deborah Stienstra, "Dancing Resistance from Rio to Beijing: Transnational Women's Organizing and United Nations Conferences, 1992–6," in Marianne H. Marchand and

constitutes the linchpin in successful campaigns to provoke a move toward greater governmental accountability. Pressure from civic advocacy or watchdog groups is most effective when "combined either with substantial and sustained social mobilization (to put pressure on officials and to protect accusers), or else with other, more systematized, forms of institutionalizing voice, to achieve a more substantial movement in the direction of genuine accountability."[93]

Confronting World Bank Projects: Accountability Within Transnational Coalitions

Much transnational activism attempts to connect local and global activists and to respond to the needs of a marginalized local – or worldwide – constituency. But accountability relationships within transnational coalitions are complex because of their internal power relationships. In essence, some transnational coalitions are more closely connected and accountable to a constituency than others. Accountability within coalitions constitutes a significant issue in transnational social movement organizing. Because such coalitions typically confront either states or international financial institutions (such as multilateral development banks) that are themselves accused of being unaccountable, activist coalitions' own accountability is sometimes put at issue by the target of the campaign.

One of the challenges facing civil society organizations hoping to hold governments and global institutions accountable is that the civic groups themselves may lack democratic accountability in their own operations.[94] Internally, they may meet only procedural criteria for accountability, featuring perfunctory elections, minimal transparency about their operations and finances, and a board composed of the founders' friends.[95] They may have little to no contact with their ostensible constituency – and therefore are unable "to answer to stakeholders for their actions and omissions," much less to take direction from those stakeholders who are affected by the NGO's activities (or lack of same). Civil society groups' failure to abide by principles of accountability can undermine trust in those organizations across the board and provide fuel for governments aiming to delegitimate

Anne Sisson Runyan, eds., *Gender and Global Restructuring: Sightings, Sites and Resistances* (London: Routledge, 2000), p. 223.

[93] Goetz and Jenkins, p. 96.
[94] Scholte, "Civil Society and Democratically Accountable Global Governance," pp. 230–2.
[95] Ibid., pp. 230–1.

opponents.[96] Transnational coalitions composed of large, funded, Western or "Northern" NGOs and smaller domestic NGOs and grassroots groups in a state undergoing a development project are likely to be subject to similar critiques.

Resistance to multilateral bank-funded projects or their impacts can be effective in stopping funding for a project, whether or not the transnational coalition involved exhibits good internal accountability. But the most effective coalitions, in terms of meeting the needs of people directly affected by such projects and of building the potential for making states more accountable to their populations in the longer term, are those that are internally accountable to the grassroots in the affected area.

In a study of North-South "advocacy partnerships" aimed at making World Bank projects more environmentally responsible, David Wirth finds that some advocacy coalitions bringing together Northern- and Southern-based groups are more empowering of the Southern groups than are others, and that such partnerships vary in their degree of accountability to local communities.[97] Several cases serve to illustrate the fragility of transnational coalition advocacy as an instrument of meeting local needs. The following section explores four cases of transnational coalition advocacy aimed at influencing World Bank (and state) policy on development projects, with an eye toward evaluating the coalitions in each case for their capacity to meet the needs of the local constituency in whose name they initially took up the banner of protest.

Transnational Advocacy Without Accountability: The Kedung Ombo Dam (Indonesia) and the Sierra Madre Forest (Mexico)

Built with the aid of a $156 million World Bank loan, Indonesia's Kedung Ombo Dam was finished in January 1989, resulting in the involuntary displacement of several thousand people, none of whom were compensated for their land at the price that they had been promised.[98] The injustice of their resettlement and submarket compensation did not pass unnoticed. Local farmers' protests began roughly two years prior to the dam's completion (and the corollary flooding of their territory) as a demand for proper compensation. Initially, villagers seeking compensation for their land sought

---

[96] Ibid.

[97] David A. Wirth, "Partnership Advocacy in World Bank Environmental Reform," in Fox and Brown, eds., *The Struggle for Accountability*, p. 59.

[98] Villagers were offered compensation for their land at one-tenth of its value. See Bruce Rich, *Mortgaging the Earth: The World Bank, Environmental Impoverishment, and the Crisis of Development* (Boston: Beacon Press, 1995), pp. 149–50.

out local legal aid organizations and then Indonesian NGOs in the capital. These national NGOs "reached out to partners" in the advanced industrial countries, creating a transnational alliance that served the purpose of spreading information and applying pressure on the World Bank and the Indonesian government.[99]

As the protest reached the national level, however, Indonesian NGOs' concerns shifted to other issues, such as democratization, while internationally the campaign took on an anti-big-dam tone, although the villagers affected had not protested against the building of the dam per se. Although a transnational alliance of sorts was formed with the Kedung Ombo villagers' plight as its impetus, the components of that alliance were insufficiently responsive to the expressed needs of the local farmers. Instead, the national and transnational NGOs brought in issues on their own agendas, risking political repercussions for the villagers. The campaign's accountability to its least powerful participants was flawed at best.

Despite the distortion of local goals, the Kedung Ombo campaign was not a failure at the transnational level. The Kedung Ombo experience "may have contributed" to the World Bank initiating a set of guidelines intended to prevent such stark resettlement and compensation problems in the future, including a plan to create more space for NGO voices in project development.[100] The World Bank also responded to the protests by sending a mission to Kedung Ombo and raising complaints with the Indonesian government.

With respect to accountability within transnational civic coalitions, the alliance formed in response to the Kedung Ombo Dam issue provides compelling evidence that although pressure at the local, national, and international levels can be useful, such "alliances" can provoke a repressive reaction from the target state against domestic activists. When the international campaign drew attention to the government's failure to resettle and compensate the local villagers properly, ultimately leading the World Bank to confront the Indonesian government, this infuriated Indonesian President Suharto, who, in turn, sought to punish and more closely control the NGOs involved[101] – a response not unlike that of the Nigerian government's to the Ogoni movement's receipt of foreign support. Given Indonesia's repressive regime, Suharto's response provoked understandable anxiety among the grassroots groups, who then sought to distance

---

[99] Augustinus Rumansara, "Indonesia: The Struggle of the People of Kedung Ombo," in Fox and Brown, eds., *The Struggle for Accountability*, p. 126.

[100] Ibid., p. 127.

[101] Ibid., p. 137.

themselves from the national NGOs: "Local groups told the press that INGI [the International NGO Group on Indonesia, including foreign and Indonesian NGOs], not they, were responsible for 'airing dirty linen abroad,' so it appeared that INGI was losing its base inside the country."[102] Driving the rupture between the local and national/international NGOs was the fact that university students in Indonesia had organized in the name of solidarity with the villagers, but in fact campaigned not only for compensation for the villagers but also for "clean government, transparency in development policy decision making, human rights, and democratization," provoking the government's hard-line response.[103]

"Downward" accountability within the Kedung Ombo campaign was lacking. At the international level, the Kedung Ombo issue "was packaged to fit within the context of a global environmental NGO campaign theme: an 'anti-big dam campaign,'" bringing in issues from resettlement to human rights to environmental protection. As Augustinus Rumansara, an experienced development specialist active in Indonesia writes, "It is not clear that the shift from the issue of 'compensation' to 'democratization' and 'no more big dams' directly benefited the people in Kedung Ombo, nor is it clear to what extent NGOs 'represented' the people of Kedung Ombo in the campaign."[104] Indeed, language barriers and a general lack of power meant that the grassroots groups "played a very limited direct role in the legal strategy and the effort to lobby officials" in the Indonesian government, and were "not involved at all in the international campaign."[105] Thus, the "lines of accountability within the international campaign [were] complex and [were] not easily drawn from international NGO to local NGO to affected community."[106] Transnational campaigns could be strengthened (and the chances of state repression diminished) if the planning process incorporated participants at every tier of the campaign: "grassroots groups with local NGOs, local NGOs with national NGO networks, and national NGO networks with international NGO networks."[107] As is clear from other studies of transnational alliances, the failure of transnational organizers to work closely with "those on the ground who are most knowledgeable about their own circumstances" can leave the priorities of those at the most local and marginalized level unaddressed.[108]

[102] Ibid., p. 140.
[103] Ibid., p. 141.
[104] Ibid., p. 141.
[105] Ibid., pp. 137–8.
[106] Ibid., p. 141.
[107] Ibid., p. 146.
[108] Tripp, pp. 297, 308.

A second transnational alliance seeking to change the course of a World Bank loan was the early-1990s protest campaign against the Sierra Madre Forestry project, "a World Bank–Mexican government venture intended to modernize the forestry industry of northern Mexico."[109] In this case, a "local church-based human rights organization began tracking this project because of concerns over its environmental and social impact on the indigenous groups in the area."[110] The local NGO aimed to "redesign the project to increase economic benefits for the area" (because the project guaranteed no jobs for indigenous people), not to cancel the project entirely.[111] After linking up with an environmentalist NGO in Washington, D.C., the local group was sidelined, as U.S. NGOs adopted the issue. Pressure on the World Bank to withdraw support for the project combined with "macroeconomic factors" that made the project unfeasible, and it was canceled. The transnational alliance's environmental aims were fulfilled, but "the economic development goals of the local NGO [became] impossible to achieve" because the project was nixed.[112] There had been almost no involvement of the indigenous groups in whose name the transnational campaign was launched: "[The] indigenous people affected were used briefly to lend legitimacy to the environmental campaign. They felt exploited and withdrew from further involvement, and so lost an opportunity to pursue their interests."[113] Downward accountability in this campaign was insufficient, and the indigenous groups' needs remained unmet.

Transnational Advocacy with Accountability: The Mount Apo Geothermal Plant (Philippines) and the Narmada River Dam (India)

By contrast, the transnational alliance formed in the late 1980s to defeat World Bank funding to build a geothermal power plant in the Philippines exhibited clear lines of accountability between local and foreign activist partners. Although the Philippine government proceeded with the project anyway, the transnational campaign successfully convinced the Bank to

---

[109] Jane Covey, "Accountability and Effectiveness in NGO Policy Alliances," in Michael Edwards and David Hulme, eds., *Beyond the Magic Bullet: NGO Performance and Accountability in the Post–Cold War World* (West Hartford, CT: Kumarian Press, 1996), p. 203.

[110] Ibid., p. 203.

[111] Ibid., p. 203; Maria Teresa Guerrero, Cyrus Reed, Brandon Vegter, "The Forest Industry in the Sierra Madre of Chihuahua: Social, Economic, and Ecological Impacts," Commission on Solidarity and Defense of Human Rights, AC., and Texas Center for Policy Studies, July 2000, p. 24, accessed May 23, 2007, at http://www.texascenter.org/publications/forestry.pdf.

[112] Covey, p. 204.

[113] Ibid., p. 206.

withdraw funding to build the Mount Apo geothermal plant, which was predicted to have a negative environmental and social impact on indigenous inhabitants of the region.[114] Unlike the Kedung Ombo Dam and Sierra Madre Forest campaigns, however, the voices of the local people most closely affected did not disappear from the campaign. Instead, the transnational coalition was led by Philippine NGOs, whose major transnational partner was the Philippine Development Forum (PDF), a U.S.-based organization with access to the World Bank. Within the transnational campaign, the decision-making procedure was transparent, and information flow in both directions was thorough. Decisions were "evaluated through...Solidarity Conferences attended solely by Philippine-based groups." These gatherings functioned as "mechanisms to ensure accountability to the local communities, build consensus on demands, strategy and tactics, and develop a coherent division of labor."[115]

Although the division of labor empowered the "Northern" partners in the campaign to act as the "articulator or messenger for the Southern members," while the latter provided the data to their transnational allies for use in talks with the World Bank (a division of labor similar to that in the Argentine and Mexican human rights movements), the accuracy of the "message" was maintained because participants at all levels prioritized accountability to the grassroots in their campaign. Antoinette Royo, an environmental lawyer in Manila, explored three "dimensions" of accountability in the campaign: within the Philippine campaign (to the local indigenous people), within the transnational alliance (PDF accountability to the Philippine campaign and the local communities it represented), and within the PDF. She found that the lines of accountability to the local population were well maintained.[116] In effect, the campaign used its "unified front" as a transnational organizing tool, "where the national, regional and local task forces worked together to implement a coordinated opposition and to provide international campaigners with the ammunition for their communications with the [multilateral development banks] or international aid agencies."[117] The fact that the campaign failed to prevent the Philippine government from building the geothermal plant suggests that, in this case, the World Bank's management showed

---

[114] Antoinette G. Royo, "The Philippines: Against the People's Wishes, the Mt. Apo Story," in Fox and Brown, eds., *The Struggle for Accountability*, p. 151.
[115] Ibid., pp. 151, 65.
[116] Ibid., pp. 164–7.
[117] Ibid., p 173.

more accountability to the grassroots than did the domestic national political leaders who chose to proceed with the project.

The late-1980s movement opposing the World Bank's loan to India for a major dam on the Narmada River constitutes a second positive case of "partnership advocacy" between Northern and Southern groups, although the case is complex on the internal accountability front.[118] As with the Mount Apo campaign, local and transnational movements cooperated. At the local level, grassroots activists threatened to drown rather than leave their homes so that the dam could flood their villages, increasing the "efficacy of [their] Northern partners on behalf of their Indian constituents."[119] The campaign eventually led to the Bank convening the Morse Commission, an independent review of the Narmada project conducted by experts in the field. The commission's investigation resulted in a recommendation that the Bank retreat from funding the project further until certain "benchmark" conditions could be met by the Indian government to "remedy environmental and resettlement shortcomings."[120] India's executive director at the Bank ultimately asked that the Bank "cancel the remaining disbursements of $170 million, and announced that the government of India would finance the remainder of the project by itself." Although the Bank then asserted its "confidence that India had nonetheless satisfied the benchmark conditions...for the continued receipt of funds under the loan," the NGO campaign was regarded as a success in that it helped provoke reforms such as the creation of the Inspection Panel (see Chapter 2 of this book) and an improved policy of information sharing with the public.[121]

The Narmada campaign, however, cannot be categorized as featuring unambiguously high accountability to the grassroots, because after 1988 the local movement split. Some organizations (such as Arch-Vahini) continued their previous efforts to work for improved resettlement and rehabilitation benefits for those "tribals" displaced by the dam, while others (such as Narmada Bachao Andolan) that had previously supported the struggle to

---

[118] The World Bank funding was arranged in 1985 and continued through March 1993; dam construction started in 1987. See William F. Fisher, "Development and Resistance in the Narmada Valley," in William F. Fisher, ed., *Toward Sustainable Development? Struggling over India's Narmada River* (Armonk, NY: M. E. Sharpe, 1995), p. 12. Fisher's chapter details the resistance movement that spurred the World Bank's reevaluation of the project.

[119] Wirth, p. 62.

[120] Thomas A. Blinkhorn and William T. Smith, "India's Narmada: River of Hope," in Fisher, ed., *Toward Sustainable Development?* p. 108; Wirth, pp. 63-4.

[121] Wirth, pp. 64-5.

improve the resettlement package now dismissed the rehabilitation benefits
as false promises, protesting instead against the dam project in its entirety.[122]
Initially, the groups pressing for better compensation had collaborated
successfully with transnational NGOs (such as Oxfam) to pressure the
World Bank and the Indian government to improve the rehabilitation and
resettlement package, meeting at least some of the needs of those slated
for resettlement.[123] After 1988, the (now) anti-dam organizations also
worked closely with transnational NGOs (such as the Environmental
Defense Fund), arguing that the project was environmentally unwise and
of dubious economic benefit, and that local people ostensibly "opposed
the project" (because, as these groups argued, "rehabilitation and resettlement was impossible in principle").[124] Mass protests (including the "We
will drown but we will not move" events)[125] led to the Bank's reevaluation
of the project and ultimately to an end to World Bank funding. But as it
withdrew its financial support, the World Bank also lost its influence over
the project, including the resettlement component, which deteriorated after
the Bank's involvement in the project ended.[126] This outcome dismayed the
pro-compensation activists, who wanted Bank support for their ongoing
efforts to ensure fair compensation for displaced villagers.[127] Whether the
anti-dam activists or the pro-compensation activists better represented the
wishes and interests of the local "oustees" is disputed, making the transnational campaign after 1988 either a case of high or low levels of grassroots
accountability, depending on the perspective of the movement activists in
question.[128]

Even when international financial institutions (IFIs) can be successfully
pressured to improve or comply with their own standards of accountability, states, of course, make the determining choices about which projects
to pursue. Transnational coalitions making use of grassroots protest and
including local activists as full partners in the campaign set a standard
for local organizing that can be reactivated in the event of future lapses in
governmental or IFI accountability.

[122] Fisher, "Development and Resistance," pp. 22–3.
[123] Anil Patel, "What Do the Narmada Valley Tribals Want?" in Fisher, ed., *Toward Sustainable Development?* p. 187.
[124] Ibid., p. 191.
[125] See Medha Paktar, "The Struggle for Participation and Justice: A Historical Narrative," in Fisher, ed., *Toward Sustainable Development?* p. 171.
[126] Patel, pp. 197–8.
[127] Fisher, "Development and Resistance," p. 33.
[128] For opposing perspectives, see the Patel and Paktar chapters in Fisher, ed., *Toward Sustainable Development?*

Building Accountability Within Transnational Coalitions That Target Development Banks

Despite the uneven outcomes of the North-South partnerships in these campaigns, David Wirth sees Northern representation of Southern interests at the World Bank or to the U.S. government as being "often a more effective mechanism for Third World activists to achieve success than is dialogue with their own governments," echoing the "boomerang" strategy that Keck and Sikkink described.[129] For the boomerang to stay on course, however, the transnational coalitions must practice good internal accountability. "Multinational NGOs" – such as Greenpeace – have branches in multiple countries, including developing states, and hold yearly meetings of their affiliates. This practice builds accountability, because at such meetings agreement is achieved on an agenda, and campaign strategy can be developed.[130] The involvement of local affiliates in decision making should help to avoid the use of tactics likely to alienate the local population.

The preceding briefly considered cases can be classified according to the degree of their internal accountability. Jane Covey, for instance, categorizes alliances as "grassroots-centered," "NGO-centered," and "mixed."[131] The Sierra Madre and Kedung Ombo cases could be characterized as NGO-centered alliances. In such coalitions, "[a]ccountability to the grassroots tends to be weak, since the alliance is formed primarily to achieve NGO-defined policy goals."[132] By contrast, the Mount Apo case exhibited a "high level of grassroots accountability" evidenced by the "task forces" present at all levels. These were designed to support the aims "defined by indigenous people and farmers," in contrast to the Sierra Madre case, where "there was little accountability to affected people [and] NGOs pursued their own priorities."[133]

Establishing accountability within coalitions is not a straightforward process. The greater the geographic and political distance between coalition members (e.g., grassroots groups and international advocacy NGOs), the more difficult it may be to establish accountability and trust.[134] Project campaigns successful at garnering legitimacy tend to have grassroots groups at their center, as opposed to campaigns "organized and strongly

[129] Wirth, p. 59,
[130] Ibid., p. 61.
[131] Covey, p. 211.
[132] Ibid., p. 212.
[133] Ibid., p. 209.
[134] L. David Brown and Jonathan A. Fox, "Accountability Within Transnational Coalitions," in Fox and Brown, eds., *The Struggle for Accountability*, p. 441.

influenced by international NGOs," as was the coalition protesting Indonesia's Kedung Ombo Dam.[135] Not surprisingly, "when the coalition is defined to require the resources of grassroots movements, it is more likely that their interests will be taken into account in decisions," and that mutual influence will be the norm. This was true in the Philippines to a greater extent than in the Indonesian case.[136]

Unfortunately, high accountability "between NGOs and the communities they work with is...elusive."[137] First, "NGO accountability procedures are most often designed to meet donor needs rather than grassroots objectives," meaning that NGOs, like governments seeking IFI loans, are primarily accountable to the source of their funding.[138] Second, grassroots groups, national NGOs, and international (or Northern) advocacy NGOs differ along spectrums of power, and can bring to the coalition highly diverse goals, ideologies, and interests.[139] Yet establishing accountability within the coalition is important, because the "[b]alanced power relations and mutual influence" that accompany accountability can then foster trust among coalition participants, building social capital and laying the groundwork for future collaboration on campaigns.[140] Such future campaigns might confront development banks or governments in an attempt to hold influential institutions accountable to the population. For this reason, "policy alliances must strengthen grassroots participation if people are to develop the staying power required to build democratic societies."[141]

Effective campaigns against Bank-funded development projects do not necessarily require that a transnational coalition exhibit high internal

---

[135] Ibid., p. 448.

[136] Ibid., pp. 452–3, 456.

[137] Covey, p. 201. Obstacles to achieving accountability within transnational coalitions exist on several fronts. For a set of criteria by which to judge protest campaigns' internal political accountability, see Lisa Jordan and Peter Van Tuijl, "Political Responsibility in Transnational NGO Advocacy," *World Development*, Vol. 28, No. 12 (2000), pp. 2051–65.

[138] Covey, p. 201.

[139] Brown and Fox, p. 440.

[140] Ibid., p. 473. See also Jonathan Fox and John Gershman, "The World Bank and Social Capital: Lessons from Ten Rural Development Projects in the Philippines and Mexico," *Policy Sciences*, No. 33 (2000), pp. 399–419.

[141] Covey, p. 200. Well-integrated transnational activism can also monitor the effectiveness of World Bank–funded poverty-reduction programs – such as loans for social services – in particular countries. Neither the Bank nor borrower governments tend to measure program performance outcomes (such as the impact of rural health clinics). Joint efforts among local, national, and transnational activists to make program outcomes transparent can spur improvements in governmental accountability. See Jonathan Fox, "Vertically Integrated Policy Monitoring: A Tool for Civil Society Advocacy," *Nonprofit and Voluntary Sector Quarterly*, Vol. 30, No. 3 (September 2001), pp. 616–27.

accountability. The Sierra Madre case (and, to some extent, the Kedung Ombo case) show that campaigns can still win significant victories at the transnational level with neither local involvement nor grassroots strength. In fact, there is no evident causal connection between the degree of a campaign's internal accountability and its success, either at the transnational level (stopping IFI funding for a project) or at the domestic level (achieving the goals of the local community, whether those entail changing the policies adversely affecting the community, or stopping the project entirely).

However, the accountability of such alliances to grassroots groups is of central importance for democracy building and state accountability down the line. In the absence of grassroots protest, pressure on the state itself to behave more accountably is much less strong. Unaccountable transnational alliances thus have little impact on "deepening civil society and broadening democratic participation," which are key elements in holding state leaders accountable.[142] Civic participation is important to accountability even in stable, democratic states. There, the bonds of accountability are strengthened when the public participates in the policy-making process, both by lobbying the legislature and by commenting on the regulations generated by the executive branch to implement laws. If a population lacks the habit of civic activism, it will be in a weak position when it comes to holding its government accountable in these ways later on.[143] In this view, the corollary to Barrington Moore's famous dictum, "No bourgeois, no democracy," might be, "No civic activists, no consolidated democracy."[144] Participation in internally accountable transnational coalitions thus provides transferable skills that can be used by civic activists in their own countries to increase governmental accountability, whether or not those states have a democratic process in place. Transnational organizing that fosters grassroots mobilization – in ways consonant with the choices of local activists – should reinforce the connections, skills, and practices that help citizens struggle to achieve human rights and social justice at home.

TRANSNATIONAL NGOS AND SERVICE PROVISION

A significant number of transnational nongovernmental organizations supply social services rather than social change. These NGOs, which "deliver

[142] Covey, p. 212.

[143] Susan Rose-Ackerman, *From Elections to Democracy: Building Accountable Government in Hungary and Poland* (New York: Cambridge University Press, 2005), p. 22.

[144] Barrington Moore, Jr., *Social Origins of Dictatorship and Democracy* (Boston: Beacon Press, 1966), p. 418.

more official development assistance than the entire UN system (excluding the World Bank and the International Monetary Fund)," increasingly step in where states have abandoned ship, "delivering the services – in urban and rural community development, education, and health care – that faltering governments can no longer manage."[145] Although they may appear apolitical, offering charitable assistance rather than pressing for accountable behavior on the part of governments and transnational financial institutions, the work of these NGOs, too, reveals accountability dilemmas.

First, when foreign-financed NGOs in the developing world take on the provision of typically public services (such as schooling and health care), they are, in effect, freeing state leaders to direct their resources to enrich themselves, to finance wars, or to bolster their repressive apparatus.[146] Counterintuitively, with the help of NGOs, such states can more freely disassociate themselves from accountability to society. Funding domestic NGOs that provide welfare services or encourage economic self-help may also be the preference of foreign donors, who prefer financing such projects to funding broader initiatives to address and protest against structural economic inequalities.[147] NGOs, then, can indirectly accommodate existing systems of inequality perpetuated by national governments rather than promote governmental accountability by organizing popular pressure for it.

A second – and more common – accountability dilemma arises when NGOs step in to replace states that have abdicated their social welfare responsibilities. Such NGOs find themselves in the role of "public service sub-contractors" funded by foreign donors.[148] These NGOs rapidly become dependent on and accountable to their donors, not to those receiving their services.[149] This results in two distinct but related phenomena: the precedence of "upward" over "downward" accountability, and a demobilizing tendency in the NGOs' activism itself.

---

[145] Jessica T. Mathews, "Power Shift," *Foreign Affairs*, Vol. 76, No. 1 (January/February 1997), p. 53.

[146] Norimitsu Onishi, "Nongovernmental Organizations Show Their Growing Power," *New York Times*, March 22, 2002, p. A10.

[147] James Richter, "The Global and the Local: A Framework for Analyzing Local Activism," unpublished manuscript, 2002.

[148] Thomas G. Weiss, ed., *Beyond UN Subcontracting: Task Sharing with Regional Security Arrangements and Service-Providing NGOs* (New York: St. Martin's Press, 1998), cited in Julie Mertus, "From Legal Transplants to Transformative Justice: Human Rights and the Promise of Transnational Civil Society," *American University International Law Review*, Vol. 14. No. 5 (1999), pp. 1372–3.

[149] Mertus, pp. 46–7.

At the Mercy of Funders: Upward Versus Downward Accountability

One of the risks of transnationally funded service provision is that local groups receiving it are at the mercy of their funders' shifting agendas. In 2002, for instance, Russian women' crisis centers addressing the needs of survivors of domestic violence found themselves on perilous financial ground when transnational donors' priorities swung from countering domestic violence to fighting sex trafficking. Many centers were not prepared to change their focus, and the number of functioning crisis centers declined.[150]

Another case of service to marginalized women put at risk by changeable donor agendas is that of Durjoy Nari Sangha, a Bangladeshi NGO seeking to empower sex workers. With the aid of a grant from a U.S. government–funded transnational NGO starting in 1998, the group opened twenty drop-in centers where sex workers could get condoms and gather to talk about protection from HIV and other matters. According to Hazera Bagum, a member of Durjoy Nari Sangha, the funding stopped in December of 2005 and the drop-in centers had to close their doors. A documentary film produced by the Network of Sex Work Projects claimed that the funding was cut because the international NGO in question, in order to receive funds from the U.S. President's Emergency Plan for AIDS Relief (PEPFAR), had signed the "PEPFAR pledge" prohibiting PEPFAR funds from being used to "promote or advocate the legalization or practice of prostitution and sex trafficking." The "pledge" further mandated that any organization receiving PEPFAR funds must "explicitly" oppose prostitution and sex trafficking.[151] Presumably, funding Durjoy Nari Sangha – in essence, a sex-worker empowerment organization – would no longer be an option for a transnational NGO acceding to the pledge.

At issue is the notion of "upward" and "downward" accountability; the former flows from the NGO (transnational or otherwise) to "donors, trustees and host governments," and the latter between NGOs and "their partners, beneficiaries, staff, and supporters."[152] Based on a study of

---

[150] See Janet Johnson, *Gender Violence in Russia: The Politics of Feminist Intervention* (Bloomington: Indiana University Press, 2009).

[151] H.R. 1298, Public Law 108–25, "United States Leadership Against HIV/AIDS, Tuberculosis, and Malaria Act of 2003," May 27, 2003, accessed November 27, 2007, at http://frwebgate.access.gpo.gov/cgi-bin/getdoc.cgi?dbname=108_cong_public_laws& docid=f:publ025.108.pdf; Network of Sex Work Projects, "Taking the Pledge," 2007, accessed May 24, 2007, at http://sexworkerspresent.blip.tv/file/181155/.

[152] Michael Edwards and David Hulme, "Introduction: NGO Performance and Accountability," in Edwards and Hulme, eds., *Beyond the Magic Bullet*, p. 8.

accountability among NGOs in the development field, David Hulme and Michael Edwards find NGO accountability lacking, in part because NGOs and their donors have an interest in putting forth an image of success.[153] Downward accountability may be less strong than upward accountability in part because the financial relationship between NGOs and their benefactors necessitates a certain amount of reporting, whereas NGOs do not tend to report to their beneficiaries or "constituents."[154]

Writing about NGO accountability in Bangladesh, for instance, Syed Hashemi found that "upward" accountability prevails over "downward" accountability to the impoverished recipients of NGO services. This upward accountability to foreign donors (on whom Bangladeshi NGOs depend) accompanies a tendency to "[skew] NGO activities toward donor-driven agendas for development rather than indigenous priorities," leaving NGOs vulnerable and more interested in taking guidance from above than from below.[155] "[O]nly through the development of a system of [downward] accountability to the poor can NGOs truly transform themselves into organizations of the poor" – and thereby be in a position to "struggle for empowerment" actively rather than merely providing economic aid.[156] Instead, in Bangladesh, the government's repression of NGOs and demands for "greater accountability" to the state have been accompanied by a decrease in NGOs' actively organizing the poor to push for greater state accountability to the poor population.[157]

Demobilization: Advocates or Activists?

Demobilization constitutes a third dilemma of transnational service provision, where NGOs provide immediate material aid but do not actively protest against the root causes (national and transnational) of the gap in services to marginalized people. Considerable evidence from the development field points to a tension within and among NGOs between service provision and organizing for social change (e.g., democratization and fighting poverty).[158] The structures for putting each task into practice are different – if not antithetical to each other. Witness, for instance,

---

[153] Ibid., p. 9.
[154] Ibid., p. 14.
[155] Syed Hashemi, "NGO Accountability in Bangladesh: Beneficiaries, Donors, and the State," in Edwards and Hulme, eds., *Beyond the Magic Bullet*, p. 129.
[156] Ibid., p. 131.
[157] Ibid., p. 127.
[158] See Edwards and Hulme, eds., *Beyond the Magic Bullet*.

the organizational hierarchy deemed necessary for bringing in funds to implement services, as opposed to the less hierarchical, decentralized structure often used by groups doing grassroots organizing.[159] Funding an NGO through foreign grants can therefore transform an organization's structure and even its purpose. The reliance of "Southern" NGOs on Northern ones for funding in the development field typically brings with it the Northern groups' requirements for "strict financial accountability." This leaves little flexibility for the recipient organizations, which occupy much of their time with writing reports for donors.[160]

Michael Edwards and David Hulme, the editors of a study exploring accountability relations between NGOs and the communities they serve, conclude that various pressures for "upward accountability" and "performance measurement" lead NGOs to adopt projects whose success can be quantified, and that this has "damaging effects on the ability of NGOs to be catalysts for social change."[161] In short, downward accountability is "nearly always weaker than upward accountability."[162] This weakness can be attenuated only by "[i]ncreasing the involvement of grassroots constituencies (beneficiaries and supporters)."[163] But, despite the large increases in funding available to NGOs between the mid-1980s and mid-1990s, "very few NGOs (Northern or Southern)...have...become more transparent or accountable to their different constituencies."[164]

The problems of donor-driven activism, reliance on outside funding sources rather than a local constituency, upward rather than downward accountability, and demobilization (in favor of service provision and/or more elite forms of organizing) do not exclusively afflict transnational social movements and NGOs in the global South. An identical set of problems plagues social justice organizations in the United States, for example, giving rise to growing criticism of the "non-profit industrial complex."[165]

---

[159] Edwards and Hulme, "Introduction," p. 6.
[160] Zie Gariyo, "NGOs and Development in East Africa," in Edwards and Hulme, eds., *Beyond the Magic Bullet*, p. 158.
[161] Michael Edwards and David Hulme, "Beyond the Magic Bullet? Lessons and Conclusions," in Edwards and Hulme, eds., *Beyond the Magic Bullet*, p. 254.
[162] Ibid., p. 254–5.
[163] Ibid., p. 256.
[164] Ibid., p. 260.
[165] For a wide-ranging series of essays critical of foundation funding and the nonprofit industrial complex, see INCITE! Women of Color Against Violence, eds., *The Revolution Will Not Be Funded: Beyond the Non-Profit Industrial Complex* (Cambridge, MA: South End Press, 2007).

CONCLUSION

Transborder civic organizing occurs for a variety of reasons, all of which center around improving an institution's accountability – broadly construed – to a population. Some campaigns seek to alter state policies on behalf of – or, more productively, in concert with – local organizers. Transnational civil society also operates at the "global governance" level, aiming to force transnational economic institutions to live up to – or improve – their own standards of accountability to the people their policies affect. Transnational civic organizing in the form of campaigns against environmentally unsound World Bank policies, for instance, constitutes an attempt to enforce the Bank's accountability to a worldwide, if diffuse, community.

Given the considerable influence exerted globally both by states and international financial institutions, the advent of a counterweight in the form of transnational civic coalitions would appear to be a positive development. Yet the attempt to get transnational entities such as multilateral development banks, multinational corporations, and governments abroad to behave accountably may distract activists from local and national public politics, given their limited amounts of energy, time, and resources. Charles Tilly cautions, "To that extent [transnational organizing] will weaken connections between activists' trust networks and those smaller-scale sites of public politics."[166] Other scholars are also apprehensive about the side-effects of "globalization from below" on national-level political participation, seeing a decline in "participatory citizenship" alongside an increase in NGO activism at the transnational level. As Alison Brysk and Gershon Shafir write, "Civil society organizations have the potential to restore political participation, but in the process they may be transferring the effective arena of debate from national elections and competition for individual voters to a 'new aristocracy' of global activists."[167]

Will transnational activists focus on the transnational and lose sight of the need to hold local and national political institutions accountable for their behavior? Although activists may form cross-border coalitions, engage in activism aimed at influencing transnational institutions, and "participate in common themes across the world," this "does not mean... that transnational activism is displacing activists' domestic involvements

[166] Tilly, *Trust and Rule*, p. 159.
[167] Alison Brysk and Gershon Shafir, "Introduction: Globalization and the Citizenship Gap," in Alison Brysk and Gershon Shafir, eds., *People out of Place: Globalization, Human Rights, and the Citizenship Gap* (New York: Routledge), p. 7.

or escaping national constraints."[168] The hallmark of contemporary transnational activism is that it is rooted in domestic politics. Although domestic and international activism influence each other, the latter has not displaced the former, and largely centers around states (and the international institutions in which states participate). Activists thus move easily from engaging in campaigns against the World Bank to organizing during domestic election campaigns.[169] This fact highlights the importance of grassroots involvement in transnational protests against World Bank projects, for example. The experience of participating in internally accountable transnational campaigns could conceivably contribute to grassroots activists' empowerment in national politics – a plus for expanding democratic accountability.

States, IFIs, multinational corporations (MNCs), and other targets of transnational NGOs frequently lob the label of "illegitimacy" at NGOs, because NGOs' own accountability to a constituency is not self-evident.[170] One set of analysts examining global governance posed the issue starkly: "Just whom do these NGOs represent? And should decisions that affect many interests and often billions of people be shaped or blocked by their actions?"[171] L. David Brown, Sanjeev Khagram, Mark H. Moore, and Peter Frumkin provide three views on these questions. First, the lack of an explicit relationship to a constituency makes NGOs' representativeness questionable. If transnational NGO coalitions indeed "represent the world's citizens (or even a substantial part of them), their interventions arguably may increase the democratic accountability of the target institutions. But this representativeness is a difficult claim to substantiate. And international NGO alliances might reduce democratic accountability if they promoted policies that ran against the interests of their constituents."[172] Several cases where transnational NGOs fought to cancel Bank-funded projects, against the interests and objectives of local communities, underline the relevance of this concern. Maintaining a clear connection to grassroots needs is therefore essential to increasing target institutions' accountability effectively.

[168] Tarrow, p. 209.
[169] Ibid., p. 212.
[170] On the increasing pressure on NGOs to demonstrate their own transparency and accountability to constituents, see Goetz and Jenkins, pp. 102–7.
[171] L. David Brown, Sanjeev Khagram, Mark H. Moore, and Peter Frumkin, "Globalization, NGOs, and Multisectoral Relations," in Joseph S. Nye and John D. Donahue, eds., *Governance in a Globalizing World* (Washington: Brookings Institution Press, 2000), p. 286.
[172] Ibid., pp. 286–7.

A second way of looking at transnational NGO accountability regards these organizations as "represent[ing] transcendental purposes rather than particular groups or individuals" – that is, they represent "fundamental human rights," the observance of which is a sign of accountability. From this perspective, NGOs promoting human rights "are advancing democratic governance." Finally, the third approach suggests that whatever the legitimacy of transnational NGOs themselves, if they are acting to push an institution to "live up to its own policies and standards for practice," then the NGOs are acting in the service of accountability.[173] A thorough interrogation of transnational coalitions' internal accountability might result in the reordering of transnational campaign priorities and in a greater focus on abuses by national governments, not transnational economic institutions.

Transnational pressures for human rights, combined with local grassroots organizing, can successfully contribute to a national government's decision to change its policies and practices and thereby become more accountable to its population. By contrast, another type of transnational organizing takes the form of what I call "elite" or "leisure" advocacy, where activists are largely divorced from the people on whose behalf the campaign is organized. There are certainly cases where this kind of activism is warranted. In those instances, the safety of marginalized people would be at great risk if they organized publicly at the domestic level – such as women organizing for equal treatment under Taliban rule in 1990s Afghanistan. In such cases, the "boomerang" technique makes perfect sense, mobilizing educated, "cosmopolitan" foreigners who possess the spare time in which to sign Internet petitions and lobby their legislators to pressure the offending state. Any changes that a state introduces as a result, however, may fall by the wayside once the transnational advocacy campaign dies down. Rather than facilitating large-scale mobilization to pressure authoritarian states for change, transnational activism that remains at the elite level does little to further the sense of empowerment and citizenship necessary to hold states accountable and promote democratization over the longer term.

[173] Ibid., p. 287.

7

Conclusion

Altered States and Altered Citizens

The preceding chapters tell a sobering tale. In many of its forms, globalization has had detrimental effects on accountability to citizens. Even where transnational forces – primarily transnational social movements and judicial institutions – have had positive effects on governmental accountability, those effects are quite limited, and significant accountability gaps persist. Impunity remains an enormous problem in our national and transnational governing institutions alike.

Under what conditions do transnational forces promote or debilitate governmental accountability? To some extent, the answer revolves around sovereignty. Transnational forces and institutions are destructive to accountability when they constrain a government's autonomy by restricting information and limiting policy choices on issues where the public could otherwise assert itself. In those instances (such as when International Monetary Fund [IMF] agreements controlling economic policy extend beyond the term of the current government, or when private military companies' contracts undergo scrutiny by the executive branch, but not the legislature), transnational institutions limit popular sovereignty as well as state autonomy. By the same token, transnational institutions enhance popular sovereignty when they encourage the expansion of political participation and freedom of information. They may do so by enabling elections, as Executive Outcomes initially helped to do in Sierra Leone, or by fostering human rights education in states with low levels of democratic accountability, as the UN did in Cambodia, or simply by increasing the availability of information about governmental actions and providing more opportunities for informed political participation, especially among marginalized citizens.[1] Transnational forces are also conducive to accountability building when they disrupt a state's claim of national sovereignty as a cover for human rights violations and other forms of citizen oppression. A government responsive to the demands of a transnational social movement or to a decision by the European Court of Human Rights (ECHR), for instance, may appear to lose sovereignty, but only because it is being pushed to acknowledge concretely the rights of its citizens and therefore to increase *popular* sovereignty. In terms of their own practices, transnational forces promote accountability when they expand access to information and participation to those affected by their policies. They do the reverse when they restrict information under the rubric of confidentiality and when they invoke the combined sovereignty of member states as an excuse for doing so (such as when international financial institutions [IFIs] refuse to make loan information public).

Cross-border civic organizing often arises where governments and transnational institutions have restricted the exercise of public participation in decision making or in response to actions taken by transnational institutions that lack external accountability. As the reach of supraterritorial governance institutions has grown, attention has been drawn to their political accountability, both internal and external. Under pressure from activists, some transnational institutions have developed limited accountability mechanisms, such as the World Bank's Inspection Panel and NAFTA's National Administrative Offices (NAOs). Whether they are paragons or black holes of accountability, however, transnational institutions inevitably create space for grassroots groups interested in promoting it. The ECHR, for example, provides a mechanism through which a handful of Russian grassroots human rights advocacy groups can pursue their goals. Those groups generate cases for the Court, hoping its decisions will foster more accountable Russian state behavior. Likewise, through its policy choices and loans, the World Bank backhandedly creates opportunities for transnational citizen coalitions to form and then provides a venue at the Inspection Panel to hear their complaints. Transborder institutions and the "imagined community"[2] of transborder "citizens" appear to go hand in hand.

That the globalization of economic liberalism (in the form of multinational corporation [MNC] expansion, IMF intervention, and so on)

---

[1] Anne-Marie Goetz and Rob Jenkins, *Reinventing Accountability: Making Democracy Work for Human Development* (New York: Palgrave Macmillan).

[2] Benedict Anderson, *Imagined Communities: Reflections on the Origin and Spread of Nationalism* (London: Verso, 1991).

gives rise to resistance is in a dialectical sense inevitable. Yet those who oppose and those who promote globalization of this type share an important perspective on the world. The people James Rosenau calls "Resistant Globals" (such as the Seattle "antiglobalization" protestors) may clash ideologically with those he labels "Affirmative Globals" (who favor free trade and the other tenets of economic neoliberalism), but both groups view their worlds with "large-scale, nonterritorial orientations."[3] In other words, both camps in the debate over economic globalization exhibit a firm belief in a global community, differing profoundly over whether that community constitutes primarily an opportunity for building market relations or building accountability relations.

As global governance institutions expand and transnational activist coalitions rise and fall, scholars question the nature of the global activist community, wondering whether something like a global consciousness is arising in support of an expanded notion of accountability. Widespread evidence of transnational organizing for environmental and social justice – typically demanding accountability from transnational institutions, MNCs, and powerful countries – suggests that the activists in local communities, whether they are aware of it or not, affiliate themselves with a broader political community whose borders have little to do with the formal division of territory into states. Concerned about issues ranging from peace to pollution, their community is no smaller than humanity as a whole.[4]

The existence of this nonterritorial community and the nonterritorial institutions that increasingly govern it raises profound questions about sovereignty, accountability, and democracy. As discussed in previous chapters, the most central of these is the problem of supraterritorial institutions and external accountability. Because transnational decision-making institutions are not coterminous with the territory of a state, democratic theory provides us with "no way empirically to determine definitively who is (significantly) affected by a decision," or, to use Anne-Marie Goetz and Rob Jenkins's term, who the legitimate accountability-seekers are.[5] The group "relevantly affected" by decisions had been traditionally defined as the

[3] James N. Rosenau, *Distant Proximities: Dynamics Beyond Globalization* (Princeton: Princeton University Press, 2003), p. 137.
[4] Paul Hawken, *Blessed Unrest: How the Largest Movement in the World Came into Being and Why No One Saw It Coming* (New York: Viking, 2007).
[5] Michael Goodhart, "Europe's Democratic Deficits Through the Looking Glass: The European Union as a Challenge for Democracy," *Perspectives on Politics* Vol. 5, No. 3 (September 2007), p. 575.

citizens of an internationally recognized, sovereign state, but states now share the decision-making arena with transnational institutions.[6] Moreover, the very concept of democracy is historically linked to the notion of state sovereignty. Transnational governance institutions, whether economic, political, military, or judicial, cannot, therefore, be democratic as the term is traditionally understood.[7] If it is "unclear" in a theoretical sense how supraterritorial entities could be construed as democratic, then it is also unclear how they could be held externally accountable.[8] Transnational civic activists, however, appear to be undeterred by this theoretical muddle. Cross-border activists organizing against a wide range of injustices seem to regard empathy and conscience, rather than national sovereignty, as the determinants of their community boundaries.

GLOBAL CONSCIOUSNESS AND GLOBAL CONSCIENCE: FROM ADVOCACY TO ALLIANCE

If you have come to help me, you are wasting your time. But if you have come because your liberation is bound up with mine, then let us work together.
                                    – Aboriginal activist group, Queensland, 1970s[9]

Transnational organizing takes many forms. These range from short-term advocacy coalitions attempting to influence international institutions (such as the transnational coalitions that protest World Bank–financed projects) to what Dieter Rucht calls "distant issue" organizing, where activists in the "West" mobilize on issues that have at most a peripheral relationship to their own lives and well-being.[10] Such transnational "solidarity" cannot be explained by a narrow rational choice model, calculating the material costs and benefits of participation.[11] Exploring distant issue protests

---

[6] Ibid., p. 575; also see Jan Aart Scholte, *Globalization: A Critical Introduction* (New York: Palgrave), pp. 262–7.

[7] Goodhart, p. 575.

[8] Ibid.

[9] This quote, famously emblazoned on a 1994 poster, is often attributed to "Lila Watson, aboriginal activist." The poster designer provides a more accurate back story, accessed November 27, 2007, at http://northlandposter.com/blog/2006/12/18/lila-watson-if-you-have-come-to-help-me-you-are-wasting-your-time-but-if-you-have-come-because-your-liberation-is-bound-up-with-mine-then-let-us-work-together/.

[10] Dieter Rucht, "Distant Issue Movements in Germany: Empirical Description and Theoretical Reflections," in John A. Guidry, Michael D. Kennedy, and Mayer N. Zald, eds., *Globalizations and Social Movements: Culture, Power, and the Transnational Public Sphere* (Ann Arbor: University of Michigan Press, 2000), p. 79.

[11] Ibid., p. 102.

in West Germany from 1950 to 1994, Rucht found the highest levels of activism on matters of peace (50.7 percent of all distant-issue protests) and democracy or human rights (34 percent of all distant-issue protests). This evidence of fairly extensive, largely altruistic activism on these issues speaks to the possibility that some people regard wide swaths of the world as falling within their realm of moral concern and common conscience.[12]

Distant issue organizing on human rights and democracy suggests that any given local fight for political accountability can have foreign backing – which can play a powerful role in transforming accountability relationships on the ground. Consider the role of transnational organizing in the struggle against apartheid in South Africa. Although none would dispute that the lion's share of the success in overturning apartheid should be credited to South Africans' decades-long domestic struggle against racist oppression, the anti-apartheid movement has simultaneously been judged by its participants as "truly transnational."[13] Regardless of location, participants in the anti-apartheid struggle, while engaged in local actions (such as pushing their universities to divest from companies doing business in or with South Africa), saw themselves as part of a "transnational antiracist community."[14] Given the anti-apartheid campaign and other transborder activist efforts, Gay Seidman considers that

something important seems to be happening in the realm of social activists' vision of their constituencies and audiences. The shared networks, shared information, shared strategies – *above all, the shared sense of moral connectedness and the construction of an identity that extends beyond national borders* – suggest that somehow activists in these movements are increasingly likely to define their concerns in a way that is emphatically not limited to the single territorially defined community. There is at least a normative vision of a collective identity that goes beyond borders.[15]

---

[12] Ibid., p. 91.

[13] Gay W. Seidman, "Adjusting the Lens: What Do Globalizations, Transnationalism, and the Anti-Apartheid Movement Mean for Social Movement Theory?" in Guidry, Kennedy, and Zald, eds., *Globalizations and Social Movements*, p. 340. Together, foreign governments, corporations, and activists exerted significant international pressure that helped topple the apartheid regime. See Robert M. Price, *The Apartheid State in Crisis: Political Transformation in South Africa 1975–1990* (New York: Oxford University Press, 1991).

[14] Seidman, "Adjusting the Lens," p. 350.

[15] Ibid., p. 354, my emphasis. The transnational "collective identity" among antisexist or feminist activists, which Valentine Moghadam traces to the mid-1980s and the third UN world conference on women, is to some degree analogous to the antiracist organizing community that coalesced around apartheid. Valentine M. Moghadam, *Globalizing Women: Transnational Feminist Networks* (Baltimore: Johns Hopkins University Press), p. 1). Also see Myra Marx Ferree and Aili Mari Tripp, eds., *Global Feminism: Transnational*

Because such activists do not necessarily share the same background or experience, this collective "identity" may be better described as an amorphous "transnational community." In the case of transnational feminist organizing, writes Chandra Mohanty, these "imagined communities of women with divergent histories and social locations [are] woven together by the political threads of opposition to forms of domination that are not only pervasive but also systemic."[16] Activists are thus drawn together by a commitment to struggle against unjust – and unaccountable – hierarchies of power rather than by some precisely shared experience of oppression. In a recent example of such a commitment, South African dock workers made common cause with Zimbabwean human rights activists when, in April 2008, the former refused to unload a shipment of Chinese weapons that had arrived in Durban Harbor, destined for Zimbabwe. There, the ruling party had refused to admit defeat in hotly contested national elections and was in the midst of a violent crackdown against its opposition. As a spokesperson for the Congress of South African Trade Unions explained, trade unionists in South Africa would not facilitate the transmission of "weapons that could be used to kill and maim our fellow workers and Zimbabweans."[17] This gesture of transnational solidarity is emblematic of a cross-border identity opposing governments that rule by force.

The expression of such transnational "identities" has historical roots. The twentieth century in particular constitutes a period during which international organizations – particularly those focusing on peace, humanitarian and development aid, crosscultural communication, the environment, and human rights – flourished, making "efforts to establish interconnections among nations and peoples so as to develop a sense of global community."[18] Here, the term "global community" denotes

the building of transnational networks that are based upon a *global consciousness*, the idea that there is a wider world over and above separate states and national societies, and that individuals and groups, no matter where they are, share certain

Women's Activism, Organizing, and Human Rights (New York: New York University Press, 2006).

[16] Chandra Talpade Mohanty, *Feminism Without Borders: Decolonizing Theory, Practicing Solidarity* (Durham: Duke University Press, 2003), pp. 46–7, cited in Kathy Davis, *The Making of* Our Bodies, Ourselves: *How Feminism Travels Across Borders* (Durham: Duke University Press, 2007).

[17] Celia W. Dugger, David Barboza, and Alan Cowell, "Opposition 'Clear Victor' in Zimbabwe, U.S. Says," NYTimes.com, April 25, 2008, accessed August 7, 2008, at http://www.nytimes.com/2008/04/25/world/africa/25zimbabwe.html?hp.

[18] Akira Iriye, *Global Community: The Role of International Organizations in the Making of the Contemporary World* (Berkeley: University of California Press, 2002), p. viii.

interests and concerns in that wider world. This consciousness has to be given some institutional form if it is to become effective – hence the role of international organizations.[19]

From the establishment of the American Friends Service Committee (AFSC) in 1917 to Amnesty International in 1961, such organizations provide historical evidence of a transnational community of concern for human rights.[20] Some of these groups explicitly support a universal right to accountability. The AFSC, for instance, describes itself as "committed to supporting 'poor people in representing their own interests in global decision making.'"[21] Other transnational institutions, such as the International Criminal Court, similarly embody "a reflection of shared consciences that transcend national boundaries."[22] Transborder activism based on a community of conscience might be well equipped to confront rights-violating governments as well as unaccountable transnational political and economic institutions. Hypothetically, activists sharing consciousness of any given injustice and motivated by a "shared conscience" could be mobilized to counter manifestations of political and economic impunity around the world.

A global conscience, however, presupposes a global or transborder consciousness about particular injustices. What is the mechanism for the formation of a global consciousness on any given issue? Transnational consciousness – or awareness – of an injustice is typically the result of globalization and constitutive of it; issues are framed transnationally, and large-scale transnational social movements are thus mobilized. A successful transnational frame tends to draw on "global consciousness" – the "conception of the world as a single place."[23] Global consciousness is not a novel phenomenon, although until quite recently it resided largely in the realm of elites. Now, however, "most people on the planet have a degree of global consciousness, that is, some awareness and knowledge of what goes on in distant places and that this may have an effect on their lives."[24]

---

[19] Ibid., p. 8, emphasis mine.
[20] Ibid., p. 112. The idea of a shared consciousness or identity regarding human rights norms may be regarded as one manifestation of cultural globalization. A large literature exists on cultural globalization and identity, including on resistance to the spread of Western, corporate culture. For a useful analysis of this subject, see Douglas W. Blum, *National Identity and Globalization: Youth, State, and Society in Post-Soviet Eurasia* (New York: Cambridge University Press, 2007).
[21] Quoted in Iriye, p. 198.
[22] Ibid., p. 205.
[23] Thomas Olesen, "The Uses and Misuses of Globalization in the Study of Social Movements," *Social Movement Studies*, Vol. 4, No. 1 (May 2005), p. 54.
[24] Ibid., p. 54.

Building on this global consciousness, successful transnational activists frame a local or national-level issue in ways that "make it relevant to an audience outside the concrete physical territory." This occurs, for instance, when a human rights violation in a particular country is "framed in terms of universal human rights." Similarly, when some issue with a "global" nature (e.g., disease or pollution) arises, activists can easily frame these as affecting the globe, not just one locale.[25] Ideas such as human rights norms are also "localized" by "national and local actors who participate in transnational conferences and other events and bring home what they learn." These activists, academics, and government officials are the "key players" helping to "translate" international human rights ideas to local people.[26]

But to what extent does a shared, globalized conscience exist as a precondition motivating people to take action against injustice? In a U.S. poll published in 1999, 77 percent of respondents agreed with the statement, "I regard myself as a citizen of the world as well as a citizen of the United States."[27] Such a "cosmopolitan" identity, internationalist in viewpoint, where identity is not fully rooted in the state, was similarly embraced by a "small but not insignificant" proportion of citizens surveyed in the 1990s across seventy countries. The World Values Surveys across that decade revealed that 15 percent of respondents felt "close to their continent or 'the world as a whole' in their primary identity."[28] The relatively small number of people embracing a "global identity" does not negate the potential for a citizenship of conscience as a counterweight to unaccountable states and transborder governance institutions. Indeed, the potential for a transborder movement supporting political accountability in all states and transnational institutions may lie in the possibility of transnational communities founded on shared conscience and empathy (such as the antiracist community described by Seidman).[29] As a global "community of concern"

---

[25] Ibid., p. 54.

[26] Sally Engle Merry, *Human Rights and Gender Violence: Translating International Law into Local Justice* (Chicago: University of Chicago Press), p. 20.

[27] Quoted in Rosenau, p. 84.

[28] Pippa Norris, "Cosmopolitan Citizens," in Joseph S. Nye and John D. Donahue, eds., *Governance in a Globalizing World* (Washington: Brookings Institution Press, 2000), pp. 159–61. In some scholars' view, Norris's research finds the feeling of "collective identity, or solidarity" at "negligible levels" – a different interpretation of the survey results. Robert O. Keohane and Joseph S. Nye, Jr., "Introduction," in Nye and Donahue, eds., *Governance in a Globalizing World*, p. 29.

[29] Seidman, "Adjusting the Lens," p. 350. Of course, shared transnational identity per se is no guarantee of a counterweight to impunity of action. A transnational militant "jihadist"

expands, it changes the international opportunity structure for local NGOs and social movement organizers, increasing the likelihood that their concerns will be heard by their own governments as well as within transnational institutions.

As historian Eric Hobsbawm observed, "In real life, identities, like garments, are interchangeable or wearable in combination rather than unique, and, as it were, stuck to the body."[30] New information – about human rights abuses, for instance – can provoke the acquisition of a new identity shared with others similarly motivated to act. The globalization of computer technology in particular enables the creation of shared identities based on issue awareness, as well as facilitating action based on empathy and conscience. The Internet and other communications revolutions in recent years have facilitated the "formation and sustenance of networks among like-minded people who in earlier, pre-Internet times could never have converged."[31] In fact, the Internet era has "coincided with an apparent fourfold increase in the number of NGOs. That is, *transnational social activity* is increasing dramatically."[32] One antidote to impunity may therefore be the creation of transnational virtual communities of conscience, insisting on accountability wherever impunity is in evidence. Indeed, technological revolutions have long lent hope to those on the side of accountability. In the 1850s, abolitionist William Lloyd Garrison appreciated the new power and speed of the latest revolution in technology – the railroad – and the way it had opened "new markets for Truth as well as merchandise."[33]

Although high costs continue to restrict computer technology to a relatively wealthy segment of the global population, Internet access is starting to democratize. Even in authoritarian regimes that limit access to the Internet and to the content of particular websites, hackers have managed to circumvent government censorship. The expansion of Internet accessibility opens up a world of options for cross-border organizing and virtual community building. In a relatively recent development, massively multiplayer on-line role-playing games (MMORPGs), such as Eve Online, have

---

identity, for instance, may strengthen the hand of those who disdain accountability to human rights norms.

[30] Eric Hobsbawm, "Identity Politics and the Left," *New Left Review*, Vol. 217 (1996), pp. 38–47, at p. 41, cited in Rosenau, p. 188.

[31] Rosenau, p. 268.

[32] Keohane and Nye, "Introduction," p. 29. Emphasis in the original.

[33] Quoted in Henry Mayer, *All on Fire: William Lloyd Garrison and the Abolition of Slavery* (New York: St. Martins Press, 1998), p. 427.

brought together up to thirty-seven thousand participants simultaneously.[34] If such numbers can be mobilized for game playing, perhaps large-scale real-time web forums could be similarly organized on pressing matters of human rights and other accountability issues.[35] Evidence of political activism arising within on-line role-playing games has already surfaced, such as a gay pride march organized within the most popular MMORPG, World of Warcraft, and nationalist protest rallies virtually attended by tens of thousands of players in a Chinese on-line game called Fantasy Westward Journey.[36]

Large-scale real-world activism, too, has found a home on the web. Avaaz, a massive on-line community that campaigns for human rights and to prevent further global warming, spent a year mobilizing its members in advance of the UN's climate change conference in Bali in December 2007. There, when Japan, the United States, and Canada blocked agreement on the reduction of carbon emissions, the Avaaz network leapt into action. Over three hundred thousand Avaaz members were mobilized within three days, producing a flood of emails and phone calls to the relevant government officials and conference delegates, as well as an 180,000-signature petition, printed in the *Jakarta Post* and distributed to all the Bali conference delegates. The recalcitrant governments were successfully pressured to join the consensus. In a setting designed for negotiation at some remove from the public eye, Internet-facilitated organizing had enabled "people power" to influence the proceedings.[37]

From obstinate authoritarian states, to narrow, exclusionary, fundamentalist identities, there are many obstacles to making governing institutions more accountable and participatory. Still, some scholars see grounds for optimism in progressive social movements attempting to hold transnational and state institutions accountable, as well as in institutions such as the United Nations and European Union, where conflicts are occasionally resolved and where norms that support accountable behavior (such as observance of human rights at the state level) are, at least at times, promulgated.[38] Other means to address accountability gaps,

---

[34] See http://myeve.eve-online.com/mb/news.asp?nid=1649.

[35] A first step would be to provide web access in areas and to people who typically lie beyond the reach of these technologies.

[36] See Henry Jenkins, "From Participatory Culture to Participatory Democracy," March 5, 2007, accessed December 6, 2007, at http://www.henryjenkins.org/2007/03/from_participatatory_culture_t.html.

[37] Avaaz.org, "Bali: People Power Confronts Climate Change," accessed August 7, 2008, at http://www.avaaz.org/en/bali_report_back/.

[38] Held et al., p. 452.

particularly in transnational institutions, include altering those institutions' decision-making processes.

David Held, Anthony McGrew, David Goldblatt, and Jonathan Perraton summarize three ways of thinking about democratizing globalization processes. The first is a liberal-internationalist position, favoring the "reform of existing structures of global governance" as a means of handling global problems and crises. The second seeks to move decision making closer to the ground level, empowering communities to make their own choices and to make connections with other local communities, creating social movements "which challenge the authority of states and international agencies [through] a politics of resistance and empowerment."[39] The third, labeled "cosmopolitanism," seeks "to specify the principles and the institutional arrangements for making accountable those sites and forms of power which presently operate beyond the scope of democratic control," arguing in effect that the globalized world will require people to maintain "multiple citizenships" in their local, regional, and global communities. As "cosmopolitan citizens," people will need to "gain access to, mediate between, and render accountable the social, economic and political processes and flows that cut across and transform their traditional community boundaries."[40] International as well as national decision-making processes would become matters for public participation and debate in an "international public sphere."[41]

This "cosmopolitan" system of global governance would rest on the provision of "diverse and multiple democratic public forums" at the city, national, world-regional, and global (transnational) levels, to counter the external accountability problem of stakeholders being absent from decision-making processes and to enhance the possibility that decision makers will be held accountable by those affected.[42] A similar proposal imagines the development of "global issue networks (GINs)" for any given policy problem of importance; such issue networks would include representatives from states affected, from the business community, and from international nongovernmental organizations (INGOs), as the particular policy issue dictates, and would be responsible for developing norms and then

[39] Ibid., pp. 447–9.
[40] Ibid., pp. 449–50.
[41] Ibid., p. 451; Marc Lynch, "Globalization and International Democracy" (a review essay), *International Studies Review*, Vol. 2, No. 3 (Fall 2000), p. 97.
[42] David Held, "Democratic Accountability and Political Effectiveness from a Cosmopolitan Perspective," *Government and Opposition*, Vol. 30, No. 2 (April 2004), pp. 364, 376.

holding states accountable through public pressure.[43] Without enforcement power, however, such a network might be of little utility – and deciding who should be represented in it renews some of the original issues of stakeholder inclusiveness.[44]

It is here that the issue of citizenship's basis reenters the picture. Held's preference is for the development of a new way of conceiving of citizenship, one that reflects the extraterritorial nature of policy and its effects, and that rests on "the availability and clarity of the principles of democracy and human rights." Citizenship would no longer be exclusively associated with a state recognizing a particular set of "rights and duties," but would reflect "an alternative principle of world order in which all persons have equivalent rights and duties in the cross-cutting spheres of decision-making which affect their vital needs and interests."[45] The grounds for establishing such "citizenship" would, of necessity, be conscience-based rather than territorial.

Likewise, there is hope for the closing of external accountability gaps in the long term development of global "networks of connection, and empathy, ...so that democratic publics in powerful states demand that the interests of people in weaker states be taken into account."[46] In effect, if powerful states (and transnational institutions) cannot be held externally accountable by those who are affected, perhaps they can be held accountable by those who *care* that others outside are affected.[47]

To the extent that the community of people concerned about extending human rights (including the right to participate in governance) grows, pressure for accountability on governing institutions – state and supraterritorial alike – will intensify. It is then that the balance of entries on the impunity-accountability ledger may shift. As globalization in all of its guises facilitates a growth in consciousness, so too should we expect – and hope for – the enlargement of our perceived community of concern. As the groups of people to whom we extend our empathy expand, more people may develop not just a global consciousness, but a global conscience.

[43] Ibid., pp. 378–80.
[44] Ibid., p. 380.
[45] Ibid., p. 386.
[46] Robert O. Keohane, "Global Governance and Democratic Accountability," in David Held and Mathias Koenig-Archibugi, eds., *Taming Globalization: Frontiers of Governance* (Oxford: Polity Press/Blackwell, 2003), p. 155.
[47] To the extent that conscience can work against impunity, conscience needs to be local (or national) as well as global. As Goetz and Jenkins point out, oppression occurs not only within the boundaries of official government agencies and institutions, but is widespread within societies as well. See Goetz and Jenkins, p. 14.

In a transnational world, we are all rapidly becoming each other's agents – and each other's principals. Global citizenship entails accountability to one another. Bad news *should* trouble us, wherever it occurs. Rather than paying to return the newspaper to its box, however, global "citizens" may be inspired to direct their resources toward improving the news – through acts of solidarity against oppression. As Alice Walker writes, "Only justice can stop a curse."[48] And only accountability will spell the end of impunity.

[48] Alice Walker, "Only Justice Can Stop A Curse," in Pam McAllister, ed., *Reweaving the Web of Life* (Philadelphia: New Society, 1982), pp. 262–5.

Bibliography

Abouharb, M. Rodwan, and David Cingranelli. *Human Rights and Structural Adjustment*. Cambridge, UK: Cambridge University Press, 2007.
"The Human Rights Effects of World Bank Structural Adjustment, 1981–2000." *International Studies Quarterly*, 50 (2006), pp. 233–62.

Abramovich, Victor. "Social Protection Conditionality in World Bank Structural Adjustment Loans: The Case of Argentina's Garden Program (Pro–Huerta)." In Dana Clark, Jonathan A. Fox, and Kay Treakle, eds., *Demanding Accountability: Civil Society Claims and the World Bank Inspection Panel*. Lanham, MD: Rowman & Littlefield, 2003. pp. 191–210.

ADHOC (Cambodia Human Rights and Development Association). Accessed November 21, 2007 at: http://www.bigpond.com.kh/users/adhoc/about_adhoc/about_adhoc.htm.

AFL-CIO et al. "Responsible Reform of the World Bank," April 2002. Accessed July 17, 2007, at http://www.bicusa.org/bicusa/issues/Responsible_Reform_of_the_20_World_Bank.pdf.

Alesina, Alberto, and Beatrice Weder. "Do Corrupt Governments Receive Less Foreign Aid?" *American Economic Review*, Vol. 92, No. 4 (September 2002), pp. 1126–37.

Alexander, Nancy C. "Paying for Education: How the World Bank and the International Monetary Fund Influence Education in Developing Countries." *Peabody Journal of Education*, Vol. 76, Nos. 3, 4 (2001), pp. 285–338.

Alexander, Robin, and Peter Gilmore. "The Emergence of Cross-Border Labor Solidarity." In Rachael Kamel, and Anya Hoffman, eds., *The Maquiladora Reader: Cross-Border Organizing Since NAFTA*. Philadelphia: American Friends Service Committee, 1999. pp. 67–73.

Almond, Mark. "How the West Helps the Vote-Riggers." *New Statesman* (March 11, 2002), pp. 29–30.

Alpert, Arnie. "Bringing Globalization Home Is No Sweat." In John Feffer, ed., *Living in Hope: People Challenging Globalization*. London: Zed, 2002. Pp. 37–52.

Aman, Alfred. *The Democracy Deficit: Taming Globalization Through Law Reform*. New York: New York University Press, 2004.

Amnesty International USA. "AI on Human Rights and Labor Rights." In Frank J. Lechner and John Boli, eds., *The Globalization Reader*. Malden, MA: Blackwell, 2000. Pp. 187–90.

"About Amnesty International." Accessed November 24, 2007, at http://www.amnestyusa.org/About_Us/page.do?id=1101195&n1=2.

"Governments Worldwide Attack Human Rights in the Name of Fighting Terror with Deadly Consequences, Amnesty International to Assert During 2006 Annual Report Release." May 23, 2006. Accessed November 23, 2007, at http://www.amnestyusa.org/annualreport/.

"Annual Report 2006: Outsourcing Facilitating Human Rights Violations." Accessed November 23, 2007, at http://www.amnestyusa.org/annualreport/2006/overview.html.

"Annual Report 2007: The State of the World's Human Rights." Accessed November 24, 2007, at http://thereport.amnesty.org/eng/Facts-and-Figures.

"And Compares Democracy To Potatoes." RFE/RL Newsline, February 6, 2006.

Anderson, Benedict. *Imagined Communities: Reflections on the Origin and Spread of Nationalism*. London: Verso, 1991.

"Appealing in Strasbourg Comes with a Heavy Price." *Jamestown Foundation: Chechnya Weekly*, Vol. 7, No. 4 (January 26, 2006). Accessed March 24, 2006, at http://www.jamestown.org/publications_details.php?volume_id=416&issue_id=3598&article_id=2370707.

Associated Press. "Abusive G.I.'s Not Pursued, Survey Finds." *New York Times*, February 23, 2006, p. A8.

"Dagestani Rights Activist Seeks Asylum in Ukraine," July 30, 2006. Accessed August 7, 2006, at http://groups.yahoo.com/group/chechnya-sl/message/49175.

Avaaz.org. "Bali: People Power Confronts Climate Change." Accessed August 7, 2008, at http://www.avaaz.org/en/bali_report_back/.

Avant, Deborah D. *The Market for Force: The Consequences of Privatizing Security*. New York: Cambridge University Press, 2005.

Baguiya, Mme. Kaniba. "One Pledge at a Time: Stopping Excision in Mali." *Peacework*, April 2005. Accessed May 16, 2007, at http://www.peaceworkmagazine.org.

Balakrishnan, Radhika. "Why MES with Human Rights? Integrating Macroeconomic Strategies with Human Rights." Marymount Manhattan College, 2005.

Barber, Benjamin R. "A Failure of Democracy, Not Capitalism." *New York Times*, July 29, 2002, p. A23.

Barnett, Michael, and Martha Finnemore. *Rules for the World: International Organizations in Global Politics*. Ithaca: Cornell University Press, 2004.

Barstow, David et al. "Security Companies: Shadow Soldiers in Iraq." *New York Times*, April 19, 2004, pp. A1, A11.

Baum, Dan. "Nation Builders for Hire." *New York Times Magazine*, June 22, 2003, pp. 32–7.

Bazilli, Susan. "Reflections of a Global Women's Activist." *Human Rights Dialogue* (Carnegie Council on Ethics and International Affairs), Summer 2000, pp. 12–13.

Becker, Elizabeth. *When the War Was Over: Cambodia and the Khmer Rouge Revolution*. New York: PublicAffairs, 1998.

Bedont, Barbara. "The Renewed Popularity of Rule of Law: Implications for Women, Impunity, and Peacekeeping." In Dyan Mazurana, Angela Raven-Roberts, and Jane Parpart, eds., *Gender, Conflict and Peacekeeping*. Lanham, MD: Rowman & Littlefield, 2005. Pp. 89–92.

Bellona. "Sutyagin Case." Accessed August 10, 2006, at http://www.bellona.org/subjects/Sutyagin_case.

Benjamin, Mark, and Michael Scherer. "'Big Steve' and Abu Ghraib." Salon.com, March 31, 2006. Accessed March 31, 2006, at http://www.salon.com/news/feature/2006/03/31/big_steve/print.html.

Bieber, Florian. *Post-War Bosnia: Ethnicity, Inequality and Public Sector Governance*. New York: Palgrave Macmillan, 2006.

"The Birth of the Pledge Against Excision." Accessed November 24, 2007, at http://www.stopexcision.net/s10.html.

Bissell, Richard E. "The Arun III Hydroelectric Project, Nepal." In Clark, Fox, and Treakle, eds., *Demanding Accountability: Civil Society Claims and the World Bank Inspection Panel*. Pp. 25–44.

Black, Stephanie. "About the Film." 2001. Accessed November 27, 2007, at http://www.lifeanddebt.org/about.html.

Blinkhorn, Thomas A., and William T. Smith. "India's Narmada: River of Hope." In William Fisher, ed., *Toward Sustainable Development?: Struggling over India's Narmada River*. Armonk, NY: M. E. Sharpe, 1995. Pp. 89–112.

Blom, Lance Cpl. Lukas J. "U.S. Criminal Justice System Travels Overseas." Marine Corps Air Station Iwakuni, Japan, April 22, 2005. Accessed February 9, 2006, at www.usmc.mil/marinelink/mcn2000.nsf/0/1A9407432D9D802D85256FE900247928?opendocument.

Blum, Douglas W. *National Identity and Globalization: Youth, State, and Society in Post-Soviet Eurasia*. New York: Cambridge University Press, 2007.

Boas, Taylor C. and Jordan Gans–Morse. "Neoliberalism: From New Liberal Philosophy to Anti-Liberal Slogan." *Studies in Comparative International Development*, Vol. 44, No. 2. forthcoming, Summer 2009.

Bob, Clifford. *The Marketing of Rebellion: Insurgents, Media, and International Activism*. New York: Cambridge University Press, 2005.

Brinkley, Joel, and James Glanz. "Contractors in Sensitive Roles, Unchecked." *New York Times*, May 7, 2004, p. A12.

Broad, Robin, ed. *Global Backlash: Citizen Initiatives for a Just World Economy*. Lanham, MD: Rowman and Littlefield, 2002.

Broder, John M., and James Risen. "Armed Guards in Iraq Occupy a Legal Limbo." *New York Times*, September 20, 2007. Accessed December 13, 2008, at http://www.nytimes.com/2007/09/20/world/middleeast/20blackwater.html?_r=1&scp=1&sq=Armed_20Guards%20in%20Iraq%20Occupy%20a%20Legal%20Limbo%st=cse.

Bronfenbrenner, Kate. "We'll Close! Plant Closings, Plant-Closing Threats, Union Organizing and NATFA." *Multinational Monitor*, Vol. 18, No. 3, March 1997. Accessed July 6, 2006, at http://multinationalmonitor.org/hyper/mm0397.04.html.

Brown, L. David, and Jonathan A. Fox. "Accountability within Transnational Coalitions." In Fox, and Brown, eds., *The Struggle for Accountability: The World Bank, NGOs, and Grassroots Movements*. Pp. 439–83.

Brown, L. David, Sanjeev Khagram, Mark H. Moore, and Peter Frumkin. "Globalization, NGOs, and Multisectoral Relations." In Joseph S. Nye and John D. Donahue, eds., *Governance in a Globalizing World*. Washington: Brookings Institution Press, 2000. Pp. 271–96.

Brown, MacAlister, and Joseph J. Zasloff. *Cambodia Confounds the Peacemakers 1979–1998*. Ithaca: Cornell University Press, 1998.

Brown, Stephen. "Authoritarian Leaders and Multiparty Elections in Africa: How Foreign Donors Help to Keep Kenya's Daniel arap Moi in Power." *Third World Quarterly*, Vol. 22, No. 5 (October 2001), pp. 725–39.

Brysk, Alison, and Gershon Shafir, eds. *People Out of Place: Globalization, Human Rights, and the Citizenship Gap*. New York: Routledge, 2004.

"Introduction: Globalization and the Citizenship Gap." In Brysk, and Shafir, *People Out of Place: Globalization, Human Rights, and the Citizenship Gap.* Pp. 3–10.

Bureau of African Affairs, U.S. Department of State. "Background Note: Sierra Leone." October 2007. Accessed November 24, 2007, at http://www.state.gov/r/pa/ei/bgn/5475.htm.

Burkov, Anton. "Implementation of the Convention for the Protection of Human Rights and Fundamental Freedoms in Russian Courts." *Russian Law: Theory and Practice* 1 (2006), pp. 68–76. Accessed September 8, 2006, at http://www.sutyajnik.ru/rus/library/articles/2006/russian_law_2006.pdf.

The Impact of the European Convention for the Protection of Human Rights and Fundamental Freedoms on Russian Law. Stuttgart: ibidem–Verlag, 2007.

[Burkov, A.L.] ed. *Primenenie Evropeiskoi konventsii o zashchite prav cheloveka v sudakh Rossii*. Ekaterinburg: Izdatel'stvo Ural'skogo Universiteta, 2006. Accessed November 24, 2007. at http://www.sutyajnik.ru/rus/library/sborniki/echr6/.

[Burkov, Anton Leonidovich.] "Detention of Mentally Ill Persons in the Russian Federation under Article 5 of the European Convention on Human Rights." In A. Umland, ed., *The Implementation of the European Convention on Human Rights in Russia: Philosophical, Legal, and Empirical Studies (Soviet and Post–Soviet Politics & Society)*, Vol. 1, 2004, pp. 121–143. Accessed August 10, 2006 at http://www.sutyajnik.ru/cgi-bin/articles.php?pub_id=11.

Burkov, Anton, and Anna Demeneva. "Probable Legal Consequences of Rakevich v. Russia." *Human Rights Law Review Student Supplement*, Human Rights Law Center, School of Law, University of Nottingham (August 2004), pp. 7–11. Accessed August 10, 2006, at http://www.sutyajnik.ru/eng/news/2004/HRLR_Student_Supplement_2004.pdf.

Cambodia Office of the High Commissioner of Human Rights (COHCHR). "Continuing Patterns of Impunity in Cambodia." October 2005. Accessed July 27, 2006, at http://cambodia.ohchr.org/Documents/Reports/Thematic%20reports%20by%20SRSG/English/242.pdf.

"Cambodian Human Rights Activist Launches His Own Political Party." Khmer.org, July 31, 2007, accessed December 2, 2008, at http://khmer.org/doc/o,article,74,584,0,1443,0.htm.

Campbell, Greg. "Blood Diamonds." *Amnesty Now* (Fall 2002), pp. 4–7.

Capaccio, Tony. "U.S. Military Tightens Rules for Contractors in Combat Zones." Bloomberg.com, October 27, 2005.

Cassen, Bernard. "To Save Society." In Frank J. Lechner and John Boli, eds., *The Globalization Reader*. Malden, MA: Blackwell, 2000. Pp. 14–16.

Center for Constitutional Rights. "CCR Files Lawsuit Against Private Contractors for Torture Conspiracy." Press Release, June 9, 2004. Accessed November 23, 2007, at http://ccrjustice.org/newsroom/press–releases/ccr–files–lawsuit–against–private–contractors–torture–conspiracy.

"The Center for Constitutional rights Credits Pressure from Advocacy Group and Public with CACI International Withdrawal from Iraq." Accessed November 23, 2007, at http://web.archive.org/web/20051130080938/http://www.ccr-ny.org/v2/reports/report.asp?ObjID=5Ar4fA7mMX&Content=633.

"Saleh v. Titan: Timeline." Accessed November 23, 2007. at http://ccrjustice.org/ourcases/current-cases/saleh-v.-titan.

Central Bank of Nigeria. *Economic Report for the First Quarter of 2006*. Accessed November 21, 2007. at http://www.cenbank.org/out/publications/reports/rd/2006/mrp-03-06.pdf.

Central Intelligence Agency. *The World Factbook: Cambodia*, November 15, 2007. Accessed November 21, 2007, at http://https://www.cia.gov/library/publications/the–world–factbook/geos/cb.html.

Chandler, David. *Bosnia: Faking Democracy After Dayton*. London: Pluto Press, 1999.

"How State-Building Weakens States." October 24, 2005. Accessed November 21, 2007, at http://www.spiked–online.com/Articles/0000000CADDB.htm.

Chandler, David, ed. *Peace Without Politics?: Ten Years of State-Building in Bosnia*. Abington, Oxon, New York: Routledge, 2005.

"Ten Years On: Who's Running Bosnia?" November 23, 2005. Accessed November 21, 2007, at http://www.spiked-online.com/Articles/0000000CAE83.htm.

Chazan, Guy. "Benched in Russia's Courts, a Judge Speaks Up – and Gets Fired." *Wall Street Journal*, August 5, 2004, p. A1. Accessed November 23, 2007, at http://courses.wcupa.edu/rbove/eco343/040Compecon/Soviet/Russia/040805legal.txt.

"In Russia, Grim Case Spotlights Distress of Justice Denied." *Wall Street Journal*, April 26, 2006, pp. A1, A14.

Cherednichenko, E. G. "Postanovlenie, g. Ioshkar-Ola." 16 ianvaria, 2006. Accessed November 24, 2007, at http://www.sutyajnik.ru/rus/echr/rus_judgments/distr/orlov_16_01_2006.pdf.

"Chief Judge Calls for Check on Kremlin's Power." RFE/RL Newsline, January 24, 2006.

Chivers, C. J. "Putin Urges Plan to Reverse Slide in the Birthrate." *New York Times*, May 11, 2006, p. A6.

Cichowski, Rachel A. "Courts, Rights, and Democratic Participation." *Comparative Political Studies*, Vol. 39, No. 1 (2006), pp. 50–75.

The European Court and Civil Society: Litigation, Mobilization and Governance. Cambridge, UK: Cambridge University Press, 2007.

Cilliers, Jakkie, and Richard Cornwell. "Africa – from the Privatisation of Security to the Privatisation of War?" In Jakkie Cilliers, and Peggy Mason, eds., *Peace, Profit or Plunder: The Privatization of Security in War-Torn African Societies.* Pretoria: Institute for Security Studies, 1999. Pp. 227–43.

Clark, Dana. "Singrauli: An Unfulfilled Struggle for Justice." In Clark, Fox, and Treakle, eds., *Demanding Accountability: Civil Society Claims and the World Bank Inspection Panel.* Pp. 167–90.

"Understanding the World Bank Inspection Panel." In Clark, Fox, and Treakle, eds., *Demanding Accountability: Civil Society Claims and the World Bank Inspection Panel.* Pp. 1–24.

Clark, Dana, and Kay Treakle. "The China Western Poverty Reduction Project." In Clark, Fox, and Treakle, eds., *Demanding Accountability: Civil Society Claims and the World Bank Inspection Panel.* Pp. 211–45.

Clean Clothes Campaign. "Nike Supplier Closes Unionized Factory, Shifts Work to Vietnam." *Peacework* (October 2007), p. 17.

CM/Inf/DH(2006)19. "Non-enforcement of Domestic Judicial Decisions in Russia: General Measures to Comply with the European Court's Judgments." June 6, 2006.

CNN. "U.S. Expects More Attacks in Iraq." May 6, 2004. Accessed November 23, 2007, at http://www.cnn.com/2004/WORLD/meast/03/31/iraq.main/.

Cohen, Roger. "Germany: Arms for Women." *New York Times*, January 12, 2000.

Coker, Christopher. "Outsourcing War." In Daphné Josselin, and William Wallace, eds., *Non-state Actors in World Politics.* Basingstoke: Palgrave, 2001. Pp. 189–202.

Collier, Paul. "Learning from Failure: The International Financial Institutions as Agencies of Restraint in Africa." In Andreas Schedler, Larry Diamond, and Marc F. Plattner, eds., *The Self-Restraining State: Power and Accountability in New Democracies.* Boulder: Lynne Rienner, 1999. Pp. 313–30.

Committee on Government Reform (Minority Office). "Iraq Reconstruction: All Investigations." Accessed November 23, 2007, at http://web.archive.org/web/20060210170146/http://www.democrats.reform.house.gov/investigations.asp?Issue=Iraq+Reconstruction.

Committee to Protect Journalists. "Russia: Journalist Goes on Trial for Satirizing Putin." September 21, 2006. Accessed September 28, 2006, at http://www.cpj.org/news/2006/europe/russia21sept06na.html.

"CPJ Fears Silencing of Critical Web Site on Chechnya." October 13, 2006. Accessed November 9, 2006, at http://www.cpj.org/news/2006/europe/russia13oct06na.html.

"Russia: Thirteen Murders, No Justice." November 2006. Accessed November 9, 2006, at http://cpj.org/reports/2006/11/russia-murders.php/.

Compa, Lance. "Another Look at NAFTA." In Broad, ed., *Global Backlash: Citizen Initiatives for a Just World Economy.* Pp. 135–9.

"The Conception of the Russian Academy of Justice." Moscow, 2000. Accessed November 24, 2007, at https://www.abanet.org/ceeli/special_projects/jtc/russia_raj_concept.pdf.

Council of Europe. "About the Committee of Ministers." Accessed November 23, 2007, at http://www.coe.int/T/CM/aboutCM_en.asp.

"The ECHR in Practice." Accessed November 23, 2007, at http://www.coe.int/T/E/Com/About_Coe/Brochures/fiche_dhc.asp.

Council of Europe/Committee of Ministers. "Execution of (ECHR) Judgments" website. Accessed December 2, 2008, at http://www.coe.int/T/E/Human_rights/execution/.

Council of Europe/European Court of Human Rights. "Yearly Surveys of Activities, 1998–2005." Accessed March 27, 2006, from Reports at http://www.echr.coe.int/ECHR.

Covey, Jane. "Accountability and Effectiveness in NGO Policy Alliances." In Edwards, and Hulme, eds., *Beyond the Magic Bullet: NGO Performance and Accountability in the Post–Cold War World*. Pp. 198–214.

Cowell, Alan. "Rights Group Criticizes U.S. over 'Outsourcing' in Iraq." *New York Times*, May 24, 2006, p. A12.

Coy, Patrick. "Cooperative Accompaniment and Peace Brigades International in Sri Lanka." In Jackie Smith, Charles Chatfield, and Ron Pagnucco, eds., *Transnational Social Movements and Global Politics*. Syracuse: Syracuse University Press, 1997. Pp. 81–100.

Crawley, Vince. "U.S. 'Disappointed' by Defeat of Bosnian Constitutional Reforms." Washington File, U.S. Department of State, April 28, 2006. Accessed October 17, 2007, at http://usinfo.state.gov/xarchives/display.html?p=washfile-english&y=2006&m=April&x=20060428134331MVyelwarCo.9095423&t=is/is-latest.html.

Crisp, Brian F., and Michael J. Kelly. "The Socioeconomic Impacts of Structural Adjustment." *International Studies Quarterly*, 43 (1999), pp. 533–52.

Cronin, Bruce. "The Two Faces of the United Nations: The Tension Between Intergovernmentalism and Transnationalism." *Global Governance*, 8 (2002), pp. 53–71.

Crossette, Barbara. "U.N. Report Says New Democracies Falter." *New York Times*, July 24, 2002, p. A8.

Crowfoot, John. "Postscript" to Anna Politkovskaya, *A Dirty War: A Russian Reporter in Chechnya*. London: Harvill Press, 1999.

"Cry for Action: Shameful Neglect and the Search for Hope in AIDS–Ravaged Africa: An Interview with Stephen Lewis." *Multinational Monitor*, Vol. 28, No. 2 (March–April 2007). Accessed July 31, 2008, at http://www.multinationalmonitor.org/mm2007/032007/interview–lewis.html.

CURIA. "The Court of Justice of the European Communities." Accessed June 25, 2008, at http://curia.europa.eu/en/instit/presentationfr/index_cje.htm.

Curphey, Shauna. "Amnesty Pushing Nations to End Gender Violence." Women's E-News, March 19, 2004. Accessed April 12, 2007, at http://www.womensenews.org/article.cfm?aid=1755.

Curtis, Grant. *Cambodia Reborn*. Washington: Brookings Institution Press, 1998.

"Dagestanskii pravozashchitnik Osman Boliev uekhal iz Rossii i poprosil ubezhishcha v predstavitel'stve verkhovnogo komissara OON po bezhentsam v Kieve." July 28, 2006. Accessed November 24, 2007, at http://www.echo.msk.ru/news/325065.html.

Dahl, Robert A. *Dilemmas of Pluralist Democracy.* New Haven: Yale University Press, 1982.

"Can International Organizations Be Democratic? A Skeptic's View." In Ian Shapiro, and Casiano Hacker-Cordon (eds.), *Democracy's Edges.* Cambridge, UK: Cambridge University Press, 1999. Pp. 19–36.

Danilenko, Gennady M. "Implementation of International Law in Russia and Other CIS States." 1998. Accessed March 27, 2006, at http://www.nato.int/acad/fellow/96–98/danilenk.pdf.

Davis, Kathy. *The Making of Our Bodies, Ourselves: How Feminism Travels Across Borders.* Durham: Duke University Press, 2007.

De Grauwe, P., and F. Camerman. "How Big Are the Big Multinational Companies?" *Tijdschrift voor Economie en Management,* Vol. XLVII, No. 3 (2002), pp. 311–26.

Demeneva, A.V. "Ispolneniiu ne podlezhit." Kommersant–Den'gi, No. 37 (2005). Accessed July13, 2006, at http://www.sutyajnik.ru/rus/library/articles/2005/ispolneniu_ne_podkezhit.htm.

Demeneva, A. V., and L. M. Churkina. "Primenenie Konventsii o zashchite prav cheloveka i osnovnykh svobod iuristami Ural'skogo tsentra konstitutsionnoi i mezhdunarodnoi zashchity prav cheloveka: opyt i rekomendatsii." In Burkov, ed., *Primenenie Evropeiskoi konventsii o zashchite prav cheloveka v sudakh Rossii.* Pp. 77–97.

Department of Peacekeeping Operations (DPKO) Fact Sheet. February 2008. Accessed December 2, 2008, at http://www.un.org/Depts/dpko/factsheet.pdf.

Diamond, Larry, and Leonardo Morlino. "The Quality of Democracy: An Overview." *Journal of Democracy,* Vol. 15, No. 4 (October 2004), pp. 20–31.

Diamond, Larry, Marc F. Plattner, and Andreas Schedler. "Introduction." In Schedler, Diamond, and Plattner, *The Self-Restraining State: Power and Accountability in New Democracies.* Pp. 1–10.

"Diamonds: A Rebel's Best Friend." BBC News, May 15, 2000. Accessed September 28, 2006, at http://news.bbc.co.uk/1/hi/world/africa/745194.stm.

"Djarawélé and the Fifth Person Principle." Accessed November 24, 2007, at http://www.stopexcision.net/s1.html.

Dline, Irina, and Olga Schwartz. "The Jury Is Still Out on the Future of Jury Trials in Russia." *East European Constitutional Review,* Vol. 11, Nos. 1/2 (Winter/Spring 2002), pp. 104–10.

Dollarhide, Maya. "Sexual Abuse: The UN Under Fire." *Voices–Unabridged: The E–Magazine on Women and Human Rights Worldwide,* No. 11 (February–April, 2007). Accessed April 25, 2007, at http://www.voices-unabridged.org/article.php?id_article=169&numero=11.

Downie, Sue. "The United Nations in East Timor: Comparisons with Cambodia." In Damien Kingsbury, ed., *Guns and Ballot Boxes: East Timor's Vote for Independence.* Victoria, Australia: Monash Asia Institute, 2000. Pp. 117–34.

Doyle, Mark. "UK Backs Sierra Leone Border Force." BBC News, January 16, 2002. Accessed February 10, 2006, at http://news.bbc.co.uk/1/hi/world/africa/1763030.stm.

"Bringing Justice to Sierra Leone." BBC News, January 17, 2002. Accessed November 22, 2007, at http://news.bbc.co.uk/1/hi/world/africa/1765611.stm.

Doyle, Michael W. *UN Peacekeeping in Cambodia: UNTAC's Civil Mandate.* Boulder, CO: Lynne Rienner, 1995.

"DPKO's Comprehensive Strategy on Sexual Exploitation and Abuse." Accessed April 19, 2007 at http://www.un.org/Depts/dpko/CDT/strategy.html.

"Draft: Official Statement of the Permanent Representative of the Russian Federation to the Council of Europe at the meeting of the Committee of Ministers of the Council of Europe concerning the Action Plan as regards execution by the Russian Federation of the judgments of the European Court of Human Rights in the cases of Khashiyev and Akayeva v. Russia (nos. 57942/00 and 57945/00), Isayeva, Yusupova and Bazayeva v. Russia (nos. 57947/00, 57948/00 and 57949/00, and Isayeva v. Russia (no. 57950/00)." Accessed August 8, 2006, at http://www.londonmet.ac.uk/londonmet/library/u70061_3.pdf.

Drake, Paul W. "Introduction: The Political Economy of Foreign Advisers and Lenders in Latin America." In Paul W. Drake, ed., *Money Doctors, Foreign Debts, and Economic Reforms in Latin America from the 1890s to the Present.* Wilmington: Scholarly Resources Inc., 1994. Pp. xi–xxxiii.

Dubnov, Vadim. "The Russian Mutiny." *New Times* (June 2006). Accessed July 6, 2006 at: http://www.newtimes.ru/eng/detail.asp?art_id=708.

Dugger, Celia W. "In Africa, Free Schools Feed a Different Hunger." *New York Times*, October 24, 2004. Accessed July 31, 2008, at http://www.nytimes.com/2004/10/24/international/africa/24africa.html?pagewanted=1&_r=1&sq=user%20fees%20october%202000%20congress&st=cse&oref=slogin&scp=2.

Dugger, Celia W. "World Bank Chief Outlines a War on Fraud." *New York Times*, April 12, 2006, p. A7.

Dugger, Celia W., David Barboza, and Alan Cowell. "Opposition 'Clear Victor' in Zimbabwe, U.S. Says." NYTimes.com, April 25, 2008. Accessed August 7, 2008, at http://www.nytimes.com/2008/04/25/world/africa/25zimbabwe.html?hp.

Easterly, William. "IMF and World Bank Structural Adjustment Programs and Poverty." World Bank, 2001.

Easton, Peter, Karen Monkman, and Rebecca Miles. "Social Policy from the Bottom Up; Abandoning FGC in Sub-Saharan Africa." *Development in Practice*, Vol. 13, No. 5 (November 2003), pp. 445–58.

Edwards, Michael, and David Hulme. "Beyond the Magic Bullet? Lessons and Conclusions." In Edwards, and Hulme, eds., *Beyond the Magic Bullet: NGO Performance and Accountability in the Post–Cold War World.* Pp. 254–66.

"Introduction: NGO Performance and Accountability." In Edwards, and Hulme, eds., *Beyond the Magic Bullet: NGO Performance and Accountability in the Post–Cold War World.* Pp. 1–20.

Edwards, Michael, and David Hulme, eds. *Beyond the Magic Bullet: NGO Performance and Accountability in the Post–Cold War World.* West Hartford, CT: Kumarian Press, 1996.

"Embattled Oligarch Sent to Pack Boxes." RFE/RL Newsline, April 4, 2006.

Enloe, Cynthia. *The Curious Feminist: Searching for Women in a New Age of Empire.* Berkeley: University of California Press, 2004.

Globalization and Militarism. Lanham, MD: Rowman & Littlefield, 2007.

Erinys. "Oil Protection Force Article." Accessed November 23, 2007, at http://www.erinysinternational.com/NewsInformation-Articles.asp.

European Convention on Human Rights. Accessed November 23, 2007, at http://
www.hri.org/docs/ECHR50.html#C.Art14.

European Court of Human Rights. "Organization of the Court." Accessed November
23, 2007, at http://www.echr.coe.int/ECHR/EN/Header/The+Court/The+Court/
Organisation+of+the+Court/.

Searchable Database. Accessed November 8, 2008, at http://cmiskp.echr.coe.
int/.

"Survey of Activities: 2005." Accessed November 8, 2007, at http://www.echr.coe.
int/NR/rdonlyres/4753F3E8–3ADo–42C5–B294–0F2A68507FCo/o/2005_
SURVEY__COURT_.pdf.

"Survey of Activities: 2006." Accessed November 8, 2007, at http://www.
echr.coe.int/NR/rdonlyres/69564084–9825–430B–9150–A9137DD22737/o/
Survey_2006.pdf.

"Case of Burdov v. Russia," Judgment, May 7, 2002. Accessed December 13,
2008, at http://cmiskp.echr.coe.int/tkp197/view.asp?action=html&documentId=
698326&portal=hbkm&source=externalbydocnumber&table=F69A27FD8FB
86142BFo1C1166DEA398649.

"Case of Kalashnikov v. Russia," Judgment, July 15, 2002. Accessed December 13,
2008, at http://cmiskp.echr.coe.int/tkp197/view.asp?action=html&documentId=
698483&portal=hbkm&source=externalbydocnumber&table=F69A27FD8FB
86142BFo1C1166DEA398649.

"Case of Rakevich v. Russia," Judgment, October 28, 2003. Accessed December 13,
2008, at http://cmiskp.echr.coe.int/tkp197/view.asp?action=html&documentId=
699291&portal=hbkm&source=externalbydocnumber&table=F69A27FD8FB
86142BFo1C1166DEA398649.

"Case of Gusinskiy v. Russia," Judgment, May 19, 2004. Accessed December 13,
2008, at http://cmiskp.echr.coe.int/tkp197/view.asp?action=html&documentId=
699643&portal=hbkm&source=externalbydocnumber&table=F69A27FD8FB
86142BFo1C1166DEA398649.

"Case of Fedorov and Fedorova v. Russia," Judgment, October 13, 2005.
Accessed December 13, 2008, at http://cmiskp.echr.coe.int/tkp197/view.asp?
action=html&documentId=787923&portal=hbkm&source=externalbydocnu
mber&table=F69A27FD8FB86142BFo1C1166DEA398649.

"Case of Dolgova v. Russia," Judgment, March 2, 2006. Accessed December 14,
2008, at http://cmiskp.echr.coe.int/tkp197/view.asp?action=html&documentId=
793001&portal=hbkm&source=externalbydocnumber&table=F69A27FD8FB
86142BFo1C1166DEA398649.

"First Section Decision as to the Admissibility of Application no. 8269/02 by
Sutyazhnik Against Russia." March 2, 2006. Accessed November 24, 2007,
at http://www.sutyajnik.ru/rus/cases/sutyajnik_v_russia/decision.html.

Press Release by ECHR Registrar, "Chamber Judgment Menesheva v. Russia."
March 9, 2006. Accessed March 29, 2006, at http://www.echr.coe.int/Eng/
Press/2006/March/ChamberjudgmentMeneshevavRussia090306.htm.

"Case of Bazorkina v. Russia," Judgment, July 27, 2006. Accessed December 13,
2008, at http://cmiskp.echr.coe.int/tkp197/view.asp?action=html&documentId=
807138&portal=hbkm&source=externalbydocnumber&table=F69A27FD8FB
86142BFo1C1166DEA398649.

Press Release by ECHR Registrar, "Chamber Judgment: Bazorkina v. Russia."
  July 27, 2006. Accessed December 13, 2008, at http://cmiskp.echr.coe.int/
  tkp197/view.asp?action=html&documentId=807136&portal=hbkm&source=
  externalbydocnumber&table=F69A27FD8FB86142BF01C1166DEA398649.
"Case of Bitiyeva and X v. Russia," Judgment, June 21, 2007. Accessed
  December 15, 2008, at http://cmiskp.echr.coe.int/tkp197/view.asp?action=
  html&documentId=819060&portal=hbkm&source=externalbydocnumber&
  table=F69A27FD8FB86142BF01C1166DEA398649.
"European Court of Human Rights Finds Against Russia...." RFE/RL Newsline,
  July 16, 2002.
"European Court of Human Rights Rules in Favor of a Russian National Bolshe-
  vik Party Member." *In Their Own Voices: Eurasian Human Rights Digest*,
  No. 11 (February 27–March 6, 2006).
"European Court of Human Rights Statistics 2004." April 2005. Accessed
  March 27, 2006, at http://www.echr.coe.int/NR/rdonlyres/F2B964EE-
  57C5-4C86-8B8F-8B4B6095D89C/0/MicrosoftWordstatisticalcharts_
  2004__internet_.pdf.
"European Court of Human Rights Upholds Verdict Against Russia." RFE/RL
  Newsline, November 2, 2005.
"European Court for Human Rights Rejects Russian Appeal." RFE/RL Newsline,
  July 19, 2005.
"European Court Rules Against Russia in Chechnya Cases." RFE/RL Newsline,
  February 25, 2005.
"European Court Says Police Mistreated Russian Woman." RFE/RL Newsline,
  March 10, 2006.
"European Court Tells Russia to Pay Torture Victim." RFE/RL Newsline,
  February 1, 2006.
Evangelista, Matthew. *The Chechen Wars*. Washington: Brookings Institution
  Press, 2002.
Evans, Peter. "The Eclipse of the State? Reflections on Stateness in an Era of
  Globalization." *World Politics*, October 1997, pp. 62–87.
Fearon, James D. "Electoral Accountability and the Control of Politicians: Select-
  ing Good Types Versus Sanctioning Poor Performance." In Adam Przeworski,
  Susan C. Stokes, and Bernard Manin, eds., *Democracy, Accountability, and
  Representation*. New York: Cambridge University Press, 1999. Pp. 55–97.
Fergusson, Ian F. "The WTO, Intellectual Property Rights, and the Access
  to Medicines Controversy." Congressional Research Service, November
  5, 2007. Accessed June 12, 2008, at http://italy.usembassy.gov/pdf/other/
  RL33750.pdf.
Ferree, Myra Marx, and Aili Mari Tripp, eds. *Global Feminism: Transnational
  Women's Activism, Organizing, and Human Rights*. New York: New York
  University Press, 2006.
The Final Report of the Truth & Reconciliation Commission of Sierra Leone
  (2002–2007). Accessed March 9, 2007, at http://trcsierraleone.org/drwebsite/
  publish/v3a-c2.shtml?page=5.
Finer, Jonathan. "Security Contractors in Iraq Under Scrutiny After Shootings."
  Washington Post Foreign Service, September 10, 2005, p. A1. Accessed

February 9, 2005, at http://www.washingtonpost.com/wp-dyn/content/article/2005/09/09/AR2005090902136.html.

Finn, Peter. "German Women Gain Job Parity in Military." *Washington Post,* January 3, 2001. Accessed March 23, 2006, at http://www.globalpolicy.org/socecon/inequal/2001/0103pf.htm.

   "In Russia, Trying Times for Trial by Jury." *Washington Post,* October 31, 2005, p. A12. Accessed March 27, 2006, at http://www.washingtonpost.com/wp-dyn/content/article/2005/10/30/AR2005103001026_pf.html.

Fish, M. Steven. *Democracy Derailed in Russia.* New York: Cambridge University Press, 2005.

Fish, M. Steven, and Omar Choudhry. "Democratization and Economic Liberalization in the Postcommunist World." *Comparative Political Studies,* Vol. 40 (2007), pp. 254–82.

Fisher, William F. "Development and Resistance in the Narmada Valley." In Fisher, ed., *Toward Sustainable Development?: Struggling Over India's Narmada River.* Pp. 3–46.

Fisher, William F., ed. *Toward Sustainable Development?: Struggling Over India's Narmada River.* Armonk, NY: M.E. Sharpe, 1995.

Fisher, William F., and Thomas Ponniah, eds. *Another World Is Possible: Popular Alternatives to Globalization at the World Social Forum.* London: Zed, 2003.

Fisher, Jr., Richard D. "Don't Railroad Cambodia's Democrats." September 15, 1998. Accessed November 21, 2007, at http://www.heritage.org/Research/AsiaandthePacific/BG1220.cfm.

Fix-Fierro, Hector, and Sergio Lopes-Ayllon. "Communication Between Legal Cultures: The Case of NAFTA's Chapter 19 Binational Panels." Unpublished manuscript, Instituto de Investigaciones Juridicas de la Universidad Nacional Autonoma de Mexico, Mexico City, 1997.

Foreign Policy Editors. "The Top Ten Stories You Missed in 2005: The New Coalition of the Willing." ForeignPolicy.com, December 2005. Accessed February 9. 2006, at http://www.foreignpolicy.com/story/cms.php?story_id=3315.

Fox, Jonathan. "Vertically Integrated Policy Monitoring: A Tool for Civil Society Advocacy." *Nonprofit and Voluntary Sector Quarterly,* Vol. 30, No. 3 (September 2001), pp. 616–627.

   "Advocacy Research and the World Bank: Propositions for Discussion." *Development in Practice,* Vol. 12, No. 4 (November 2003), pp. 519–27.

[Fox, Jonathan A.] "When Does Reform Policy Influence Practice? Lessons from the Bankwide Resettlement Review." In Fox, and Brown, eds., *The Struggle for Accountability: The World Bank, NGOs, and Grassroots Movements.* Pp. 303–344.

   "Introduction: Framing the Inspection Panel." In Clark, Fox, and Treakle, eds., *Demanding Accountability: Civil Society Claims and the World Bank Inspection Panel.* Pp. xi–xxxi.

Fox, Jonathan, and John Gershman. "The World Bank and Social Capital: Lessons from Ten Rural Development Projects in the Philippines and Mexico." *Policy Sciences,* No. 33 (2000), pp. 399–419.

Fox, Jonathan A., and L. David Brown, eds. *The Struggle for Accountability: The World Bank, NGOs, and Grassroots Movements.* Cambridge, MA: MIT Press, 1998.

"Assessing the Impact of NGO Advocacy Campaigns on World Bank Projects and Policies." In Fox, and Brown, eds., *The Struggle for Accountability: The World Bank, NGOs, and Grassroots Movements.* Pp. 485–551.

"Introduction." In Fox and Brown, eds., *The Struggle for Accountability: The World Bank, NGOs, and Grassroots Movements.* Pp. 1–48.

Fox, Jonathan A., and Kay Treakle. "Concluding Propositions." In Clark, Fox, and Treakle, eds., *Demanding Accountability: Civil Society Claims and the World Bank Inspection Panel.* Pp. 279–86.

Freedom House. "Freedom in the World, 2007." Accessed June 28, 2007, at http://www.freedomhouse.org/template.cfm?page=363&year=2007.

Fried, Jonathan. "In Guatemala, Things Go Worse with Coke." *Multinational Monitor*, Vol. 5, No. 4 (April 1984). Accessed July 6. 2006, at http://multinationalmonitor.org/hyper/issues/1984/04/fried.html.

Friedman, Thomas. "The New Human Rights." *New York Times*, July 30, 1999.

Frundt, Henry J. "Guatemala in Search of Democracy." *Journal of Interamerican Studies and World Affairs*, Vol. 32, No. 3 (Autumn 1990), pp. 24–74.

Galtung, Fredrik. "Transparency International's Network to Curb Global Corruption." In Gerald E. Caiden, O. P. Dwivedi, and Joseph Jabbra, eds., *Where Corruption Lives.* Bloomfield, CT: Kumarian Press, 2001. Pp. 189–206.

Gardiner, Nile. "The UN Peacekeeping Scandal in the Congo: How Congress Should Respond." Heritage Foundation, March 22, 2005. Accessed February 22, 2007, at http://www.heritage.org/Research/InternationalOrganizations/hl868.cfm.

Gariyo, Zie. "NGOs and Development in East Africa." In Edwards, and Hulme, eds., *Beyond the Magic Bullet: NGO Performance and Accountability in the Post–Cold War World.* Pp. 156–65.

Garuda, Gopal. "The Distributional Effects of IMF Programs: A Cross–Country Analysis." *World Development*, 28 (2000), pp. 1031–51.

Gauslaa, Jon. "European Court Takes Action." September 30, 2005. Accessed August 10, 2006, at http://www.bellona.org/english_import_area/international/russia/envirorights/pasko/40027.

Gberie, Lansana. *A Dirty War in West Africa: the RUF and the Destruction of Sierra Leone.* Bloomington: Indiana University Press, 2005. Accessed March 7, 2007, at books.google.com.

Gélinas, Jacques B. "The Pillars of the System." In Broad, ed., *Global Backlash: Citizen Initiatives for a Just World Economy.* Pp. 106–11.

Gereffi, Gary. "The Elusive Last Lap in the Quest for Developed-Country Status." In James Mittelman, ed., *Globalization: Critical Reflections.* Boulder: Lynne Rienner, 1997. Pp. 53–81.

Gill, Stephen. "Globalization, Democratization, and the Politics of Indifference." In James Mittelman, ed., *Globalization: Critical Reflections.* Boulder: Lynne Rienner, 1997. Pp. 205–28.

Glanz, James, and Alissa J. Rubin. "From Errand to Fatal Shot to Hail of Fire to 17 Deaths." *New York Times*, October 3, 2007. Accessed December 3, 2008, at http://www.nytimes.com/2007/10/03/world/middleeast/03firefight. html?scp=1&sq=From%20Errand%20to%20Fatal%20Shot%20to%20 Hail%20of%20Fire&st=cse.

Global Exchange. "How the International Monetary Fund and the World Bank Undermine Democracy and Erode Human Rights: Five Case Studies." September 2001. Accessed March 1, 2006, at http://www.globalexchange. org/campaigns/wbimf/imfwbReport2001.html.

Goetz, Anne-Marie. "Gender and Accountability." Lecture at Fletcher School, Tufts University, April 10, 2006.

Goetz, Anne-Marie, and Rob Jenkins. *Reinventing Accountability: Making Democracy Work for Human Development*. New York: Palgrave Macmillan, 2005.

Goldstein, Judith, Miles Kahler, Robert O. Keohane, and Anne-Marie Slaughter. "Introduction: Legalization and World Politics." *International Organization*, Vol. 54, No. 3 (June 2000), pp. 385–99.

Goldstone, Richard J. "International Jurisdiction and Prosecutorial Crimes." In David Barnhizer, ed., *Effective Strategies for Protecting Human Rights: Economic Sanctions, Use of National Courts and International Fora and Coercive Power*. Burlington, VT: Ashgate, 2001. Pp. 113–23.

Gonzalez, David. "Latin Sweatshops Pressed by U.S. Campus Power." *New York Times*, April 4, 2003, p. A3.

Goodhart, Michael. "Europe's Democratic Deficits Through the Looking Glass: The European Union as a Challenge for Democracy." *Perspectives on Politics*, Vol. 5, No. 3 (September 2007), pp. 567–84.

Goodman, Amy (with David Goodman). *The Exception to the Rulers: Exposing Oily Politicians, War Profiteers, and the Media That Love Them*. New York: Hyperion, 2004.

Goolsbee, Austan. "Count Ethnic Divisions, Not Bombs, to Tell if a Nation Will Recover from War." *New York Times*, July 20, 2006, p. C3.

Gottesman, Evan. *Cambodia After the Khmer Rouge: Inside the Politics of Nation Building*. New Haven: Yale University Press, 2002.

Gray, Andrew. "Development Policy, Development Protest: The World Bank, Indigenous Peoples, and NGOs." In Fox and Brown, eds., *The Struggle for Accountability: The World Bank, NGOs, and Grassroots Movements*. Pp. 267–301.

Greider, William. "Wawasan 2020." In Frank J. Lechner and John Boli, eds., *The Globalization Reader*. Malden, MA: Blackwell, 2000. Pp. 148–54.

Griffin, Keith. "Economic Globalization and Institutions of Global Governance." *Development and Change*, Vol. 34, No. 5 (2003), pp. 789–808.

Guerrero, Maria Teresa, Cyrus Reed, and Brandon Vegter. "The Forest Industry in the Sierra Madre of Chihuahua: Social, Economic, and Ecological Impacts." Commission on Solidarity and Defense of Human Rights, AC., and Texas Center for Policy Studies, July 2000. Accessed May 23, 2007, at http://www. texascenter.org/publications/forestry.pdf.

Guidry, John A., Michael D. Kennedy, and Mayer N. Zald, eds. *Globalizations and Social Movements: Culture, Power, and the Transnational Public Sphere*. Ann Arbor: University of Michigan Press, 2000.

H.R. 1298, Public Law 108–25, "United States Leadership Against HIV/AIDS, Tuberculosis, and Malaria Act of 2003." May 27, 2003. Accessed November 27, 2007, at http://frwebgate.access.gpo.gov/cgi-bin/getdoc.cgi?dbname=108_cong_public_laws&docid=f:publ025.108.pdf.

Habib, Mohsin, and Leon Zurawicki. "Corruption and Foreign Direct Investment." In Transparency International, *Global Corruption Report 2004*. London: Pluto Press, 2004. Pp. 313–15.

Hanson, Stephen E. "Defining Democratic Consolidation." In Richard D. Anderson, Jr., M. Steven Fish, Stephen E. Hanson, and Philip G. Roeder, eds., *Postcommunism and The Theory of Democracy*. Princeton: Princeton University Press, 2001. Pp. 126–51.

Hardt, Michael, and Antonio Negri. *Empire*. Cambridge, MA: Harvard University Press, 2000.

Hartung, William D. "Soldiers vs. Contractors: Emerging Budget Reality?" World Policy Institute, February 10, 2006. Accessed March 10, 2006, at http://www.worldpolicy.org/projects/arms/reports/soldiers.html.

Hashemi, Syed. "NGO Accountability in Bangladesh: Beneficiaries, Donors, and the State." In Edwards, and Hulme, eds., *Beyond the Magic Bullet: NGO Performance and Accountability in the Post–Cold War World*. Pp. 123–31.

Hawken, Paul. *Blessed Unrest: How the Largest Movement in the World Came into Being and Why No One Saw It Coming*. New York: Viking, 2007.

Hayden, Tom, and Charles Kernaghan. "Pennies an Hour, and No Way Up." *New York Times*, July 6, 2002, p. A27.

Heckscher, Zahara. "Long Before Seattle: Historical Resistance to Economic Globalization." In Broad, ed., *Global Backlash: Citizen Initiatives for a Just World Economy*. Pp. 86–91.

Held, David. "Democratic Accountability and Political Effectiveness from a Cosmopolitan Perspective." *Government and Opposition*, Vol. 30, No. 2 (April 2004), pp. 364–91.

Held, David, Anthony McGrew, David Goldblatt, and Jonathan Perraton. *Global Transformations: Politics, Economics and Culture*. Stanford: Stanford University Press, 1999.

Hellwig, Timothy, and David Samuels. "Voting in Open Economies: The Electoral Consequences of Globalization." *Comparative Political Studies*, Vol. 40 (2007), pp. 283–306.

Hersh, Seymour M. "Torture at Abu Ghraib." New Yorker, May 10, 2004. Accessed February 3, 2006, at http://www.newyorker.com/printables/fact/040510fa_fact.

Hirsch, John. *Sierra Leone: Diamonds and the Struggle for Democracy*. Boulder: Lynne Rienner, 2001.

Hobsbawm, Eric. "Identity Politics and the Left." *New Left Review*, Vol. 217 (1996), pp. 38–47.

  The Age of Capital 1848–1875. London: Weidenfeld & Nicholson, 2000.

Hochschild, Adam. *King Leopold's Ghost*. Boston: Houghton Mifflin, 1998.

  Bury the Chains: Prophets and Rebels in the Fight to Free an Empire's Slaves. Boston: Houghton Mifflin, 2005.

Hoge, Warren. "Report Finds U.N. Isn't Moving to End Sex Abuse by Peacekeepers." *New York Times*, October 19, 2005, p. A5.

Holmes, Stephen. "Introduction: Reforming Russia's Courts." *East European Constitutional Review*, Vol. 11, Nos. 1/2 (Winter/Spring 2002), pp. 90–1.

Holt, Kate, and Sarah Hughes. "Sex and Death in the Heart of Africa." Refugees International, May 25, 2004. Accessed February 22, 2007, at http://www.refugeesinternational.org/content/article/detail/1093.

Horowitz, Donald. "Ethnic Conflict Management for Policymakers." In Joseph Montville, ed., *Conflict and Peacemaking in Multiethnic Societies*. Lexington, MA: Lexington Books, 1990. Pp. 115–30.

Howe, Herbert M. *Ambiguous Order: Military Forces in African States*. Boulder: Lynne Rienner, 2001.

"Human Rights Activist Arrested in Daghestan." RFE/RL Newsline, November 21, 2005.

Human Rights Watch. "The 'Sixth Division': Military-Paramilitary Ties and U.S. Policy in Colombia." 2001. Accessed November 1, 2007, at http://www.hrw.org/reports/2001/colombia/1.htm.

"Russia: World Report, 2005." Accessed March 24, 2006, at http://hrw.org/english/docs/2005/01/13/russia9867.htm.

"Hun Sen Systematically Silences Critics." January 4, 2006. Accessed November 21, 2007, at http://www.hrw.org/english/docs/2006/01/04/cambod12360.htm.

Hunter, David, Cristian Opaso, and Marcos Orellana. "The Biobio's Legacy: Institutional Reforms and Unfulfilled Promises at the International Finance Corporation." In Clark, Fox, and Treakle, eds., *Demanding Accountability: Civil Society Claims and the World Bank Inspection Panel*. Pp. 115–43.

ICFTU Online. "Action by World Bank's IFC on Workers' Rights a Major Step Forward." February 22, 2006. Accessed February 26, 2006, at http://www.icftu.org/displaydocument.asp?Index=991223448&Language=EN.

"... In Case Called Precedent–Setting." RFE/RL Newsline, July 16, 2002.

INCITE! Women of Color Against Violence, eds. *The Revolution Will Not Be Funded: Beyond the Non-Profit Industrial Complex*. Cambridge, MA: South End Press, 2007.

Independent Evaluation Office (IEO/IMF). "Evaluation of Structural Conditionality in IMF-Supported Programs." May 17, 2005, p. 2. Accessed November 27, 2007, at http://www.ieo-imf.org/eval/ongoing/051805.pdf.

"IMF Exchange Rate Policy Advice 1999–2005." May 17, 2007.

Informatsionnoe agenstvo PRIMA-News. "Rossiiskii sud vynes reshenie na osnovanii Evropeiskoi konventsii o pravakh cheloveka." January 1, 2006.

Inspection Panel. "Inspection Panel Investigation Report: Uganda – Private Power Generation (Bujagali) Project," August 29, 2008. Accessed December 15, 2008, at http://internationalrivers.org/en/node/3568.

Interfax. "Juries Are Too Lenient – Russian Supreme Court Head." April 9, 2006. Accessed August 7, 2006, at http://www.interfax.ru/e/B/politics/28.html?id_issue=11494330.

"Journalists' Organizations Call for Criminal Liability for Libel to Be Abolished." June 20, 2006. Accessed August 8, 2006, at http://feeds.moscownews.net/?rid=1c30d14da74c31ac&cat=871e5a31f6912bb3&f=1.

"Interim Resolution ResDH(2003)123 Concerning the Judgment of the European Court of Human Rights of 15 July 2002, Final on 15 October 2002, in the Case of Kalashnikov Against the Russian Federation." June 4, 2003.

"Interim Resolution ResDH(2006)1 Concerning the Violations of the Principle of Legal Certainty Through the Supervisory Review Procedure ("Nadzor") in Civil Proceedings in the Russian Federation – General Measures Adopted and Outstanding Issues." Adopted by the Committee of Ministers on February 8, 2006.

International Commission of Jurists. "Russian Federation: Tax Order Threatens Leading Human Rights Organization." Press Release, July 31, 2006. Accessed November 24, 2007, at http://www.icj.org/IMG/PR_Russia_Protection_Centre.pdf.

International Monetary Fund (IMF). "Articles of Agreement of the International Monetary Fund," Article XII. Accessed July 29, 2008, at http://www.imf.org/external/pubs/ft/aa/aa12.htm#5.

"IMF Executive Directors and Voting Power." Accessed July 6, 2008, at http://www.imf.org/external/np/sec/memdir/eds.htm.

"Structural Conditionality in Fund–Supported Programs." February 16, 2001. Accessed June 11, 2008, at http://www.imf.org/external/np/pdr/cond/2001/eng/struct/cond.pdf.

"Financing the Fund's Operations." April 11, 2001. Accessed July 6, 2008, at http://www.imf.org/external/np/tre/ffo/2001/fin.htm.

"What Is the IMF?" September 30, 2006. Accessed November 27, 2007, at http://www.imf.org/external/pubs/ft/exrp/what.htm#do.

"IMF Quotas: A Factsheet." October 2007. Accessed November 27, 2007, at http://www.imf.org/external/np/exr/facts/quotas.htm.

"IMF Members' Quotas and Voting Power, and IMF Board of Governors." November 2007. Accessed November 27, 2007, at http://www.imf.org/external/np/sec/memdir/members.htm.

International Transport Workers' Federation. "What Do FOCs Mean to Seafarers?" Accessed November 15, 2007, at http://www.itfglobal.org/flags–convenience/flags–convenien–184.cfm.

Interparliamentary Union. "Legislation and Other National Provisions: Mali." Accessed November 24, 2007, at http://www.ipu.org/wmn–e/fgm–prov–m.htm.

Iriye, Akira. *Global Community: The Role of International Organizations in the Making of the Contemporary World*. Berkeley: University of California Press, 2002.

"It's in Our Hands: Stop Violence Against Women." London: Amnesty International Publications, 2004. Accessed November 24, 2007, at http://web.amnesty.org/web/web.nsf/8bad1ff50703146980256e32003c42f0/2def35f72df aa2f980256e320038f366/$FILE/SVAW%20report%20ENGLISH.pdf.

Jack, Andrew. *Inside Putin's Russia: Can There Be Reform Without Democracy?* New York: Oxford University Press, 2006.

Jackson, Karl ed. *Cambodia 1975–1978: Rendezvous with Death*. Princeton: Princeton University Press, 1989.

"Jailed Nuclear Scientist Appeals to European Court of Human Rights." RFE/RL Newsline, January 6, 2006.

James, John S. "WTO Accepts Rules Limiting Medicine Exports to Poor Countries." *AIDS Treatment News*, September 12, 2003. Accessed June 12, 2008, at http://www.thebody.com/content/art31751.html.

Jenkins, Henry. "From Participatory Culture to Participatory Democracy." March 5, 2007. Accessed December 6, 2007, at http://www.henryjenkins. org/2007/03/from_participatatory_culture_t.html.

Jensen, Nathan. "Democratic Governance and Multinational Corporations; Political Regimes and Inflows of Foreign Direct Investment." *International Organization*, Vol. 57, No. 3 (2003), pp. 587–616.

Johnson, Janet. *Gender Violence in Russia: The Politics of Feminist Intervention.* Bloomington: Indiana University Press, 2009.

Johnston, David. "Immunity Deals Offered to Blackwater Guards." NYTimes.com, October 29, 2007. Accessed December 3, 2008, at http://www.nytimes.com/ 2007/10/30/washington/30blackwater.html?_r=1&scp=1&sq=immunity% 20deals%20offered%20to%20blackwater%20guards&st=cse.

Johnston, David, and John M. Broder. "F.B.I. Says Guards Killed 14 Iraqis Without Cause." NYTimes.com, November 14, 2007. Accessed December 3, 2008, at http://www.nytimes.com/2007/11/14/world/middleeast/14blackwater.html? cp=1&sq=F.B.I.%20Says%20Guards%20Killed%2014%20Iraqi&st=cse.

Jordan, Lisa, and Peter Van Tuijl. "Political Responsibility in Transnational NGO Advocacy." *World Development*, Vol. 28, No. 12 (2000), pp. 2051–65.

Jordan, Pamela A. "Russia's Accession to the Council of Europe and Compliance with European Human Rights Norms." *Demokratizatsiya*, Spring 2003, pp. 281–96.

  Defending Rights in Russia: Lawyers, the State, and Legal Reform in the Post-Soviet Era. Vancouver: University of British Columbia Press, 2006.

Josselin, Daphné. "Back to the Front Line? Trade Unions in a Global Age." In Daphné Josselin, and William Wallace, eds., *Non-state Actors in World Politics*. Basingstoke: Palgrave, 2001. Pp. 169–86.

"Journalist Goes on Trial for Calling Putin 'Russia's Phallic Symbol." RFE/RL Newsline, September 22, 2006.

"Judges Sworn in for Khmer Rouge." BBC News, July 3, 2006. Accessed July 5, 2006, at http://news.bbc.co.uk/2/hi/asia-pacific/5140032.stm.

Jusu-Sheriff, Yasmin. "Sierra Leonean Women and the Peace Process." Conciliation Resources, September 2000. Accessed September 20, 2006, at http:// www.c-r.org/our-work/accord/sierra-leone/women-peace.php.

Kahler, Miles. "Defining Accountability Up: the Global Economic Multilaterals." *Government and Opposition*, Vol. 39, No. 2 (April 2004), pp. 132–58.

Kahn, Jeffrey. "A Marriage of Convenience: Russia and the European Court of Human Rights." RFE/RL Russian Political Weekly, June 19, 2002.

Kamel, Rachael, and Anya Hoffman, eds. *The Maquiladora Reader: Cross-Border Organizing Since NAFTA*. Philadelphia: American Friends Service Committee, 1999.

Kamm, Henry. *Cambodia: Report from a Stricken Land*. New York: Arcade, 1998.

Keck, Margaret E., and Kathryn Sikkink. *Activists Beyond Borders: Advocacy Networks in International Politics*. Ithaca: Cornell University Press, 1998.

Keohane, Robert O. "Global Governance and Democratic Accountability." In David Held, and Mathias Koenig-Archibugi, eds., *Taming Globalization: Frontiers of Governance.* Oxford, UK: Polity Press/Blackwell, 2003. Pp. 130–59.

Keohane, Robert O., Andrew Moravcsik, and Anne-Marie Slaughter. "Legalized Dispute Resolution: Interstate and Transnational." *International Organization*, Vol. 54, No. 3 (June 2000), pp. 457–88.

Keohane, Robert O., and Joseph S. Nye, Jr. *Power and Interdependence: World Politics in Transition.* Boston: Little, Brown & Co., 1977.

"Introduction." In Joseph S. Nye and John D. Donahue, eds., *Governance in a Globalizing World.* Washington: Brookings Institution Press, 2000. Pp. 1–41.

Khaleeli, Jehan, and Sarah Martin. "Addressing the Sexual Misconduct of Peacekeepers." Refugees International, September 23, 2004. Accessed February 2, 2006, at http://www.refugeesinternational.org/content/article/detail/4047/.

"Khasaviurtovskii sud Dagestana opravdal pravosashchitnika Bolieva." May 18, 2006. Accessed May 22, 2006, at http://www.kavkaz.memo.ru/newstext/news/id/1002460.html.

"Khmer Rouge Trials Ready to Start." BBC News, June 13, 2007. Accessed October 17, 2007, at http://news.bbc.co.uk/1/hi/world/asia-pacific/6747143.stm.

"Khodorkovskii Appeals to European Court of Human Rights...as Lawyer Assails Prison Conditions." RFE/RL Newsline, December 5, 2005.

Kiernan, Ben. *The Pol Pot Regime: Race, Power, and Genocide in Cambodia Under the Khmer Rouge, 1975–79.* New Haven: Yale University Press, 1996.

Koenig-Archibugi, Mathias. "Introduction: Globalization and the Challenge to Governance." In Held, and Koenig-Archibugi, eds., *Taming Globalization: Frontiers of Governance.* Pp. 1–17.

"Transnational Corporations and Public Accountability." *Government and Opposition*, Vol. 39, No. 2 (April 2004), pp. 234–59.

Kotova, Anna. "Pravo est', a garantii otsutstvuiut." *Ezh-Iurist*, No. 25 (June 2005). Accessed July 12, 2006, at www.sutyajnik.ru/rus/library/articles/2006/ezh_urist.pdf.

Kozenko, Alexey. "Taxes Can Deal Death Blow to NGOs." *Kommersant*, August 2, 2006. Accessed November 24, 2007, at http://www.kommersant.com/page.asp?idr=528&id=694490.

Kposowa, Augustine. "Erosion of the Rule of Law as a Contributing Factor in Civil Conflict: The Case of Sierra Leone." *Police Practice and Research*, Vol. 7, No. 1 (March 2006), pp. 35–48.

Kramer, Mark. "Rights and Restraints in Russia's Criminal Justice System." Program on New Approaches to Russian Security (PONARS) Policy Memo No. 289, May 2003.

Krasnov, Mikhail. "Is the 'Concept of Judicial Reform' Timely?" *East European Constitutional Review*, Vol. 11, Nos. 1/2 (Winter/Spring 2002), pp. 92–4.

Krugman, Paul. "For Richer: How the Permissive Capitalism of the Boom Destroyed American Equality." *New York Times Magazine*, October 20, 2002.

Lacey, Marc. "For Ugandan Girls, Delaying Sex Has Economic Cost." *New York Times*, August 18, 2003, p. A4.

Lancaster, John. "In Bow to WTO, India Targets Drug Copying." *Washington Post*, March 24, 2005, p. E6. Accessed June 12, 2008, at http://www.washingtonpost.com/wp-dyn/articles/A61757-2005Mar23.html.

"Last Sierra Leone Rebels Disarm." BBC News, January 13, 2002. Accessed September 28, 2006, at http://news.bbc.co.uk/1/hi/world/africa/1757912.stm.

Lederer, Edith M. "Bosnia Administrator Calls for Normality." Associated Press, April 18, 2006. Accessed April 20, 2006, at http://www.washingtonpost.com/wp-dyn/content/article/2006/04/18/AR2006041801475.html.

Levinson, Jerome I. "NAFTA's Labor Agreement: Lessons." In Broad, ed. *Global Backlash: Citizen Initiatives for a Just World Economy*. Pp. 142–9.

Lewis, Peter M. "Economic Reform and the Discourse of Democracy in Africa: Resolving the Contradictions." In Crawford Young and Mark Beissinger, eds., *Beyond State Crisis? Postcolonial Africa and Post-Soviet Eurasia in Comparative Perspective*. Washington: Woodrow Wilson Center Press, 2002. Pp. 291–320.

LICADHO (Cambodian League for the Promotion and Defense of Human Rights). "Civil Society Members Show Support for Detainees." January 16, 2006. Accessed July 27, 2006, at http://www.licadho.org/articles/20060116/34/index.html.

   Threats to Human Rights Defenders in Cambodia, 2005: Briefing Paper. June 2006. Accessed June 29, 2006, at http://www.licadho.org/reports/files/85HRDefenders2005.pdf.

Life and Debt. "About the Film." Accessed November 18, 2007, at www.lifeanddebt.org.

Lillie, Nathan. "A Global Union for Global Workers: The International Transport Workers' Federation and the Representation of Seafarers on Flag of Convenience Shipping." Ph.D. dissertation, Cornell University, New York State School of Industrial and Labor Relations, 2003.

Lobe, Jim. "Unions Assail WTO for Ignoring Worker Rights." OneWorld.net, 2003. Accessed June 12, 2008, at http://www.commondreams.org/headlines03/0908-02.htm.

Lumpe, Lora. "U.S. Foreign Military Training." *Foreign Policy in Focus Special Report* (May 2002), pp. 12–13.

Lyall, Sarah. "Aid Workers Are Said to Abuse Girls." *New York Times*, May 9, 2006, p. A8.

Lynch, Colum. "U.N. Faces More Accusations of Sexual Misconduct." *Washington Post*, Sunday, March 13, 2005, p. A22. Accessed February 2, 2006, at http://www.washingtonpost.com/wp-dyn/articles/A30286-2005Mar12.html.

Lynch, Marc. "Globalization and International Democracy" (a review essay). *International Studies Review*, Vol. 2, No. 3 (Fall 2000), pp. 91–101.

Margolin, Jean-Louis. "Cambodia: The Country of Disconcerting Crimes." In Stéphane Courtois, Nicolas Werth, Jean-Louis Panné, Andrzej Paczkowski, Karel Bartosek, and Jean–Louis Margolin, *The Black Book of Communism: Crimes, Terror, Repression*. Cambridge, MA: Harvard University Press, 1999. Pp. 577–635.

"Marii El Group Protests Violations by Procurator's Office." *Russian Regional Report*, Vol. 10, No. 20 (November 23, 2005). Accessed August 17, 2006, at http://www.mari.ee/eng/news/soc/2005/11/01.htm.

Martin, Brian. *Justice Ignited: The Dynamics of Backfire*. Lanham, MD: Rowman & Littlefield, 2006.

Martin, Sarah. "Must Boys Be Boys? Ending Sexual Exploitation and Abuse in UN Peacekeeping Missions." Refugees International, October 2005. Accessed February 22, 2007, at http://www.refugeesinternational.org/content/publication/detail/6976/.

"Must Boys Be Boys? Confronting Sexual Exploitation and Abuse in UN Peacekeeping Operations." Lecture at Fletcher School, Tufts University, February 1, 2006.

Mason, Michael. "The World Trade Regime and Non-Governmental Organisations: Addressing Transnational Environmental Concerns." London: LSE Research Online, 2003. Accessed June 11, 2008, at http://eprints.lse.ac.uk/571/1/RPESA-no84(2003).pdf.

Mason, T. David. *Caught in the Crossfire: Revolutions, Repression, and the Rational Peasant*. Lanham, MD: Rowman & Littlefield, 2004.

Massing, Michael. "In Failed States, Can Democracy Come Too Soon?" *New York Times*, February 23, 2003, p. A17.

Mathews, Jessica T. "Power Shift." *Foreign Affairs*, Vol. 76, No. 1 (January/February 1997), pp. 50–66.

Mayer, Henry. *All on Fire: William Lloyd Garrison and the Abolition of Slavery*. New York: St. Martins Press, 1998.

McCargo, Duncan. "Cambodia: Getting Away with Authoritarianism?" *Journal of Democracy*, Vol. 16, No. 4 (October 2005), pp. 98–112.

McConnell, Tristan. "All-Female Unit Keeps Peace in Liberia." *Christian Science Monitor*, March 21, 2007. Accessed April 20, 2007, at http://peacejournalism.com/ReadArticle.asp?ArticleID=17876.

McFadyen, Jacqueline. "NAFTA Supplemental Agreements: Four Year Review." Working Paper 98–4, Institute for International Economics. Accessed July 3, 2006, at http://www.iie.com/publications/wp/wp.cfm?ResearchID=145.

McLucas, Susan. "Conscientious Objection to Female Genital Mutilation in Mali." *Peacework* (May 2007), p. 11.

"Report from Mali Project: January 8–March 7, 2008." On file with author.

Mekay, Emad. "World Bank Weighs Risks of Anti-Graft Drive." Inter Press Service News Agency, June 2, 2006. Accessed July 5, 2006, at http://www.ipsnews.net/news.asp?idnews=33476.

"The Menace That Wasn't." *The Economist*, November 13, 2004, pp. 59–60.

Mendelson, Sarah. *Barracks and Brothels: Peacekeepers and Human Trafficking in the Balkans*. Washington: CSIS Press, 2005.

Merry, Sally Engle. *Human Rights and Gender Violence: Translating International Law into Local Justice*. Chicago: University of Chicago Press, 2005.

Mertus, Julie. "From Legal Transplants to Transformative Justice: Human Rights and the Promise of Transnational Civil Society." *American University International Law Review*, Vol. 14, No. 5 (1999), pp. 1335–89.

Migdal, Joel. "Strong States, Weak States: Power and Accommodation." In Myron Weiner and Samuel P. Huntington, eds., *Understanding Political Development.* Boston: Little, Brown, 1987.

Military Professional Resources International (MPRI). Online at http://www.mpri.com/channels/home.html. Accessed November 24, 2007.

Miller, T. Christian. *Blood Money: Wasted Billions, Lost Lives, and Corporate Greed in Iraq.* Boston: Little, Brown, 2006.

Mittelman, James H. *The Globalization Syndrome: Transformation and Resistance.* Princeton: Princeton University Press, 2000.

Mittelman, James, ed., *Globalization: Critical Reflections.* Boulder: Lynne Rienner, 1997.

Moghadam, Valentine M. *Globalizing Women: Transnational Feminist Networks.* Baltimore: Johns Hopkins University Press, 2005.

Mohanty, Chandra Talpade. *Feminism Without Borders: Decolonizing Theory, Practicing Solidarity.* Durham: Duke University Press, 2003, as cited in Davis, *The Making of Our Bodies, Ourselves: How Feminism Travels Across Borders.*

Moore, Deborah, and Leonard Sklar. "Reforming the World Bank's Lending for Water." In Fox and Brown, eds., *The Struggle for Accountability: The World Bank, NGOs, and Grassroots Movements.* Pp. 345–90.

Moore, Patrick. "Bosnia–Herzegovina: What Future for Bosnia?" Radio Free Europe/Radio Liberty, July 18, 2005. Accessed August 3, 2006, at http://www.rferl.org/featuresarticle/2005/07/601fffd2–75d7–4e00–9659–4c93defa6194.html.

Moore, Barrington, Jr. *Social Origins of Dictatorship and Democracy.* Boston: Beacon Press, 1966.

Moravcsik, Andrew. "The Origins of Human Rights Regimes: Democratic Delegation in Postwar Europe." *International Organization,* Vol. 54, No. 2 (Spring 2000), pp. 217–52.

"Is There a 'Democratic Deficit' in World Politics? A Framework for Analysis." *Government and Opposition,* Vol. 39, No. 2 (April 2004), pp. 336–63.

Mosely, Layna, and Saika Uno. "Racing to the Bottom or Climbing to the Top? Economic Globalization and Collective Labor Rights." *Comparative Political Studies,* Vol. 40, (2007), pp. 923–48.

Murphy, Ray. "International Criminal Accountability and the International Criminal Court." Columbia International Affairs Online (CIAO), November 2004. Accessed June 25, 2008, at http://se1.isn.ch:80/serviceengine/FileContent?serviceID=PublishingHouse&fileid=598B0548–DAA5–FFED–A435–D9DE8EDEEF9A&lng=en.

"Museum Director Convicted of Inciting Religious Hatred." RFE/RL Newsline, March 29, 2005.

Mydans, Seth. "Nurturing Democracy from the Grass Roots." *New York Times,* June 13, 1999, p. 5.

"Cambodian Leader Rules as If from the Throne." *New York Times,* March 19, 2002, p. A3.

"Killing Fields of Cambodia Now in Court." *New York Times,* November 21, 2007, pp. A1, A6.

Myers, Steven Lee. "Verdict in Russian Courts: Guilty Until Proven Guilty." *New York Times*, June 20, 2004, Week in Review, p. 3.

Mynott, Adam. "Politics Sinks Kenya's War on Graft." BBC News, September 14, 2007. Accessed October 10, 2007, at http://news.bbc.co.uk/2/hi/africa/6993826.stm.

Neou, Kassie, with Jeffrey C. Gallup. "Field Report: Conducting Cambodia's Elections." *Journal of Democracy*, Vol. 10, No. 2 (1999), pp. 152–64.

Network of Sex Work Projects. "Taking the Pledge." 2007. Accessed May 24, 2007, at http://sexworkerspresent.blip.tv/file/181155/.

News Agency Sutyajnik-Press. "Rakevich v. Russia." October 28, 2003. Accessed March 25, 2006, at http://www.sutyajnik.ru/eng/news/2004/r_v_r.html.

Norris, Pippa ed. *Critical Citizens: Global Support for Democratic Government.* Oxford, UK: Oxford University Press, 1999.

"Cosmopolitan Citizens." In Joseph S. Nye and John D. Donahue, eds., *Governance in a Globalizing World.* Washington: Brookings Institution Press, 2000. Pp. 155–77.

Nye, Joseph S., Jr., et al. *The "Democracy Deficit" in the Global Economy: Enhancing the Legitimacy and Accountability of Global Institutions* (A Report to the Trilateral Commission). Washington, Paris, Tokyo: Trilateral Commission, 2003.

Obi, Cyril I. "Global, State, and Local Intersections: Power, Authority, and Conflict in the Niger Delta Oil Communities." In Thomas Callaghy, Ronald Kassimir, and Robert Latham, eds., *Intervention and Transnationalism in Africa.* Cambridge, UK: Cambridge University Press, 2001. Pp. 173–93.

Odinkalu, Chidi Anselm. "Why More Africans Don't Use Human Rights Language" *Human Rights Dialogue*, Vol. 2, No. 1 (Winter 1999). Accessed March 10, 2006, at http://www.cceia.org/resources/publications/dialogue/2_01/articles/602.html.

O'Donnell, Guillermo. "Horizontal Accountability in New Democracies." In Schedler, Diamond, and Plattner, eds., *The Self-Restraining State: Power and Accountability in New Democracies.* Pp. 29–51.

Office of the High Representative (OHR). "General Information." Accessed December 12, 2008, at http://www.ohr.int/ohr-info/gen-info/#1.

"History and Mandate of the OHR North/Brcko." August 28, 2001. Accessed November 21, 2007, at http://www.ohr.int/ohr–offices/brcko/history/default.asp?content_id=5531.

"Introduction." February 28, 2007. Accessed November 21, 2007, at http://www.ohr.int/ohr–info/gen–info/default.asp?content_id=38519.

"The Peace Implementation Council and Its Steering Board." Accessed December 12, 2008, at http://www.ohr.int/ohr-info/gen-info/#6.

Office of the Senior Coordinator for International Women's Issues, Office of the Under Secretary for Global Affairs, U.S. Department of State. "Mali: Report on Female Genital Mutilation (FGM) or Female Genital Cutting (FGC)." June 2001. Accessed May 16, 2007, at http://www.state.gov/g/wi/rls/rep/crfgm/10105.htm.

Office to Monitor and Combat Trafficking in Persons, US Department of State. "Trafficking in Persons Report." June 3, 2005. Accessed February 22, 2007, at http://www.state.gov/g/tip/rls/tiprpt/2005/46606.htm.

Olesen, Thomas. "The Uses and Misuses of Globalization in the Study of Social Movements." *Social Movement Studies*, Vol. 4, No. 1 (May 2005), pp. 49–63.

"Oligarch Wins Suit Against Russia at European Court." RFE/RL Newsline, May 20, 2004.

Onishi, Norimitsu. "Nongovernmental Organizations Show Their Growing Power." *New York Times*, March 22, 2002, p. A10.

  "For Sierra Leone Ballot, Hope Trumps Despair." *New York Times*, May 13, 2002, p. 3.

   "Where Battered People Find Wholeness in a Ballot." *New York Times*, May 15, 2002, p. A4.

Ostrow, Joel, M. Georgiy A. Satarov, and Irina M. Khakamada. *The Consolidation of Dictatorship in Russia: An Inside View of the Demise of Democracy.* Westport, CT: Praeger, 2007.

Pace, Eric. "Jose Figueres Ferrer Is Dead at 83, Led Costa Ricans to Democracy." *New York Times*, June 9, 1990. Accessed August 8, 2008, at http://query.nytimes.com/gst/fullpage.html?res=9C0CEFD81639F93AA35755C0A966958260.

Paktar, Medha. "The Struggle for Participation and Justice: A Historical Narrative." In Fisher, ed., *Toward Sustainable Development?: Struggling Over India's Narmada River.* Pp. 157–78.

Pamfilova, E. A. "Predislovie" (Preface). In Burkov, ed., *Primenenie Evropeiskoi konventsii o zashchite prav cheloveka v sudakh Rossii.* Accessed November 24, 2007, at http://www.sutyajnik.ru/rus/library/sborniki/echr6/foreword.htm.

Paris, Roland. *At War's End: Building Peace After Civil Conflict.* New York: Cambridge University Press, 2004.

Pastor, Manuel, Jr. "The Effects of IMF Programs in the Third World: Debate and Evidence from Latin America." *World Development*, Vol. 15 (1987), pp. 365–91.

  The International Monetary Fund and Latin America: Economic Stabilization and Class Conflict. Boulder: Westview Press, 1987.

Pastor, Robert. "The Third Dimension of Accountability: The International Community in National Elections." In Schedler, Diamond, and Plattner, eds., *The Self-Restraining State: Power and Accountability in New Democracies.* Pp. 123–42.

Patel, Anil. "What Do the Narmada Valley Tribals Want?" In Fisher, ed., *Toward Sustainable Development?: Struggling over India's Narmada River.* Pp. 179–200.

Peace Brigades International. "Organizations in Guatemala." March 2000. Accessed November 21, 2007, at http://web.archive.org/web/20060906163221/http://www.peacebrigades.org/guate.html.

Pech, Khareen. "Executive Outcomes: A Corporate Conquest." In Cilliers and Mason, eds., *Peace, Profit or Plunder: The Privatization of Security in War-Torn African Societies.* Pp. 81–109.

Peou, Sorpong. *Intervention and Change in Cambodia: Towards Democracy?* New York: St Martin's Press, 2000.

Perlez, Jane. "A Nation-Building Project Comes Apart in East Timor." *New York Times*, July 14, 2006, p. A4.

Peterson, V. Spike, and Anne Sisson Runyan. *Global Gender Issues*, 2nd edition. Boulder: Westview Press, 1999.

Petritsch, Wolfgang. "Decision Removing Ante Jelavic from His Position as the Croat Member of the BiH Presidency." March 7, 2001. Accessed October 18, 2007, at http://www.ohr.int/decisions/removalssdec/default.asp?content_id=328.

Petrova, Anna. "Sud prisiazhnykh" [Trial by Jury]. Fond 'Obshchestvennoe mnenie,' April 6, 2006. Accessed April 12, 2006, at http://bd.fom.ru/report/map/projects/dominant/domo614/domto614_4/do61423.

Pevehouse, Jon C. *Democracy from Above: Regional Organizations and Democratization.* Cambridge, UK: Cambridge University Press, 2005.

Plattner, Marc F. "Globalization and Self-Government." *Journal of Democracy*, Vol. 13, No. 3 (July 2002), pp. 54–67.

Polgreen, Lydia. "World Bank Reaches Pact with Chad over Use of Oil Profits." *New York Times*, July 15, 2006, p. A5.

Polgreen, Lydia, and Celia W. Dugger. "Chad's Oil Riches, Meant for Poor, Are Diverted." *New York Times*, February 18, 2006, pp. A1, A6.

Politkovskaya, Anna. *A Dirty War: A Russian Reporter in Chechnya.* London: Harvill Press, 1999.

A Russian Diary. New York: Random House, 2007.

Pomorski, Stanislaw. "In a Siberian Criminal Court." *East European Constitutional Review*, Vol. 11, Nos. 1/2 (Winter/Spring 2002), pp. 111–116.

Posner, Paul. "Development and Collective Action in Chile's Neoliberal Democracy." Conference paper presented at "Democracy in Latin America Thirty Years After Chile's 9/11." State University of New York (SUNY)–Albany, October 10–12, 2003.

"Development and Collective Action in Chile's Neoliberal Democracy." *Political Power and Social Theory*, Vol. 18, 2007, pp. 85–129.

State, Market and Democracy in Chile: The Constraint of Popular Participation. New York: Palgrave Macmillan, 2008.

"Prazdnik prishel na 'ulitsu' sutiazhnikov...ili Rukovodstvo k deistviiu dlia obshchestvennykh ob'edinenii Rossii." May 17, 2005. Accessed August 23, 2006, at http://www.sutyajnik.ru/rus/news/2005/05/17–1.htm.

Price, Robert M. *The Apartheid State in Crisis: Political Transformation in South Africa 1975–1990.* New York: Oxford University Press, 1991.

Project on International Courts and Tribunals. "African Court of Human and Peoples' Rights." Accessed November 23, 2007, at http://www.pict–pcti.org/courts/ACHPR.html.

"Project Stop Excision: Collaborating Groups in Mali." Accessed November 24, 2007, at http://stopexcision.net/groupsinMali.html.

Rainsy, Sam. "A Farcical Justice." December 22, 2005. Accessed November 21, 2007, at http://www.samrainsyparty.org/national_assembly/2005/dec/051222_statement.htm.

Randall, Vicky, and Robin Theobald. *Political Change and Underdevelopment: A Critical Introduction to Third World Politics,* 2nd edition. London: Macmillan, 1998.

Refugees International. "Sexual Exploitation in Liberia: Are the conditions ripe for another scandal?" April 20, 2004. Accessed February 22, 2007, at http://www.refugeesinternational.org/content/article/detail/957.

Reno, William. "Privatizing War in Sierra Leone." *Current History*, May 1997, pp. 227–30.

Warlord Politics in African States. Boulder: Lynne Rienner, 1998.

"The Failure of Peacekeeping in Sierra Leone." *Current History* (May 2001), pp. 219–25.

"Mafiya Troubles, Warlord Crises." In Crawford Young, and Mark Beissinger, eds., *Beyond State Crisis? Postcolonial Africa and Post-Soviet Eurasia in Comparative Perspective.* Washington: Woodrow Wilson Center Press, 2002. Pp. 105–27.

Reporters Without Borders. "In 'Grotesque' Sentence Court Fines Website Editor for Insulting Putin." October 27, 2006. Accessed November 9, 2006, at http://www.rsf.org/article.php3?id_article=19473.

"Worldwide Press Freedom Index: 2006." Accessed November 23, 2007, at http://www.rsf.org/article.php3?id_article=19384.

Reuters. "President of Sierra Leone Wins Re-election by a Wide Margin." *New York Times,* May 20, 2002, p. A8.

"Revised Draft Model Memorandum of Understanding Between the United Nations and [Participating State] Contributing Resources to [the United Nations Peacekeeping Operation]." Note by the Secretary General, October 3, 2006, p. 3. Accessed April 19, 2007, at http://daccessdds.un.org/doc/UNDOC/GEN/N06/553/30/PDF/N0655330.pdf?OpenElement.

RIA Novosti. "Trial By Jury Provides Too Many Acquittals – Supreme Court Head." April 7, 2006. Accessed April 12, 2006, at http://en.rian.ru/russia/20060407/45428737.html.

"State Duma Backs Delay in Introducing Jury Trials in Chechnya." November 15, 2006. Accessed November 23, 2006, at http://en.rian.ru/russia/ 20061115/55674530.html.

Rich, Bruce. *Mortgaging the Earth: The World Bank, Environmental Impoverishment, and the Crisis of Development.* Boston: Beacon Press, 1995.

Richter, James. "The Global and the Local: A Framework for Analyzing Local Activism." Unpublished manuscript, 2002.

Riedl, Andrew. "Stop Famine in Niger." *Peacework* (August 2005), p. 11.

Riise, Thomas, and Kathryn Sikkink. "The Socialization of International Human Rights Norms into Domestic Practices: Introduction." In Thomas Riise, Stephen C. Ropp, and Kathryn Sikkink, eds., *The Power of Human Rights: International Norms and Domestic Change* (Cambridge, UK: Cambridge University Press, 1999).

Riley, Stephen. "Review: Sierra Leone Politics: Some Recent Assessments." *Africa: Journal of the International African Institute,* Vol. 52, No. 2 (1982), pp. 106–9.

Risen, James. "Command Errors Aided Iraq Abuse, Army Has Found." *New York Times,* May 3, 2004, pp. A1, A11.

"Iraq Contractor in Shooting Case Makes Comeback." *New York Times,* May 10, 2008, pp. A1, A9.

Robberson, Tod. "Employees Not Convinced Whistle-Blowers Are Safe." *Dallas Morning News,* February 9, 2007. Accessed August 13, 2008, at http://www.contractormisconduct.org/ass/contractors/59/cases/690/761/veritas–capital–dyncorp–in–bosnia_dmn.pdf.

Robertson, James (United States District Judge). "Saleh, et al, Plaintiffs, v. Titan Corporation, et al., Defendants." Memorandum Order, United States District Court for the District of Columbia, June 29, 2006. Accessed March 21, 2007, at http://www.burkepyle.com/Saleh/June–29–2006–order–on–motion–to–dismiss.pdf.

Rodrigues, Maria Guadalupe Moog. "The Planafloro Inspection Panel Claim: Opportunities and Challenges for Civil Society in Rondonia, Brazil." In Clark, Fox, and Treakle, eds., *Demanding Accountability: Civil Society Claims and the World Bank Inspection Panel*. Pp. 45–68.

Rogers, Tim. "Private Military Firms Find Golden Goose." *Z Magazine*, Vol. 18, No. 3, March 2005. Accessed December 4, 2008, at http://www.zcommunications.org/zmag/viewArticle/14006.

Rohde, David. "Indian Contract Workers in Iraq Complain of Exploitation." *New York Times*, May 7, 2004, p. A14.

Rohter, Larry. "Brazilians Find Political Cost for Help from I.M.F." *New York Times*, August 11, 2002, p. 3.

Rose-Ackerman, Susan. *From Elections to Democracy: Building Accountable Government in Hungary and Poland*. New York: Cambridge University Press, 2005.

Rosenau, James N. *Distant Proximities: Dynamics Beyond Globalization*. Princeton: Princeton University Press, 2003.

Ross, Robert J. S. "The 'Race to the Bottom' in Imported Clothes." *Dollars and Sense*, January/February 2002, pp. 46–7.

"The Declining Average Wage in Imported Clothes." *Dollars and Sense* (July 2002), p. 6.

Slaves to Fashion. Ann Arbor: University of Michigan Press, 2004.

Ross, Will. "Liberia Gets All-Female Peacekeeping Force." BBC News, Liberia, January 31, 2007. Accessed March 1, 2007, at http://news.bbc.co.uk/2/hi/africa/6316387.stm.

Royo, Antoinette G. "The Philippines: Against the People's Wishes, the Mt. Apo Story." In Fox and Brown, eds., *The Struggle for Accountability: The World Bank, NGOs, and Grassroots Movements*. Pp. 151–79.

Rubin, Alissa J., and Paul von Zielbauer. "The Judgment Gap." *New York Times*, October 11, 2007, pp. A1, A12.

Rubin, Elizabeth. "An Army of Their Own." *Harper's*, February 1997, p. 45

Rucht, Dieter. "Distant Issue Movements in Germany: Empirical Description and Theoretical Reflections." In Guidry, Kennedy, and Zald, eds., *Globalizations and Social Movements: Culture, Power, and the Transnational Public Sphere*. Pp. 76–105.

Rumansara, Augustinus. "Indonesia: The Struggle of the People of Kedung Ombo." In Fox and Brown, eds., *The Struggle for Accountability: The World Bank, NGOs, and Grassroots Movements*. Pp. 123–49.

"Russia Appeals Ruling of European Court." *Moscow Times*, November 15, 2006, p. 3.

"Russian Cases Most Numerous At European Human Rights Court." RFE/RL Newsline, January 25, 2000.

"Russian Government Rejects Registration of Russian Justice Initiative." November 23, 2006. Accessed December 7, 2006, at http://www.srji.org/en/news/2006/11/23/.

"Russian NGO Receives Tax Bill For Foreign Grants." RFE/RL Newsline, July 25, 2006.

"Russians Have 22,000 Complaints Pending in Strasbourg." RFE/RL Newsline, April 21, 2005.

"Russia Sets Record with Number of Lawsuits Filed at Strasbourg Court." PRAVDA.Ru: http://english.pravda.ru/, 5 November 2005. Accessed July 28, 2006, at http://www.londonmet.ac.uk/index.cfm?FADB56DF–966B–43FB–B73C–7B97CC42645F.

"Russia Suffers Another Loss at European Court of Human Rights." RFE/RL Newsline, April 8, 2005.

Saleh v. Titan Corporation, Third Amended Class Action Complaint. Accessed November 23, 2007, at http://ccrjustice.org/files/Saleh_3rdamendedcomplaint.pdf.

Sandoz, Yves. "Private Security and International Law." In Cilliers and Mason, eds., *Peace, Profit or Plunder: The Privatization of Security in War-Torn African Societies*. Pp. 201–26.

Scahill, Jeremy. *Blackwater: The Rise of the World's Most Powerful Mercenary Army*. New York: Nation Books, 2007.

   "Bush's Shadow Army." *The Nation*, April 2, 2007. Accessed March 21, 2007, at http://www.thenation.com/doc/20070402/scahill.

Schanman, Gary. "Technologically Transmitted Smut: On the Cutting Edge of Technology, 'Cyber-sex' Is Big Business." *Monroe Street Journal*, February 10, 1997. Accessed November 15, 2007, at http://www.umich.edu/~msjrnl/backmsj/021097/tech.html.

Schedler, Andreas. "Conceptualizing Accountability." In Schedler, Diamond, and Plattner, eds., *The Self-Restraining State: Power and Accountability in New Democracies*. Pp. 13–28.

   "Restraining the State: Conflicts and Agents of Accountability." In Schedler, Diamond, and Plattner, eds., *The Self-Restraining State: Power and Accountability in New Democracies*. Pp. 333–350.

Scheier, Rachel. "Soldier Verdict Spotlights Rape in Ugandan Camps." Women's E-news, May 29, 2006. Accessed June 2, 2006, at http://www.womensenews.org/article.cfm?aid=2756.

Schmitt, Eric. "Iraq Abuse Trial Is Again Limited to Lower Ranks." *New York Times*, March 23, 2006, pp. A 1, A 20.

Schmitter, Philippe. "The Ambiguous Virtues of Accountability." *Journal of Democracy*, Vol. 15, No. 4 (October 2004), pp. 47–60.

Schmitter, Philippe, and Terry Lynn Karl. "What Democracy Is...and Is Not." *Journal of Democracy*, Vol. 2, No. 3 (Summer 1991), pp. 75–88.

Schmitz, Hans Peter. "When Networks Blind: Human Rights and Politics in Kenya." In Thomas Callaghy, Ronald Kassimir, and Robert Latham, eds., *Intervention and Transnationalism in Africa: Global-Local Networks of Power*. Cambridge, UK: Cambridge University Press, 2001. Pp. 149–172.

   "Domestic and Transnational Perspectives on Democratization." *International Studies Review*, No. 6 (2004), pp. 403–26.

Scholte, Jan Aart. *Globalization: A Critical Introduction*. New York: Palgrave, 2000.

   "Civil Society and Democratically Accountable Global Governance." *Government and Opposition*, Vol. 39, No. 2 (April 2005), pp. 211–33.

Schrader, Esther. "U.S. Companies Hired to Train Foreign Armies." *Los Angeles Times*, April 14, 2002, p. A1. Accessed August 24, 2006, at http://www.globalpolicy.org/security/peacekpg/training/pmc.htm.

Secretary General of the United Nations. "Special Measures for Protection from Sexual Exploitation and Sexual Abuse." June 15, 2007. Accessed November 1, 2007, at http://documents-dds-ny.un.org/doc/UNDOC/GEN/N06/360/40/pdf/N0636040.pdf?OpenElement.

Seidman, Gay W. "Adjusting the Lens: What Do Globalizations, Transnationalism, and the Anti-apartheid Movement Mean for Social Movement Theory?" In Guidry, Kennedy, and Zald, eds., *Globalizations and Social Movements: Culture, Power, and the Transnational Public Sphere*, Pp. 339–57.

"Deflated Citizenship: Labor Rights in a Global Era." In Alison Brysk and Gershon Shafir, eds., *People Out of Place: Globalization, Human Rights, and the Citizenship Gap*. Pp. 109–29.

Sen, Amartya. *Development as Freedom*. New York: Anchor, 1999.

Sengupta, Somini. "African Held for War Crimes Dies in Custody of a Tribunal." *New York Times*, July 31, 2003, p. A6.

Sesay, Max. "Security and State – Society Crises in Sierra Leone and Liberia." In Caroline Thomas and Peter Wilkin, eds., *Globalization, Human Security and the African Experience*. Boulder: Lynne Rienner, 1999. Pp. 145–61.

Shain, Yossi, and Lynn Berat, "The International Interim Government Model Revisited." In Yossi Shain and Juan Linz, eds., *Between States: Interim Governments and Democratic Transitions*. New York: Cambridge University Press, 1995. Pp. 63–75.

Shapiro, Ian, and Casiano Hacker-Cordón, eds. *Democracy's Edges*. Cambridge, UK: Cambridge University Press, 1999.

Shawcross, William. *Cambodia's New Deal*. Washington: Carnegie Endowment for International Peace, 1994.

Shotton, Anna. "A Strategy to Address Sexual Exploitation and Abuse by United Nations Peacekeeping Personnel." *Cornell International Law Journal*, Vol. 39, No. 1 (Winter 2006), pp. 97–107.

Shultz, Jim. "Bechtel vs. Bolivia: The People Win!" *Peacework* (February 2006). Accessed July 18, 2007, at http://www.peaceworkmagazine.org/pwork/0602/060208.htm.

Sierra Leone Web. "News Archives: July 26, 2002." Accessed September 28, 2006, at http://www.sierra–leone.org/slnews0702.html.

"News Archives: July 28, 2002." Accessed September 28, 2006, at http://www.sierra–leone.org/slnews0702.html.

Silber, Laura, and Allan Little. *Yugoslavia: Death of a Nation*. New York: T.V. Books, 1996.

Silverstein, Ken. *Private Warriors*. New York: Verso: 2000.

Simons, Marlise. "Trial of Liberia's Ex-Leader Languishes Amid Delays, Bureaucracy, and Costs." *New York Times*, August 27, 2007, p. A6.

Simpson, Cam, and Aamer Madhani. "Iraq: War Fuels Human Labor Trade." *Chicago Tribune*, October 13, 2005. Accessed February 8, 2006, at www.corpwatch.org/article.php?id=12688.

Singer, P. W. *Corporate Warriors: The Rise of the Privatized Military Industry.*
    Ithaca: Cornell University Press, 2003.
    "Nation Builders and Low Bidders in Iraq." *New York Times*, June 15, 2004, p.
        A23.
    "The Law Catches Up to Private Militaries, Embeds." DefenseTech.org, January 3,
        2007. Accessed March 7, 2007, at http://www.defensetech.org/archives/003123.
        html.
Sini Sanuman. "Press Release: Malian Government Gives Nod to Anti-FGM
    Movement: Public Discussion Begins at the Legislature to Outlaw Excision."
    October 4, 2007. On file with author.
Smith, Kathleen E. *Remembering Stalin's Victims.* Ithaca: Cornell University
    Press, 1996.
Snyder, Jack. *From Voting to Violence: Democratization and Nationalist Con-
    flict.* New York: W.W. Norton, 2000.
Solomon, Richard H. *Exiting Indochina.* Washington: US Institute of Peace Press,
    2000.
Somers, Jean. "Debt: The New Colonialism." In Bill Bigelow and Bob Peterson,
    eds., *Rethinking Globalization: Teaching for Justice in an Unjust World.* Mil-
    waukee: Rethinking Schools Press, 2002. Pp. 78–81.
SourceWatch. "Aegis Defence Services." Accessed November 23, 2007, at http://
    www.sourcewatch.org/index.php?title=Aegis_Defence_Services.
Secretary General of the United Nations. "Special Measures for Protection from
    Sexual Exploitation and Sexual Abuse." Report of the Secretary General,
    May 24, 2006. Accessed December 13, 2008, at http://daccessdds.un.org/doc/
    UNDOC/GEN/N06/360/40/PDF/N0636040.pdf?OpenElement.
Sperling, Valerie. *Organizing Women in Contemporary Russia.* Cambridge, UK:
    Cambridge University Press, 1999.
    "Introduction." In Valerie Sperling, ed., *Building the Russian State.* Boulder:
        Westview Press, 2000. Pp. 1–23.
Stack, Jr., John F. "Human Rights in the Inter–American System." In Mary L.
    Volcansek, ed., *Law Above Nations: Supranational Courts and the Legali-
    zation of Politics.* Gainesville: University Press of Florida, 1997. Pp. 99–117.
Stevenson, Linda S. "Confronting Gender Discrimination in the Mexican Work-
    place: Women and Labor Facing NAFTA with Transnational Contention."
    Women & Politics, Vol. 26, No. 1 (2004), pp. 71–97.
    "Gender Equality and Globalization: Cooperation and Conflict." Unpublished
        paper, presented at Women's Caucus for Political Science APSA Pre-Conference,
        Washington, 2005.
Stevenson, Richard W. "A Chief Banker for Nations at the Bottom of the Heap."
    New York Times, September 14, 1997, Section 3, p. 1.
Stienstra, Deborah. "Dancing Resistance from Rio to Beijing: Transnational
    Women's Organizing and United Nations Conferences, 1992–6." In Mari-
    anne H. Marchand and Anne Sisson Runyan, eds., *Gender and Global
    Restructuring: Sightings, Sites and Resistances.* London: Routledge, 2000.
    Pp. 209–24.
Stiglitz, Joseph. "Globalization and Development." In Held and Koenig-Archibugi,
    eds., *Taming Globalization: Frontiers of Governance.* Pp. 47–67.

[Stiglitz, Joseph E.] *Globalization and Its Discontents*. New York: W.W. Norton, 2002.

Stiles, Kendall W. "The IMF and Economic Development: Book Review." *Perspectives on Politics*, Vol. 2, No. 3, September 2004, p. 644.

Stinchcombe, Arthur. "On the Virtues of the Old Institutionalism." *Annual Review of Sociology*, Vol. 23 (1997), pp. 1–19.

Stix, Bob. "Boycott Coke." *Multinational Monitor*, Vol. 5, No. 5 (May 1984). Accessed July 6, 2006, at http://www.multinationalmonitor.org/hyper/issues/1984/05/newsroundup.html.

Stokes, Susan C. "What Do Policy Switches Tell Us About Democracy?" In Przeworski, Stokes, and Manin, eds., *Democracy, Accountability, and Representation*. Pp. 98–130.

"Supreme Court Upholds Dismissal of Judge for Criticizing Prosecutors." RFE/RL Newsline, January 20, 2005.

"Sutyagin Loses Another Appeal...As Attorneys Pin Hopes on European Court." RFE/RL Newsline, August 18, 2004.

Sutyajnik. "2005 Annual Report." Accessed November 24, 2007, at http://www.sutyajnik.ru/rus/reports/2005/eng/cons.htm.

"Poniatovskii protiv Pravitel'stva." Accessed July 12, 2006, at http://www.sutyajnik.ru/rus/cases/p_v_gov.

Tagliabue, John. "As Multinationals Run the Taps, Anger Rises over Water for Profit." *New York Times*, August, 26, 2002, p. 1.

Taguba Report/Hearing Article 15–6 Investigation of the 800th Military Police Brigade. Accessed November 23, 2007, at http://www.globalsecurity.org/intell/library/reports/2004/800–mp–bde.htm.

Tannenbaum, David. "Obsessed: The Latest Chapter in the World Bank's Privatization Plans." *Multinational Monitor*, Vol. 23, No. 9 (September 2002). Accessed November 27, 2007, at http://multinationalmonitor.org/mm2002/02september/sept02corp1.html.

Tarrow, Sidney. *The New Transnational Activism*. New York: Cambridge University Press, 2005.

Thompson, Ginger and James Risen. "Plea by Blackwater Guard Helps Indict Others." NYTimes.com, December 8, 2008. Accessed December 15, 2008, at http://www.nytimes.com/2008/12/09/washington/09blackwater.html?_r=1&hp.

Tickner, J. Ann. "Feminist Perspectives on Security in a Global Economy." In Thomas and Wilkin, eds., *Globalization, Human Security and the African Experience*. Pp. 41–58.

Tilly, Charles. "Reflections on the History of European State–Making." In Charles Tilly, ed., *The Formation of National States in Western Europe*. Princeton: Princeton University Press, 1975. Pp. 3–83.

Coercion, Capital, and European States, AD 990–1990. Cambridge, MA: Basil Blackwell, 1990.

Contention and Democracy in Europe, 1650–2000. New York: Cambridge University Press, 2004.

Trust and Rule. New York: Cambridge University Press, 2005.

Toporkov, Roman. "Ostrye problemy kruglogo stola." *Vechernii Tomsk*, December 6, 2005.

Tostevin, Matthew. "Votes Cast in Sierra Leone." *Boston Globe*, May 15, 2002, p. A10.

Trafficking Victims Protection Reauthorization Act of 2005. Accessed November 23, 2007, at http://www.state.gov/g/tip/rls/61106.htm.

Traynor, Ian. "The Privatisation of War." *The Guardian*, December 10, 2003. Accessed February 9, 2006, at www.guardian.co.uk/print/0,3858,4815701–103681,00.html.

Treakle, Kay, and Elias Diaz Peña. "Accountability at the World Bank: What Does It Take? Lessons from the Yacyretá Hydroelectric Project, Argentina/Paraguay." In Clark, Fox, and Treakle, eds., *Demanding Accountability: Civil Society Claims and the World Bank Inspection Panel*. Pp. 69–91.

Treakle, Kay, Jonathan A. Fox, and Dana Clark. "Lessons Learned." In Clark, Fox, and Treakle, eds., *Demanding Accountability: Civil Society Claims and the World Bank Inspection Panel*. Pp. 247–77.

Tripp, Aili Mari. "Challenges in Transnational Feminist Mobilization." In Ferree and Tripp, eds., *Global Feminism: Transnational Women's Activism, Organizing, and Human Rights*. Pp. 296–312.

Udall, Lori. "The World Bank and Public Accountability: Has Anything Changed?" In Fox and Brown, eds., *The Struggle for Accountability: The World Bank, NGOs, and Grassroots Movements*. Pp. 391–436.

UNAMSIL. "United Nations Mission in Sierra Leone." Accessed November 22, 2007, at http://www.un.org/Depts/dpko/unamsil/body_unamsil.htm.

United Nations Conference on Trade and Development (UNCTAD), "World Investment Report 2002: TNCs and Export Competitiveness," Geneva, United Nations, 2002, as cited in Mathias Koenig-Archibugi, "Transnational Corporations and Public Accountability," *Government and Opposition*, Vol. 39, No. 2 (April 2004), p. 234.

United Nations Department of Information. "Sierra Leone: Consolidating a Hard-Won Peace." 2005. Accessed November 22, 2007, at http://www.un.org/events/tenstories/story.asp?storyID=1400.

United Nations Development Program (UNDP). *Human Development Report 2005: International Cooperation at a Crossroads: Aid, Trade and Security in an Unequal World* (2005). Accessed November 27, 2007, at http://hdr.undp.org/en/reports/global/hdr2005/.

Beyond Scarcity: Power, Poverty, and the Global Water Crisis. New York: Palgrave Macmillan, 2006.

United Nations High Commissioner for Refugees (UNHCR) and Save the Children–UK. "Sexual Violence & Exploitation: The Experience of Refugee Children in Guinea, Liberia and Sierra Leone." February 2002. Accessed February 22, 2007, at http://www.savethechildren.org.uk/scuk_cache/scuk/cache/cmsattach/1550_unhcr–scuk_wafrica_report.pdf.

United Nations Mission in Bosnia and Herzegovina. "Bosnia and Herzegovina – UNMIBH – Mandate." Accessed November 17, 2007, at http://www.un.org/Depts/dpko/missions/unmibh/mandate.html.

United Nations Mission in Liberia (UNMIL). Conduct and Discipline Unit. Accessed November 23, 2007, at http://unmil.org/content.asp?ccat=cdu.

United Nations Transitional Authority in Cambodia (UNTAC). Accessed November 21, 2007, at http://www.un.org/av/photo/subjects/untac.htm.

"U.N. Ousts Peacekeepers in Sex Case." *New York Times*, November 3, 2007, p. A10.

US Code, Title 18 Crimes and Criminal Procedure, Chapter 212, Military Extra-territorial Jurisdiction (MEJA). Accessed November 23, 2007, at http://www.access.gpo.gov/uscode/title18/partii_chapter212_.html.

U.S. Department of Defense Inspector General's Office. "Assessment of DOD Efforts to Combat Trafficking in Persons: Phase II: Bosnia-Herzegovina and Kosovo." December 8, 2003. On file with author.

U.S. Department of Defense. Instruction Number 5525.11, March 3, 2005. Accessed February 3, 2006, at http://www.ipoaonline.org/uploads/05–03–03%20MEJA%20Instructions%20i55251%201x=DoD.pdf.

U.S. Department of State, "Cambodia Human Rights Practices, 1993." January 31, 1994 Accessed July 20, 2006, at http://dosfan.lib.uic.edu/ERC/democracy/1993_hrp_report/93hrp_report_eap/Cambodia.html.

U.S. Department of State, Bureau of Democracy, Human Rights, and Labor. *Country Reports on Human Rights Practices: Russia (2006)*, March 6, 2007. Accessed November 8, 2007, at http://www.state.gov/g/drl/rls/hrrpt/2006/78835.htm.

Vandenberg, Martina. *Hopes Betrayed: Trafficking of Women and Girls to Bosnia and Herzegovina for Forced Prostitution*. Human Rights Watch, November 2002. Accessed November 23, 2007, at http://www.hrw.org/reports/2002/bosnia/Bosnia1102.pdf.

"Peacekeeping, Alphabet Soup, and Violence Against Women in the Balkans." In Dyan Mazurana, Angela Raven–Roberts, and Jane Parpart, eds., *Gender, Conflict and Peacekeeping*. Lanham, MD: Rowman & Littlefield, 2005. Pp. 150–167.

[Vandenberg, Martina E.] "Out of Bondage." *Legal Times*, February 14, 2005. Accessed December 1, 2008, at http://www.jenner.com/files/tbl_s20Publications/RelatedDocumentsPDFs1252/889/Legal_Times_Vandenberg_021405.pdf.

Vandenberg, Martina, and Sarah Mendelson. Comments on DFARS Case 2004–D017, Defense Federal Acquisition Regulation Supplement; Combating Trafficking in Persons, August 22, 2005. On file with author.

"Vast Majority of Russians Have No Faith in Judicial Independence." RFE/RL Newsline, June 3, 2005.

Vianna, Aurelio, Jr. "The Inspection Panel Claims in Brazil." In Clark, Fox, and Treakle, eds., *Demanding Accountability: Civil Society Claims and the World Bank Inspection Panel*. Pp. 145–65.

Vincent, Andrew. *Theories of the State*. Oxford: Basil Blackwell, Ltd., 1987.

Volcansek, Mary L. "Supranational Courts in a Political Context." In Volcansek, ed., *Law Above Nations: Supranational Courts and the Legalization of Politics*. Pp. 1–19.

Von Zielbauer, Paul. "Marines' Trials in Iraq Killings Are Withering." *New York Times*, August 30, 2007, pp. A1, A10.

Vreeland, James. *The IMF and Economic Development*. New York: Cambridge University Press, 2003.

Wade, Robert Hunter. "The Disturbing Rise in Poverty and Inequality: Is It All a 'Big Lie'?" In Held and Koenig-Archibugi, eds., *Taming Globalization: Frontiers of Governance*. Pp. 18–46.

Wadhams, Nick. "Civilian Employees, Not Soldiers, Will Be Big Problem as United Nations Tackles Sex Abuse, Official Says." Associated Press, March 15, 2005. Accessed February 22, 2007, at http://www.refugeesinternational.org/content/article/detail/6356.

Walker, Alice. "Only Justice Can Stop A Curse." In Pam McAllister, ed., *Reweaving the Web of Life*. Philadelphia: New Society, 1982. Pp. 262–5.

Walker, Kristen. "Moving Gaily Forward? Lesbian, Gay and Transgender Human Rights in Europe." *Melbourne Journal of International Law*, Vol. 2, No. 1 (June 2001), pp. 122–43.

Wayne, Leslie. "America's For-Profit Secret Army." *New York Times*, October 13, 2002, Section 3, pp. 1, 10–11.

Weber, Max. "Politics as a Vocation." In H.H. Gerth and C. Wright Mills, eds., *From Max Weber: Essays in Sociology*. New York: Oxford University Press, 1958. Pp. 77–128.

Weigle, Marcia. *Russia's Liberal Project*. University Park: Pennsylvania State University Press, 2000.

Weiss, Thomas G. ed. *Beyond UN Subcontracting: Task Sharing with Regional Security Arrangements and Service-Providing NGOs*. New York: St. Martin's Press, 1998.

Wells, Jonathon, Jack Meyers, Maggie Mulvihill. "U.S. Ties to Saudi Elite May Be Hurting War on Terrorism: Businesses Weave Tangled Web with Saudis." *Boston Herald*, December 10, 2001, pp. 1, 6–7.

Weston, Burns H., Robin Ann Lukes, and Kelly M. Hnatt. "Regional Human Rights Regimes: A Comparison and Appraisal." In Richard Pierre Claude and Burns H. Weston, eds., *Human Rights in the World Community*, 2nd edition. Philedelphia: University of Pennsylvania Press, 1992. Pp. 244–55.

Whitmore, Brian. "Concerns Raised About Russia Chairing Council of Europe." RFE/RL Newsline, May 22, 2006.

Whitworth, Sandra. *Men, Militarism and UN Peacekeeping: A Gendered Analysis*. Boulder: Lynne Rienner, 2004.

"Widow of Slain Duma Deputy Convicted in Retrial." RFE/RL Newsline, November 29, 2005.

Wilkin, Peter. "Human Security and Class in a Global Economy." In Thomas and Wilkin, eds., *Globalization, Human Security and the African Experience*. Pp. 23–40.

Williams, Heather. "Of Labor Tragedy and Legal Farce: The Han Young Factory Struggle in Tijuana, Mexico." *Social Science History*, No. 27 (2003), pp. 525–50.

Williamson, Hugh. "Globalizing Trade Unions: An Interview with Bill Jordan." *Multinational Monitor*, Vol. 17, No. 6 (June 1995). Accessed February 26, 2006, at http://multinationalmonitor.org/hyper/issues/1995/06/mm0695_11.html.

Williamson, John. "What Washington Means by Policy Reform." In John Williamson, ed., *Latin American Adjustment: How Much Has Happened?* Washington: Institute for International Economics, 1990. Accessed June 11, 2008, at http://www.iie.com/publications/papers/paper.cfm?researchid=486.

Wirth, David A. "Partnership Advocacy in World Bank Environmental Reform." In Fox and Brown, eds., *The Struggle for Accountability: The World Bank, NGOs, and Grassroots Movements.* Pp. 51–79.

Wolfowitz, Paul. "Good Governance and Development: A Time for Action." Jakarta, Indonesia, April 11, 2006. Accessed July 5, 2006, at http://web.worldbank.org/WBSITE/EXTERNAL/NEWS/0,contentMDK:20883752~pagePK:34370~piPK:42770~theSitePK:4607,00.html.

Woods, Ngaire, and Amrita Narlikar. "Governance and the Limits of Accountability: the WTO, the IMF, and the World Bank." *International Social Science Journal*, Vol. 53, No. 170 (2001), pp. 569–83.

Woolf, Virginia. *Three Guineas*. Harvest Books, 1963.

Worden, Leon. "Iraqis Sue SCV Translator." The-Signal.com. Accessed November 23, 2007, at http://www.scvhistory.com/scvhistory/signal/iraq/sg061004a.htm.

World Bank. "Governance and Anti–Corruption." Accessed December 4, 2008, at http://www.worldbank.org/wbi/governance/.

   Advancing Social Development: A World Bank Contribution to the Social Summit. Washington: World Bank, 1995.

   Accountability at the World Bank: The Inspection Panel, 10 Years On. Washington: World Bank, 2003. Pp. 58–68.

   "News Release: World Bank Board Discusses Investigation by the Independent Inspection Panel of Power Project in Uganda," December 12, 2008. Accessed December 15, 2008, at http://siteresources.worldbank.org/EXTINSPECTIONPANEL/Resources/Bujagali_Press_Release_Final_121208_Clean.pdf.

   "Questions and Answers: Government Indicators." Accessed November 27, 2007, at http://info.worldbank.org/governance/kkz2005/q&a.htm#2.

Wright, Tom. "U.S. Defends Itself on Inmate Abuse." *New York Times*, May 9, 2006, p. A11.

Zisk, Kimberly Marten. *Enforcing the Peace: Learning from the Imperial Past*. New York: Columbia University Press, 2004.

Interviews

Brad Adams, Director of Human Rights Watch's Asia Division, and Chief of the Legal Assistance Unit of the UN High Commission for Human Rights [Cambodia] from May 1995–September 1998, phone interview by author, July 26, 2006.

Anton Burkov, attorney, Urals Center for Constitutional and International Protection of Human Rights (Russia), phone interview by author, August 23, 2006.

Evan Gottesman, Deputy Director of the American Bar Association's Law and Democracy project in Cambodia in the mid-1990s, phone interview by author, July 3, 2006.

Jennifer Green, staff attorney at the Center for Constitutional Rights, phone interview by author, March 31, 2006.

Diederik Lohman, Senior Researcher, Human Rights Watch, phone interview by author, July 20, 2006.

Sarah Martin, Senior Advocate, Refugees International, phone interview by author, March 29, 2007.

Susan McLucas, Director of Healthy Tomorrow and General Secretary of Sini Sanuman, interview by author, August 31, 2006, in Somerville, Massachusetts.

Index